ACADEMIC SKILLS PROBLEMS

The Guilford School Practitioner Series

EDITORS

STEPHEN N. ELLIOTT, Ph.D.
University of Wisconsin–Madison

JOSEPH C. WITT, Ph.D.
Louisiana State University, Baton Rouge

Recent Volumes

Academic Skills Problems

DIRECT ASSESSMENT AND INTERVENTION

SECOND EDITION

◆◆◆

Edward S. Shapiro, Ph.D.

◆

THE GUILFORD PRESS
New York   London

© 1996 The Guilford Press
A Division of Guilford Publications, Inc.
72 Spring Street, New York, NY 10012

Printed in the United States of America

This book is printed on acid-free paper.

Last digit is print number: 9 8 7 6 5 4 3 2

Library of Congress Cataloging-in-Publication Data

Shapiro, Edward S. (Edward Steven), 1951–
    Academic skills problems : direct assessment and intervention /
Edward S. Shapiro. — 2nd ed.
      p.   cm. — (The Guilford school practitioner series)
    Includes bibliographical references and index.
    ISBN 1-57230-093-0
    1. Remedial teaching.   2. Basic education.   3. Educational tests
and measurements.   I. Title.   II. Series.
LB1029.R4S5   1996
372.4'3—dc20   95-28
                                                CIP

Preface

◆

In the years since the publication of the first edition of this text, education professionals have expressed significant interest in the use of alternative methods to published, standardized, norm-referenced tests in the evaluation of academic skills. Included among these alternative methods is curriculum-based assessment (CBA). Designed to evaluate student academic skills directly from instructional material, CBA has been increasingly accepted as a process for providing a link between assessment and intervention.

When the first edition of this book was published, the model I advocated was still in its evolution. Several different models of CBA were being promoted at the time and the relationship among them was not always evident. Although the cornerstones of my model, assessing the instructional environment, determining a student's placement in the curriculum, and conducting progress monitoring to evaluate outcome, had been established, a conceptual approach that tied these processes together into a unified method for evaluating academic skills problems had not been delineated. Shortly after the first edition appeared in 1989, I published an article entitled "An Integrated Model for Curriculum-Based Assessment," which represented several years of developing, field-testing, and evaluating a four-step model of CBA. It defined a conceptual process for conducting assessment of academic skills using the methods described in the first edition. This edition represents the outcomes of the ongoing development and refinement of that conceptual model.

Readers familiar with the first edition will notice several changes in the techniques I describe. First, the entire assessment process is now focused on four essential steps: assessing the academic environment, determining a student's placement in the curriculum of instruction, designing and implementing modifications in the instructional process, and evaluating both short- and long-term progress. Detailed description of each of the four steps is provided. Second, since the publication of the first edition, there have been significant changes in the way the instruction of reading and math is conducted. In reading, many schools have moved from using a basal reading series in a skills-based approach to using a literature-based reading series in a whole-language, holistic method of teaching. Math curricula have increasingly emphasized problem solving over computation. The teaching of spelling is often integrated into instruction in written language. These changes in the way many children are being taught required some rethinking of CBA methods. Although many questions still remain about the use of CBA within these approaches to the instructional process, I have attempted in this edition to address some of these issues in the assessment methods I recommend. Finally, case examples of both assessment and intervention strategies have been provided, and I have added a case illustrating the full four-step model. The entire text contains updated references, forms, and reproducible materials that should permit the interested reader to implement quickly and easily the techniques described throughout the book.

The text remains useful to all school-based practitioners. School psychologists, special education teachers, educational consultants, general educators, reading and curriculum specialists, and school administrators who have an interest in the evaluation of academic skills should find the second edition of the book highly valuable. In addition, students training to enter a school-based profession should find this an excellent source for understanting these evolving methods.

Like all authors, I have many people to thank for facilitating the development of this book. Most important, I want to thank the many graduate students at Lehigh University with whom I have worked over the years. They have provided ongoing opportunities to field-test, refine, and improve my ideas. Having access to these built-in critics has truly been an inspiration for my efforts. Second, I want to thank the many colleagues around the country who have offered positive and constructive comments on the first edition. I have listened and hope I have responded to most of their common criticisms. Last, but never least, I want to thank my family who once again remained highly supportive of my professional efforts. Without the love and support of my wife, Sally, and two adolescent sons, Dan and Jay, I would not have been able to complete this work. My family have always been and remain a strong inspriration in my life's work to improve the lives of children who may be less fortunate than my own.

Contents

◆

CHAPTER 1

♦♦♦

Introduction

♦

Brian, a second-grade student at Salter Elementary School, was referred to the school psychologist for evaluation. The request for evaluation noted that he was easily distracted and was having difficulty in most academic subjects. Background information reported on the referral request indicated that he was retained in kindergarten and was on the list this year for possible retention. As a result of his difficulties sitting still during class, his desk has been removed from the area near his peers and placed adjacent to the teacher's desk. Brian currently receives remedial math lessons.

Maria was in the fifth grade at Carnell Elementary School. She had been in a self-contained classroom for learning-disabled students since second grade and was currently doing very well. Her teacher referred her to determine her current academic status and potential for increased mainstreaming.

Both of these cases are samples of the many types of referrals for academic problems faced by school personnel. How should the team proceed to conduct the evaluations? The answer to this question lies clearly in how the problems are conceptualized. Most often, the multidisciplinary team will view the problem within a diagnostic framework. In Brian's case, the primary question asked would be whether he is eligible for special education services and if so, in which category. In Maria's case, the question would be whether her skills have improved sufficiently to suggest that she will be successful in a less restrictive setting. In both cases, the methodology employed in conducting this type of traditional assessment is similar.

Typically, the school psychologist would administer an individual intelligence test (usually the Wechsler Intelligence Scale for Children—Third Edition [WISC-III; Wechsler, 1991]), an individual achievement test (such as the Peabody Individual Achievement Test—Revised [PIAT-R; Markwardt, 1989] or the Wechsler Individual Achievement Test

1

[WIAT; Weschler, 1992]), and a test of visual–motor integration (usually the Bender–Gestalt). Often, the psychologist would add some measure of personality such as projective drawings. Other professionals, such as educational consultants or educational diagnosticians, might assess the child's specific academic skills by administering norm-referenced achievement tests such as the Woodcock–Johnson Psychoeducational Battery—Revised (Woodcock & Johnson, 1989, 1990), the Key Math—Revised (Connoley, 1988), or other diagnostic instruments. Based on these test results, a determination of eligibility (in the case of Brian) or evaluation of academic performance (in the case of Maria) would be made.

When Brian was evaluated in this traditional way, the results revealed that he was not eligible for special education. Not surprisingly, Brian's teacher requested that the multidisciplinary team make some recommendations for remediating his skills. From this type of assessment, it was very difficult to make specific recommendations. The team suggested that since Brian was not eligible for special education, he was probably doing the best he could in his current classroom. They did note that his phonetic analysis skills appeared weak and recommended that some consideration be given to switching him to a less phonetically oriented approach to reading.

When Maria was assessed, the data showed that she was still substantially below grade levels in all academic areas. Despite having spent the last 3 years in a self-contained classroom for students with learning disabilities, Maria had made minimal progress when compared to peers of similar age and grade. As a result, the team decided to not increase the amount of time that she be mainstreamed for academic subjects.

In contrast to viewing the referral problems of Brian and Maria as diagnostic problems, one could also conceptualize their referrals as questions of "which remediation strategies would be likely to improve academic skills." Seen in this way, the assessment process involves a very different set of methodologies. First, to identify remediation strategies, one must have a clear understanding of both the child's mastery of skills that were taught as well as carefully examining the instructional environment in which learning had occurred. To do this, one must look to the material that was actually instructed, the curriculum, rather than to a set of tasks that may or may not actually have been taught (i.e., standardized tests). Second, a clear understanding of the instructional ecology is attained only through methods of direct observation, teacher and student interviewing, and examination of student-generated products such as worksheets. When the assessment is conducted from this perspective, the results are more directly linked to developing intervention strategies.

When Brian was assessed in this way, it was found that he was appropriately placed in the curriculum materials in both reading and math. Deficiencies in mastery of basic addition and subtraction facts were identified. In particular, specific problems in spelling and written expression were noted, and specific recommendations for instruction in capitalization and punctuation were made. Moreover, the assessment team suggested that Brian's seat be moved, as it was found that he really was not as distractible as the teacher had indicated.

Results of Maria's direct assessment were more surprising and in direct contrast to the traditional evaluation. Although it was found that Maria was appropriately placed in the areas of reading, math, and spelling, examination of her skills in the curriculum showed that she probably could be successful in the lowest reading group within a regular classroom. In particular, it was found that she had attained fifth-grade math skills within the curriculum, despite scoring below grade level on the standardized test.

The focus of the present text is on the direct assessment and intervention methodologies available for the evaluation and remediation of academic problems. Specifically, detailed descriptions of conducting a behavioral assessment of academic skills (as developed by Shapiro, 1990, and Shapiro and Lentz, 1985, 1986) are presented. Direct interventions derived primarily from the research in behavior analysis and academic engaged time are also presented.

BACKGROUND, HISTORY, AND RATIONALE FOR ACADEMIC ASSESSMENT AND INTERVENTION

The percentage of children experiencing academic problems consistently has been of concern to school personnel. Over the past 15 years, the percentage nationally of students who have been identified and classified as learning-disabled and are receiving services for learning disabilities has risen from 2.30% to 5.21% of the population between 1978 and 1993, according to the 1994 *16th Annual Report to Congress on the Implementation of the Education of the Handicapped Act*. In comparison, the percentage of students served under other handicapping conditions has remained stable. Although much of the increase may be due to different ways of defining and assessing students believed to have learning disabilities, a significant number of students are having substantial difficulties mastering basic academic skills. These concerns have been extended beyond special education, with the increased interest in development of competency-based testing and remediation in regular education.

Ownby, Wallbrown, D'Atri, and Armstrong (1985) examined the patterns of referrals made for school psychological services within a small school system (school population = 2,800). Across all grade levels except preschool and kindergarten (where few total referrals were made), refer-rals for academic problems exceeded referrals for behavior problems by almost 5 to 1.

Clearly, there are significant needs for effective assessment and inter-vention strategies to address academic problems in school-age children. Indeed, the number of commercially available standardized achievement tests (e.g., Salvia & Ysseldyke, 1995) suggests that evaluation of academic progress has been a long-standing concern among educators. Goh, Tes-low, and Fuller (1981), in an examination of testing practices of school psychologists, provided additional evidence regarding the number and range of tests used in assessments conducted by school psychologists. A replication of the Goh et al. (1981) study 10 years later found few differ-ences (Hutton, Dubes, & Muir, 1992). Similarly, an extensive literature ex-ists regarding empirically based intervention strategies that have been found to be successful with various academic problems (e.g., Algozzine & Maheady, 1986; Stoner, Shinn, & Walker, 1991).

Despite the historically strong concern about assessing and remediat-ing academic problems, there remains significant controversy about the most effective methods for conducting useful assessments and for choosing the most effective intervention strategies. In particular, longtime dissatis-faction with commercially available, norm-referenced tests has been evi-dent among educational professionals (e.g., Heller, Holtzman, & Messick, 1982; Hively & Reynolds, 1975; Shepard, 1991; Wiggins, 1989) . Likewise, strategies that attempt to remediate identified deficient learning processes have not been found to be useful in effecting change in academic perfor-mance (e.g., Arter & Jenkins, 1979; Good, Vollmer, Creek, Katz, & Chowdhri, 1993)

ASSESSMENT AND DECISION MAKING FOR ACADEMIC PROBLEMS

Salvia and Ysseldyke (1995) define assessment as "the process of collecting data for the purpose of (1) specifying and verifying problems, and (2) mak-ing decisions about students" (p. 5). They identify five types of decisions that can be made from assessment data: referral, screening, classification, instructional planning, and monitoring pupils' progress. They also add that decisions about the effectiveness of programs (program evaluation) can be made from assessment data.

Not all assessment methodologies for evaluating academic behavior can equally address each of the types of decisions needed. For example, norm-referenced instruments may be useful for classification decisions but not very valuable for decisions regarding instructional programming. Likewise, criterion-referenced tests that offer intrasubject comparisons may be useful in identifying relative strengths and weaknesses of academic performance but may not be sensitive to monitoring student progress within a curriculum. Clearly, use of a particular assessment strategy should be linked to the type of decision one wishes to make. A methodology that can be used across types of decisions would be extremely valuable.

It seems logical that the various types of decisions described by Salvia and Ysseldyke should require the collection of different types of data. Unfortunately, an examination of the state of practice in assessment suggests that this is not the case. Goh et al. (1981) reported data suggesting that regardless of the reason for referral, most school psychologists administer an individual intelligence test, a general test of achievement, a test of perceptual–motor performance, and a projective personality measure. A replication of the Goh et al. (1981) study 10 years later found that little had changed. Psychologists still spent more than 50% of their time engaged in assessment. Hutton, et al. (1992) noted that the emphasis on intelligence tests noted by Goh et al. (1981) had lessened, whereas the use of achievement tests had increased. Hutton et al. (1992) also found that the use of behavior rating scales and adaptive behavior measures had increased somewhat. Ysseldyke, Regan, Thurlow, and Schwartz (1981) likewise noted that whether the expected decision was determination of an educational classification or the development of strategies for intervention, a similar standard test battery was administered. Clearly, the use of standardized tests in this way is inconsistent with the mandates of Public Law 94-142 and individualization of services.

In this chapter, an overview of the conceptual issues of academic assessment and remediation are provided. The framework upon which behavioral assessment and intervention for academic problems are based is described. First, however, the current state of academic assessment and intervention is examined.

TYPES OF ASSESSMENT METHODS

Norm-Referenced Tests

One of the most common methods of evaluating academic skills involves the administration of published norm-referenced, commercial, standardized tests. These measures contain items that sample specific academic skills within a content area. Scores on the test are derived by comparing the results for the child being tested to scores obtained by a large, nonclinical, same-age/same-grade sample of children. Various types of standard scores are used to describe the relative standing of the target child against the normative sample.

The primary purpose of norm-referenced tests is to make comparisons with "expected" responses. Collection of norms gives the assessor a reference point for identifying the degree to which the responses of the identified student differ significantly from those of the average same-age/same-grade peer. This information may be useful when making special education eligibility decisions, since degree of deviation from the norm is an important consideration in meeting requirements for various handicaps.

There are different types of norm-referenced tests of academic achievement. Some measures provide broad-based assessments of academic skills, such as the Wide Range Achievement Test—Third Edition (WRAT-III; Wilkinson, 1993); the PIAT-R (Markwardt, 1989); the WIAT (Wechsler, 1992); or the Kaufman Test of Educational Achievement (K-TEA; Kaufman & Kaufman, 1985). These tests each contain various subtests that assess reading, math, and spelling, and provide overall scores for each content area. Other norm-referenced tests, such as the Woodcock Reading Mastery Test—Revised (Woodcock, 1987), are designed to be more diagnostic and offer scores on subskills within the content area, such as passage comprehension, word recognition, or phonetic analysis.

Despite the popular and widespread use of norm-referenced tests for assessing academic skills, a number of significant problems may severely limit their usefulness. If a test is to evaluate a student's acquisition of knowledge, then the test should assess what was taught within the curriculum of the child. If there is little overlap between the curriculum and the test, a child's failure to show improvement on the measure may not necessarily reflect failure to learn what was taught. Instead, the child's failure may only be related to the test's poor correlation with the curriculum in which the child was instructed. In a replication and extension of the work of Jenkins and Pany (1978), Shapiro and Derr (1987) examined the degree of overlap between five commonly used basal reading series and four commercial, norm-referenced achievement tests. At each grade level (first through fifth), the number of words appearing on each subtest and in the reading series were counted. The resulting score was converted to a standard score (mean = 100, $SD = 15$), percentile, and grade equivalent, using the standardization data provided for each subtest. Results of this analysis are reported in Table 1.1. Across subtests and reading series, there appeared to be little and inconsistent overlap between the words appearing in the series and on the tests.

Although these results suggest that the overlap between what is taught and what is tested on reading subtests is questionable, the data examined by Shapiro and Derr (1987) and Jenkins and Pany (1978) were hypothetical. It certainly is possible that such poor overlap does not actually exist, since the achievement tests are designed only as samples of skills and

TABLE 1.1. Overlap between Basal Reader Curricula and Tests

	PIAT				WRAT-R				K-TEA				WRM			
	RS	GE	%tile	SS	RS	GE	%tile	SS	RS	GE	%tile	SS	RS	GE	%tile	SS
Ginn-720																
Grade 1	23	1.8	58	103	40	1M	47	99	14	1.6	37	95	38	1.8	38	96
Grade2	28	2.8	50	100	52	2M	39	96	23	2.6	42	97	69	2.5	33	94
Grade 3	37	4.0	52	101	58	2E	27	91	27	3.2	32	93	83	3.0	24	90
Grade 4	40	4.4	40	96	58	2E	16	85	27	3.2	16	85	83	3.0	10	81
Grade 5	40	4.4	25	90	61	3B	12	82	28	3.4	9	80	83	3.0	4	74
Scott, Foresman																
Grade 1	20	1.4	27	91	39	1M	41	97	12	1.5	27	91	33	1.8	30	92
Grade 2	23	1.8	13	83	44	1E	16	85	17	1.9	18	86	63	2.3	27	91
Grade 3	23	1.8	7	78	46	2B	4	73	17	1.9	5	70	63	2.3	9	80
Grade 4	23	1.8	3	72	46	2B	1	67	17	1.9	2	70	63	2.3	2	70
Grade 5	23	1.8	1	65	46	2B	.7	59	17	1.9	1	66	63	2.3	.4	56
Macmillan-R																
Grade 1	23	1.8	58	103	35	1B	30	92	13	1.6	32	93	42	1.9	44	98
Grade 2	24	2.0	20	87	41	1M	10	81	18	2.0	19	87	58	2.2	22	89
Grade 3	24	2.0	9	80	48	2B	5	76	21	2.3	12	82	66	2.4	10	81
Grade 4	24	2.0	4	74	48	2B	2	70	21	2.3	5	75	67	2.5	3	72
Grade 5	24	2.0	2	69	50	2M	1	65	21	2.3	2	70	67	2.5	2	69

(Cont.)

TABLE 1.1. (Cont.)

	PIAT				WRAT-R				K-TEA				WRM			
	RS	GE	%tile	SS	RS	GE	%tile	SS	RS	GE	%tile	SS	RS	GE	%tile	SS
Keys to Reading																
Grade 1	24	2.0	68	107	41	1M	50	100	15	1.7	42	97	42	1.9	44	98
Grade 2	28	2.8	50	100	51	2M	37	95	20	2.2	27	91	68	2.5	33	94
Grade 3	35	3.8	47	99	59	3B	30	92	24	2.7	19	87	84	3.1	26	91
Grade 4	35	3.8	26	91	59	3B	18	86	24	2.7	9	80	84	3.1	11	82
Grade 5	35	3.8	14	84	59	3B	8	79	25	2.8	5	76	84	3.1	4	74
Scott, Foresman—Focus																
Grade 1	23	1.8	58	103	35	1B	30	92	13	1.6	32	93	37	1.8	35	94
Grade 2	25	2.2	28	91	46	2B	21	88	17	1.9	18	86	56	2.1	20	89
Grade 3	27	2.6	21	88	49	2B	6	77	20	2.2	10	81	68	2.5	11	82
Grade 4	28	2.8	11	82	54	2M	8	79	22	2.4	6	77	76	2.8	7	78
Grade 5	28	2.8	6	77	55	2E	4	73	24	2.7	4	64	81	2.9	3	72

Note. The grade equivalent scores "B, M, E" for the WRAT-R refer to the assignment of the score to the beginning, middle, or end of the grade level. RS, raw scores; GE, grade equivalent; SS, standard score (mean = 100; *SD* = 15); PIAT, Peabody Individual Achievement Test; WRAT-R, Wide Range Achievement Test—Revised; K-TEA, Kaufman Test of Educational Achievement; WRM, Woodcock Reading Mastery Test. From "An Examination of Overlap between Reading Curricula and Standardized Achievement Tests" by E. S. Shapiro and T. F. Derr, 1987, *Journal of Special Education, 21*, pp. 60–61. Copyright 1987 by Pro-Ed, Inc. Reprinted by permission.

not as direct assessments. Good and Salvia (1988) and Bell, Lentz, and Graden (1992) have provided evidence with actual students evaluated on common achievement measures that there is inconsistent overlap between the basal reading series employed in their studies and the different measures of reading achievement.

In the Good and Salvia (1988) study, a total of 65 third- and fourth-grade students who were all being instructed in the same basal reading series (Allyn & Bacon Pathfinder Program, 1978), were administered four reading subtests: the Reading Vocabulary subtest of the California Achievement Test (CAT; Tiegs & Clarke, 1970), the Word Knowledge subtest of the Metropolitan Achievement Test (MAT; Durost, Bixler, Wrightsone, Prescott, & Balow, 1970), the Reading Recognition subtest of the Peabody Individual Achievement Test (PIAT; Dunn & Markwardt, 1970), and the Reading subtest of the Wide Range Achievement Test (WRAT; Jastak & Jastak, 1978). Results of their analysis showed significant differences in test performance for the same students on different reading tests, predicted by the test's content validity.

Using a similar methodology, Bell et al. (1992) examined the content validity of three popular achievement tests: Reading Decoding subtest of the K-TEA), Reading subtest of the Wide Range Achievement Test—Revised (WRAT-R; Jastak & Wilkinson, 1984), and the Word Identification subtest of the Woodcock Reading Mastery Tests—Revised (WRMT-R; Woodcock, 1987). All students ($n = 181$) in the first and second grades of two school districts were administered these tests. Both districts used the Macmillan-R (Smith & Arnold, 1986) reading series. Results showed dramatic differences across tests when a word-by-word content analysis (Jenkins & Pany, 1978) was conducted. Perhaps more importantly, significant differences were evident across tests for students within each grade level. For example, as seen in Table 1.2, students in one district obtained an average standard score of 117.19 ($M = 100$, $SD = 15$) on the WRMT-R and a score of 102.44 on the WRAT-R, a difference of a full standard deviation.

Problems of overlap between test and text content are not limited to the area of reading alone. For example, Shriner and Salvia (1988) conducted an examination of the curriculum overlap between two elementary mathematics curricula and two commonly used norm-referenced standardized tests (Key Math, and Iowa Tests of Basic Skills) across grades 1–3. An assessment of the correspondence for content as well as the type of learning required revealed a lack of content correspondence at all levels.

One potential difficulty with poor curriculum–test overlap is that test results from these measures may be interpreted as indicative of a student's failure to acquire skills taught. This conclusion may contribute to more

TABLE 1.2. Student Performance Scores on Standardized Achievement Tests in Districts One and Two

Group	n	Test		
		WRMT-R	K-TEA	WRAT-R
		District One		
Grade 1	52			
M		117.19	110.31	102.44
SD		17.65	15.67	1.55
Grade 2	47			
M		112.61	104.04	103.68
SD		14.98	13.34	11.02
Total	99			
M		115.11	108.76	102.3
SD		15.91	14.74	11.79
		District Two		
Grade 1	40			
M		113.08	105.23	100.2
SD		14.57	13.02	12.31
Grade 2	42			
M		108.6	108.86	99.26
SD		14.96	13.04	12.42
Total	82			
M		110.78	106.06	99.73
SD		14.86	12.98	12.29

Note. From "Effects of Curriculum–Test Overlap on Standardized Achievement Test Scores: Identifying Systematic Confounds in Educational Decision Making," by P. F. Bell, F. E. Lentz, Jr., and J. L. Graden, 1992, *School Psychology Review, 21,* p. 651. Copyright 1992 by the National Association of School Psychologists. Reprinted by permission.

dramatic decisions, such as changing an educational placement. Unfortunately, if the overlap between what is tested and what is taught is questionable, then the use of these measures to examine student change across time is problematic.

Despite potential problems in curriculum–test overlap, norm-referenced tests are still useful for deciding the relative standing of an individual within a peer group. Although this type of information is valuable in making eligibility decisions, it may have limited use in other types of assessment decisions. An important consideration in assessing academic skills is to determine how much progress students have made across time. This requires that periodic assessments be conducted. Because norm-referenced tests are developed as samples of skills and therefore are limited in the numbers of items that sample various skills, the frequent repetition of these measures results in significant bias. Indeed, these measures were never designed to be repeated at frequent intervals without compromising the integrity of the test. Use of norm-referenced tests to assess student progress is not possible.

In addition to the problem of bias from frequent repetition of the tests, the limited skills assessed on these measures may result in very poor sensitivity to small changes in student behavior. Typically, norm-referenced tests contain items that sample across a large array of skills. As students are instructed, gains evident on a day-to-day basis may not appear on the norm-referenced test, since these skills may not be reflected on test items.

Another problem related to norm-referenced tests is their inability to contribute effectively to decisions about programmatic interventions. Although norm-referenced tests were never designed to be used to make educational recommendations for remediation, they continue to be employed frequently in this way by school psychologists. In a survey, Thurlow and Ysseldyke (1982) found that the WISC-R, WRAT, and Bender–Gestalt were reported by school psychologists to be most useful in making intervention recommendations, whereas teachers reported the WISC-R, PIAT, and Key Math test to be valuable. With the exception of perhaps the Key Math, all of these tests were being used for a purpose (instructional planning) for which they were never designed.

Overall, norm-referenced tests may have the potential to contribute to decisions regarding eligibility for special education. Because these tests provide a standardized comparison across peers of similar age or grade, the relative standing of students can be helpful in identifying the degree to which the assessed student is deviant. Unfortunately, norm-referenced tests cannot be sensitive to small changes in student behavior, were never designed to contribute to the development of intervention procedures, and may not relate closely to what is actually being taught. These limitations may severely limit the usefulness of these measures for academic evaluations.

Criterion-Referenced Tests

Another method for assessing academic skills is to examine a student's mastery of specific skills. This procedure requires comparison of student performance against an absolute standard that reflects acquisition of a skill, rather than the normative comparison made to same-age/same-grade peers that is employed in norm-referenced testing. Criterion-referenced tests are instruments referenced to domains of behavior and can offer intrasubject rather than intersubject comparisons.

Scores on criterion-referenced measures are interpreted by examining the particular skill assessed and then deciding whether the score meets a criterion that reflects student mastery of that skill. By looking across the different skills assessed, one is able to determine the particular components of the content area assessed (e.g., reading, math, social studies) that represent strengths and weaknesses in a student's academic profile. One problem with some criterion-referenced tests is that it is not clear how the criterion representing mastery was derived. Although it seems that the logical method for establishing this criterion may be a normative comparison (i.e., criterion = number of items passed by 80% of same-age/same-grade peers), most criterion-referenced tests establish the acceptable criterion score on the basis of logical rather than empirical analysis.

Excellent examples of criterion-referenced instruments are a series of inventories developed by Brigance. Each of these measures is designed for a different age group with the Brigance Inventory for Early Development (Brigance, 1978) containing subtests geared for preschool children, the Brigance Diagnostic Inventory of Basic Skills (Brigance, 1977) for elementary-age students, and the Brigance Diagnostic Inventory of Essential Skills (Brigance, 1981) aimed at secondary-age students. The inventories cover a wide range of subskills that are linked to specific behavioral objectives. Table 1.3 provides a list of the individual subtests for the Inventory of Basic Skills.

Although criterion-referenced tests appear to address some of the problems with norm-referenced instruments, they may only be useful for certain types of assessment decisions. For example, criterion-referenced measures may be excellent tests for screening decisions. Because we are interested in identifying children who may be at risk for academic failure, the use of a criterion-referenced measure should provide a direct comparison of the skills present in our assessed student against the range of skills expected by same-age/same-grade peers. In this way, we can easily identify those students who have substantially fewer or weaker skills and target these students for more in-depth evaluation.

By contrast, criterion-referenced tests usually are not helpful in making decisions about educational classifications. If criterion-referenced measures are to be used to make such decisions, it is critical that skills expected to be present in nonhandicapped students be identified. Because these measures do not typically have a normative base, it becomes difficult to make statements about a student's relative standing to peers. For example, to use a criterion-referenced test in kindergarten screening, it is necessary to know the type and level of subskills that children should possess as they enter kindergarten. If this information were known, the obtained score of a specific student could be compared to the expected score, and a decision regarding probability for success could be derived. Of course, the

TABLE 1.3. Partial List of Skills Assessed on the
Brigance Inventory of Basic Skills

I. Readiness .
   Color Recognition
   Visual Discrimination
   Visual Motor Skills
   Fine Motor Skills
   Articulation of Sounds
   Counting
   Alphabet
   Number Recognition
   Number Comprehension

II. Reading
   Word Recognition
   Reading Levels
   Word Analysis
   Vocabulary

III. Language Arts
   Handwriting
   Grammar Mechanics
   Spelling
   Reference Skills

IV. Math
   Numbers
   Operations
   Decimals
   Measurement

---

empirical verification of this score would be necessary, since the identification of subskills needed for kindergarten entrance would most likely be obtained initially through teacher interview. Clearly, although criterion-referenced tests could be used to make classification decisions, they typically are not employed in this way.

Perhaps the decision to which criterion-referenced tests can contribute significantly is the identification of target areas for the development of educational interventions. Given that these measures contain assessments of subskills within a behavioral domain, they may be useful in identifying the specific strengths and weaknesses of a student's academic profile. The measures do not, however, offer direct assistance in the identification of intervention strategies that may be successful in remediation. Instead, by suggesting a student's strengths, they may aid in the development of interventions capitalizing on these subskills to remediate weaker areas of academic functioning. It is important to remember that criterion-referenced tests can tell us what a student can and cannot do, but they do not tell us what variables are related to the student's success or failure.

One area in which criterion-referenced tests appear problematic is in decisions regarding monitoring of student progress. It would seem logical that since these measures only make intrasubject comparisons, they would be valuable for monitoring student progress across time. Unfortunately, these tests share with norm-referenced measures the problem of curriculum–test overlap. Most criterion-referenced measures have been developed by examining published curricula and pulling a subset of items together to assess a subskill. As such, student gains in a specific curriculum may or may not be related directly to performance on the criterion-referenced test. Tindal et al. (1985) found that although criterion-referenced instruments may be useful for assessing some academic skills, not all measures showed strong relationships to student progress in a curriculum. Thus, these measures may be subject to some of the same biases raised in regard to norm-referenced tests (Armbruster, Stevens, & Rosenshine, 1977; Bell et al., 1992; Good & Salvia, 1988; Jenkins & Pany, 1978; Shapiro & Derr, 1987).

Another problem related to monitoring student progress is the limited range of subskills included in a criterion-referenced test. Typically, most criterion-referenced measures contain a limited sample of subskills as well as a limited number of items assessing any particular subskill. These limitations make the repeated use of the measure over a short period of time questionable. Furthermore, the degree to which these measures may be sensitive to small changes in student growth is unknown. Using criterion-referenced tests to assess student progress may therefore be problematic.

Criterion-referenced tests may be somewhat useful for decisions regarding program evaluation. These types of decisions involve examination of the progress of a large number of students across a relatively long period of time. As such, any problem of limited curriculum–test overlap or sensitivity to short-term growth of students would be unlikely to affect the outcome. For example, one could use the measure to determine the percentage of students in each grade meeting the preset criteria for different subskills. Such a normative comparison may be of use in evaluating the instructional validity of the program.

Strengths and Weaknesses of Norm- and Criterion-Referenced Tests

In general, criterion-referenced tests appear to have certain advantages over norm-referenced measures. These tests have strong relationships to intrasubject comparison methods and strong ties to behavioral assessment strategies (Cancelli & Kratochwill, 1981). Furthermore, because the measures offer assessments of subskills within broader areas, they may provide useful mechanisms for the identification of remediation targets in the development of intervention strategies. Criterion-referenced tests may also be particularly useful in the screening process.

Despite these advantages, the measures do not appear to be applicable to all types of educational decision making. Questions of educational classification, monitoring student progress, and developing intervention strategies may not be addressed adequately with these measures alone. Problems of curriculum–test overlap, sensitivity to short-term academic growth, and selection of subskills assessed may all act to limit the potential use of these instruments.

Clearly, what is needed in the evaluation of academic skills is a method that more directly assesses student performance within the academic curriculum. Both norm-referenced and criterion-referenced measures provide an indirect evaluation of skills by assessing students on a sample of items taken from expected grade-level performance. Unfortunately, the items selected may not have strong relationships to what students were actually asked to learn. More importantly, because the measures provide samples of behavior, they may not be sensitive to small gains in student performance across time. As such, they cannot directly tell us whether our present intervention methods are succeeding.

Equally important is the failure of these measures to take into account the potential influence the environment may have on student academic performance. Both norm-referenced and criterion-referenced instruments may tell us certain things about a student's individual skills, but little about variables that affect academic performance, such as instructional methods for presenting material, feedback mechanisms, classroom structure, competing contingencies, and so forth (Lentz & Shapiro, 1986).

What is needed in the assessment of academic skills is a methodology that can more directly assess both the student's skills and the academic environment. This methodology also needs to be able to address most or all of the types of educational decisions identified by Salvia and Ysseldyke (1995).

Direct Assessment of Academic Skills

A large number of assessment models have been derived for the direct evaluation of academic skills (e.g., Blankenship, 1985; Deno, 1985; Gickling & Havertape, 1981; Howell, Fox, & Morehead, 1993; Salvia & Hughes, 1990; Shapiro, 1989; Shapiro & Lentz, 1986). All of these models have in common the underlying assumption that *one should test what one teaches*. As such, the contents for the assessments employed for each model are based on the instructional curriculum. In contrast to the potential problem of poor overlap between the curriculum and the test in other forms of academic assessment, evaluation methods that are based on the curriculum offer direct evaluations of student performance on material that students are expected to acquire. Thus, the inferences that may have to be made with more indirect assessment methods are avoided.

Despite the underlying commonality of the various models of direct assessment, each model has provided a somewhat different emphasis to the evaluation process. In addition, somewhat different terms have been used by these investigators to describe their respective models. Fuchs and Deno (1991) classified all models of curriculum-based assessment as either general outcome measurement or specific subskill-mastery models. General outcome measurement models use standardized measures that have acceptable levels of reliability and validity. The primary objective of the model is to index long-term growth in the curriculum and across a wide range of skills. Although outcomes derived from this model may suggest when and if instructional modifications are needed, the model is not directly designed to suggest what those specific instructional modifications should be.

Measures used in a general outcome measurement model are presented in a standardized format. Material for assessment is controlled for difficulty by grade levels and may or may not come directly from the curriculum of instruction (Fuchs & Deno, 1994). Typically, measures are presented as brief, timed samples of performance, using rate as the primary metric to determine outcome.

In contrast, specific subskill-mastery models do not use standardized measures. Instead, measures are criterion referenced and usually based on the development of a skill hierarchy. The primary objective of this model is to determine if students are meeting the short-term instructional objectives of the curriculum. The measures may or may not have any relationship to the long-term goals of mastering the curriculum.

Specific subskill-mastery models require a shift in measurement with the teaching of each new objective. As such, measures are not standardized from one objective to the next. Generally, these measures are teacher made, and the metric used to determine student performance can vary widely from accuracy to rate to analysis of error patterns. The model is designed primarily to provide suggestions for the types of instructional modifications that may be useful in teaching a student.

One specific subskill mastery model is Blankenship's (1985) model of "curriculum-based assessment" (CBA). Student performance is evaluated on individual instructional objectives. CBAs can be developed for any part of the curriculum and can include any number of objectives the teacher wishes to assess. Testing on similar objectives is repeated over several days to provide stable indications of student performance. From these CBAs, instructional objectives are derived. Periodic assessment using a CBA is employed to determine whether the student has mastered the content instructed.

In another subskill-mastery model of CBA, Gickling and his colleagues (Gickling & Havertape, 1981; Gickling & Rosenfield, 1995; Gickling & Thompson, 1985; Rosenfield & Kuralt, 1990) concentrate on the selection of instructional objectives and content based on assessment. In particular, this model tries to control the level of instructional delivery carefully, so that student success is maximized. To accomplish this task, academic skills are evaluated in terms of student "knowns" and "unknowns." Adjustments are then made in the curriculum to keep students at an "instructional" level, as compared to "independent" or "frustrational" levels (Betts, 1946). I (Shapiro, 1992) provide a good illustration of how this model of CBA can be applied to a student with problems in reading fluency.

Howell, et al. (1993) have provided a subskill-mastery model called "curriculum-based evaluation" that is wider in scope and application than either Blankenship or Gickling's models. In the model, Howell et al. (1993) concentrate on the development of intervention strategies using task analysis, skill probes, direct observation, and other evaluation tools. Extensive suggestions for intervention programs that are based on curriculum-based evaluation are offered for various subskills such as reading comprehension, decoding, mathematics, written communication, and social skills. In addition, details are provided for decision making in changing intervention strategies.

Among general outcome models of CBA, the assessment model that has had the most substantial research base is that developed by Deno and his colleagues at the University of Minnesota (e.g., Deno, 1985). Derived from some earlier work on "data-based program modification" (Deno & Mirkin, 1977), Deno's model, called "curriculum-based measurement" (CBM) is primarily designed as a progress-monitoring system rather than as a system designed to develop intervention strategies. The most common use of this model employs repeated and frequent administration of skill probes taken from the curriculum in which the child is being instructed. Some research has shown that the model is equally effective in monitoring student progress when a curriculum not matched to the student's instruction is used as well (Fuchs & Deno, 1994). The skill assessed in giving the probes (e.g., oral reading rates) is not necessarily the skill being instructed but is viewed as a "vital sign" that reflects improvement and acquisition of curriculum content. Deno and his colleagues have provided a large, extensive, and impressive database that substantiates the value of this system for screening decisions, eligibility decisions, progress monitoring, and program evaluation (e.g., Deno, Marston, & Mirkin, 1982; Deno, Marston, & Tindal, 1986; Deno, Mirkin, & Chiang, 1982; Fuchs, Deno, & Mirkin, 1984; Fuchs & Fuchs, 1986a; Fuchs, Fuchs, Hamlett, Phillips, & Bentz, 1994; Shinn, Habedank, Rodden-Nord, & Knutson, 1993).

Although each of these models offers useful and important alternatives to norm- and criterion-referenced testing, they all primarily focus on the evaluation of student academic performance to examine student skills. Certainly, the importance of assessing individual academic skills cannot be denied. However, it seems equally important to examine the instructional environment in which the student is being taught. Lentz and I (Shapiro, 1987a, 1990; Shapiro & Lentz, 1985, 1986) provided a model for academic assessment that incorporated the evaluation of the academic environment as well as student performance. Calling our model "behavioral assessment of academic skills," we (Shapiro, 1989; Shapiro & Lentz, 1985, 1986) drew on the principles of behavioral assessment employed for assessing social–emotional problems (Mash & Terdal, 1981; Ollendick & Hersen, 1984; Shapiro & Kratochwill, 1988) but applied them to the evaluation of academic problems. Teacher interviews, systematic direct observation, and an examination of student-produced academic products, played a significant part in the evaluation process. Specific variables examined for the assessment process were selected from the research on effective teaching (e.g., Denham & Lieberman, 1980) and applied behavior analysis (e.g., Sulzar-Azaroff & Mayer, 1986). In addition, the methodology developed by Deno and his associates was used to evaluate individual student performance, but was combined with the assessment of the instructional environment in making recommendations for intervention. Indeed, it is this assessment of the instructional ecology that differentiates our model from other models of curriculum-based assessment.

In a refinement of this model, I (Shapiro, 1990) described a four-step process for the assessment of academic skills that integrates several of the existing models of CBA. As illustrated in Figure 1.1, the process begins with an evaluation of the instructional environment through the use of systematic observation, teacher interviewing, student interviewing, and a review of student-produced academic products. The assessment continues by determining the student's current instructional level in curriculum materials. Next, instructional modifications designed to maximize student success are implemented with ongoing assessment of the acquisition of instructional objectives (short-term goals). The final step of the model involves the monitoring of student progress toward long-term (year-end)

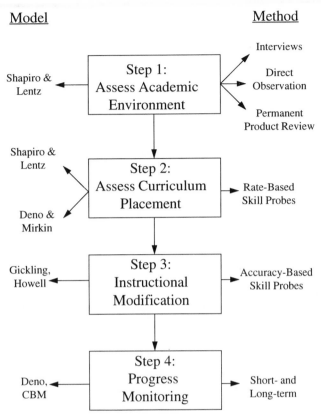

FIGURE 1.1. Integrated model of curriculum-based assessment. Adapted from "An Integrated Model for Curriculum-Based Assessment" by E. S. Shapiro, 1990, *School Psychology Review, 19*, p. 331. Copyright 1990 by the National Association of School Psychologists. Adapted by permission of the author.

curriculum goals. The model integrates several existing models of CBA into a systematic methodology for conducting direct academic assessment. The model will be described in more detail in Chapter 3.

One of the important considerations in adopting a new methodology for conducting academic assessment is the degree to which the proposed change is acceptable to consumers who will use the method. Substantial attention in the literature has been given to the importance of the acceptability of intervention strategies recommended for school- and home-based behavior management (e.g., Clark & Elliott, 1988; Miltenberger, 1990; Reimers, Wacker, Cooper, & deRaad, 1992; Reimers,

Wacker, Derby, & Cooper, 1995; Witt & Elliott, 1985). We (Eckert, Shapiro, & Lutz, 1995; Shapiro & Eckert, 1994) extended the concept of treatment acceptability to assessment acceptability. Using a measure derived from the Intervention Rating Profile (Witt & Martens, 1983), the studies demonstrated that both teachers and school psychologists found CBA, compared to use of standardized, norm-referenced tests, to be relatively more acceptable in conducting academic skills assessments. We (Shapiro & Eckert, 1993) also showed in a nationally derived sample that 46% of school psychologists surveyed indicated that they had used some form of CBA in their work. However, our survey also revealed that school psychologists still had limited knowledge of the actual methods used in conducting a CBA. Overall, these studies suggest that CBA is highly acceptable to the consumers (teachers and school psychologists) and is assuming an increasingly prominent role in the assessment methods of psychologists.

Conclusions and Summary

Strategies for the assessment of academic skills range from the more indirect, traditional norm- and criterion-referenced methods through direct assessment, which is based on the curriculum in which the student is being instructed. Clearly, the type of decision to be made must be tied to the particular assessment strategy employed. Although some traditional assessment methods may be useful for making eligibility decisions, these strategies are sorely lacking in their ability to assist evaluators in recommending appropriate remediation procedures or in their sensitivity to improvements in academic skills over short periods of time. Many alternative assessment strategies designed to provide closer links between the assessment data and intervention methods are available. Although these strategies may also be limited for certain types of decision making, their common core of using the curriculum as the basis for assessment allows these methods to be employed more effectively for several different types of decisions.

INTERVENTION METHODS FOR ACADEMIC SKILLS

Remediation procedures developed for academic problems can be conceptualized on a continuum from indirect to direct procedures. Those techniques that attempt to improve academic performance by improving underlying learning processes can be characterized as indirect interventions. In particular, interventions based on "aptitude–treatment interactions" (ATIs) would be considered indirect methods of intervention. In contrast, direct interventions attempt to improve the area of academic skill by directly teaching that particular skill. These types of interventions usually are based on examination of variables that have been found to have direct relationships to academic performance.

Indirect Interventions for Academic Skills

Most indirect interventions for remediating academic skills are based on the assumed existence of ATIs. The basis of the concept of ATI is that different aptitudes require different treatment. If one properly matches the correct treatment to the correct aptitude, then gains will be observed in the child's behavior. Assuming that there are basic cognitive processes that must be intact for certain academic skills to be mastered, it seems logical that identification and remediation of aptitudes would result in improved academic behavior.

In reading, for example, it may be determined from an assessment that a student's failure to acquire mastery of reading is based on poor phonetic analysis skills. Furthermore, the evaluation may show that the student possesses a preference for learning in the visual over auditory modality. Given this information, it may be predicted that the student will succeed if instruction is based more on a visual than on a phonetic approach to reading. In this example, the aptitude (strength in visual modality) is matched to a treatment procedure (change to a more visually oriented reading curriculum) in hopes of improving the student's skills.

Probably one of the most extensive uses of the ATI concept for remediating academic problems has been in the area of process remediation. Intervention strategies that are aimed at process remediation attempt to instruct students in those skills felt to be prerequisites to successful academic performance. For example, if a student having difficulty in reading is assessed to have poor auditory discrimination skills, process remediation strategies would specifically work at teaching the child to make auditory discriminations more effectively. The underlying assumption is that reading skills would show improvement once auditory discrimination is also improved.

Despite the logical appeal of process remediation, studies specifically examining the validity of the method have not been very encouraging. Arter and Jenkins (1979), in a comprehensive, critical, and detailed analysis of both process assessment and remediation programs (called "DD-PT," Differential Diagnosis–Prescriptive Teaching, by Arter & Jenkins), have reported that there is almost no support for the validity of the assessment measures employed to identify specific aptitudes, nor for the remediation programs that are matched to the results of these assessments. Arter and Jenkins (1979) furthermore state:

> We believe that until a substantive research base for the DD-PT model has been developed, it is imperative to call for a moratorium on advocacy of DD-PT, on classification and placement of children according to differential ability tests, on the purchase of instructional materials and programs that claim to improve these abilities, and on coursework designed to train DD-PT teachers. (p. 550)

Cronbach and Snow (1977) similarly reported the limited empirical support of ATIs. Kavale and Forness (1987), in a meta-analysis from 39 studies searching for aptitude–treatment interactions related to modality assessment and instruction, found no substantial differences between students receiving instruction linked to assessed modality of learning and those receiving no special instruction.

Although support for ATI approaches to remediation are questionable, their presence continues to be felt in the literature. An excellent example is the publication of the Kaufman Assessment Battery for Children (K-ABC; Kaufman & Kaufman, 1983). The measure was designed based on the hypothesized structure of information processing that divides mental functioning into sequential and simultaneous processing (Das, Kirby, & Jarman, 1975, 1979). Included within the interpretative manual are remedial techniques that describe how to teach skills in reading, spelling, and mathematics differentially, based on whether a child's skills are stronger in sequential or simultaneous processing. Although these remediation strategies are not attempting to train underlying cognitive processes directly (they are not teaching children to be better sequential processors), the specific intervention is clearly linked to a specific aptitude. In fact, Kaufman and Kaufman (1983) specifically recommend this approach.

It is somewhat surprising, given the strong empirical basis upon which the K-ABC was developed, that so little attention was given to empirical evaluation of the recommended ATI approach to remediation. One of the few published studies examining the K-ABC's approach to remediation was reported by Ayres and Cooley (1986). Two procedures were developed based directly on Kaufman and Kaufman's (1983) recommended remediation strategies suggested in the K-ABC interpretative manual. One strategy used a sequential processing approach, whereas the other used a simultaneous approach. Students who were differentiated as simultaneous or sequential processors on the K-ABC were divided such that half of each group were trained on tasks matched to processing mechanisms and half on unmatched tasks. The results of the study were startling. Although an aptitude–treatment interaction was found, it was in the opposite direction of that predicted based on the K-ABC!

Good et al. (1993) replicated and extended the previous study, working with first- and second-grade students. Carefully controlling for some of the methodological limitations of previous studies, Good et al. designed instructional programs that emphasized sequential or simultaneous processing modes. After identifying 7 students with strengths in simultaneous processing and 21 with strengths in sequential processing, each student was taught vocabulary words, using each of the two methods of instruction. Results of this carefully conducted study were consistent with previous research (Ayres & Cooley, 1986; Ayres, Cooley, & Severson, 1988), failing to support the K-ABC instructional model.

Despite the consistent findings that indirect interventions based on ATIs are not very effective at remediating academic problems, significant efforts are still being made to use this paradigm to explain academic failure (Gordon, DeStefano, & Shipman, 1985). It appears that the logical appeal of the model may still be outweighing its empirical support. Clearly, for the "moratorium" suggested by Arter and Jenkins (1979) to occur, alternative models for academic remediation that appear to have a significant database must be examined.

Direct Interventions for Academic Problems

Interventions for academic problems are considered direct if responses targeted for change are identical to those observed in the natural environment. For example, in reading, interventions that specifically address such reading skills as comprehension, phonetic analysis, or sight vocabulary are considered direct interventions. This is in contrast to indirect interventions, which may target cognitive processes (e.g., sequencing) that are assumed to underlie and be prerequisite to acquisition of the academic skill.

The types of direct interventions employed for academic skills have been derived from two sets of research. One set of intervention strategies has emerged from basic educational research that has explored the relationship of time variables to academic performance (e.g., Denham & Lieberman, 1980; Rosenshine, 1981). In particular, the time during which students are actively engaged in academic responding, or "engaged time," has been consistently found to have significant relationships to academic performance. Berliner (1979), in data reported from the Beginning Teacher Education System (BTES), found wide variations across classrooms in the amount of time students actually spend in engaged time. Frederick, Walberg, and Rasher (1979), in comparing engaged time and scores on the Iowa Tests of Basic Skills among 175 classrooms, found moderately strong correlations ($r = .54$). Greenwood and his associates at the Juniper Garden's Children's Project in Kansas City have examined academic engaged time by focusing on student opportunities to respond. Using the Code for Instructional Structure and Student Academic Response (CISSAR) and its derivatives (MS-CISSAR and ESCAPE), a number of studies have demonstrated the direct relationships between engagement rates and academic performance (e.g., Berliner, 1988; Fisher & Berliner, 1985; Goodman, 1990; Greenwood, 1991; Hall, Delquadri, Greenwood, & Thurston, 1982; Myers, 1990; Pickens & McNaughton, 1988; Stanley & Greenwood, 1983; Thurlow, Ysseldyke, Graden, & Algozzine, 1983, 1984; Ysseldyke, Thurlow, Christenson, & McVicar, 1988; Ysseldyke, Thurlow, Mecklenberg, Graden, & Algozzine, 1984).

A number of academic interventions designed specifically to increase opportunities to respond have been developed. In particular, the use of peer tutoring and cooperative learning strategies have been developed for this purpose (e.g., Delquadri, Greenwood, Stretton, & Hall, 1983; Greenwood, Carta, & Hall, 1988; Greenwood, Terry, Arreaga-Mayer, & Finney, 1992; Johnson & Johnson, 1985; Phillips, Fuchs, & Fuchs, 1994; Slavin, 1983a).

Another line of research that has resulted in the development of direct interventions for academic problems is applied behavior analysis. There has been a long and successful history of interest in academic remediations by researchers in behavior analysis. Examination of the literature reveals hundreds of studies in which academic skills were the targets for remediation. Contingent reinforcement has been applied for increasing accuracy of reading comprehension (e.g., Lahey & Drabman, 1973; Lahey, McNees, & Brown, 1973), improving oral reading rates (Lovitt, Eaton, Kirkwood, & Perlander, 1971), formation of numbers and letters (Hasazi & Hasazi, 1972), arithmetic computation (Lovitt, 1978), spelling (Lovitt, 1978), and creative writing (Campbell & Willis, 1978). Other variables of the instructional environment, such as teacher attention and praise (Hasazi & Hasazi, 1972), free time (Hopkins, Schultz, & Garton, 1971), access to peer tutors (Delquadri, et al., 1983), tokens or points (McLaughlin, 1981), and avoidance of drill (Lovitt & Hansen, 1976a) have all been found to be effective in modifying academic behavior of students. In addition, other procedures, such as group contingencies (Goldberg & Shapiro, 1995; Shapiro & Goldberg, 1986), monitoring of student progress (Fuchs, Deno, & Mirkin, 1984; McCurdy & Shapiro, 1992; Stowitschek, Lewis, Shores, & Ezzell, 1981), self-management (Piersal & Kratochwill, 1979; Shapiro & Cole, 1994; Szykula, Saudargas, & Wahler, 1981), public posting of performance (Van Houten, Hill, & Parsons, 1975), and positive practice (Ollendick, Matson, Esvelt-Dawson, &

Shapiro, 1980), have all been employed as direct interventions for academic problems.

Clearly, the range of variables that can be modified within the instructional environment is impressive. More importantly, in most of these studies, changes in academic behaviors were present without concern about supposed prerequisite, underlying cognitive skills.

CHAPTER 2

◆◆◆

Choosing Targets for Academic Assessment and Remediation

◆

When a child is referred for academic problems, the most important questions facing the evaluator are "What do I assess?" and "What behavior(s) should be targeted for intervention?" As simple and straightforward as these questions seem to be, the correct responses to these inquiries are not as logical as one might think. For example, if a child is reported to be showing difficulties in sustaining attention to task, it seems logical that one would assess the child's on-task behavior and design interventions to increase attention to task. The literature, however, suggests that this would not be the most effective approach to solving this type of problem. If a child is not doing well in reading skills, one obviously should assess reading skills to determine whether the selected intervention is effective. But reading is an incredibly complex skill consisting of many subskills. What is the most efficient way to determine student progress? Clearly, the selection of behaviors for assessment and intervention is a critical decision in remediating academic problems.

   The complexity of target behavior selection for assessment and intervention is reflected in a number of articles published in a special issue of *Behavioral Assessment* (Vol. 7, No. 1). For example, Evans (1985) suggests that identifying targets for clinical assessment requires an understanding of the interactions among behavioral repertoires. He argues for the use of a systems model to plan and conduct appropriate target behavior selection in the assessment process. Kazdin (1985) likewise points to the known constellations of behavior, which suggest that focus on single targets for assessment or remediation would be inappropriate. Kratochwill (1985b) has discussed the way in which target behaviors are selected through behavioral consultation. He notes the issues related to using verbal behavior as the source for target behavior selection as problematic.

Nelson (1985) has pointed to several additional concerns in the selection of targets for behavioral assessment. The choice of behaviors may be based on both nonempirical and empirical guidelines. For example, McFall (1976) recommends choosing positive behaviors that need to be increased over negative behaviors that need to be decreased. Likewise, when a child presents several disruptive behaviors, the one chosen for intervention may be the one that is the most irritating to the teacher or causes the most significant disruption to other students.

Target behaviors may also be selected empirically by using normative data. Those behaviors that are evident in peers but not in the targeted child may then become the targets for assessment and intervention. Other empirical methods for choosing target behaviors have included use of regression equations (McKinney, Mason, Perkerson, & Clifford, 1975), identification of known groups of children who are considered to be demonstrating effective behavior (McFall, 1976; Nelson, 1985), experimental manipulation of different behaviors to determine which result in the best effects (e.g., Broussard & Northrup, 1995; Cooper, Wacker, Sasso, Reimers, & Donn, 1990; Cooper et al., 1992; Lalli, Browder, Mace, & Brown, 1993; Mace, Page, Ivancic, & O'Brien, 1986; Wahler & Fox, 1980), and use of the triple-response mode system (Cone, 1978). Clearly, selection of behaviors for assessment and intervention for nonacademic problems considers both the individual behavior and the environmental context in which it occurs to be equally important. There appears to be a tendency in assessing academic problems, however, not to consider the instructional environment or to consider it only rarely when a child is referred for academic problems (but see Bijou & Grimm, 1972; Greenwood, Carta, & Atwater, 1991; Lentz & Shapiro, 1986). Traditional assessment measures, both norm-referenced and criterion-referenced, and many models of curriculum-based assessment (CBA; e.g., Deno, 1985), make decisions about a child's academic skills without adequate consideration of the instructional environment in which these skills have been taught. Unfortunately, a substantial literature has demonstrated that a child's academic failure may reside in the instructional environment rather than in the child's inadequate mastery of skills (Lentz & Shapiro, 1986; Thurlow, Ysseldyke, Wotruba, & Algozzine, 1993). Indeed, if a child fails to master an academic skill, it directly suggests potential failure in the instructional methodologies.

SELECTING TARGETS FOR ASSESSMENT

We (Lentz & Shapiro, 1985) have listed several basic assumptions in assessing academic problems. Each assumption is consistent with a behavioral approach to assessment and recognizes the important differences between assessment for academic problems and assessment for behavioral–emotional problems (in which behavioral methods more typically are used).

1. *Assessment must reflect an evaluation of the behavior in the natural environment.* Behavioral assessment emphasizes the need for collecting data under conditions that most closely approximate the natural conditions under which the behavior originally occurred. A child can perform academically in many ways, including individual seatwork, teacher-led small-group activities, teacher-led large-group activities, independent or small peer groups at learning centers, teacher-led testing activities, cooperative groups, peer-tutoring dyads, and so forth. Each of these instructional arrangements may result in differential academic performance under the same task. Whatever method is chosen for the assessment of academic skills, the procedure should be closely related to the way in which the behavior of interest occurs during the regular instructional period.

2. *Assessment should be idiographic rather than nomothetic.* The concerns that often drive the assessment process are the identification and evaluation of potential intervention procedures that may assist the remediation process. In assessing academic skills, it is important to determine how the targeted student is performing against a preintervention baseline rather than normative comparisons. In this way, any changes in performance subsequent to interventions can be observed. Although normative comparisons are important in making eligibility decisions and for setting goals, intraindividual rather than interindividual comparisons remain the primary focus of the direct assessment of academic skills.

3. *What is taught and expected to be learned should be what is tested.* One of the significant problems with traditional norm-referenced testing, as noted in Chapter 1, is the potential lack of overlap between the instructional curriculum and the content of achievement tests (Bell et al., 1992; Good & Salvia, 1988; Jenkins & Pany, 1978; Martens, Steele, Massie, & Diskin, 1995; Shapiro & Derr, 1987). In the behavioral assessment of academic skills, it is important that there be significant overlap between the curriculum and the test. Without such overlap, it is difficult to separate a child's failure on these tests due to inadequate mastery of the curriculum from failure to teach material covered on the test.

4. *The results of the assessment should be strongly related to planning interventions.* A primary purpose of any assessment is to identify those strategies that may be successful in remediating the problem. When assessing academic skills, it is important that the assessment methods provide some indications of potential intervention procedures.

5. *Assessment methods should be appropriate for continuous monitoring of student progress, so that intervention strategies can be altered as indicated.* Because the assessment process is idiographic and designed to evaluate behavior across

time, it is critical that the measures employed be sensitive to change. Indeed, whatever methods are chosen to assess academic skills, these procedures must be capable of showing behavioral improvement (or decrements), regardless of the type of intervention selected. If the intervention chosen is effective at improving a child's math computation (e.g., single-digit subtraction), the assessment method must be sensitive to any small fluctuations in the student's performance. It is also important to note that, because of the frequency with which these measures are employed, they must be brief, repeatable, and usable across types of classroom instructors (e.g., teachers, aides, peers, parents).

6. *Measures used need to be based upon empirical research and to have adequate validity.* Like all assessment measures, methods used to conduct direct assessment of academic skills must meet appropriate psychometric standards. From a traditional perspective, this would require that the measures display adequate test–retest reliability and internal consistency, sufficient content validity, and demonstrated concurrent validity. In addition, because these measures are designed to be consistent with behavioral assessment, the measures should also meet standards of behavioral assessment, such as interobserver agreement, treatment validity, and social validity. Although there have been substantial research efforts to provide a traditional psychometric base for direct assessment measures (e.g., Shinn, 1988) there have been few efforts to substantiate the use of the measures from a behavioral assessment perspective (Lentz, 1988); however, see Derr and Shapiro (1989) and Derr-Minnici and Shapiro (1992).

7. *Measures should be useful in making many types of educational decisions.* Any method used for assessing academic skills should contribute across different types of decisions (Salvia & Ysseldyke, 1985). Specifically, the assessment should be helpful in screening, setting individual educational plan (IEP) goals, designing interventions, determining eligibility for special services, and evaluating special services.

The keys to selecting the appropriate behaviors for assessing academic problems are their sensitivity to small increments of change, their ability to reflect improvement in more molar areas of academic skills (e.g., reading), the curriculum validity of the observed behaviors (match between the assessment measure and the instructional objectives), their ability to assist in the development of intervention strategies, the ability to meet appropriate psychometric standards, and the inclusion of both the academic environment and individual skills in the assessment process. Interestingly, an examination of the literature from somewhat different perspectives (cognitive psychology, educational psychology, applied behavior analysis, and special education) provides significant support for the selection of specific classes of behavior from which one should chose the appropriate targets for evaluation of both the academic environment and the individual's skills.

Assessing the Academic Environment

Academic Engaged Time

Considerable effort has been given to the identification of the critical instructional variables affecting student mastery of basic skills. Much of this research was derived from Carroll's (1963) model of classroom learning, which hypothesized that learning is a function of time engaged in learning relative to the time needed to learn. Although a few researchers have examined issues related to the time needed for learning (e.g., Gettinger, 1985), most efforts have concentrated on the relationship of engaged time to academic performance (Caldwell, Huitt, & Graeber, 1982; Goodman, 1990; Karweit, 1983; Karweit & Slavin, 1981).

One of the most significant projects that examined relationships between time and academic achievement was the Beginning Teacher Evaluation Study (BTES; Denham & Lieberman, 1980). Observations were conducted on the entire instructional day in second- and fifth-grade classrooms across a 6-year period. Data were collected on the amount of time allocated for instruction, how the allocated time was actually spent, and the proportion of time that students spent actively engaged in academic tasks within the allocated time. From the BTES was derived the concept of "academic learning time" (ALT), a variable that incorporates allocated time, engaged time, and success rate.

Berliner (1979), in data reported from the BTES study, compared the amount of allocated time (time assigned for instruction) and engaged time (time actually spent in academic tasks) in second- and fifth-grade classrooms. Although there were wide variations in levels of performance across classes, many were found to have under 100 cumulative hours of engaged time across a 150-day school year. Frederick et al. (1979) examined engaged time and scores on the Iowa Tests of Basic Skills among 175 classrooms in Chicago and found engagement rates and achievement scores to be moderately correlated ($r = .54$). The importance of engaged time has led to a number of studies examining the levels of student engagement across special education classrooms. Leinhardt, Zigmond, and Cooley (1981) examined engagement rates within reading instruction periods of self-contained classrooms for students with learning disabilities. Results of their investigation noted that reading behavior was significantly predicted by pretest scores, teacher instructional variables, and teacher contact. However, students were found to spend only 10% of their academic day in oral or silent reading activities with teachers, averaging 16 minutes daily of actual direct instruction. Haynes and Jenkins (1986), examining resource rooms for students with learning disabilities, found similar results, with students engaged in silent or oral reading activities only 44% of the time scheduled for reading within the resource room. Similarly, most student time (54%) in these settings was spent in individual seatwork.

In a review of the engaged time literature, Gettinger (1986) noted that there appears to be "a positive association between academic engaged time and learning" (p. 9). She does offer substantial caution, however, that the literature is far from definitive and that other factors that may interact with engaged time (e.g., time needed for learning) need continued investigation. Despite these cautions, it appears that academic engaged time may be a critical variable for the assessment of academic skills. Indeed, Gettinger offers a significant number of excellent recommendations for increasing engaged time that have been supported by research. These suggestions include increasing direct instruction and reducing reliance on independent seatwork, improving teacher monitoring of student performance, reducing student behaviors that compete with engaged time (such as off-task), increasing teacher feedback to students, improving classroom organization, frequent monitoring of student progress, and adhering to the schedule of planned academic activities.

Although there is clear evidence of the importance of engaged time and its relationship to academic achievement, the translation of engaged time to targets for academic assessment is not as direct as it appears. Greenwood and his associates (e.g., Greenwood, Delquadri, & Hall, 1984) at the Juniper Garden's Children's Project have examined engaged time by focusing on opportunities to respond. "Opportunity to respond" is a concept that incorporates the antecedent–behavior relationships surrounding the instructional process. Specifically, the concept includes the academic environment or ecology along with the student response. Thus, measurement of opportunities to respond must include assessment of the instructional environment along with the child's responses. Greenwood and his colleagues have developed a series of observational codes matched to different educational settings designed to provide a detailed analysis of these variables. The Code for Instructional Structure and Student Academic Response (CISSAR; Stanley & Greenwood, 1981) is used for the assessment of non-special education students in regular education settings; the Code for Instructional Structure and Student Academic Response—Mainstream Version (MS-CISSAR; Carta, Greenwood, Schulte, Arrega-Mayer, & Terry, 1988) is used for assessing identified special education students within mainstream settings; and the Ecobehavioral System for Complex Assessments of Preschool Environments (ESCAPE; Carta, Greenwood, & Atwater, 1985) is used for assessing students within kindergarten and preschool settings. These codes have been configured for computerized data collection and analysis using laptop computers into a system called the Ecobehavioral Assessment Systems Software (E-BASS; Greenwood, Carta, Kamps, & Delquadri, 1993). Table 2.1 provides a listing of the CISSAR categories and codes. Similar sets of codes are used for the MS-CISSAR and ESCAPE. As one can see, the code is extremely complex and offers substantially detailed information about teacher and student behavior. Greenwood, Delquadri, and Hall (1984) make clear that the concept of "opportunities to respond" is not identical to the more typical observational category of on-task behavior common to many direct observational data-collection systems. The key difference is the active responding involved in opportunities to respond, compared to the more passive response of on-task behavior.

A large number of studies have been conducted using the CISSAR, MS-CISSAR, and ESCAPE (e.g., Ager & Shapiro, 1995; Carta, Atwater, Schwartz, & Miller, 1990; Friedman, Cancelli, & Yoshida, 1988; Greenwood, Carta, Kamps, Terry, & Delquadri, 1994; Greenwood, Delquadri, & Hall, 1989; Hall et al., 1982; Kamps, Leonard, Dugan, & Boland, 1991; Stanley & Greenwood, 1983; Thurlow, Ysseldyke, Graden, & Algozzine, 1983, 1984; Ysseldyke, Thurlow, Mecklenberg, Graden, & Algozzine, 1984). Researchers consistently have found results similar to those from the BTES and other studies suggesting that the levels of academic engaged time are surprisingly low. In addition, Thurlow et al. (1983, 1984), and Ysseldyke et al. (1984) also found few differences in engagement rates across types of learning-disabled services. Other studies that have used less complex processes for recording engaged time have achieved similar results (e.g., Gettinger, 1984; Leach & Dolan, 1985; McConnell et al., 1984).

It is clear that any assessment of academic skills must include a variable that either assesses engaged time directly or provides a close approximation of engagement rate. Although observational codes that assess engagement directly do exist (e.g., CISSAR), these codes may be unnecessarily complex for clinical use. What is critical in the behavior or behaviors selected for assessment that represent engaged time is that they clearly should show the level of *active* student responding and not simply be measures of on-task time alone. Two codes that provide such a variable and have been found to be very useful for classroom observation are the State-Event Classroom Observation System (SECOS; Saudargas, 1992) and the Behavioral Observation of Students in Schools (B.O.S.S.; Shapiro, 1996). Furthermore, it is also possible that approximations of engaged time can be obtained by combining observations on interrelated behaviors that together represent academic engaged time. The observational systems described in the present text take this approach by collecting data about a child's academic behavior from various sources (teacher interview, student interview, direct observation, permanent products) and combining these

TABLE 2.1. CISSAR Categories, Descriptions, and Codes

Ecological categories	Number of codes	Description	Codes
Activity	12	Subject of instruction	Reading, mathematics, spelling, handwriting, language, science, social studies, arts/crafts, free time, business management, transition, can't tell
Task	8	Curriculum materials or the stimuli set by the teacher to occasion responding	Readers, workbook, worksheet, paper/pencil, listen to lecture, other media, teacher/student discussion, fetch/put away
Structure	3	Grouping and peer proximity during instruction	Entire group, small group, individual
Teacher position	6	Teacher's position relative to student observed	In front, among students, out of room, at desk, side, behind
Teacher behavior	5	Teacher's position relative to student observed	Teaching, no response, approval, disapproval, other talk
Student behavior categories			
Academic response	7	Specific, active response	Writing, reading aloud, reading silent, asking questions, anwering questions, academic talk, academic game play
Task management	5	Prerequisite or enabling response	Attention, raise hand, look for materials, move, play appropriate
Competing (inappropriate responses)	7	Responses that compete or are incompatible with academic or task management behavior	Disrupt, look around, inappropriate (locale, task, play) talk nonacademic, self-stimulation
Total codes	53		

Note. From "Teacher- versus Peer-Mediated Instruction: An Ecobehavioral Analysis of Achievement Outcomes" by C. R. Greenwood, G. Dinwiddie, B. Terry, L. Wade, S. Thibadeau, and J. C. Delquadri, 1984, *Journal of Applied Behavior Analysis, 17*, p. 524. Copyright 1984 by the Society for the Experimental Analysis of Behavior, Inc. Reprinted by permission.

to determine the student's level of academic responding. Detailed discussion of the use of these codes is provided in Chapter 3.

Classroom Contingencies

Academic responding does not occur in a vacuum. Each response is surrounded by various stimuli within the instructional environment that significantly affect performance. Stimuli immediately preceding the academic responses (e.g., teacher instructions), stimuli preceding the response but removed in time (e.g., studying for a test the night before), consequences immediately following the response (e.g., teacher feedback), delayed consequences (e.g., grades), and contingencies that compete against academic responses (e.g., student–student off-task, disruptive behavior) may all interact in complex ways to affect student academic performance. A significant and substantial research base has developed in applied behavior analysis that demonstrates the relationships of such variables to academic performance.

Antecedent conditions that occur immediately prior to academic responding have been investigated in a number of studies. For example, Hendrickson, Roberts, and Shores (1978) demonstrated the use of a modeling procedure for teaching sight vocabulary to children with learning disabilities. They noted in a subsequent review article that modeling can be used as either an antecedent or a consequence to the modeled response. As an antecedent procedure—for example, in sight vocabulary training—the trainer presents a word by saying, "This word is _____," and then asks the child, "What is this word?" In contrast, as a consequence, a word is presented with the examiner asking the child, "What is this word?" The correct response is modeled only if the child's response is incorrect. Hendrickson and Gable (1981) noted that antecedent modeling may have a stronger effect with younger children than older pupils.

Instructional pacing and teacher presentation during instruction have also been found to be a potentially important antecedents to academic performance. Carnine (1976) demonstrated that students answered correctly about 80% of the time when in a fast-paced condition (12 questions per minute) as compared to answering correctly 30% of the time in a slow-rate condition (5 questions per minute). Indeed, recommendations made by those advocating direct methods of instruction (e.g., Becker & Carnine, 1981; Rosenshine, 1979) suggest that students will be more attentive to a fast-paced instructional strategy.

Another form of immediate antecedent that appears to influence academic responding involves the use of self-talk. There has been an emerging literature that demonstrates that a child's academic responses can be altered by teaching the child to perform self-instructions. Although first applied and developed for impulsive children (Meichenbaum & Goodman, 1971), self-instruction training has been applied across populations such as preschoolers (e.g., Bornstein & Quevillon, 1976; Duarte & Baer, 1994), children with mental retardation (e.g., Johnston, Whitman, & Johnson, 1980), and elementary-age children with learning disabilities (e.g., Lloyd, 1980; Wood, Rosenberg, & Carran, 1993). In addition, the procedure has been successfully applied to academic problems (Fox & Kendall, 1983; Graham & Wong, 1993; Lloyd, Kneedler, & Cameron, 1982; Wood et al., 1993).

Although there has been substantial support for the effects of immediate antecedent stimuli on academic responding, there has been little research examining the impact of antecedent conditions that are removed in time from the academic responses but may equally affect performance. Obviously, there is a substantial problem in trying to establish causal inferences when antecedents and responses are not contiguous. This probably accounts for the lack of research conducted on such events. Still, it is common to encounter teachers who attribute a child's failure to perform in school to events that occurred some time ago. Furthermore, it seems logical that a child who arrives at school without breakfast and who has been awake most of the night listening to parents fight may not perform as well as expected, despite past evidence of skill mastery in the area being assessed. Given that these types of antecedents that are removed temporally from the response may affect academic performance, they clearly provide important variables for assessment.

In general, the types of antecedent stimuli that need to be assessed are primarily found in observation of teacher behavior and the way the instructional environment is arranged. Evaluation of the academic ecology must include some provision for the collection of data around teaching procedures. These variables include methods of presenting instructional stimuli, teacher instructions, student use of self-instructional strategies, and details about any possible temporally removed antecedents to the observed student's academic responding.

Significant effort has been devoted in the literature on applied behavior analysis to the application of consequences contingent upon academic responding. One of the simplest yet effective procedures to alter academic responding has been the use of feedback about performance. Van Houten and Lai Fatt (1981) examined the impact of public posting of weekly grades on biology tests with 12th-grade high school students. In two experiments, they demonstrated that public posting alone increased accuracy from 55.7% to 73.2% correct responses. These results are consistent with those of earlier studies examining the use of explicit timing and public posting in increasing mathematics and composition skills in regular elementary school students (Van Houten et al., 1975; Van Houten & Thompson, 1976).

Whinnery and Fuchs (1993) examined the impact of a goal-setting and test-taking feedback strategy on the performance of 40 students with learning disabilities. In both conditions, students set CBM performance goals after a 20-week intervention period. In one condition, students engaged in weekly CBM test taking, whereas no test taking was done in the other. Results showed that the group engaged in the CBM test-taking strategy had higher performance at the completion of the 20 weeks.

In another example of the impact of feedback on student academic performance, Fuchs, Fuchs, Hamlett, and Whinnery (1991) examined the effect of providing goal lines superimposed on graphs on the math performance of 40 students with learning disabilities. Results showed that providing goal-line feedback to students produced greater performance stability among students than providing graphs without goal-line feedback.

We (Skinner, Shapiro, Turco, Cole, & Brown, 1992) compared corrective feedback for completion of math problems given under either peer- or self-delivered conditions across six second-grade students. In the self-delivered condition, students were instructed to first look at the problem with its answer, cover the problem with a cardboard marker, copy the problem as they recalled it, and then compare the copied and correct responses. This procedure, called "cover, copy, and compare" was contrasted against a procedure in which peers examined student responses and provided feedback. Results showed that self-determined feedback resulted in greater performance for four of the six students.

Other forms of contingent consequences have been examined extensively in the literature. For example, Trice, Parker, and Furrow (1981) found that feedback and contingent reinforcement, using a written format for responses to reading materials, significantly improved the number of words written in replies to questions and the spelling accuracy of a 17-year-old boy with learning disabilities. Allen, Howard, Sweeney, and McLaughlin (1993) found that contingency contracting was effective at improving the academic and social behavior of three second- or third-grade elementary school students. McLaughlin and Helm (1993) used contingent access to music for two middle school students to increase the number of correct problems completed in mathematics. Several studies (Daly & Martens, 1994; Freeman & McLaughlin, 1984; Shapiro & McCurdy, 1989; Skinner & Shapiro, 1987) explored the effectiveness of reading words contiguously with a tape recording. Lovitt and Hansen (1976a) examined the use of a skipping and drilling activity contingent upon improved reading. Gettinger (1985) investigated the use of imitation to correct spelling errors. Campbell and Willis (1979) investigated the use of contingent reward for improving the creativity of writing skills. Many,

many other studies have been completed in which some form of contingent consequence has been employed to improve academic responding.

The extensive literature on consequences to academic responding suggests strongly that assessment of academic skills must include an evaluation of events following the academic responses. Included among those events are frequency and type of teacher responses to academic performance (both immediate and delayed). It is also important to assess the instructional environment to determine whether the classroom management system provides opportunities for consequences to be appropriately applied following academic responses.

Other important variables that clearly affect academic performance and are derived from applied behavior analysis are competing contingencies. These are classroom events that compete with the potential affects of antecedent–consequence relationships of academic responses. For example, if a student is frequently drawn off-task by peers asking for help, the observed student may be making fewer academic responses than are desirable. Likewise, if a target student engages in high rates of contact with other students, out-of-seat or out-of-area responses, disruptiveness, or other behaviors that prevent student academic performance, it is likely that the student's academic achievement will be limited. Although Hoge and Andrews (1987) raise some questions about the actual relationship between modifications of disruptive behavior and improvements in academic responding, it remains important in the assessment process to examine the student behaviors that may be affecting the student's academic responding. The assessment of competing contingencies, therefore, requires careful examination of student behaviors that typically occur in classrooms and are considered disruptive or related to poor academic performance. These would include such behaviors as being out of seat, student–student contacts, talking out, physical and/or verbally aggressive behavior, and general inattentiveness.

One final set of instructional environmental variables that should be assessed includes teacher expectations for students, goal setting, and progress monitoring. There is some evidence that students make greater gains in academic performance when teachers formally monitor progress across time (Fuchs, 1986; Fuchs, Deno, & Mirkin, 1984). Also, goal setting, whether performed by the teacher or the student, appears to be critical in improving academic performance (Kelley & Stokes, 1982, 1984; Lee & Tindal, 1994; Lenz, Ehren, & Smiley, 1991; Schunk & Schwartz, 1993).

Summary and Conclusions

The assessment of the academic environment requires an evaluation of those variables that have an impact upon academic performance. These variables would include behaviors that are related to academic engaged time (e.g, opportunities to respond), teacher instructional procedures (e.g., presentation style, antecedents and consequences of academic responding), competing contingencies (e.g., disruptiveness, student–student contacts), and teacher–student monitoring procedures and expectations. Although it is impossible to conclude that any one of these variables alone is critical for academic responding, the thorough examination of the academic ecology becomes a crucial portion of the evaluation of a student's academic skills.

Assessing Individual Academic Skills

There has been increasing dissatisfaction with the use of traditional methods of assessing academic performance (e.g., Carver, 1974; Hively & Reynolds, 1975; Neill & Medina, 1989; Tindal, Fuchs, et al., 1985). Typically, these procedures involve the administration of norm-referenced achievement tests before and after the implementation of an intervention. Significant questions have been raised about the value of these methods for assessing student progress (Fuchs, Fuchs, Benowitz, & Barringer, 1987), the poor overlap with instructional curricula (Bell, et al., 1992; Good & Salvia, 1988; Jenkins & Pany, 1978; Martens et al., 1995; Shapiro & Derr, 1987), and the relevance of these measures for assessing students with handicaps (Fuchs et al., 1987; Fuchs, Fuchs, & Bishop, 1992). In addition, the measures were never designed to be repeated frequently or to assist in deriving appropriate intervention strategies.

A number of alternative measurement systems have been developed for assessing academic skills. They are designed to be reliable, provide direct assessment of skills based on the curricula, are repeatable, are sensitive to student growth, and can assist in deriving appropriate strategies for academic performance (e.g., Deno & Mirkin, 1977; Gickling & Rosenfield, 1995; Gickling & Havertape, 1981; Howell et al., 1993; Idol, 1987; Lindsley, 1971; Salvia & Hughes, 1990; Shapiro, 1990; Shapiro & Lentz, 1985, 1986; White & Haring, 1980). Each of these systems is based on principles of CBA. Data are obtained directly from the instructional curriculum in which a student is being taught. Measures collected are brief and repeatable, and generally consist of timed or untimed skill probes. Critical parts of each system are the systematic graphing of the data and use of the data in educational decision making. The measures are also employed in the development of goals for IEPs and, in some cases, are used to help plan remediation strategies.

Despite the underlying similarity of the measurement systems, specific strategies employed do vary. For example, Idol-Maestas (1983) uses oral reading rates on 100 word passages in assessing reading, or she may employ simply the time needed to read the 100 words as the dependent measure. Blankenship (1985) assesses students by writing test items tied to specific instructional objectives and determines mastery of objectives based on student performance. Gickling and Havertape (1981) make instructional decisions based on the ratio of curricular material known by the student (immediate and correct responses) to material unknown by the student. This ratio is again determined by developing skill probes tied to specific instructional objectives. Howell et al. (1993) first conduct a broad-based survey assessment followed by more specific-level assessment of particular skills in order to identify potential strategies for intervention.

Among the many systems for conducting CBA, the most substantial research base documenting psychometric properties of CBA measures has been the work of Deno and his colleagues. The reliability and validity of their measurement system, called "curriculum-based measurement" (CBM), has been thoroughly investigated. In particular, concurrent validity of CBM with standardized, norm-referenced testing in reading, spelling, and written language has been examined. In addition, the correspondence between CBM and traditional assessment methods for making decisions about student eligibility for special education has been examined. Shinn (1989) provides an excellent review of the research in CBM.

The development of CBM began with an earlier effort entitled "data-based program modification" (Deno & Mirkin, 1977). This program described a methodology for special education consultants that used skill probes taken directly from the curriculum as the assessment strategy for determining student progress in academic subjects. Oral reading rates were used for assessing reading; performance on timed sheets of math problems encompassing specific computational objectives was used to assess skills in math; words spelled correctly during a timed and dictated word list assessed spelling; and words written correctly in writing a story during 3 minutes were used to assess written language. Results from these assessments were graphed and analyzed for assessing students' progress through a curriculum as well as their performance on specific objectives.

The psychometric properties of these measures in reading, spelling, and written expression were investigated in a series of studies (Deno, Marston, & Mirkin, 1982; Deno, Mirkin, & Chiang, 1982; Deno, Mirkin, Lowry, & Kuehnle, 1980). Shinn, Tindal, and Stein (1988) noted that for each measure, reliability (test–retest, internal consistency, and interscorer), and concurrent validity had to be demonstrated..

In reading, Deno, Mirkin, and Chiang (1982) compared various types of reading probe measures: the number of words read aloud from a list of words randomly taken from the basal reader; the number of words read aloud from basal reader passages; the number of correctly defined words from the basal reader; the number of correct words provided in a cloze procedure taken from the basal reader; and the number of correct words underlined in a passage. All of these measures had been used as methods of informal assessment in the evaluation of reading. Measures were examined for their correlation with numerous subtests from norm-referenced, commercially available standardized tests such as the Stanford Diagnostic Reading Test (Karlsen, Madden, & Gardner, 1975), the Peabody Individual Achievement Test, (PIAT; Dunn & Markwardt, 1970), and the Woodcock Reading Mastery Test (Woodcock, 1987). These data showed that the number of words read aloud correctly in 1 minute from either word lists or passages taken from the basal readers had the highest correlations with the various reading subtests, ranging from .73 to .91. Similarly, internal consistency and test–retest reliability, as well as inter-scorer agreement, ranged from .89 to .99.

Fuchs, Deno, and Marston (1983) examined the effects of aggregating scores on reliability of oral reading probes. Results showed that measures of correct reading rates were extremely stable across observations and that aggregation of scores had little effect in increasing reliability. For error rates, aggregation substantially improved reliability. Correlations with the Reading Recognition subtest of the Woodcock Reading Mastery Test showed that CBM was just as precise using only a single measure assessed on one occasion.

In a series of studies, Fuchs, Tindal, and Deno (1984) examined the use of 30- versus 60-second reading samples, as well as a comprehension measure. They also investigated the stability of CBM for reading in two second-grade girls. Results showed that the 30- and 60-second samples had high correlations with each other and substantially high correlations with the comprehension measure (cloze procedure). The second study, however, showed that the degree of instability in performance across time was much higher when 30-second samples rather than 60-second samples were used.

In spelling, Deno et al. (1980) found that the number of words spelled correctly or the number of correct letter sequences, a measurement procedure used in precision teaching (White & Haring, 1980), during a 2-minute period had correlations of between .80 and .96 with the Test of Written Spelling (Larsen & Hammill, 1976), the PIAT Spelling subtest (Dunn & Markwardt, 1970), and the Stanford Achievement Test Primary III (Madden, Gardener, Rudman, Karlsen, & Marwin, 1973). Reliability estimates of internal consistency, test–retest, and interscorer agreement ranged from .86 to .99. Further research by Deno et al. (1980) found that 1-, 2-, or 3-minute dictation samples all had equally strong correlations with the criterion spelling measures.

The same research strategy for written expression found that the number of words written during a writing sample was highly correlated

(> .70) with various criterion measures, such as the Test of Written Language (Hammill & Larsen, 1978), the Word Usage subtest of the Stanford Achievement Test (Madden, et al., 1973), and the Developmental Sentence Scoring System (Lee & Canter, 1971). Additional research related to stimuli used to generate writing samples (e.g., pictures, story starters, or topic sentences) and to time limits found no significant relationships between the criterion measures and CBM. As a result, Deno, Marston, and Mirkin (1982) recommended that a 3-minute response time be used with story starters.

Surprisingly, there has been very little systematic investigation into CBM measures for mathematics although it has been used as an outcome measure in numerous studies (e.g., Fuchs, Fuchs, Phillips, Hamlett, & Karns, 1995; Fuchs, Fuchs, Hamlett, & Whinery, 1991; Stoner, Carey, Ikeda, & Shinn, 1994). Although Deno and Mirkin (1977) offer some very specific recommendations for assessing computational skills, there have been few published attempts to demonstrate reliability and validity of the measures. A number of sites have adopted the Deno and Mirkin (1977) procedures of giving timed skill probes taken from specific objectives and counting the number of correct digits per minute (Germann & Tindal, 1985; Marston & Magnusson, 1985). In some settings, computational probes with a mix of operations have been employed; in others, probes of single operations have been used. Although these measures appear to be useful and valid for assessing math performance, the technical adequacy of these measures still remains largely unknown. Despite this concern, Fuchs, Hamlett, and Fuchs (1990a) have developed a computerized program for conducting CBM monitoring of students in math. In addition, Fuchs, Fuchs, Hamlett, Walz, and Germann (1993) have provided data on the expected rate of progress in math among students in general education when CBM is conducted across an entire year. Together, these types of materials allow evaluators to use CBM in math with some degree of confidence.

In a review of CBM research, Shinn (1988, 1989) describes the extensive efforts to replicate the technical adequacy findings of Deno and colleagues (Deno, Mirkin, & Chiang, 1982; Deno et al., 1980). Test–retest and alternate-form reliabilities over a 5-week period remained high for reading and spelling measures (.80–.90) and moderate for written expression (.60). Marston and Magnusson (1985), in a replication of Deno, Mirkin, et al. (1982), found that correlations between subtests of the Stanford Achievement Test, the Science Research Associates (SRA) Achievement series (Naslund, Thorpe, & Lefever, 1978), and the Ginn 720 Reading Series (Clymer & Fenn, 1979) with oral reading rates taken from basal readers showed coefficients between .80 and .90. In addition, Marston and Magnusson (1985) found correlations between teacher judgments of student achievement levels in reading to be strongest for CBM measures compared to standardized test scores.

Over the past five years, a significant shift in curriculum materials used for reading instruction has occurred. Schools are increasingly using literature-based materials and whole-language instructional methods rather than basal texts. Questions have been raised as to whether the measures typical of CBM that are derived from grade-based reading material are equally applicable when working with nongraded material typical of a literature-based reading series. Fuchs and Deno (1994) examined the necessity of deriving the assessment material directly from the curriculum of instruction. Their analysis suggests that it may not be critical that the measures developed for purposes of assessment come directly from the material being instructed. Indeed, Fuchs and Deno (1992), in a study of 91 elementary-age students, found that the oral reading rate metric was a developmentally sensitive measure regardless of the series in which the students were being instructed. However, Hintze, Shapiro, and Lutz (1994), Hintze and Shapiro (1995), and Bradley, Shapiro, Lutz, and DuPaul (in press) have found that there may be some differences in the sensitivity of CBM passages derived from literature-based and basal reading series when the measures are used to monitor progress across time. Results from these studies suggest that it is important to use passages that are carefully controlled for grade-level readability when working from a literature-based reading series. It was found, however, that CBM measures derived from basal reading material can be used to monitor student progress regardless of which type of curriculum series a student is being taught. Substantial research is still needed to clarify the potential role that CBM can play in assessing students who are being taught in a nonbasal reading series.

Significant efforts have been made to demonstrate the ability of CBM to provide effective discriminations in differentiating students with mild handicaps (learning disabilities) from students with low achievement and those in regular education. Deno, Marston, and Mirkin (1982) demonstrated that all CBMs (reading, spelling, written language) taken across students in general education classrooms, in Chapter 1 (remedial) programs, and with identified learning disabilities showed clear differences across groups. Such findings have been replicated frequently (Shinn, & Marston, 1985; Shinn, Tindal, Spira, & Marston, 1987; Shinn, Ysseldyke, Deno, & Tindal, 1986). Furthermore, CBM procedures have been used to make all eligibility decisions regarding learning disabilities in several field sites (Marston, & Magnusson, 1985; Tindal, Wesson, Deno, Germann, & Mirkin, 1985).

Beyond the data suggesting that CBM can be used reliably to discriminate categories of learning-disabled and non-learning-disabled students, an important aspect of CBM is its ability to be sensitive to student progress across time. Clearly, one of the key advantages of CBM is its repeatability over time. Indeed, Jenkins, Deno, and Mirkin (1979) have offered strong and persuasive arguments for the use of these measures in writing and setting IEP goals (see Deno et al., 1986).

Shinn, Habedank, Rodden-Nord, and Knutson (1993) demonstrated how CBM can be used potentially to impact decisions to reintegrate students from special education to general education settings. In two studies involving children in grades 3–5, CBM was used to identify special education students who performed in reading at or above those students in the low-reading groups from general education classes. Results showed that approximately 40% of the special education students could be candidates for potential reintegration using this approach.

Fuchs, Deno, and Mirkin (1984) reported an important and significant study investigating the relationship between teacher monitoring of progress and student achievement. Special education teachers in the New York City public schools were assigned randomly to either a repeated-measurement or conventional-measurement group. Those in the repeated-measurement group were trained to assess reading using 1-minute probes taken from the goal level of the basal reading series. Data from these probes were graphed and implemented using a data-utilization rule that required them to introduce program changes whenever a student's improvement across 7 to 10 measurement points appeared inadequate for reaching their goal. Teachers in the conventional measurement group set IEP goals and monitored student performance as they wished, relying predominantly on teacher-made tests, nonsystematic observation, and scores on workbook exercises. Data were obtained on a CBM of reading (using third-grade reading material), the Structural Analysis and Reading Comprehension subtests of the Stanford Diagnostic Reading Test (Karlsen et al., 1975), the Structure of Instruction Rating Scale (Deno, King, Skiba, Sevcik, & Wesson, 1983), a teacher questionnaire designed to assess progress toward reading goals and descriptions of student functioning, and a student interview.

Results of the study showed that children whose teachers used repeated measurement made significantly better academic progress. These improvements were noted not only on the passage-reading tests, which were similar to the repeated-measurement procedure, but also on decoding and comprehension measures. In addition, teachers using repeated-measurement procedures were able to write precise and specific goals for students, and students whose behavior was measured repeatedly showed significantly more knowledge about the progress they were making. In a similar study, Marston, Fuchs, and Deno (1986) directly compared the sensitivity of standardized achievement tests and CBM of reading and written language across a 10- and 16-week period. Results of their investigation showed that CBM consistently reflected student progress and was related to teacher judgments of pupil growth across time.

Fuchs and Fuchs (1986b), in a meta-analysis of formative evaluation procedures on student achievement, examined 21 studies in which evaluation procedures employed systematic examination of ongoing student progress and continual modification of instructional procedures. The analysis showed an average weighted effect size of .70. Fuchs and Fuchs suggested from their data that one can expect handicapped students whose programs are monitored to average 0.7 standard deviation units higher than nonmonitored students on evaluation measures. Results of their analysis were consistent across students' age, treatment duration, frequency of measurement, and handicapped status. In particular, the strongest effect sizes were related to use of behavior modification procedures as intervention strategies, use of data-utilization rules by teachers, and use of a graphic method for displaying data. Overall, the study by Fuchs and Fuchs provides significant evidence for the importance of monitoring student progress and using data in decision making.

Fuchs and Fuchs (1986a) also conducted a meta-analysis of studies that used different methods of measuring outcomes on IEPs. Comparisons were made between CBA methods, employing direct assessment of curriculum objectives (e.g., Blankenship, 1985; Idol-Maestas, 1983) and CBM-type methods, which assess performance on identical measures across time (e.g., Fuchs, Deno, & Mirkin, 1984). Analysis of these data showed that the largest effect size was associated with the type of measure employed, but not with the goal on which monitoring occurred. In other words, when progress toward long-term goals was measured, the use of CBM-type methods was more likely to show progress than the use of CBA methods assessing mastery of curriculum objectives. Likewise, when progress toward short-term goals was measured, methods assessing mastery of objectives were more likely to reflect progress than those measuring global performance. These findings may have significant implications for the use of CBM-type measures for planning and assessing interventions for remediation of specific academic deficiencies.

In general, there is a substantial research base justifying the use of CBA methods, particularly CBM-type, in the evaluation of academic problems. These measures appear to possess acceptable psychometric characteristics (reliability and criterion-related validity) and are sensitive to student growth. The measures appear to be important in affecting academic performance and can be useful in differentiating students with and without handicaps.

Despite the very impressive findings supporting these measures, almost all research to date has used traditional psychometric concepts of reliability and validity in justifying their use. For example, although CBM methods have been found to effectively discriminate learning-disabled, Chapter 1, and general education students (e.g., Shinn et al., 1987; Shinn et al., 1986), these measures have only been employed in the concurrent validation of discriminating students who have already been differentiated by use of more traditional methods. Essentially, to say that CBM can accurately identify students classified as learning disabled and those in need of Chapter 1 services only serves to validate the decisions made without these measures. Despite the failure of traditional standardized tests to make these discriminations accurately (Epps, McGue, & Ysseldyke, 1982; Epps, Ysseldyke, & McGue, 1984; Ysseldyke et al., 1983), the fact that CBM can accurately make the discrimination only suggests that whatever the method, current procedures are not doing that badly!

Equally important are the studies examining student progress across time using CBM. Although these studies are important and clearly suggestive of the value of such monitoring, the studies typically employ group research designs that treat individual variation as error variance. Indeed, the meta-analyses reported by Fuchs and Fuchs (1986a,1986b) only included control comparison studies.

What appear to be needed are additional investigations that approach the question of the validity of CBA methods from a more intra-subject perspective. Lentz and I (Lentz & Shapiro, 1986; Shapiro & Lentz, 1985, 1986) have conceptualized CBA as a behavioral assessment methodology. As such, validation of CBA should come through an examination of parameters such as accuracy, generalizability, and treatment validity (Cone, 1981, 1988; Cone & Hoier, 1986; Lentz, 1988). For example, to what degree does a student's oral reading rate vary when he or she reads aloud in a small group to the teacher, individually to the teacher, individually to a stranger, in a small testing room, and so forth? How closely related are a child's spelling scores when the words are taken from the basal reader versus the spelling curriculum? Do we have to make assessments from the same basal reader that the student is reading, or can we use any basal reader? If a teacher does not employ a basal reading series, can we still demonstrate student growth over time by assessing across a basal reading series? These later questions are particularly important for students with handicaps, who may be changing reading series when they return from a self-contained to a mainstreamed setting.

In an attempt to examine the accuracy of CBM, Derr and Shapiro (1989) and Derr-Minneci and Shapiro (1992) investigated the relationship between differential arrangements of how a CBA in reading is conducted. In our studies, 126 third- and fourth-grade students in general education classes were administered sets of reading passages under conditions that varied the location of the assessment, who conducted the evaluation, and whether students knew they were being timed or not. Results showed that oral reading rates were significantly different depending on the conditions of the assessment. These effects were present regardless of whether students were low-, average-, or high-ability readers. The outcome of these studies suggested that the results of a CBA in reading may be affected significantly by the methodology for data collection.

We (McCurdy & Shapiro, 1992) conducted another study to examine the impact of the way CBM data are collected on student performance in reading. Using 48 elementary-age students with learning disabilities, progress monitoring in reading was conducted for 9 weeks. Students were randomly assigned to either teacher-monitoring, peer-monitoring, or self-monitoring conditions. Analysis of the group data showed that students in all conditions made equal levels of progress across time. However, when the data were examined at an idiographic level, students in the teacher-monitoring condition showed the most progress. The study did demonstrate that students with learning disabilities were able to reliably collect CBM data on themselves and their peers, thus demonstrating the potential reduction in teachers time devoted to the data-collection process.

Although these studies have begun to answer some of the important questions that have been raised regarding CBM, continued investigation are needed. Despite this, the use of CBM appears quite promising. Indeed, as noted by Shapiro and Eckert (1993), CBA appears to have made a substantial impact on the practice of school psychologists. For example, Roberts and Rust (1994) found that school psychologists in Iowa spent a significant amount of time in CBA activities. CBA measures seem to be able to overcome many of the problems of the traditional standardized assessment instruments and have been shown in many field settings to be highly acceptable.

SELECTING TARGETS FOR REMEDIATION: LINKING ASSESSMENT TO INTERVENTION

Choosing target behaviors for remediation of academic problems is not always as simple as it seems. When behavioral assessments are conducted for nonacademic problems, the behaviors chosen for assessment are usually the direct targets for remediation. If a child is referred because of excessive talking out during group instruction, the number times the child talks out is recorded, and remediation strategies are developed specifically to reduce the talking-out behavior. If a student is referred because of low rates of peer interaction, the number of peer interactions is assessed, and interventions are implemented to increase the frequency of positive peer interactions. When the problem is academic, however, the link between what is assessed and what is targeted for remediation is not as straightforward. Although a student may have significant problems in reading, the complexity of read-ing behavior makes selection of the specific skill to be assessed quite diffi-cult. For example, a student who is a poor reader may have a deficiency in the component skill of sequencing—a problem that is viewed by some as a prerequisite skill to developing effective reading skill. If one follows the same logical linkage between the assessment and intervention strategies as in a behavioral assessment for nonacademic problems, one should probably design an intervention to remediate sequencing skills, readministering the assessment measures used to identify the deficient component skill. Despite the logical appeal of this approach, there is a substantial literature to sug-gest that such an approach may improve sequencing but not reading.

Arter and Jenkins (1979), in an extensive and comprehensive review of the literature examining the assessment and remediation in diagnos-tic–prescriptive teaching, found very few studies in which the remediation of an underlying perceptual process led to improvements in the overall academic skill of interest. Consistently, the literature showed that even when specific component skills underlying basic academic skills (such as auditory memory or perceptual–motor integration) could be adequately identified and remediated, changes would only be observed for the com-ponent skill trained (i.e., auditory memory or perceptual–motor integra-tion). Any transfer from improvements in these skills to increases in acade-mic performance in reading or math were negligible. The evidence against the use of this approach was so overwhelming that, as noted previ-ously, Arter and Jenkins have called for a moratorium on the classification and placement of children according to differential ability tests and on the use of instructional materials and programs that claim to improve these abilities. The critical issue in selecting the appropriate behaviors for assess-ment is the functional relationship between the assessed behavior and re-mediation strategies designed to improve the skill. Lahey, Vosk, and Habif (1981) noted that approaches such as the DD-PT method described by Arter and Jenkins (1979) assume that because academic skills consist of numerous components, each serving a requisite function resulting in ade-quate academic performance, the assessment and remediation process should center on these molecular skills. However, Lahey et al. (1981) noted substantial evidence suggesting that assessment targets and remediation strategies aimed at more molar levels may result in significant improve-ments in basic academic skills (Lahey, 1976; Lahey, Busemeyer, Beggs, & O'Hara, 1977; Lahey, McNees, & Brown, 1973). On the basis of their analysis, Lahey et al. (1981) suggested that measures such as standardized tests that approximate actual requirements for classroom performance, samples of permanent products from actual academic assignments, and direct observations in classrooms during instructional periods may provide the needed targets for assessments and remediation.

Hoge and Andrews (1987) have provided an extensive review of the literature on selecting targets for remediation of academic problems. Typically, studies that have aimed at improving academic skills have focused either on enhancing classroom behavior or on improving academic performance. Those looking at classroom performance have argued that academic survival skills, such as attention to task, compliance, and nondisruptive behavior, have direct and functional links to improvements in academic responding (e.g., Cobbs & Hopps, 1973; Friedling & O'Leary, 1979; Greenwood, Hops, & Walker, 1977; Greenwood et al., 1979; Hallahan, Lloyd, Kneedler, & Marshall, 1982). Others have examined the relationship of direct remediation of academic skills to both academic performance and classroom behavior (e.g., Ayllon & Roberts, 1974; Broughton & Lahey, 1978; Harris, Graham, Reid, McElroy, & Hamby, 1994; Maag, Reid, & DiGangi, 1993; Reid & Harris, 1993; Speltz, Shimamura, & McReynolds, 1982; Stevenson & Fantuzzo, 1984). Still other researchers have made direct comparisons between interventions designed to improve academic performance and interventions aimed directly at classroom behavior (e.g, Hay, Hay, & Nelson, 1977; Lam, Cole, Shapiro, & Bambara, 1994; Marholin & Steinman, 1977; Marholin, Steinman, McInnis, & Heads, 1975). According to Hoge and Andrews (1987), all of these studies clearly showed that the most direct effects upon academic performance are evident when academic performance rather than classroom behavior is the target for remediation.

What becomes clear in the selection of behaviors for assessing academic problems is the necessity for these behaviors to reflect change in the academic skill, should the selected remediation strategy be effective. Indeed, although the methods developed by Deno and his colleagues for CBA are both molar and aimed at direct assessment of academic skills, they must also be shown to be sensitive to remediation of the skills. Obviously an important question that must be raised is the process by which the intervention strategy would be selected. Over the last several years, Fuchs and colleagues (e.g., Fuchs, Fuchs, Hamlett, & Allinder, 1991a, 1991b; Fuchs, Fuchs, Hamlett, & Ferguson, 1992; Fuchs, Fuchs, Hamlett, & Stecker, 1991; Phillips, Hamlett, Fuchs, & Fuchs, 1993) have increasingly demonstrated that CBM can be used to identify a student's strengths and weaknesses in skill development and assist the teacher in selecting an intervention method that may improve a student's skills. However, although the use of CBM data as described by Deno et al. offers an excellent method for monitoring the effectiveness of academic interventions (e.g., Fuchs, Deno, & Mirkin, 1984; Fuchs & Fuchs, 1986a, 1986b), the method was not designed primarily to suggest which remediation strategies may be effective. How does one chose the intervention procedure likely to remediate the academic problem?

SELECTING INTERVENTION PROCEDURES

Choosing an appropriate remediation strategy should be based on a linkage between assessment and intervention. In choosing interventions for nonacademic problems, Nelson and Hayes (1986) describe three procedures: functional analysis, the keystone behavior strategy, and the diagnostic strategy. A fourth procedure, the template-matching strategy, is also described here.

Functional Analysis

The purpose of functional analysis is to determine empirically the relationships between the variables controlling the target behavior and subsequently to modify these behaviors. In terms of selecting a treatment strategy, the identification of specific environmental variables related to behavior change should differentially lead to the selection of various treatment procedures. Hypothetically, choosing the strategy with a functional relationship to the target behavior should result in improvement, whereas choosing strategies without a functional relationship should not result in any change in the targeted response. Functional analysis has long been suggested as a viable strategy for linking assessment and intervention in behavior analysis (e.g., Ferster, 1965), and several empirical investigations demonstrating the utility of this methodology have appeared in the literature. Based on the work of Iwata, Dorsey, Slifer, Bauman, and Richman (1982), Mace and his colleagues, in a series of studies, have provided several examples of the potential use of the functional analysis methodology.

Mace, Yankanich, and West (1988) have provided both a description and an example of the application of this methodology to the treatment of stereotypic behavior in an 8-year-old girl with profound mental retardation. The method begins with a problem identification interview with the referral source (in this case, a teacher), followed by data collection to generate a series of potential hypotheses regarding variables that may be functioning to maintain the aberrant response. These hypotheses are then evaluated through the development of analogue conditions, typically employed in an alternating treatments design. Data are graphed and examined to determine which variables are functionally related to the response, and a relevant treatment procedure based on this knowledge is then generated, implemented, and evaluated. If the analysis is accurate, the aberrant behavior should be significantly altered once the appropriate treatment procedure is implemented.

In another example of this methodology, Mace and Knight (1986) described the analysis and treatment of pica behavior in a 19-year-old individual with mental retardation. Data collected through direct observation and interviews with staff members suggested the possibility that levels of staff interaction may have been related to the pica behavior. As shown in Figure 2.1, the lowest levels of pica were evident during the condition of frequent staff interaction. Throughout this phase, the client continually wore a protective helmet with a face shield, prescribed by a physician as a mechanism for reducing pica. An additional phase was conducted to examine the relationship of pica to wearing the helmet with and without the face shield. From this analysis, it was determined that frequent interaction without the helmet was likely to result in the most significant reductions of pica behavior. Staff feedback suggested that frequent interaction would be difficult to maintain, so a treatment consisting of limited interaction plus no helmet was implemented. As evident in Figure 2.1, this treatment was successful in substantially reducing the frequency of pica behavior.

This same methodology has been applied by Mace, Browder, and Lin (1987) in reducing stereotypic mouthing and Carr, Newsom, and Binkoff (1980) in analyzing escape behavior in maintaining the aggressive responses of two children with mental retardation. In all cases, the use of functional analysis provided direct links between the process of assessment and the development of intervention strategies.

Although few studies have directly applied this methodology to the selection of effective treatment strategies for academic problems, the procedures described by Mace, Yankanich, and West (1988) seem to have direct applicability to such problems. For example, hypotheses could be generated based on direct observation and interview data collected during the initial analysis phase. These hypotheses could be tested through analogue conditions, and differential treatment procedures could be generated. From these data, one could determine the effective treatment and the functional variables related to academic performance. Thus, one student who is performing poorly in math may be found to be having problems related to competing contingencies (being drawn off-task by peers), whereas another student may need to have the level of difficulty reduced. Each of these cases would require differential interventions, which could be systematically evaluated and implemented within the classroom setting.

Broussard and Northrup (1995) demonstrated the use of functional analysis in the evaluation of three elementary-age students who were referred for extreme disruptive behavior. Based upon the descriptive assessment phase, one of three hypotheses was chosen for functional analysis; disruptive behavior was related primarily to teacher attention, peer attention, or escape from an academic task. For each student, two conditions were constructed that represented occurrences or nonoccurrences of the consequences associated with each hypothesis. For example, for the contingent teacher attention hypothesis, the evaluator made a disapproving statement (e.g., "Pay attention to your work") each time the targeted stu-

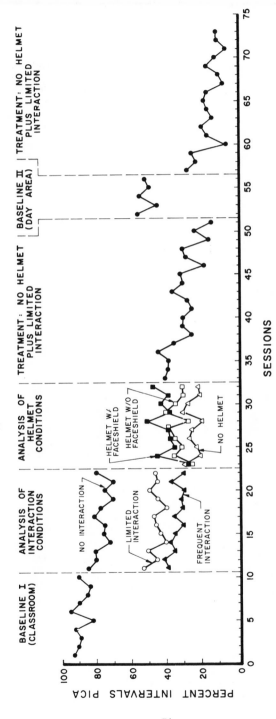

FIGURE 2.1. Pica behavior across baseline, analysis, and treatment conditions. From "Functional Analysis and Treatment of Severe Pica" by F. C. Mace and D. Knight, 1986, *Journal of Applied Behavior Analysis, 19*, p. 415. Copyright 1986 by the Society for the Experimental Analysis of Behavior, Inc. Reprinted by permission.

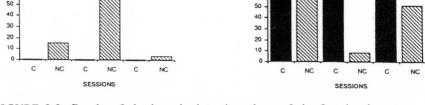

FIGURE 2.2. Results of the hypothesis-testing phase of the functional assessment process. Levels of disruptive behavior (left) and on-task responding (right) are shown for each of the four hypotheses. From "Functional Assessment, Curric-

dent engaged in a disruptive behavior. For nonoccurrence of this condition, the evaluator had the teacher provide noncontingent attention ("Good job") every 60 seconds, independent of the student's behavior. Similar conditions were constructed for the contingent peer attention and escape-from-academic-task hypotheses. Using a reversal design, the effects of the differing conditions were compared. Results of the functional analysis demonstrated that the same disruptive behaviors were controlled by differing contingencies for different students.

In another extension of functional analysis methodology, Cooper et al. (1990) conducted an analysis of variables that were maintaining behavior among children with conduct disorders. Completed in an outpatient clinic setting, the children's parents were instructed to present one of four conditions following a no- demand baseline phase, to present the children with difficult or easy tasks, and to attend or ignore appropriate behavior. Two replications of the conditions were then conducted. Results again showed that the same behavioral responses were maintained by differing sets of consequences.

In working with a 12-year-old girl with a long history of severely disruptive behavior, Dunlap, Kern-Dunlap, Clarke, and Robbins (1991) demonstrated the relationships between the student's school curriculum and her disruptive behavior. Following a descriptive analysis and data-collection process, four hypotheses were generated: (1) the student is better behaved when engaged in large-motor as opposed to fine-motor activities; (2) the student is better behaved when fine-motor and academic requirements are brief as opposed to lengthy; (3) the student is better behaved when engaged in functional activities with concrete and preferred outcomes; and (4) the student is better behaved when she has some choice regarding her activities. In the initial phase of the study, each of these hypotheses was evaluated systematically during 15-minute sessions using materials taken directly from the classroom curriculum.

Results of the analysis are shown in Figure 2.2. The test of the first hypothesis showed that the student had zero level of disruptive behavior (left side of figure) and consistently high levels of on-task behavior (right side of figure) under gross- motor conditions compared to fine-motor activities. Data from the second hypothesis showed substantially better performance under short versus long tasks. The third hypothesis test revealed that she did much better when the task was functional. The results of the

ular Revision, and Severe Behavior Problems" by G. Dunlap, L. Kern-Dunlap, S. Clarke, and F. R. Robbins, 1991, *Journal of Applied Behavior Analysis*, *24*, p. 391. Copyright 1991 by the Society for the Experimental Analysis of Behavior, Inc. Reprinted by permission.

final hypothesis showed superior performance when choice was provided in activities. Thus, the analysis of the student's performance revealed that her best performance would occur using functional, gross-motor activities of a short duration when she had a choice of tasks.

Following the assessment phase, the student's curriculum was revised to incorporate the variables associated with high rates of on-task behavior and low rates of disruptive behavior. Based on the analysis, a set of guidelines was constructed to assist the teacher in developing lesson plans for the student. Specifically, it was suggested that sessions involving fine-motor activities be of short duration (e.g., 5 minutes or less). These activities should be interspersed with gross-motor activities, since these were found to result in low levels of disruption. Whenever possible, the activities should lead to functional and concrete outcomes. In addition, the student should be offered choices regarding activities. Through the help of classroom consultants, these changes were implemented throughout the student's day.

The results were dramatic and immediate. Once the intervention was begun, classroom disruption occurred only once across 30 days of observation. Follow-up data collected up to 10 weeks later showed maintenance of this zero rate of disruption. The student also showed substantial increases in appropriate social behavior and decreases in inappropriate vocalizations.

Conducting a functional analysis in a regular classroom setting requires a high degree of expertise in behavior analysis. Clearly, such a procedure would necessitate the use of a classroom consultant who could effectively direct the classroom teacher and arrange for the analysis to be properly conducted. The outcomes of this analysis are especially useful when faced with a difficult and challenging set of behaviors that may have not responded to more common methods of analysis. Functional analysis does offer an opportunity to provide a strong idiographic analysis of student behavior.

Keystone Behavior Strategy

A second method described by Nelson and Hayes (1986) for selecting intervention strategies is the "keystone behavior strategy." This procedure is based on the notion that one may be able to identify a group of responses that have been found to be linked to a particular disorder. Within this set of responses, a particular response is identified, which if changed, would result in significant and substantial change in the overall group of responses. Thus, one attempts to identify a key response that is functionally related to all others. Nelson and Hayes noted that the primary difference between functional analysis and the keystone behavior strategy is that functional analysis is based on stimulus–response relationships, whereas the keystone strategy is based on response–response interactions.

McKnight, Nelson, Hayes, and Jarrett (1984) provided some evidence for this procedure in a study of depressed women with social skills problems, who showed improved social skills and reduced depression when treated with social skills training as compared to cognitive therapy. Similarly, those with depression and assessed cognitive distortion improved more when treated with cognitive therapy then with social skills training. Thus, assessing and treating the correct behavior was a keystone in reducing depression.

Another example of a keystone behavior is the development of language in nonverbal children with autism. Lovaas (1977) and Lovaas, Koegel, Simmons, and Long (1973) reasoned that the development of language would be a keystone behavior in the amelioration of other aberrant responses in children with autism. Thus, much of Lovaas's efforts in treating these children were aimed at teaching and establishing functional language. Despite these hypotheses, there have been few cases described in which establishing language in children with autism resulted in substantial improvement in other behaviors.

Wahler and Hann (1984), in a naturalistic evaluation of 42 mothers who received a course of therapy, compared those reporting multiple sources versus single sources of stress. Using summary reports of the mothers' discussing their children's problems with therapists, kinfolk, and friends, Wahler and Hann showed that the presence of more than a single stressor may be a keystone in the prognosis for therapy outcomes.

Although the keystone behavior strategy certainly has applicability to the selection of interventions for academic problems, no studies reported to date have specifically examined this procedure. However, Jenkins, Larson, and Fleisher (1983) and Roberts and Smith (1980) conducted studies that would be analogous to a keystone strategy in the remediation of reading problems. In the Jenkins et al. (1983) study, the relationships between reading comprehension and two instructional strategies for correcting reading errors, word supply and word drill, were examined. Results showed that drill had substantially more impact on word recognition and comprehension than word supply. Similarly, Roberts and Smith (1980) examined the effects on comprehension of interventions aimed at either increasing oral reading rate or decreasing error rate. Results suggested that improvements in rates (correct or error) did not affect comprehension. When comprehension was targeted, collateral changes did occur in both reading rates. Shapiro (1987a) showed the interrelationships between comprehension and oral reading rates when a contingent reinforcement procedure was applied differentially to these behaviors. Results of this analysis are shown in Figure 2.3.

Diagnostic Strategy

The diagnostic strategy for choosing interventions is one that is based on the traditional medical model, that is, the notion that effective diagnosis leads to effective treatment. In this model, the diagnosis is determined from the assessment information and is based on a particularly nosology, for example, the fourth edition of the *Diagnostic and Statistical Manual of Mental Disorders* (DSM-IV; American Psychiatric Association, 1994). The specific intervention plan is determined on the basis of this diagnosis. For example, an individual diagnosed as phobic might receive exposure treatment (Barlow & Wolfe, 1981), and a depressive might receive cognitive therapy (Beck, Rush, Shaw, & Emery, 1979). Treatment selection is based on known relationships between treatment effectiveness and specific disorders (Nelson, 1988).

Applications of this approach to academic problems are somewhat vague, since educators do not use the same type of nosological classifications as clinicians. However, a child diagnosed as having attention-deficit/hyperactivity disorder may be viewed as a good candidate for pharmaco-

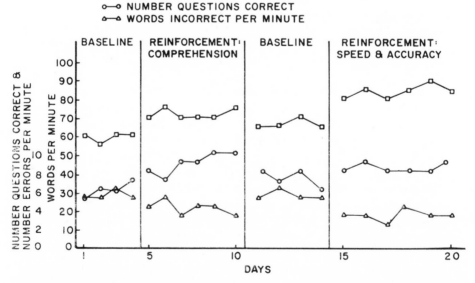

FIGURE 2.3. Collateral effects on oral reading rates and comprehension on a student in a reading program using contingent reinforcement. From "Academic Problems" by E. S. Shapiro, 1987, in M. Hersen and V. B. Van Hasselt (Eds.), *Behavior Therapy with Children and Adolescents: A Clinical Approach*, p. 377. Copyright 1987 by John Wiley & Sons, Inc. Reprinted by permission.

logical therapy to indirectly affect academic performance. Likewise, a child with a conduct disorder, who is having academic problems, may be viewed as more likely to respond to contingency management aimed at the disruptive behavior rather than at the academic performance problem (Hoge & Andrews, 1987).

Not unexpectedly, the role of the diagnostic process in the selection of intervention procedures is quite limited in behavioral assessment. There has been little evidence that effective diagnoses can be effectively made. For example, Felton and Nelson (1984) reported that six clinicians assessing the same clients had poor levels of agreement regarding controlling variables, yet had much higher levels of agreement on the treatment proposals. Clearly, the link between assessment and intervention was quite poor. Likewise, Wilson and Evans (1983) reported low levels of agreement in identifying children's problems from written protocols. Although substantial attempts to improve the reliability of psychiatric diagnosis has been made through the revision of the DSM-IV, little research has currently been done to determine if the links between assessment and intervention have improved with this latest psychiatric classification system.

In educational settings, children with academic problems are often considered for placement into special education. In a sense, the decision as to a child's eligibility for special education is a diagnostic decision, since eligibility determination is based on meeting the criteria for a specific classification (e.g., learning-disabled, behavior-disordered, educationally-handicapped). Yet these diagnostic labels have little to do with educational treatment. Indeed, substantial data suggest the instructional processes in classes for children with mild handicaps are more similar than they are different (e.g., Reynolds, 1984; Rich & Ross, 1989; Thurlow, Graden, Greener, & Ysseldyke, 1983; Thurlow, Ysseldyke, et al., 1983, 1984; Ysseldyke et al., 1984). Thus, the diagnostic–treatment link is equally weak for academic problems.

Template-Matching Strategy

Hoier and Cone (1987), Cone and Hoier (1986), and Hoier, McConnell, and Pallay (1987) describe a procedure called "template matching" that may have implications for selection of intervention strategies. Data are obtained on individuals deemed to possess effective levels of the desired behaviors. These profiles, or "templates," are compared to those individuals who are targeted for remediation in order to identify the specific behaviors that need to be remediated. Hoier (1984; cited in Hoier and Cone, 1986) compared the social skills of third- and fourth-grade students against those of classmates considered exemplary in their behavior, using primarily peer-assessment data. Discrepancies between the exemplary students' and the other students' behavior became targets for intervention. In a validation of the process, it was found that as a child's template approached the exemplary template, increases in peer interaction were evident.

Although designed primarily to identify behaviors for remediation, the procedure may have implications for choosing intervention strategies. For example, once specific behaviors are identified, one may decide on alternative treatments for differential templates. By matching the template to the treatment procedure, one may be able to make effective recommendations for interventions. Still, the applicability of these procedures to academic interventions may be somewhat questionable.

For example, we (Ager & Shapiro, 1995) used template matching to develop strategies to facilitate the transition between preschool and kindergarten for students with disabilities. Using the ESCAPE and Assessment Code/Checklist for Evaluating Survival Skills (ACCESS), templates of the expected behaviors in kindergarten classes of students without disabilities were constructed. These templates were constructed in the classrooms in which the target group of students with disabilities would be placed during the following school year. Data were then collected on the same behaviors in the preschoolers' classrooms. Using the discrepancies between the preschool and kindergarten environments, a series of interventions were implemented to more closely align the expectations of the kindergarten classroom with those of the preschool. At follow-up, those students for whom the interventions based on template matching were implemented exhibited fewer disruptive behaviors and showed high levels of independent work.

SUMMARY OF PROCEDURES FOR CHOOSING INTERVENTIONS

Despite the potential of functional analysis, the keystone behavior strategy, or template matching in applications for remediating academic problems, the current methods for choosing an intervention strategy remain largely subjective. Typically, teachers are interviewed about the child's problem; the data are examined regarding potentially important variables that may affect academic performance; the literature is consulted for studies that have previously shown the variables critical to achievement; and recommendations are made for interventions. These recommendations often are based on the teacher's experiences with other students with similar problems, past successes and failures, the range of expertise of the teacher and consultant, the structure of the classroom, the time available for remediation, the resources offered by the setting, and other variables that may or may not have direct relationships to the problem at hand. Clearly, a more empirical analysis of these effects would be worthwhile. At present, the methodology suggested by Mace et al. (1987) may have the most applicability. Still, significant work must be done to demonstrate that the procedures described for assessing and treating aberrant behavior are also applicable for assessing and treating problems in academic skill acquisition. It is important to remember that the variables surrounding an academic ecology may be significantly more complex than those surrounding behaviors such as pica or stereotypic head weaving (Lentz, 1988; Lentz & Shapiro, 1986). Furthermore, moving functional-analysis methodology into school-based applications may require additional modifications of the procedure. Despite these cautions, this method appears to offer significant promise for making the assessment–intervention link an empirically based decision.

An equally important consideration is the level of analysis at which each of the procedures are aimed. With the exception of the functional analysis, empirical support for the procedures described is based on the aggregation of data across cases. These methods rely on the ability to make effective generalizations based on assessment data. Unfortunately, almost all concerns of the practitioner are at the level of the individual. What is important is the ability to effect change in a specific student's problem. Whether the individual student is like other students with similar problems is of interest in general, but not necessarily of concern to the person conducting the assessment at that time. This makes a methodology such as functional analysis, which examines the problem at the individual student level, rather attractive.

Substantial work needs to be done to bring the decision-making process for choosing intervention strategies into line with the assessment methodology employed. Conceptually, behavioral assessment is designed to offer this link. Although the empirical link is somewhat questionable at this time, behavioral assessment continues to offer the best opportunity for using the assessment data to make one's "best guess" as to the critical elements needed for an effective intervention.

CHAPTER 3

♦♦♦

Step 1: Assessing the
Academic Environment

♦

OVERVIEW

The process of conducting an assessment of academic behavior incorporates several different methods, each designed to contribute to the overall understanding of the problem. It is important to remember that because academic responses occur in the context of an instructional environment, an effective evaluation of academic problems must contain more than just an assessment of academic skills. Procedures employed in the assessment process are those typical of behavioral assessment for nonacademic problems (interviews, direct observation, examination of permanent products) and those developed by Deno and others for curriculum-based assessment (CBA). Specifically, interviews, direct observation, and examination of permanent products provide the assessment of the academic environment, whereas the CBA procedures provide assessment of individual academic skills. Interpretation of the data, conclusions, and recommendations from the assessment require careful examination and integration of the data collected from each part of the assessment process.

Several objectives guide an assessment of academic problems. First, it is important to determine the degree to which the academic ecology is contributing to the observed academic problem (Lentz & Shapiro, 1986). Understanding how events such as instructional presentation, feedback, and class structure relate to academic responding may provide significant clues regarding potential intervention strategies for remediating the academic problems. Second, the assessment is designed to separate the degree to which the child's problem is a skills versus performance deficit. In many cases, students exhibit a "won't do" rather than "can't do" problem. These students possess the necessary skills for performance, but do not exhibit these skills when the situation for performance arises in the classroom. Other students may show similar deficits in performance; however, careful assessment reveals that their failure is due primarily to inadequate mastery of needed skills. Clearly, the remediation recommendations in each case would be different.

A third objective of the assessment for academic problems is to determine where in the curriculum the child has achieved mastery, where he or she should be instructed, and where he or she is frustrated. It is surprising to find how many times students are moved on in curricular materials despite their failure to achieve mastery of prerequisite skills. Considering that most curricula are based on principles of both repetition (spiraling) and hierarchical skills (building), failure to master certain skills will almost always lead to difficulty in subsequent parts of the curricula.

Fourth, the academic assessment should serve to assist several types of educational decisions. Salvia and Ysseldyke (1995) noted that educational assessments are used to make decisions about referral, screening, classification, instructional planning, and pupil progress. Among these, we (Lentz & Shapiro, 1985) strongly suggest that the most important purpose of an evaluation is to provide suggestions for the development of interventions aimed to remediate the problem areas.

A critical and underlying assumption of assessing academic skills is a function of environmental *and* individual variables. As such, one cannot simply focus upon the child's academic skills as the source of academic failure. It is equally important to examine events within the instructional environment that may be contributing significantly to the child's problems. In addition, careful examination of the teaching procedures, contingencies for performance, classroom structure, and other such instructional events may often suggest appropriate remediation strategies.

When academic skills are assessed, the child's academic behavior that represents the closest duplication of responses made during typical classroom instruction should be the target for evaluation. This requires that the assessment procedures be derived directly from the curriculum materials in which the child is being instructed. In this way, one is able to determine the degree to which a child has mastered what he or she has been expected to learn. Furthermore, examination of permanent products (e.g., worksheets, homework assignments, etc.) may offer significant information about the child's academic problems.

Many different terms have been used to describe the type of academic assessment under discussion. Deno and his colleagues refer to the procedure as curriculum-based measurement (CBM). Howell et al. (1993) have called it "curriculum-based evaluation." Others (Blankenship 1985; Gickling & Havertape, 1981; Idol, Nevin, & Paolucci-Whitcomb,1986; Shapiro & Lentz 1986; Tucker, 1985) have labeled the procedure "curriculum-based assessment" (CBA). Although each of these emphasizes somewhat different aspects of the evaluation process, they all have in common assessing a child's academic problems on the basis of the curriculum in which the child is instructed. One important difference, however, is that most models other than the one Lentz and I described (Shapiro, 1987b, 1989; 1990; Shapiro & Lentz, 1985, 1986) do *not* incorporate significant efforts at evaluating the academic environment along with the child's skills. Efforts to add this component to curriculum-based measurement have been offered by Ysseldyke and Christenson (1986, 1993). The model we have suggested is most consistent with the assumptions and methods of behavioral assessment. As such, our model of CBA is conceptualized as the behavioral assessment of academic skills. For the simplicity of communication, however, future mention of CBA in this text will all refer to the model we have described (Shapiro & Lentz, 1985, 1986) as "behavioral assessment of academic skills."

What Curriculum-Based Assessment Is

CBA is designed to assess individuals who have deficits in *basic academic skills*. This means that the procedures are relevant for those pupils having difficulty reading, writing, spelling, or doing math. Students of all ages, *including secondary-age students*, with deficiencies in these areas can be assessed using CBA. Students with these types of problems are found typically in the elementary grades, however. After all, once students reach the middle and high school levels, their academic skills should have progressed to the point at which they can be instructed effectively in content areas (i.e., social studies, science, history, etc.). However, we have all come across students who are failing history because they cannot read the text, or those who fail math because they cannot read the word problems. CBA is a relevant method of assessment for these students.

Attempts to bring CBA methods to content-area instruction have not been widely reported in the literature. Tindal and Parker (1989) examined the development of several possible metrics to conduct progress monitoring for students in 6th-, 8th-, and 11th-grade subject matter. Unfortunately, their attempts were not highly successful. At present, it is recommended that CBA, as described in this text, be limited to working with students who have basic skill deficiencies and are primarily in elementary level grades.

CBA can contribute to a number of decisions regarding a student with an academic problem. Specifically it can do the following:

1. Serve as an effective means for providing preplacement evaluation.
2. Determine if a student is accurately placed in curriculum materials.
3. Assist in developing strategies for remediation of academic problems.
4. Suggest changes in the instructional environment that may improve the student's performance.
5. Provide a means for setting individual educational plan (IEP) short- and long-term goals.
6. Provide a method for monitoring progress and performance of students across time.
7. Provide an empirical method for determining when an intervention is effective or not.
8. Make the assessment relevant to what the child has been expected to learn by being referenced to the curriculum.
9. Provide a potential strategy for screening students.
10. Offer an empirical method for deciding if a student needs to move to a more restrictive setting.
11. Provide accountability for teachers and psychologists when making eligibility decisions.

What Curriculum-Based Assessment Is Not

CBA is a set of new skills for purposes other than traditional psychodiagnostic assessments. Specifically, CBA is designed to assist in preplacement assessment and intervention. The data derived from CBA are intended to help make decisions regarding the variables contributing to academic performance. A significant assumption of CBA is that these variables lie *both* within the individual skills of the student *and* within the academic environment.

CBA is not designed to replace current service delivery systems completely. The legal requirements for most eligibility decisions still include the administration of norm-referenced instruments, such as individual intelligence and achievement tests. Although CBA can contribute to the decision-making process for eligibility, it cannot be used alone for making these decisions if legal mandates require specific instruments to be administered. Some school settings, however, have experimented with the use of CBA data alone for making eligibility decisions (Marston & Magnusson, 1985; Tindal, Wesson, et al., 1985).

CBA, at least the model presented here, is also not designed to evaluate problems in content areas such as American history or chemistry. Although there are CBA models that can address these areas (see Idol et al., 1986 or Howell et al., 1993), students having difficulty in these areas more often seem to have trouble in study skills or memory and require different types of assessment strategies.

Finally, it is important to remember that although the data on academic skills collected during a CBA can be on their own extremely useful, CBA, in combination with a general behavioral consultation approach, can work effectively as a method for service delivery. The integration of CBA with behavioral consultation is described elsewhere (Lentz & Shapiro, 1985; Reschly & Grimes, 1991; Rosenfield, 1987; Shapiro, 1987b).

ASSESSING THE ACADEMIC ENVIRONMENT

Overview

The assessment of the academic environment incorporates examination of variables that have been found to affect academic performance significantly. These variables include academic engaged time (scheduled time, allotted time, time on-task, opportunities to respond, response rates); events that are concurrent with engagement (instructional presentation, contingencies for performance, and classroom structure); events that are temporally removed from academic responding but may significantly influence performance (instructions, contingencies for completion, and accuracy); and teacher methods of planning and evaluation. Although all of these variables can be directly assessed through observation, it would become impractical to consistently try to observe each of these for each assessment method. As such, the use of teacher interviews, combined with direct observation of related variables such as on-task behavior, teacher attention to academic performance, and the examination of actual student products can permit the observer to examine (at least indirectly) each of the variables of concern.

Beyond these data, it is also important to determine the student's perspective on the instructional process. For example, does the student know how to access help when he or she runs into difficulty? Does the student know the objectives of the instructional lesson? What is the student's self-perception of his or her ability to successfully meet the requirements of the task? Does the student understand the instructions of the task? Answers to these types of questions may add substantially to the analysis of the instructional ecology. To obtain this information, a student interview needs to be conducted. Table 3.1 provides a list of both relevant variables for assessing the academic environment as well as which method (teacher interview, student interview, observation, or permanent products) offers data on that variable.

TABLE 3.1. Assessment Procedures for Achievement-Related Variables

Variable	Procedures
Actual placement of student in curriculum according to skill	Direct assessment using skill probes, curriculum tests, criterion-references tests
Expected placement	Teacher interview
Actual placement procedures used by teacher	Teacher interview, permanent product review
Allotted time	Teacher interview, direct observation
Opportunities to respond	Direct observation, permanent products
Active and passive engaged time	Direct observation
Student perceptions of teacher expectations	Student interview
Student academic self-efficacy	Student interview
Immediate contingencies	Direct observation
Competing contingencies	Direct observation, teacher interview, student interview
Orientation to materials	Direct observation
Teacher feedback	Direct observation, teacher interview, student interview
Teacher planning	Teacher interview

The model we have described (Shapiro & Lentz, 1985, 1986) was modified by Shapiro (1990) and was displayed in Figure 1.1 (see Chapter 1). This approach combines components from several other models of CBA and involves a four-step process: (1) assessment of the instructional environment, (2) evaluation of instructional placement, (3) instructional modification, and (4) progress monitoring. The process begins with the teacher interview. Data obtained from the interview will often suggest relevant and critical settings in which direct observation will need to be made, as well as the important areas of academic skills in need of assessment. A student interview is also conducted in conjunction with the direct observation. Finally, permanent products obtained during those observations will again help in interpreting and confirming the interview and observational data. Figure 3.1 includes a flowchart of the sequence of methods used to conduct the assessment of the academic environment.

Teacher Interviews

The first step in conducting the CBA is to interview the teacher. During the interview, information is obtained about each area of basic skills (read-

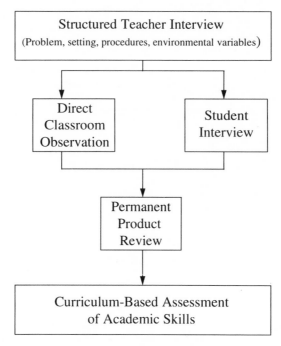

FIGURE 3.1. Flowchart of procedures for assessing academic skills.

ing, math, spelling, written language). Specifically, questions are asked about the curriculum, instructional procedures, and the child's performance. Data are sought regarding the current level and placement of the child in the curriculum, the specific materials employed for instruction, the expected levels of performance of "typical" students in the classroom, the types of instructional settings used by the teacher (large group, small group, learning centers, cooperative learning), monitoring procedures employed to assess student progress, specific contingencies for performance, and some global indications of the child's behavior during the instructional process. For these last types of data, questions are asked regarding on-task levels, homework completion, class participation, and other events that might affect academic performance.

The format for the interview process is based on the behavioral consultation process described by Bergan (1977), Bergan and Kratochwill (1990) and Kratochwill and Bergan (1990). The model incorporates the use of a series of interviews designed to identify the problem, analyze the critical variables contributing to the problem, design and implement intervention strategies, and evaluate the effectiveness of the intervention. The interview process described by the model offers a comprehensive analysis of verbal behavior and a methodology for training consultants to conduct these interviews. Bergan's interview procedures can be used reliably (Bergan, 1977; Erchul, Covington, Hughes, & Meyers, 1995; Gresham, 1984; Kratochwill, Elliott, & Busse, 1995) and the types of consultant verbalizations needed for a problem analysis interview have been validated (Gresham, 1984; Witt, 1990; Witt, Erchul, McKee, Pardue, & Wickstrom, 1991). In addition, outcome data reported by Bergan and Tombari (1975) and Miltenberger and Fuqua (1985) show the importance of effective problem identification for the problem-solving process.

Although there have been other behavioral interviewing formats for school consultation (e.g., Alessi & Kaye, 1983; Lentz & Wehmann, 1995; Witt & Elliott, 1983), the format described by Bergan appears to be most often cited in the behavioral consultation literature. For example, Graden, Casey and Bonstrom (1985) and Graden, Casey, and Christensen (1985) used Bergan's behavioral consultation model in an investigation of a pre-referral intervention program across six schools. Noll, Kamps, and Seaborn (1993) reported that a prereferral intervention program using a behavioral consultation model over a 3-year period resulted in between 43% and 64% of students referred remaining in general education class-rooms.

Appendix 3A provides a convenient form that has been developed to facilitate the teacher interview process. The section on reading is straight-forward. After identifying the specific name and type of reading series (i.e., basal, literature-based, trade books), as well as the target student's current level (for a basal series) within the series, the teacher is also asked to identify the point in the reading series that the average student in the class has reached at this time. If the teacher is having some difficulty in defining the "average student," the interviewer may want to suggest that he or she think about the students in the average or middle reading group. It is helpful to get information as specific as possible regarding the targeted student's and his or her peers' placement in the reading series, including the particular page on which the students are working currently. However, this may not be useful information if the teacher is using a literature-based rather than basal reading series.

The interviewer also asks for information about how the instructional time is allotted and divided. In reading, one needs to determine how often students are instructed in small groups, the size of the target student's group, what the expectations are for students when they are not engaged in direct teacher instruction, and other structural aspects of the teaching process. Furthermore, any specific contingencies, such as stickers, points, or rewards for completion and/or accuracy, need to be recorded.

Another important question in the interview concerns how changes are made in the instructional program. In some schools, any changes in the reading program must be cleared through the district reading specialist. This information may be influential in a teacher's decision to not alter instruction, despite a student's failure to master the given material. Equally important is information on how student performance is monitored.

The interview form also asks teachers to provide some indication of the target student's skills in certain components of reading, such as oral reading, word attack, sight vocabulary, and comprehension. In each of these areas, the teacher is asked to compare the target student to peers in the same reading group as well as those in the entire class.

Finally, the teacher is asked to complete a brief rating form describing different types of behavior problems that commonly interfere with successful academic performance. These include participation in the reading group, knowing the appropriate place in the book when called on, staying on-task and in-seat during independent seatwork, and handing in homework on time that is complete and accurate. Each of these behaviors are rated on a 5-point scale.

Content for the interview in mathematics is similar, but contains a few critical differences. The primary concern in the CBA interview for math is with computational skills. Typically, students who cannot master basic computational skills are unable to effectively master applications of mathematics, such as measurement, time, money, or geometry. Although an increased emphasis in math instruction today is placed on problem-solving skills, computational skills still provide a foundation for success in basic math. Some questions are included regarding the student's skills in the areas of math problem-solving and applications, however, the primary emphasis in the interview is the student's mastery of computational objectives. Mathematical computation tends to be taught in a consistent sequence across curricula. Skills are generally hierarchical and are taught in such a way that acquisition of one skill will provide a basis for learning later skills. For example, students are taught single-digit addition facts with sums less than 10 before sums greater than 10 are taught. Students are taught addition and subtraction without regrouping before regrouping is instructed. Typically, all students are placed within the same level of the math curriculum. Asking a teacher where a student is currently placed in the curriculum may be somewhat helpful, but it may not specifically define the computational objectives that have or have not been mastered. To determine the computational skills of the student from the teacher interview, one needs to examine the list of computational objectives for that particular district and curriculum. This can be obtained from the scope and sequence charts of the curriculum if it is not available from the district curriculum officer.

Although using the district-based list of computational objectives is ideal, the order in which these skills are instructed does not usually vary significantly. It is therefore possible to use an already existing set of objectives taken from any curriculum or district. Provided in Appendix 3B is the list of computational objectives for a small urban school district in the northeastern United States. A similar list of objectives was provided for the Pine County Minnesota Cooperative School District by Deno and Mirkin (1977). When such a list is used during the interview, the teacher is asked to mark the approximate objective the target student has mastered, the objective at which the student is being instructed, the objective at which the student is frustrated, the objective the average student in the class has mastered, and the objective at which the average student in the class is being instructed. Each of these points will play an important role in the direct assessment of math skills.

Other questions on the interview for math are identical to those on the interview for reading. Questions are asked about the instructional process (large group, small groups, independent seatwork, learning centers, cooperative learning), how progress is monitored and changes are made in instruction, what contingencies are in place for completion or accurate performance, how much time is allotted for instruction, and what problems the student may have in applications of mathematics. In addition, a similar behavior checklist is completed.

The interview for spelling is straightforward and asks questions very similar to the reading interview. An item is added, however, that asks whether the student demonstrates the same problems in spelling on homework as are evident in class. Students who may complete spelling assignments accurately only when they are assigned as homework may suggest the degree to which parents or siblings are involved in helping the student at home.

Finally, the teacher is asked to describe the types of writing assignments used in the classroom. The specific difficulties of the target student are then described in the areas of expression of thought, mechanics, grammatical usage, handwriting, and spelling. An additional opportunity is included for the teacher to express any concern about potential social–emotional adjustment problems that may be interfering with academic performance.

Figure 3.2 illustrates a completed teacher-interview form for a fourth-grade boy, Richard. In reading, the teacher indicated that Richard is currently placed in level J (book 2, grade 3) of the Houghton Mifflin basal reading series. Of the three reading groups in her class, Richard is in the middle group. Approximately 2 hours each day are allotted for language arts; this time is divided into group instruction, individual seatwork assignments, a reading center, and individual silent reading time.

TEACHER INTERVIEW FORM FOR ACADEMIC PROBLEMS

Student: __Richard__   Teacher: __Mrs. B__

Birthdate: __11/5/76__   Date: __2/24/87__

Grade: __4__   School: __Reiger__

                                         Interviewer: __K.E.__

GENERAL

Why was this student referred? __Academic difficulties__

What type(s) of academic problem(s) does this student have?
__Written language and behavior problems__

READING

Primary type of reading series used
- ☒ Basal reader
- ☐ Literature-based
- ☐ Trade books

Secondary type of reading materials used
- ☐ Basal reader
- ☐ Literature-based
- ☒ Trade books
- ☐ None

Reading series title (if applicable) __Houghton Mifflin__

  Grade level of series currently placed __3-2 (Level J)__

  Title of book in series currently placed __Weavers__

How many groups do you teach? __3__

Which group is this student assigned to? __Middle__

At this point in the school year, where is the average student in your class reading?

  Level and book __Level 3, book 2 (Level J)__

  Place in book (beginning, middle, end, specific page) __Middle__

Time allotted/day for reading __9:30–11:30__

How is time divided? (Independent seatwork? Small group? Cooperative Group?)
__Teacher-led small group, independent seat work, reading center__

How is placement in reading program determined? __Formal testing every 2 years,__
__teacher observation, classroom tests__

How are changes made in the program? __Checks in basal series and cross-referenced__
__with individual and content skills lists__

Does this student participate in Chapter 1 (remedial) reading programs? How much?
__No__

Typical daily instructional procedures __Group instruction followed by individual work__
__(reading centers, cooperative groups, silent reading)__

Contingencies for accuracy? __85%, no rewards, stars for independent reading__

Contingencies for completion? __Teacher sets goals, child completes independently__

Daily scores (if available) for past 2 weeks __None available__

Group standardized test results (if available) __None available__

FIGURE 3.2. Example of completed teacher interview form.

ORAL READING

How does he/she read orally compared to others in his/her reading group?
___ Much worse   ___ Somewhat worse   ___ About the same
_X_ Somewhat better   ___ Much better

In the class?
___ Much worse   ___ Somewhat worse   ___ About the same
_X_ Somewhat better   ___ Much better

WORD ATTACK

Does he /she attempt unknown words? _Yes_

SIGHT WORDS

How is the student's sight vocabulary, compared to others in the reading group?
___ Much worse   ___ Somewhat worse   ___ About the same
_X_ Somewhat better   ___ Much better

In the class?
___ Much worse   ___ Somewhat worse   ___ About the same
_X_ Somewhat better   ___ Much better

COMPREHENSION

How well does the student seem to understand what he/she reads, compared to others in his/her reading group?
___ Much worse   ___ Somewhat worse   ___ About the same
_X_ Somewhat better   ___ Much better

In the class?
___ Much worse   ___ Somewhat worse   ___ About the same
_X_ Somewhat better   ___ Much better

BEHAVIOR DURING READING

Rate the following areas from 1 to 5 (1 = very unsatisfactory, 3 = satisfactory, 5 = superior)

READING GROUP

a. Oral reading ability (as evidenced in reading group)	_3_
b. Volunteers answers	_4_
c. When called upon, gives correct answer	_4_
d. Attends to other students when they read aloud	_5_
e. Knows the appropriate place in book	_5_

INDEPENDENT SEATWORK

a. Stays on task	_4_
b. Completes assigned work in required time	_5_
c. Work is accurate	_4_
d. Works quietly	_4_
e. Remains in seat when required	_5_

HOMEWORK (if any)

a. Handed in on time	_5_
b. Is complete	_5_
c. Is accurate	_4_

(cont.)

FIGURE 3.2. *(cont.)*

MATHEMATICS

Curriculum series _Heath_

What are the specific problems in math? _No problems_

Time allotted/day for math _40 minutes_

How is time divided? (Independent seatwork? Small group? Large group? Cooperative groups?) _Independent seatwork, small-, large-group instruction_

For an average performing student in your class, at what point in the planned course format would you consider this student at mastery? (See computational mastery form.) _#37—Subtraction with regrouping_

For an average-performing student in your class, at what point in the planned course format would you consider this student instructional? (See computational mastery form.) _#41—Multiply with regrouping_

For an average performing student in your class, at what point in the planned course format would you consider this student frustrational? (See computational mastery form.) _#44—Divide with remainder_

For the targeted student in your class, at what point in the planned course format would you consider this student at mastery? (See computational mastery form.) _Same as average student_

For the targeted student in your class, at what point in the planned course format would you consider this student instructional? (See computational mastery form.) _Same as average student_

For the targeted student in your class, at what point in the planned course format would you consider this student frustrational? (See computational mastery form.) _Same as average student_

How is mastery assessed? _Pre- and posttest every chapter_

Describe any difficulties this student has in applying math skills (measurement, time, money, geometry, problem solving) _Some trouble with 2 × 2 digit multiplication,_ _word problems_

Are your students grouped in math? _Yes_

If so, how many groups do you have, and in which group is this student placed? _3 groups; top students_

How are changes made in the student's math program? _Based on mastery_

Does this student participate in Chapter 1 (remedial) math programs? _No_

Typical daily instructional procedures _Group instruction and independent network_

Contingencies for accuracy? _85%_

Contingencies for completion? _Based on individual goals_

Daily scores (if available) for past 2 weeks _Pre- and posttest scores available_

Group standardized test results (if available) _Not available_

BEHAVIOR DURING MATH

Rate the following areas from 1 to 5 (1 = very unsatisfactory, 3 = satisfactory, 5 = superior)

MATH GROUP (large)

a. Volunteers answers   5
b. When called upon, gives correct answer   4
c. Attends to other students when they give answers   4
d. Knows the appropriate place in math book   5

MATH GROUP (small)

a. Volunteers answers   5
b. When called upon, gives correct answer   4
c. Attends to other students when they give answers   4
d. Knows the appropriate place in math book   5

MATH GROUP (cooperative)

a. Volunteers answers   5
b. Contributes to group objectives   4
c. Attends to other students when they give answers   4
d. Facilitates others in group to participate   5
e. Shows appropriate social skills in group   3

INDEPENDENT SEATWORK

a. Stays on task   5
b. Completes assigned work in required time   5
c. Work is accurate   4
d. Works from initial directions   4
e. Works quietly   4
f. Remains in seat when required   5

HOMEWORK (if any)

a. Handed in on time   5
b. Is complete   5
c. Is accurate   4

SPELLING

Type of material used for spelling instruction:

☑ Published spelling series
    Title of series __Economy–Keys to Spelling Mastery__
☐ Basal reading series
    Title of series _____
☐ Teacher-made materials
☐ Other _____

Level of instruction (if applicable) __fourth grade__

At this point in the school year, where is the average student in your class spelling?
    Level, place in book __fourth grade or below__

Time allotted/day for spelling __25 minutes__

How is time divided? (Independent seatwork? Small group? Cooperative groups?)
__Ind. seatwork, small and large groups__

How is placement in spelling program determined? __Test at beginning of year__

(cont.)

FIGURE 3.2. *(cont.)*

How are changes made in the program? <u>Mastery of level, then advanced to next</u>
<u>highest level</u>

Typical daily instructional procedures <u>Drill every morning, 10 to higher level</u>

Contingencies for accuracy? <u>100% upon self-correction</u>

Contingencies for completion? <u>Individually set goals</u>

WRITING

Please describe the type of writing assignments you give <u>Daily assignments–journal</u>
<u>writing</u>

Compared to others in your class, does he/she have difficulty with
(please provide brief descriptions):

☑ Expressing thoughts <u>Most significant problem</u>
☐ Story length <u>No</u>
☑ Story depth <u>Yes, limited explanation</u>
☑ Creativity <u>Yes, repeats ideas throughout writing</u>

Mechanics:

☐ Capitalization
☐ Punctuation
☑ Grammar
☐ Handwriting
☑ Spelling

BEHAVIOR

Are there social–behavioral adjustment problems interfering with this student's
academic progress? (be specific) <u>Previously yes, now no</u>

Check any item that describes this student's behavior:
_____ Distracted, short attention span, unable to concentrate
_____ Hyperactive, constant, aimless movement
_____ Impulsive/aggressive behaviors, lacks self-control
_____ Fluctuating levels of performance
_____ Frequent negative self-statements
_____ Unconsciously repeating verbal or motor acts
_____ Lethargic, sluggish, too quiet
_____ Difficulty sharing or working with others

Approximately 20–25 minutes each day are devoted to small-group instruction. Richard's teacher has characterized his oral reading, sight word, and word attack skills as somewhat better than his classmates. Comprehension is also reported as somewhat better, but with difficulties related to inferential comprehension.

Examination of the entire interview reveals that the area of most concern is written language. The teacher has indicated that when daily writing assignments are given, Richard has much difficulty in expressing thoughts. Although his mechanics are good, he also shows some deficiencies in grammatical usage.

The entire interview, once an interviewer is skilled in its administration, should take no more than 15–20 minutes. It is important to become thoroughly familiar with the questions, since teachers will often provide responses in many categories when asked a single question. Although the process of interviewing teachers is common in assessment, the types of questions being asked here are not typical of most interview processes. Clearly, asking teachers to describe and think about the instructional process, to describe how they monitor student progress, and to discuss how they make decisions about moving students through the curriculum may result in unexpected defensiveness on the part of the teachers. It is essential that the purpose of this type of interview be explained to teachers prior to beginning the interview. Although asking these types of questions may appear to be potentially dangerous to maintaining effective rapport with teachers, it has been found over hundreds of cases that the common response to being asked these questions is very positive. Often, teachers will remark that they had not asked themselves these questions, which they recognize are important for understanding the students' problems.

Despite the positive testimonials regarding the method, there have not yet been any systematic investigations examining the acceptability of these types of interviews. Until such time, the user of this interview process for CBA is cautioned to be sensitive to a teacher's responses to these questions and to reassure the teacher that his or her answers to these questions are being used to help the evaluator understand the child's academic problem.

An additional adjunct to the teacher interview may be the completion of a more formal teacher-rating scale related to academic skills problems. DuPaul, Rapport, and Perriello (1991) developed the Academic Performance Rating Scale (APRS) to have teachers report their perceptions of student academic behavior. Similar measures can be found as part of the Social Skills Rating Scales—Teacher (Gresham & Elliott, 1990). A copy of the APRS, along with normative data to interpret the measure, can be found in the workbook accompanying this text (Shapiro, 1996).

From the interview and rating-scale data, one is able to discern the specific areas of academic problems, the types of settings (small groups, independent seatwork, etc.) that may differentially affect student performance, the types of instructional methods employed by the teacher, and the environmental conditions for reinforcing appropriate academic behavior. In addition, one obtains vital information regarding teacher expectations and actual student performance, along with indications in mathematics about specific types of computational deficiencies.

Although these data from the interview and rating scales are extremely valuable and useful in the assessment process, they still represent teacher report (verbal or written) and are subject to potential biases inherent in such methods of data collection. Assessing the academic environment requires the confirmation of some of these variables through direct observation. In addition, important data about the child's actual performance during the instructional period are needed.

Direct Observation

One objective of collecting data through direct observation is to provide data that may (or may not) verify the information obtained through teacher report. In particular, the direct observation data give quantitative indications about the student's reported behavior during the instructional process. For example, data collected on the levels of on-task and disruptive behavior during different formats of reading instruction (small groups vs. independent seatwork) may confirm the teacher's report that a student is substantially more disruptive when working alone then when with his or her reading group.

A second objective of direct observation is to provide data on student–teacher interactions under naturalistic conditions of instruction. It is especially important that the assessment involve evaluation not only of individual student behaviors that may be related to effective development of academic skills, but also of those types of student–student and student–teacher interactions that may be related significantly to academic performance.

Finally, given the extensive literature on the role of academic engaged time and academic performance (e.g., Goodman, 1990; Rosenshine, 1981; Rosenshine & Berliner, 1978), the direct observation of academic skills should include data collection on variables that can approximate engaged time. This would include data obtained on on-task behavior or opportunities to respond (e.g., Greenwood, Delquadri, & Hall, 1984).

In combination with direct observation, it is also important to examine the products of the student's academic performance while the direct observations were being conducted. The worksheets or academic activities that the student produces can be valuable pieces of information that allow a more accurate interpretation of the observational data. For example, although the data collected through direct observation may show that a student has a high level of on-task behavior, examination of the worksheet produced during the observation may show that the student only completed a small number of items correctly. Thus, this may be a student who has learned to appear to be working well and paying attention in class but is really struggling academically.

Procedures for collecting data systematically through direct observation have been well articulated in the literature (see Cooper, Heward, & Herron, 1987; Hintze & Shapiro, 1995; Shapiro 1987a; Sulzar-Azaroff & Mayer, 1977). After the target behaviors are identified and operationally defined, a procedure appropriate for the data-collection process is chosen. The method may involve collection of simple frequency counts of behavioral acts or may be a more complex system based on a time-sampling procedure. Although systematic observation systems can be individually tailored to each specific observational situation, this obviously can become a time consuming and inefficient procedure. Given that the behaviors of interest within instructional settings do not deviate significantly, it may be more logical and cost-efficient to use an existing observation system rather than to try to individualize the observational procedure each time a new student or behavior is observed.

Not surprisingly, a large number of observational systems have been developed and reported in the literature. Some of these systems appear to have been used in many investigations and have been found to be particularly valuable for use in school settings. Among the many coding systems available, O'Leary, Romanczyk, Kass, Dietz, and Santogrossi (1979) developed a code originally used by O'Leary, Kaufman, Kass, and Drabman (1970) in a study of the effects of loud and soft reprimands in reducing children's disruptive behavior. Their code contained nine categories of behavior, such as out of chair, playing with objects, noise, and aggression. Their procedural manual provides extensive definitions for each category, along with the needed observation forms and instructions for conducting the observations. The system has been used in studies examining hyperactive children (O'Leary, Pelham, Rosenbaum, & Price, 1976), disruptive classroom behavior (Thomas, Becker, & Armstrong, 1968), and the effects of token reinforcement on classroom behavior (O'Leary & Becker, 1967).

Another code, described by Alessi and Kaye (1983), was designed primarily to assess types of on- and off-task behavior, as well as teacher and peer response to these behaviors. Although not described in any specific research studies, the code does have an excellent training manual, including a videotape, and appears potentially useful for in-class observation of student behavior.

Saudargas and Creed (1980) developed a code designed specifically by school psychologists for school psychologists, which appears to have potential usefulness in classroom observation. Unlike the O'Leary et al. (1979) and Alessi and Kaye (1983) codes, the Saudargas and Creed code offers the opportunity to assess at least 15 different student, and 6 teacher behaviors. It also allows for behavioral categories to be added that previously were not defined by the code. Furthermore, the system has been used in at least two studies, that have found that certain behavioral categories appear to be significant discriminators of students with and without handicaps (e.g., Saudargas & Lentz, 1986; Slate & Saudargas, 1986). Additionally, normative data have been collected on the code. Because the system has been used in substantial clinical applications, as well as research studies, and appears to be an improvement over other existing systems, the code is presented in considerable detail here.

State–Event Classroom Observation System

The State–Event Classroom Observation System (SECOS; Saudargas & Creed, 1980; Saudargas, 1992) is an observational code that has been under ongoing development and revision for the past 15 years. As such, there is more than one version of the measure, although there has been little change in the substance of the code. In addition, we (Shapiro & Lentz, 1986) have developed a somewhat abbreviated version of the scale that has been employed in a major, federally funded research and training project in the state of Iowa. It is this abbreviated version that is described in detail here. (Readers interested in obtaining the most recent and complete version of the scale should write Richard A. Saudargas, Department of Psychology, University of Tennessee, Knoxville, TN 37916.)

Appendix 3C provides a copy of the observation form used for the abbreviated version of the SECOS. Before one begins the observation process, however, it is important to determine the classroom rules operating while the observations are being conducted. These rules may affect how certain behaviors are defined and can easily be obtained by either asking the teacher or looking to see whether they are posted somewhere in the room. It will also be important to find out the teacher's planned schedule of activities during the observation period. Knowing what is supposed to occur should help the observer determine the exact periods when the targeted student should be observed. Finally, it may also be useful to sketch out a seating chart, depicting where the target student is sitting in relation to peers. In addition, important components of the physical classroom structure can be noted, such as the use of learning centers, boy–girl ratios, location of teacher and aides' desks, and places where educational materials are stored. All of these data may be useful in interpreting the quantitative data to be collected.

The top of the data sheet asks for a variety of identifying information. In addition to the student's name, grade, name of school, teacher's name, and observer's name, the sheet asks for a record of the class activity. The observer should write in the exact activity observed. For example, during reading, students may be working in a workbook, engaged in silent reading, or working on assigned worksheets. Simply indicating that the activity observed was "reading" is not sufficient.

To the right of this line is a series of numbers with abbreviated codes. These represent the four most common instructional situations:

1. *ISW: TPsnt—Individual seatwork, teacher present.* The student being observed is engaged in an individual seatwork activity while the teacher is circulating around the room checking work or working with individual students. The teacher may also be seated at his or her desk.

2. *ISW: TSmGp—Individual seatwork, teacher working with a small group of students.* The student being observed is working on individual seatwork while the teacher is working with a small group of students that does not include the target student.

3. *SmGp: Tled—Small group led by the teacher.* The student being observed in this setting is part of the group of students being taught by the teacher.

4. *LgGp: Tled—Large group led by the teacher.* The student being observed in this setting is part of a large group of students, defined as at least half the class.

Occasionally, the observer will encounter a situation that is not covered by any of these four options. One common setting might be when learning centers or cooperative learning are being used. This different situation should simply be noted on the form. If the instructional arrangement changes during the observation, this change should be noted by recording the appropriate number above the time interval where the setting changes. Finally, the observer should record the specific referral problem, indicating whether it is academic or behavioral.

Before beginning the observation, the observer will need some type of timing device to keep track of the intervals. It is strongly recommended that a stopwatch *not* be used. Conducting these types of observations requires extreme vigilance to the occurrence of behavior. Using a stopwatch will require the observer to look frequently down at the watch and back up at the students. Instead of a stopwatch, the observer should use some kind of audio-cuing device. This can be an audiocassette that is cued for the appropriate intervals or a device that will make an audible sound at the set number of seconds. In either case, one should try to use a device that includes an earplug, to avoid any possible distraction the sound would create for the students in the classroom.

Typically, observations are conducted for a period of not less than 15 minutes at any one time. Some observations may last up to 30 minutes. If 15-second intervals are used, at least three sheets (60 intervals) will be needed to conduct the observation. It is suggested that the observer develop sets of recording sheets with intervals numbered 1–120, to permit the collection of data for up to 30 minutes at a time.

The next section of the form contains the behavioral categories observed for students. These behaviors are divided into "states" and "events." The last section of the form contains the behavioral categories for observing teacher behavior. All of these categories are also "events."

A "state" is a behavior in which a student can engage for different lengths of time. For example, school work (SW) could occur for only brief periods of time or throughout an entire observation. Likewise, a student may be looking around (LK) for a few seconds or for a sustained period of time.

States are coded as occurring or not occurring on a momentary time-sampling basis. The observer simply records (with a vertical line) whether the observed state is present at the instant the interval begins. The length of the observation interval can be established by the observer, but typically has been either 15 or 30 seconds. In practice, it has been found that 15-second intervals are usually optimal for accurate recording on this scale.

Sometimes, when recording states, the observer may need a few seconds to decide on all the states. During that time, the state may change. The observer should record the state that was first present. For example, when an interval begins, the target student may be engaged in schoolwork (SW) but may be looking around (LK) when the observer goes to record the behavior. In this case, the observer would record SW, not LK.

All other behaviors on the form are "events." These are defined and recorded as discrete occurrences of behavior. Thus, each time a student raises and lowers his or her hand is counted as a hand raise (RH). Each time a student calls out, a mark is made for the calling-out (CAL) behavior. During each interval, all occurrences of these events are recorded. After the state is recorded at the beginning of the interval, the observer then watches the student for the remainder of the interval, recording any events that occur. At the beginning of the next interval, the states occurring at that instant are recorded, and then any events occurring during that interval are recorded. This process is continued until the entire observation is completed.

Obviously, in order to use this code accurately, the observer must learn the definitions for each behavior. Table 3.2 provides a list of each behavioral category and its corresponding symbol. The manual available from Saudargas describes each behavior and its operational definition. Inclusive and exclusive examples of the category are provided. Figure 3.3 provides an example of the definition for schoolwork. This category is important, because its definition was written to correspond most closely to approximations of engaged time.

In addition to the student behaviors recorded, specific behavioral categories are provided for recording teacher behavior. Included are events in which teachers are interacting directly with students about schoolwork

TABLE 3.2. Saudargas Observation Code

Abbreviation	Behavior catergory
	Student behaviors
SW	Schoolwork
OS	Out of seat
LK	Looking around
SIC	Social interaction with child
SIT	Social interaction with teacher
OACT	Other activity
RH	Raise hand
CAL	Call out to teacher
AC	Approach child
OAC	Other child approach
OS	Out of seat
	Teacher behaviors
TA/SW	Teacher approach to student doing schoolwork
TA/OTH	Teacher approach to sudent doing other activity
APP	Teacher approval or praise of student behavior
DIS	Teacher disapproval of student behavior

and nonschoolwork behaviors, and places to record teacher approvals and disapprovals. In addition, special recording rules are employed for instances in which teachers address an entire class or give specific approvals or disapprovals for academic behavior, and for recording student responses to approaches from peers.

Preparing for the Observation

As previously mentioned, observations should be scheduled with the teacher, and data regarding class schedule, rules, and seating arrangements should be noted on the back of the observation form. The observer should find a place in the classroom that is unobtrusive but provides a clear view of the referred child and is close enough that the child can be overheard. However, the observer should be careful not to be disruptive or so prominent that he or she ends up distracting the target child. All materials should be ready before the observation process begins. The observer should ask the teacher before beginning the observation what can be expected to happen during the instructional period. This will be important in the examination of permanent products, which usually follows the direct observation.

During the teacher interview, the observer should have identified in-

SW: SCHOOLWORK

Schoolwork is coded when the student is engaged in a teacher-directed activity defined as follows:

1. The student is doing assigned academic work while having head and eyes oriented toward the work materials. Academic subjects are those typically found in a school curriculum: reading, language arts, social studies, science, music, mathematics, geography, art, etc.
2. In a lecture or discussion group the student must have his/her head and eyes oriented toward the person speaking.
3. The student's hand is raised when the time sampling interval begins.

Do not code as SW student behaviors which may be permissible according to the classroom rules but do not fit the three categories of SW defined above.

While this definition may seem overly strict, the definition was written this way so that judgments about the appropriateness of a specific student behavior would not have to be made or would be kept to a minimum.

SW can be coded with all other state behaviors except for LK (Looking Around) and OACT (Other Activity).

EXAMPLES CODED SW

1. Student is in reading group and is looking at book while other student is reading. (SW)
2. Student is in social studies and is looking at the teacher give a lecture. (SW)
3. After the student completes the academic work, he/she is allowed to get out a book and read. If the student gets out a book and begins reading, then SW would be coded. (SW)

EXAMPLES NOT CODED SW

1. The student is sharpening a pencil even if this is permissible according to the classroom rules. (OS and OACT)
2. Two students are interacting and you cannot tell about what they are interacting. (SIC)
3. When the time-sampling interval begins, the student is walking over to the teacher. (OS)
4. In a discussion class, the student is looking away from the person talking. (LK)

FIGURE 3.3. Behavioral definition of schoolwork (SW) from the State–Event Classroom Observation System. From *State Event Classroom System* by R. Saudargas and V. Creed, 1980, Knoxville: University of Tennessee, Department of Psychology. Copyright 1980 by Richard A. Saudargas. Reprinted by permission.

formation to be verified while observing. Specifically, this includes the actual time allotted for instruction, contingencies for accuracy and/or work completion, instructional arrangements described by the teacher, and so forth. The observer may want to jot these items down at the bottom of the observation form to serve as reminders of things to check while conducting the observations.

Conducting the Observation and Scoring the Protocol

At the beginning of the observation period, the observer should turn on the tape recorder and get ready for the first interval. As soon as the first interval is cued, a mark should be placed on the appropriate state categories.

The observer should continue to observe the student for the remainder of the interval, marking occurrences of any events during that period. As soon as the second interval is cued, the observer should move to the column marked "2" on the data sheet, record the appropriate state categories, and return to the events for the remainder of that interval. This process of moving between states and events continues until the observation is completed. If, during the observation, the instructional arrangement changes, the observer may want to stop recording during the transition period (although he or she may want to record how long the transition takes for the target student as well as some peers). Recording should be resumed once instruction has started.

The data for states and events are scored differently. For each state, the observer should add the number of intervals in which the state was recorded as present, divide by the total number of intervals observed, and multiply by 100. This will give the *percentage of intervals* in which that category of behavior occurred. Figure 3.4 shows examples of how states are scored. It is important to note that the data obtained from this type of observation are accurately reported as *percentages of intervals* and not percentages of time. Although the time-sampling procedure should be an accurate estimate of actual time, it is only an approximation and should not be reported as amount of time.

Events are scored as rate data. For each behavior, the observer should sum the number of events across the observed intervals. All occurrences of events for that category must be counted, including intervals at which the same event occurred more than once. The total number of events is divided by the *total time in minutes* of the observation, not the number of intervals. This will usually result in an integer and decimal value (e.g., 1.2 per minute) and represents the rate per minute of that category of behavior. Figure 3.4 again displays examples of event scoring on a completed coding form.

When Should Observations Be Conducted?

Observations should be planned during activities related to the child's referred problems. This is why it is particularly important to conduct the teacher interview prior to the direct observations. During the interview, the observer should be able to determine the most important instructional periods for observation. For example, if reading is the referred problem, and during the interview the teacher expresses dissatisfaction with the child's performance during group and independent seatwork activities in reading, it is important to observe the child during both of these activities. If the activities occurred consecutively (as they often do in many classrooms), the observation should be planned to cover both instructional set-

Saudargas–Creed State–Event Classroom Observation System

Sheet # ___1___

Greg (GR: 3)	11-3-87	M ⓉW T F	Start Time: 10:05
Student	Date/Yr.	Day	End: 10:10 Total: 5 min.
Riley	Reading Workbooks	① ISW: TPsnt 2. ISW: TSmGp	
School	Class Activity	3. SmGp: Tied 4. LgGp: Tied	
Mrs. Yost	R.T.	Referral: Ⓐ⒞ Beh.	
Teacher	Observer		

STATES	01	02	03	04	05	06	07	08	09	10	11	12	13	14	15	16	17	18	19	20	≥	%
SW	/					/	/		/	/	/					/	/		/	/		50
OS			/									/	/	/								20
LK		/	/	/			/										/					25
SIC							/	/														10
SIT									/	/	/											15
OACT														/								5

EVENTS	01	02	03	04	05	06	07	08	09	10	11	12	13	14	15	16	17	18	19	20	≥	Rate
RH	⊘				/												/					.6
CAL			/							/	⊘											.6
AC																						0
OCA						⊘								⊘								.4
OS					/							/	/					/				.8

TEACHER	01	02	03	04	05	06	07	08	09	10	11	12	13	14	15	16	17	18	19	20	≥	Rate
TA/SW	/																					.2
TA/OTH					/								/	/								.6
APP																/		/	/			.6
DIS			/	//								/	/									1.0

COMMENTS:_____

_____

_____

FIGURE 3.4. Example of completed observation from the State–Event Classroom Observation System.

tings. Likewise, if the teacher reports the student to be having difficulties in more than one academic area, observations may be needed in both instructional periods.

It is particularly important to be sensitive to teacher-reported discrepancies between the student's behaviors during different instructional arrangements. For example, if a teacher states in the interview that the referred student is disruptive and fails to accurately complete work during all independent seatwork activities (regardless of academic subject area), but is usually compliant and attentive during teacher-led group activities, then the observation should be planned to sample the student's behavior during independent work across academic subjects, as well as at least one occasion of teacher-led group activity. The purpose of these observations would be to confirm or disconfirm the teacher's report during the interview.

How Often Should Observations Be Conducted?

The question of how often observations should be conducted is difficult to answer. Obviously, one aspect to consider is that of time constraints on the observer. The number of observations that can be conducted is going to be partially related to the amount of time available to whoever is conducting the observation. Ideally, enough observation needs to be scheduled to give an accurate picture of the referred child's behavior and the instructional environment. The teacher interview may provide some guidance for deciding observational frequency, if the interviewer asks questions concerning the variability of student behavior. Students who are reported as different from day to day may need more observations than those reported to behave consistently. A "best-guess" recommendation is to observe for at least one full period in which problems exist, and then portions of that period on 1 or 2 other days. Spreading the observations across 2 or 3 days may be very helpful if a student's behavior is atypical on the first day of observation.

It is important to recognize that the process of conducting observations itself may alter a student's behavior in a classroom. Anyone who has conducted direct observations has had teachers tell him or her when an observation is finished that "I can't believe how good Kevin was today. He's never like this." These types of reports are critical in determining whether the observational data collected can be adequately interpreted. Following each observation, one should ask the teacher whether the student's behavior during the observation session was typical. If the teacher suggests that the student's behavior was atypical, additional observation under the same conditions will be necessary.

The primary objective of direct observation is to obtain data that are stable, conform to teacher reports, and offer an "accurate" picture of the student's typical behavior when the observer is not in the classroom. It should be kept in mind that reactivity to observation is often a transient phenomenon. Students usually habituate to observers in classrooms and act in ways that are consistent with other periods of the instructional process. The observers is cautioned, however, to try not to make it known to the target student that the object of the classroom visit is specifically to observe him or her.

Optional Observation of Comparison Children

Very often, an observer may desire to compare the behavior of the referred child to peers within his or her classroom. These data can be very useful in interpreting the results of observing the target student and can provide a type of minilocal norm. In addition, collection of data on peers may offer information about the degree of discrepancy between the target student's behavior and expected levels of behavior for other students in the classroom.

There are several ways to collect these data, all of which need to be conducted simultaneously with observing the referred student. The first step is to identify the set of children to use as a comparison. This can be done by asking the teacher prior to beginning the observation to identify some children who are "average" or who meet his or her expectations during the instructional setting to be observed. The observer should be sure that the teacher identifies students who are average, not those who represent exceptionally good behavior. The advantage of this approach is that the observer can arrange his or her data sheet to specify which children will be observed. A disadvantage, however, is that only a limited number of students will be observed, rather than a sampling across the classroom. In addition, teacher judgment obviously plays a significant role in the selection of peers.

A second procedure for selecting peers is for the observer to randomly select students from the class in which the referred child is being observed. One can choose a specific subset of children (perhaps those sitting in the referred student's proximity) and consistently observe these students, or one can randomly sample different students across the entire classroom.

Whichever method of choosing comparison students is used, the observer can systematically include these students in the observation process in different ways. One method is to mark off a subset of intervals (approximately 5 in every 20) during which only the peer comparison student(s) are observed. For example, if interval 5 is selected as a comparison interval, the observer completes the observation of the referred student during intervals 1 through 4, and then switches to the comparison child for interval 5. The choice of a specific child is based upon the method selected for identifying peers (teacher-identified, selected subset, or randomly selected). If the observer is using the random selection method, then a different student, selected randomly, is observed during the next comparison interval (e.g., interval 9).

Another way to observe peers is to alternate between the referred child in one interval and the peer-comparison child(ren) in the next. Still another way is to simultaneously observe both the referred child and a peer during each interval. This procedure obviously requires a modification of the observation form. In addition, the peer-comparison child(ren) chosen should be immediately next to the referred child. Although this last method can result in excellent comparison data, it may also result in less than accurate data collection.

Interpreting Data from the SECOS

Data collected from direct observations need to be organized in particular ways if the results are to be effectively interpreted. Typically, observations are made during one academic period, although a single observation may contain several data sheets (three sheets for a 15-minute period, 20 intervals per sheet). It is important, however, to separate observations that occur on different days, even if the same instructional activity is observed. Thus, if independent seatwork is observed during reading on Monday for 15 minutes and on Tuesday for 20 minutes, each of these sets of observations is scored independently. If observations are conducted of the same academic subject in the same day but during different instructional settings (e.g., large group led by the teacher [LgGp: Tled] vs. individual seatwork, teacher present [ISW: TPsnt]), these sets of observations should also be scored separately. The observer must be careful to check whether the instructional setting changes during an observation. For example, if during a 30-minute observation the observer finds during interval 45 that the setting goes from ISW:TPsnt to small group led by the teacher (SmGP:Tled), the data scored during intervals 1–45 should be treated separately from those scored on intervals 45–120.

When performing calculations on state data, the observer must be sure to count only the number of intervals marked for the referred student in the total number of observation intervals for that child. In other words, the intervals scored for the comparison child should be eliminated if these types of observations were made. The observer should also remember to eliminate the comparison child intervals from the calculation of event rates. Once the protocol is scored for the referred child, then similar state and event data should be calculated for the peer-comparison observations. Again, the observer must remember to eliminate the data collected on the referred child when scoring the protocol for the comparison students. Data for all comparison child intervals are combined, even if different students are observed across intervals.

Once all data are compiled for the various observation categories arranged by instructional setting, the observer is ready to interpret the data. Appendix 3D provides a form that may help to facilitate and structure the interpretation process.

States. The most significant state behavior observed in the SECOS is probably SW (schoolwork). Examination of the definition employed suggests that SW is an approximation of engaged time, because periods of student nondisruptive, but nonactive responding (e.g., thinking while looking away from work), are not scored as SW. As such, the first item examined is the SW level compared to the allocated time for instruction. Thus, if individual seatwork is allocated for approximately 40 minutes per day in reading, and the aggregated (across observations of individual seatwork) percentage of SW is 40, then it seems reasonable to believe that the student is not making good use of the available instructional and practice time.

An important component to interpreting the level of SW is related to the products that result during the individual work period. It is critical to examine the permanent products (e.g., worksheets, workbook pages, writing assignments, math sheets, etc.) that the student produced during the observation. For example, if the student during the work session is found to have a 40% SW level, but completes all the work with 80% accuracy, then the problem may lie more with the assignment than with the student. On the other hand, if the student is found to complete 50% of the work with low levels of accuracy, this may imply that the student lacks sufficient skills to accurately complete the assignment accurately. Still further, examination of permanent products may show that the student only completes 50% of the assignment, but with 100% accuracy. This may suggest either that the student has a problem with rate of performance (accurate but too slow), or that the student lacks sufficient motivation to try and move faster (in which case the contingencies for reinforcement need to be examined).

Understanding why a student may have lower than expected levels of SW will also be facilitated by examining what the student is doing instead of working. For example, if the student is found to have high levels of looking around (LK), it may suggest that the child is passively not paying attention to the assignment. Alternatively, if the student has high levels of other activity (OACT), it may suggest that the student is actively engaged in activities, but not those required by the teacher. Finally, if the student shows high levels of social interaction with children (SIC), it may suggest that the student's interactions with peers may be interfering with assignment completion. By anecdotally noting the quality of these interactions (aggressive? passive?) and the content (Are they discussing the assignment?), the observer can determine the possible reasons for the high levels of peer interaction.

Another important comparison is between the level of SW in different types of instructional settings. Differences between group and individual seatwork assignments may suggest that a student has the most difficulty under only certain types of instructional conditions.

Finally, one needs to examine the relationship of SW and social interaction with teacher (SIT). Finding that the only intervals of SW are those in which SIT is simultaneously recorded may suggest that the student cannot sustain SW without direct attention from the teacher. This would also be the case if SW occurred primarily when SIC was recorded.

Events. The data produced by events are rates. For example, if Phil is found to have raised his hand five times during a 10-minute observation, his rate of hand raising (RH) is expressed as 0.5 hand raises per minute. It is important to "translate" rate data to meaningful units when reporting such information to others. For example, instead of saying Phil had an RH rate of 0.5 per minute, one could say that he raised his hand about once every 2 minutes.

Interpretation of event data on the SECOS is designed to provide information about the levels and types of student–student and student–teacher interactions in the classroom. First, the student contacts of the teacher can be examined. One of the most common complaints of teachers seems to be that children will call out without raising their hand. Information about this type of interaction is provided in the RH, out-of-seat (OS), and call out to teacher (CAL) categories. An important part of the analysis is the number of times a teacher responds to a student's initiation of these behaviors. This is indicated on the SECOS by the circling of individual events. For example, in a 40-minute observation of individual seatwork, James may be found to have called out six times, all of which resulted in a teacher response, and to have raised his hand four times, only one of which resulted in his being called on by the teacher. The implication of this pattern is that the best way for James to get the teacher's attention is to call out. Thus, the teacher may actually be reinforcing the inappropriate behavior of calling out.

The second type of interaction of interest is student–student contact. By comparing the levels of other child approach (OCA) and approach child (AC), important information about events that may be competing with completion of work can be obtained. In addition, a student who is found to have low levels of SW but is often being approached by others, may be having periods of non-SW because he or she is being pulled off-task by peers.

A final type of classroom interaction that is important is teacher-initiated contacts with students. Because the way in which teachers contact students can strongly influence student on-task levels, it is important to compare the frequency with which the teacher contacts a student when the student is engaged in SW (TA/SW) compared to when the student is engaged in other activity (TA/OTH). Low levels of SW may be partially explained if high levels of TA/OTH are found, suggesting that teacher attention for non-SW behavior may need to be altered. Likewise, finding high levels of TA/SW despite frequent student attempts to contact the teacher may suggest an effective classroom management program.

A second type of teacher contact observed on the SECOS is approvals and disapprovals. Looking at the frequency of overall approval and disapproval, the division of these rates for academic versus social behavior, and the target of the approvals and disapprovals (the entire class or the referred student) may offer a variety of additional clues to understanding the academic environment.

Finally, drawing conclusions about what events in the classroom affect student performance must go beyond the effects of teacher attention. It is very important to remember that other data collected during the interview and observed (somewhat anecdotally) during the systematic data collection may play critical roles in the student's academic performance. Perhaps the most critical would be contingencies for work, such as feedback about accuracy, rewards, having to make up work, homework assignments, and so forth. The presence of these needs to be noted during the observation and considered during the analysis of the observational data.

Normative Data. The use of normative data to interpret observational codes presents a dilemma. On the one hand, the observer may want to know how the level of performance observed for the targeted student compares against performance levels that may be expected for same-age peers observed elsewhere under similar conditions. On the other hand, such information may be irrelevant since a local context is needed to accurately interpret the data. Given this dilemma, the collection of data on peers from the same classroom as the target student is important. However, establishing whether the target student's behavior is within the level expected against similar-age peers on a larger scale can offer helpful feedback to teachers and evaluators.

Haile-Griffey, Saudargas, Hulse-Trotter, and Zanolli (1993) completed SECOS observations on 486 children across grades 1–5 in general education classrooms from one school district in eastern Tennessee. Children were all engaged in independent seatwork while their teacher worked at his or her desk or conducted a small-group activity in which the targeted student did not partake. Data for six state and six event behaviors are re-

TABLE 3.3. Normative Results for Six State Behaviors from the SECOS

	SW	LK	OACT	SIC	SIT	OS
Grade 1						
$\overline{X}$ (SD)	58.4 (17.4)	18.5 (11.7)	10.7 (10.1)	8.3 (10.5)	1.3 (2.8)	8.1 (11.6)
Grade 2						
$\overline{X}$ (SD)	67.9 (17.4)	13.6 (10.1)	9.1 (9.7)	5.2 (7.2)	0.8 (1.9)	8.5 (10.8)
Grade 3						
$\overline{X}$ (SD)	69.0 (15.1)	12.2 (9.0)	9.7 (8.7)	4.6 (5.7)	1.4 (3.3)	7.1 (8.9)
Grade 4						
$\overline{X}$ (SD)	73.9 (15.7)	11.1 (7.7)	6.4 (6.4)	5.7 (8.2)	0.8 (1.8)	5.2 (8.5)
Grade 5						
$\overline{X}$ (SD)	70.4 (15.1)	10.8 (7.2)	8.1 (8.2)	6.5 (8.0)	1.3 (4.2)	6.8 (1.0)

Note. SW, schoolwork; LK, looking around; OACT, other activity; SIC, child interactions; SIT, teacher interactions; OS, out of seat. From *The Classroom Behavior of Elementary School Children during Independent Seatwork: Establishing Local Norms* by L. Haile-Griffey, R. A. Saudargas, K. Hulse-Trotter, and K. Zanolli, 1994, Unpublished manuscript, Department of Psychology, University of Tennessee, Knoxville, TN. Reprinted by permission of the authors.

ported in Tables 3.3 and 3.4. (For a complete set of normative data contact Richard A. Saudargas, Department of Psychology, University of Tennessee, Knoxville, TN 37996.) These data allow an evaluator to compare the obtained rates of behavior on the SECOS for their particular targeted student against a large, normative database suggesting typical levels of performance. It is important to remember, however, that these normative

TABLE 3.4. Normative Results for Six Event Behaviors from the SECOS

	AC	OCA	TA/SW	TA/OTH	RH	CAL
Grade 1						
$\overline{X}$ (SD)	.28 (.31)	.25 (.26)	.02 (.04)	.02 (.04)	.03 (.08)	.03 (.06)
Grade 2						
$\overline{X}$ (SD)	.20 (.25)	.19 (.21)	.01 (.03)	.01 (.04)	.02 (.05)	.02 (.05)
Grade 3						
$\overline{X}$ (SD)	.18 (.23)	.16 (.21)	.01 (.05)	.01 (.03)	.01 (.02)	.03 (.05)
Grade 4						
$\overline{X}$ (SD)	.20 (.27)	.16 (.17)	.01 (.03)	.01 (.02)	.02 (.05)	.02 (.04)
Grade 5						
$\overline{X}$ (SD)	.23 (.35)	.21 (.26)	.03 (.06)	.01 (.03)	.02 (.04)	.02 (.04)

Note. AC, approach child; OCA, other child approach; TA/SW, teacher approach to child engaged in schoolwork; TA/OTH, teacher approach to child not engaged in schoolwork. From *The Classroom Behavior of Elementary School Children during Independent Seatwork: Establishing Local Norms* by L. Haile-Griffey, R. A. Saudargas, K. Hulse-Trotter, and K. Zanolli, 1994, Unpublished manuscript, Department of Psychology, University of Tennessee, Knoxville, TN. Reprinted by permission of the authors.

data can only be interpreted correctly when observed under conditions of independent seatwork.

Behavioral Observation of Students in Schools

Although the SECOS can provide a rich set of data about interactions in the classroom, the measure is still highly complex and difficult to master. Becoming competent with the code requires many hours of instruction and practice. Unfortunately, many practicing school psychologists lack the time and opportunity to effectively master such a coding system.

In addition, although the SW category of the SECOS provides an indication of a student's engaged time, the measure fails to detail exactly how the engaged time is divided. As noted in the ecobehavioral assessment measures developed by Greenwood et al. (E-BASS; 1993, see Chapter 2), it is important to observe exactly how students who are on-task are spending their time. Thus, observation systems designed for periods of academic work need to more carefully determine whether students are actively or passively interacting with their academic tasks.

Given the difficulties of asking practitioners to learn overly complex codes like the SECOS or E-BASS, I (Shapiro, 1996) developed a simple observational code that was designed to assess key components of student academic performance. The code necessarily makes some compromises in limiting the range of behavioral categories that are included. However, the code is designed to provide detail about the nature of a student's on- and off-task behavior. A brief description of the code is provided here with a full and detailed description for its use in the workbook accompanying this text.

The B.O.S.S. divides on-task behavior into two components: active and passive engaged time (see Appendix 3E). Three subtypes of off-task behavior are observed: verbal, motor, and passive. In addition, data are collected on the teacher's directed instruction toward the targeted student. The code is also arranged to collect data on peer comparison students.

Active and passive engaged time are collected as momentary time samples, identical to the state behaviors of the SECOS. Off-task behaviors are collected using a partial-interval recording system. Teacher-directed instruction is sampled once per minute, also using a partial-interval recording system.

Each behavioral category is carefully defined through examples of occurrence and nonoccurrence in the B.O.S.S. manual (Shapiro, 1996). For example, both Active Engaged Time (AET) and Passive Engaged Time (PET) require that the student first be "on-task," defined as attending to his or her work or assigned task/activity. If the on-task student is actively writing, raising his or her hand, reading aloud, answering questions, talking to others (peers or teacher) concerning academics, or flipping through a book (e.g., a dictionary), an occurrence of AET would be scored. Similarly, if the student is on-task but his or her behavior is passive, such as reading silently, listening to the teacher or peer, looking at the blackboard during instruction, or looking at academic materials, an occurrence of PET is scored.

As each 15-second interval begins, the student is scored for the presence or absence of AET–PET. During the remainder of the interval, off-task behaviors (motor, verbal, or passive) are scored as soon as they occur. Unlike the event coding of the SECOS, the B.O.S.S. requires only that the behavior has occurred, not a count of its frequency. In other words, if during an interval a student gets out of his or her seat and talks to a peer, a mark would be placed in the off-task motor (OFT-M) and off-task verbal (OFT-V) categories. However, if the student in the same interval then talked to a second peer, only a single mark, indicating the behavior had occurred would be scored.

Every fifth interval, the observer using the B.O.S.S. is instructed to randomly select a different non-target student in the class to observe. Also in that interval, any teacher directed instruction to the class is marked. Thus, when the observation is completed, the B.O.S.S. provides data on the targeted student, a peer-comparison score, and a score on the estimated time the teacher spent instructing the class.

The data from the B.O.S.S. offers information about the nature of a student's on-task and off-task behavior. Although less detailed than the SECOS, the measure provides important insight into the level of engagement that a student is showing in his or her classroom. Not provided in the B.O.S.S. is extensive information on the student–student or student–teacher contact patterns. Although this information is certainly important, obtaining such data does make the observation code extremely complex to learn. It has been my clinical experience over many years that the data obtained through the B.O.S.S. offers the essential data needed to more clearly understand the aspects of the educational environment that may be impacting on student performance.

Readers who are interested in learning the B.O.S.S. are encouraged to obtain the workbook that accompanies this text. In that workbook, the entire B.O.S.S. manual, forms, and other materials necessary to master the B.O.S.S. are included.

STUDENT INTERVIEW

The perspective of the student is also important in gaining a full understanding of the academic environment. The degree to which students understand the instructions given by teachers for assignments, the degree to which students know how to access help if they are having problems answering questions, and the knowledge of classroom rules are all critical to accurately interpreting the outcomes of direct observations. Additionally, students can provide an indication of possible sources of confusion in academic instruction that can offer potential targets for designing remediation strategies.

To learn more about student perspectives of the academic environment, an interview of the student is conducted in conjunction with the completion of a systematic direct observation. Questions are asked related to the degree to which students understand the expectations of the teacher for the specific assignment that was completed during the observation, the student's self-confidence that they can complete the assigned work accurately, whether the student feels they are given sufficient time to complete their assignment, and the degree to which they feel they are included in classroom discussions.

Although many student interview forms are available, one from the The Instructional Environment Scale (TIES; Ysseldyke & Christensen, 1987) has been found to be especially useful (see Figure 3.5). The TIES student interview is conducted typically after the student has completed an independent work assignment. Questions on the form are asked in reference to the specific work assignment. At times, it is also necessary to ask the student more general questions after group assignments are completed. In those cases, the form provided in Figure 3.6 may be useful.

PERMANENT PRODUCT REVIEW

The final step in an analysis of the instructional environment involves a review of permanent products. In almost every classroom, students produce materials as part of the learning process. These may be worksheets from workbooks, xeroxed worksheets developed by the teacher, compositions, tests, quizzes, reports, and other such academic activities. All of these materials represent potentially important information that can assist the evaluator in learning more about a student's academic performance under the naturally occurring contingencies of the classroom. Analysis of these materials can offer valuable information about the areas of a student's strengths and weaknesses. In addition, because these materials were produced under naturally occurring classroom conditions, they may offer important insights into whether a student is performing differently on different types of tasks.

For example, Figure 3.7 shows the results of a first-grade student's attempt to complete a required written-language assignment. Looking at the top panel, it becomes evident that this student is using phonetic analysis in

1. I want you to tell me what you needed to do on these assignments.
   a. What did your teacher want you to learn?
   b. What did your teacher tell you about why these assignments are important?
   c. What did you have to do?
   d. Show me how you did the work. (Have the student explain a sample item.)

2. I am going to ask you several questions. In each case, I want you to tell me your answser by using this scale, where 1 means "not very much" and 4 means "very much."
   a. Sometimes students understand their assignments. Sometimes they don't. Show me how well you understand the assignment. 1 2 3 4
   b. How much did you believe you could do the assignment? 1 2 3 4
   c. How interesting is this work for you? 1 2 3 4

3. Now I have some other questions.
   a. Sometimes students cannot finish their work, and sometimes they have extra time. How much time do you usually get to finish your work: too little (1), just about right (2), or too much (3)? 1 2 3
   b. Does your teacher call on you to answer questions in class: never (1), not much (2), a lot (3)? 1 2 3

4. What does your teacher expect you to do when he or she gives these assignments:
   a. If you are confused?
   b. If you are done with your work?

5. What does your teacher tell you about:
   a. Completing your work? (What happens if your work is not done?)
   b. Getting the answers correct? (What happens if you make mistakes?)
   c. Having neat papers? (What happens if you are messy?)

6. Student success rate:
   a. Number of questions completed _____
   b. Number of correct answers _____
   c. Total number of questions assigned _____
   d. Success rate_____
   e. Kind of errors made by the student _____

FIGURE 3.5. The Instructional Environment Scale (TIES) student interview form. From *The Instructional Environment Scale* by J. Ysseldyke and S. Christenson, 1987. Copyright 1987 by Pro-Ed, Inc. Reprinted by permission.

trying to write unknown words. The student also shows some letter reversals (backwards "p" in "play") as well as poor letter formation (look at the lowercase "d"). Knowledge of irregular endings (such as "y" in "funny" and "play") is not evident. However, the student does understand the concept of punctuation (notice the use of a comma after "TV"). Using these and many other such written- language activities, patterns of the student's strengths and weaknesses become evident.

A permanent product review can also be very useful when combined with systematic, direct observation. For example, a systematic observation during which a student was asked to complete a page of math problems using the B.O.S.S. may show that the student was passively engaged for

Student Name _____

Subject   _____

Date   _____

STUDENT-REPORTED BEHAVIOR ____ None completed for this area

Understands expectations of teacher	☐ Yes	☐ No	☐ Not sure
Understands assignments	☐ Yes	☐ No	☐ Not sure
Feels he/she can do the assignments	☐ Yes	☐ No	☐ Not sure
Likes the subject	☐ Yes	☐ No	☐ Not sure
Feels he/she is given enough time to complete assignment	☐ Yes	☐ No	☐ Not sure
Feels he/she is called upon to participate in discussions	☐ Yes	☐ No	☐ Not sure

General comments:

Questions used to guide interview:

Do you think you are pretty good in _____?

If you had to pick one thing about _____ you like, what would it be?

If you had to pick one thing about _____ you don't like, what would it be?

What do you do when you are unable to solve a problem or answer with your assignment in _____?

Do you enjoy working with other students when you are having trouble with your assignment in _____?

Does the teacher call on you too often? Not often enough? In _____?

FIGURE 3.6.   General student interview.

over 90% of the intervals. However, an examination of the worksheet produced during that observation reveals that the student only completed 3 out of 20 problems. Thus, although the student was highly engaged, the rate of work completion is so slow that the student is likely to be failing mathematics tests. Clearly, the combination of permanent product reviews along with other data collected can be a helpful method for evaluators to better understand the nature of the classroom demands and their outcomes on performance.

SUMMARY AND CONCLUSIONS

In this chapter, the initial portion of conducting an academic assessment was presented. Specifically, procedures for a structured teacher interview, student interview, and conducting direct observations were presented. Along with an examination of permanent products, these data combine to

FIGURE 3.7. Example of written-language assignment used for permanent product review. Upper panel: "Watch TV, and go outside and play"; lower panel: "When I make a funny face."

offer an assessment of the instructional environment. The next portion of the assessment, evaluating a students' academic skills for purposes of instructional placement, is presented in the next chapter.

Teacher Interview Form for Academic Problems

Student: _____   Teacher: _____

Birthdate: _____   Date: _____

Grade: _____   School: _____

Interviewer: _____

GENERAL

Why was this student referred? _____

What type(s) of academic problem(s) does this student have?

_____

READING

Primary type of reading series used

☐ Basal reader
☐ Literature-based
☐ Trade books

Secondary type of reading materials used

☐ Basal reader
☐ Literature-based
☐ Trade books
☐ None

Reading series title (if applicable) _____

   Grade level of series currently placed _____

   Title of book in series currently placed _____

How many groups do you teach? _____

Which group is this student assigned to? _____

At this point in the school year, where is the average student in your class reading?

   Level and book _____

   Place in book (beginning, middle, end, specific page) _____

Time allotted/day for reading _____

How is time divided? (Independent seatwork? Small group? Cooperative groups?)

_____

How is placement in reading program determined? _____

_____

How are changes made in the program? _____

_____

Does this student participate in Chapter 1 (remedial) reading programs? How much?

_____

Typical daily instructional procedures _____

_____

Contingencies for accuracy? _____

Contingencies for completion? _____

Daily scores (if available) for past 2 weeks _____

Group standardized test results (if available) _____

ORAL READING

How does he/she read orally compared to others in his/her reading group?
___ Much worse   ___ Somewhat worse   ___ About the same
___ Somewhat better   ___ Much better

In the class?
___ Much worse   ___ Somewhat worse   ___ About the same
___ Somewhat better   ___ Much better

WORD ATTACK

Does he/she attempt unknown words? ____

SIGHT WORDS

How is the student's sight vocabulary, compared to that of others in his/her reading group?
___ Much worse   ___ Somewhat worse   ___ About the same
___Somewhat better   ___ Much better

In the class?
___ Much worse   ___ Somewhat worse   ___ About the same
___ Somewhat better   ___ Much better

COMPREHENSION

How well does the student seem to understand what he/she reads, compared to others in his/her reading group?
___ Much worse   ___ Somewhat worse   ___ About the same
___ Somewhat better   ___ Much better

In the class?
___ Much worse   ___ Somewhat worse   ___ About the same
___ Somewhat better   ___ Much better

BEHAVIOR DURING READING

Rate the following areas from 1 to 5 (1 = very unsatisfactory, 3 = satisfactory, 5 = superior)

READING GROUP

    a. Oral reading ability (as evidenced in reading group)   ____
    b. Volunteers answers   ____
    c. When called upon, gives correct answer   ____
    d. Attends to other students when they read aloud   ____
    e. Knows the appropriate place in book   ____

INDEPENDENT SEATWORK

    a. Stays on task   ____
    b. Completes assigned work in required time   ____
    c. Work is accurate   ____
    d. Works quietly   ____
    e. Remains in seat when required   ____

HOMEWORK (if any)

    a. Handed in on time   ____
    b. Is complete   ____
    c. Is accurate   ____

MATHEMATICS

Curriculum series _____

What are the specific problems in math? _____

_____

Time allotted/day for math _____

How is time divided? (Independent seatwork? Small group? Large group? Cooperative groups?) _____

For an average performing student in your class, at what point in the planned course format would you consider this student at mastery? (See computational mastery form.) _____

For an average-performing student in your class, at what point in the planned course format would you consider this student instructional? (See computational mastery form.) _____

For an average performing student in your class, at what point in the planned course format would you consider this student frustrational? (See computational mastery form.) _____

For the targeted student in your class, at what point in the planned course format would you consider this student at mastery? (See computational mastery form.)

_____

For the targeted student in your class, at what point in the planned course format would you consider this student instructional? (See computational mastery form.)

_____

For the targeted student in your class, at what point in the planned course format would you consider this student frustrational? (See computational mastery form.)

_____

How is mastery assessed? _____

Describe any difficulties this student has in applying math skills? (measurement, time, money, geometry, problem solving) _____

_____

Are your students grouped in math? _____

If so, how many groups do you have, and in which group is this student placed?

_____

How are changes made in the student's math program? _____

Does this student participate in Chapter 1 (remedial) math programs? _____

Typical daily instructional procedures _____

Contingencies for accuracy? _____

Contingencies for completion? _____

Daily scores (if available) for past 2 weeks _____

Group standardized test results (if available) _____

BEHAVIOR DURING MATH

Rate the following areas from 1 to 5 (1 = very unsatisfactory, 3 = satisfactory, 5 = superior)

MATH GROUP (large)

a. Volunteers answers ____
b. When called upon, gives correct answer ____
c. Attends to other students when they give answers ____
d. Knows the appropriate place in math book ____

MATH GROUP (small)

a. Volunteers answers ____
b. When called upon, gives correct answer ____
c. Attends to other students when they give answers ____
d. Knows the appropriate place in math book ____

MATH GROUP (cooperative)

a. Volunteers answers ____
b. Contributes to group objectives ____
c. Attends to other students when they give answers ____
d. Facilitates others in group to participate ____
e. Shows appropriate social skills in group ____

INDEPENDENT SEATWORK

a. Stays on task ____
b. Completes assigned work in required time ____
c. Work is accurate ____
d. Works from initial directions ____
e. Works quietly ____
f. Remains in seat when required ____

HOMEWORK (if any)
   a. Handed in on time   ⎯⎯
   b. Is complete   ⎯⎯
   c. Is accurate   ⎯⎯

SPELLING

Type of material used for spelling instruction:

   ☐ Published spelling series
      Title of series _____
   ☐ Basal reading series
      Title of series _____
   ☐ Teacher-made materials
   ☐ Other _____

Level of instruction (if applicable) _____

At this point in the school year, where is the average student in your class spelling?
   Level, place in book _____

Time allotted/day for spelling _____

How is time divided? (Independent seatwork? Small group? Cooperative groups?)_____

How is placement in spelling program determined? _____

How are changes made in the program? _____
_____

Typical daily instructional procedures _____

Contingencies for accuracy? _____

Contingencies for completion? _____

WRITING

Please describe the type of writing assignments you give _____
_____

Compared to others in your class, does he/she have difficulty with (please provide brief descriptions):

   ☐ Expressing thoughts _____
   ☐ Story length _____
   ☐ Story depth _____
   ☐ Creativity _____

Mechanics:
   ☐ Capitalization
   ☐ Punctuation
   ☐ Grammar
   ☐ Handwriting
   ☐ Spelling

Teaching procedures (describe): _____

_____

BEHAVIOR

Are there social–behavioral adjustment problems interfering with this student's academic progress? (be specific) _____

Check any item that describes this student's behavior:

_____ Distracted, short attention span, unable to concentrate

_____ Hyperactive, constant, aimless movement

_____ Impulsive/aggressive behaviors, lacks self-control

_____ Fluctuating levels of performance

_____ Frequent negative self-statements

_____ Unconsciously repeating verbal or motor acts

_____ Lethargic, sluggish, too quiet

_____ Difficulty sharing or working with others

Computation Skills Mastery Curriculum from a Small Urban School District in the Northeastern United States*

GRADE 1

1. Add two one-digit numbers: sums to 10
2. Subtract two one-digit numbers: combinations to 10

GRADE 2

3. Add two one-digit numbers: sums 11–19
4. Add a one-digit number to a two-digit number—no regrouping
5. Add a two-digit number to a two-digit number—no regrouping
6. Add a three-digit number to a three-digit number—no regrouping
7. Subtract a one-digit number from a one or two digit number: combinations to 18
8. Subtract a one-digit number from a two-digit number—no regrouping
9. Subtract a two-digit number from a two-digit number—no regrouping
10. Subtract a three-digit number from a three-digit number—no regrouping
11. Multiplication facts—0's, 1's, 2's

GRADE 3

12. Add three or more one-digit numbers
13. Add three or more two-digit numbers—no regrouping
14. Add three or more three- and four-digit numbers—no regrouping
15. Add a one-digit number to a two-digit number with regrouping
16. Add a two-digit number to a two-digit number with regrouping
17. Add a two-digit number to a three-digit number with regrouping from the 10's column only.
18. Add a two-digit number to a three-digit number with regrouping from the 100's column only.
19. Add a two-digit number to a three-digit number with regrouping from 10's and 100's columns
20. Add a three-digit number to a three-digit number with regrouping from the 10's column only
21. Add a three-digit number to a three-digit number with regrouping from the 100's column only
22. Add a three-digit number to a three-digit number with regrouping from the 10's and 100's columns

23. Add a four-digit number to a four-digit number with regrouping in one to three columns
24. Subtract two four-digit numbers—no regrouping
25. Subtract a one-digit number from a two-digit number with regrouping
26. Subtract a two-digit number from a two-digit number with regrouping
27. Subtract a two-digit number from a three-digit number with regrouping from 10's column only
28. Subtract a two-digit number from a three-digit number with regrouping from the 100's column only
29. Subtract a two-digit number from a three-digit number with regrouping from 10's and 100's columns
30. Subtract a three-digit number from a three-digit number with regrouping from 10's column only
31. Subtract a three-digit number from a three-digit number with regrouping from 100's column only
32. Subtract a three-digit number from a three-digit number with regrouping from 10's and 100's columns
33. Multiplication facts—3–9

GRADE 4

34. Add a five- or six-digit number to a five- or six-digit number with regrouping in any columns
35. Add three or more two-digit numbers with regrouping
36. Add three or more three-digit numbers with regrouping
37. Subtract a five- or six-digit number from a five- or six-digit number with regrouping in any columns
38. Multiply a two-digit number by a one-digit number with no regrouping
39. Multiply a three-digit number by a one-digit number with no regrouping
40. Multiply a two-digit number by a one-digit number with no regrouping
41. Multiply a three-digit number by a one-digit number with regrouping
42. Division facts—0–9
43. Divide a two-digit number by a one-digit number with no remainder
44. Divide a two-digit number by a one-digit number with remainder
45. Divide a three-digit number by a one-digit number with remainder
46. Divide a four-digit number by a one-digit number with remainder

GRADE 5

47. Multiply a two-digit number by a two-digit number with regrouping
48. Multiply a three-digit number by a two-digit number with regrouping
49. Multiply a three-digit number by a three-digit number with regrouping

♦♦♦

Blank Form for the State–Event Classroom Observation System (SECOS)*

Sheet # _____

_____ (GR: ____)   _____   M T W T F   Start Time: _____
Student   Date/Yr.   Day   End: _____ Total: _____

_____   _____   1. ISW: TPsnt   2. ISW: TSmGp
School   Class Activity   3. SmGp: Tied   4. LgGp: Tied

_____   _____   Referral: Ac. _____ Beh. _____
Teacher   Observer

STATES	01	02	03	04	05	06	07	08	09	10	11	12	13	14	15	16	17	18	19	20	≤	%
SW																						
OS																							
LK																							
SIC																							
SIT																							
OACT																							

EVENTS	01	02	03	04	05	06	07	08	09	10	11	12	13	14	15	16	17	18	19	20	≤	Rate
RH																							
CAL																							
AC																							
OCA																							
OS																							

TEACHER	01	02	03	04	05	06	07	08	09	10	11	12	13	14	15	16	17	18	19	20	≤	Rate
TA/SW																							
TA/OTH																							
APP																							
DIS																							

COMMENTS:_____

_____

_____

*From *State–Event Classroom Observation System* by R. Saudargas and V. Creed, 1980, Knoxville: University of Tennessee, Department of Psychology. Reprinted by permission.

◆◆◆

Form for Analyzing Direct Observations Using the SECOS

Student's name _____

Conditions of observation _____

Subject(s) observed _____

States

1. SW level versus allocated time for instruction:_____

_____

2. SW level versus permanent product data:_____

_____

3. SW level in groups versus individual seatwork:_____

_____

4. Type and level of non-SW behavior:_____

_____

5. SW and SIT behavior:_____

_____

Events

1. Type and level of student contact of teacher: _____

_____

2. Type and level of student–student contact: _____

_____

3. Type and level of contact teacher of student: _____

_____

4. Teacher contacts during SW versus postwork contingencies: _____

_____

Data for comparison student(s) _____

_____

_____

_____

Blank Form for the Behavioral Observation of Students in Schools (B.O.S.S.)

Child Observed: _____
Date: _____
Observer: _____
Time of Observation _____

Academic Subject: _____
Setting: ISW:TPsnt   SmGp:TPsnt
            ISW:TSmGp   LgGp:TPsnt
          Other: _____

Moment	1	2	3	4	5*	6	7	8	9	10*	11	12	13	14	15*	S	P	T
AET																		
PET																		
Partial																		
OFT-M																		
OFT-V																		
OFT-P																		
TDI																		

Moment	16	17	18	19	20*	21	22	23	24	25*	26	27	28	29	30*	S	P	T
AET																		
PET																		
Partial																		
OFT-M																		
OFT-V																		
OFT-P																		
TDI																		

Moment	31	32	33	34	35*	36	37	38	39	40*	41	42	43	44	45*	S	P	T
AET																		
PET																		
Partial																		
OFT-M																		
OFT-V																		
OFT-P																		
TDI																		

Moment	46	47	48	49	50*	51	52	53	54	55*	56	57	58	59	60*	S	P	T
AET																		
PET																		
Partial																		
OFT-M																		
OFT-V																		
OFT-P																		
TDI																		

	Target Student			Peer Comparison			Teacher
	S AET ___	% AET ___		S AET ___	% AET ___		S TDI ___
	S PET ___	% PET ___		S PET ___	% PET ___		% TDI ___
Total Intervals	S OFT-M ___	% OFT-M ___		S OFT-M ___	% OFT-M ___		Total Intervals
Observed	S OFT-V ___	% OFT-V ___		S OFT-V ___	% OFT-V ___		Observed
___	S OFT-P ___	% OFT-P ___		S OFT-P ___	% OFT-P ___		___

CHAPTER 4

♦♦♦

Step 2: Assessing Instructional Placement

♦

After the teacher interview, direct observation, student interview, and examination of permanent products have been completed, the evaluator is now ready to conduct the evaluation of student academic performance. This is done by administering a series of probes taken directly from the curriculum materials in which the student is being instructed. Materials for this part of the evaluation can be selected on the basis of the information gathered during the teacher interview and the review of permanent products. For example, examination of the last student mastery test in math (chapter test, unit test, end-of-book test) may provide indications of which types of computational probes need to be given. Likewise, teacher-reported information, such as the student's current placement in the basal reading series, helps to establish which reading probes to give. Data obtained about the expected and actual levels of performance will further guide the construction of test probes.

Assessment in some academic areas will be very similar across children (although books from which specific probes are taken will vary according to the curriculum being instructed); however, different types of probes may be used in different cases. For example, in reading, some cases may only involve administration of passages from the texts; other cases may require basal word lists and/or probes of phonics in addition to passages.

It is important to recognize that although the specific data collected on academic performance may vary according to the needs of an individual case, the procedures employed for the data-collection process should be the same. Described in the next section of this chapter are step-by-step instructions for assessing individual academic skills using curriculum-based assessment (CBA).

READING

Conducting an evaluation of reading has two major objectives:

1. To determine if the student is appropriately placed in the curriculum materials. Many times, students fail to master material but are passed on through the reading series without any remedial efforts.
2. To establish baseline reading levels that can serve as comparison points for monitoring progress through the reading curriculum.

The assessment of reading skills involves the administration of short oral reading probes taken from the basal reading series in which the student is being instructed. A reading CBA is very similar to an Individual Reading Inventory (IRI). The one critical difference is that an IRI is not typically taken from a specific curriculum, but is usually cross-curricular. Additionally, IRI's are not usually designed to be sensitive to continual measurement across time.

Using a Basal versus Literature-Based Series

One of the issues that frequently arises in conducting an evaluation of placement in the reading curriculum is whether a literature-based or basal reading series needs to be used. Basal reading series are designed with some control for grade-based readability. Thus, the approximate grade level for each book of a basal series is indicated by the publisher. Although within each book the readability of material will vary greatly, the overall grade levels noted by the publisher of the reading series are used to determine the reading level of that particular book of the series. Literature-based reading series are anthologies of literature and are not designed to have careful control of graded reading levels. In other words, a book used in the third grade of a series may vary widely in its readability. No attempt is made to control vocabulary or skill development, as is done in basal reading series. School districts have increasingly moved toward the use of literature-based reading series combined with whole-language instruction in reading.

In conducting an evaluation of instructional placement in reading, it is important to use a set of reading passages that are controlled for readability level, regardless of which reading series is used for instruction. In cases in which a student is being taught in a basal reading series, the passages used for assessment can come directly from this material. When a student is being taught in a literature-based reading series, it is recommended that a comparable basal reading series or a set of passages controlled for readability by grade level be used. It is possible to use the literature-based series, but one needs to carefully check the readability level of the passage before using it in the assessment. Passages used should be ± 1 grade level from the level that the evaluator is assessing. In other words, if the evaluator is assessing grade 2, the passage should range in readability from grades 1–3.

Determining the readability of passages can be done with the use of current computer technology. Most word processing programs (e.g., WordPerfect™, Microsoft Word™) offer a built-in readability formula that can be accessed easily. Common formulas used to calculate readability include the Fry (1968), Gunning (1952), and Flesch (1957) indices. These values offer some general indication of the difficulty level of the reading passages.

In general, the purpose of this step in the assessment process is to determine a student's instructional reading level within curriculum materials. When working in a literature-based reading series, the assessment process may require the use of material that is outside the curriculum of instruction, such as a comparable basal reading series. Given that the objective is to find out where in a graded set of materials a student's reading skills fall, this approach is perfectly acceptable. Evaluators should not be concerned about the apparent lack of a link to the curriculum of instruction, given that the reading material used for assessment is likely to be comparable to the instructional material.

Constructing Oral Reading Probes

1. For each book in a reading series, the evaluator should select three 150–200 word passages (for first through third grades, 50- to 100-word passages)—one from the beginning, one from the middle, and one from the end. This will provide a total of three passages for each book in the basal reading series. To facilitate the scoring process, the evaluator should retype the passage on a separate sheet with corresponding running word counts placed in the right-hand margin.

For preprimers and primers, shorter passages may be used. In addition, the differentiations between preprimers may not be salient enough to warrant separate probes for each individual book. In these cases, it is recommended that only the last of the preprimer books be used for purposes of assessment.

Another issue that sometimes emerges is that a basal reading series may have more than one level assigned to a single book. Although it is only necessary to assess by book, and not level, some examiners may wish to create a series of probes for each level within the book. This is a perfectly acceptable practice, but may lengthen the assessment period considerably.

Passages selected should not have a lot of dialogue, should be text (not poetry or plays), and should not have many unusual or foreign words. It is not necessary to select passages only from the beginning of stories within the text.

2. The evaluator should make two copies of each passage selected. One passage will be used for the child to read and the other copy will be used to score the child's oral reading. The evaluator may consider covering his or her copy with a transparency or laminating the probe so that the copy can be reused.

3. For each probe, the evaluator should develop a set of five to eight comprehension questions. These questions should include at least one "who," "what," "where," "why," and inference-type question. Although comprehension questions will be developed for each probe, only one passage from each level of the series will be used in the assessment. Idol et al. (1986) and Howell et al. (1993) offer excellent suggestions for developing comprehension questions.

The issue of whether to administer comprehension questions in a CBA is rather controversial. Results of a number of validation studies have consistently suggested that evaluating comprehension is usually redundant to assessing oral reading rate (e.g., Deno, Mirkin, & Chiang, 1982). Correlations between measures of comprehension and oral reading rate are consistently higher than .70. Many practitioners, however, are very uncomfortable with not assessing comprehension skills. Anyone working with students referred for academic problems has come across occasional students known as "word callers." These pupils have superb decoding skills and may read very fluently, yet have significant deficiencies in reading comprehension. Failure to assess comprehension skills for such a student could lead one to erroneous conclusions about the student's reading level. Many practitioners accurately point out that the process of reading itself is a matter of comprehension and not fluent oral reading. Essentially, these individuals are questioning the content validity of this measurement procedure.

Given the amount of time the assessment of comprehension adds to the evaluation process, this is not a small matter to resolve. There is a significant portion of the literature that would permit one to ignore the assessment of comprehension altogether. However, all of this literature is correlational in nature and is difficult to apply to individual cases. Clearly, one will miss the mark for some students if comprehension is not assessed.

The numbers of students who fall into the "word caller" category are probably quite small and do not justify the time it takes to add a full assessment of comprehension in every case. Typically, students who have poor oral reading skills have comprehension levels that are equal to or lower than their reading fluency levels. Thus, for those students who are referred for reading problems and found to have oral reading rates substantially below expectations, an assessment of comprehension is unnecessary and not recommended.

Despite the evidence that oral reading rate will typically reflect the top levels of reading comprehension, making an assessment of comprehension unnecessary, it is recommended that a screen for comprehension problems be part of the CBA. This is done by randomly selecting one of the three passages at each level of the series and administering a comprehension check only for that passage. In this way, the evaluator can feel more comfortable with the relationship between oral reading rate and comprehension. The comprehension screen will also provide the evaluator with additional information on the depth of a student's reading difficulties.

The comprehension screen is not designed to take the place of a needed full evaluation of a student's reading comprehension skills. The key indicator for when comprehension should be assessed is most likely found in comparing teacher interview data and the reason for referral against the observed oral reading rate. Should a student be referred for a reading problem and be found to have oral reading rates consistent with grade-level expectations, a full assessment of comprehension skills is necessary to confirm the suspected reading problem. Assuming that the reason for referral is valid, an assessment of comprehension skills should reveal a significant reading deficiency. If this is not found, then one needs to question the validity of the reason for referral.

Administration and Scoring of Oral Reading Probes

1. The evaluator should begin with the book in which the child is currently placed. (Which book this is should have been indicated during the teacher interview.)

2. For each book of the basal reading series, the evaluator administers first the probe from the beginning, then the one from the middle, and finally the one from the end.

Before beginning the assessment, the evaluator should tell the child that he or she is going to be asked to read and should do his or her best. If the evaluator is going to ask comprehension questions for that particular passage, the child should be told before beginning that he or she will be asked a few questions after the passage is read. The evaluator should then give a copy of the first probe to the child, make sure the stopwatch is ready, instruct the child to read aloud, and start the watch.

As the child reads, the evaluator should mark the following errors on the sheet:

a. An error of omission should be marked if the student leaves out an entire word. For example, if the line is "The cat drinks milk," and the student reads, "The drinks milk," the evaluator should mark an error. If the student omits the entire line, the evaluator should redirect the student to the line as soon as possible and mark one error. If the evaluator cannot redirect the student, the omission should be counted as one error and not as an error for each word missed.

b. An error of substitution should be marked if the student says the wrong word. If the student mispronounces a proper noun, the evaluator should count it as an error the first time, but should accept as correct all subsequent presentations of the same noun. For example, if the line is "John ran home," and if the student says "Jan" instead of "John" four times, it is counted as only one error.

If the student deletes suffixes such as "-ed" or "-s" in speech patterns, the deletion should not be counted as an error. The evaluator may, however, choose to make a note of it for subsequent oral language instruction. If a student mispronounces a word, the evaluator should give the child the correct word, and instruct the child to go to the next word if he or she hesitates.

   c. An error of addition should be marked if the student adds a word or words not in the passage.

   d. Repetition of words should not be marked as errors.

   e. Self-correction should not be marked as an error.

   f. After a pause of 5 seconds, the evaluator should supply the word and count the pause as an error.

Note: If comprehension questions are administered, the evaluator should proceed to paragraph 3a.

3. At the end of a minute, the evaluator should stop the child. If the child is in the middle of a sentence, he or she should be allowed to finish, but in either case, the evaluator should mark where the child is at the end of a minute on the probe.

4. The evaluator should count the number of words that the child gets correct in a minute, as well as the number of errors. If the child reads for a minute, then the number of words (correct or incorrect) is the rate per minute. If the child finishes the passage before the minute is up, the rate should be computed as follows:

$$\frac{\text{Number of words (correct or errors)}}{\text{Number of seconds read}} \times 60 = \text{Words per minute}$$

The evaluator should now proceed to paragraph 5.

3a. The evaluator should allow the child to finish reading the *entire probe*, marking where the child is at the end of each minute. The evaluator should allow the child to look at the probe while the comprehension questions are asked. It is important to make a note of whether the child rereads or scans the probe when answering the questions. This information may be useful in determining if the child has effective strategies for retrieving information recently read. The percentage of questions answered correctly is the comprehension score for that probe.

4a. The evaluator should count the total number of words read correctly in the passage, as well as the number of errors. These numbers are divided by the total time the child takes to read the entire passage, using the following formula:

$$\frac{\text{Number of words (correct or errors)}}{\text{Number of seconds read}} \times 60 = \text{Words per minute}$$

5. Following the scoring procedures outlined, the evaluator should score each probe. The *median* correct, *median* errors, and comprehension score are the child's scores on that book. The median score is the *middle* of the three scores on the probes.

The reason the median score is used, rather than the mean, is to control for any potential effects of difficulty of passages within a book. Although there should not be significant changes across the three probes from a single book, one may occasionally have selected a passage that is either too easy or too hard in comparison to the overall level of the particular book. Using the median score controls for any variance that may be due to such an extreme score.

6. Using the criteria for placement, the evaluator should move either up or down the series and give the next set of three probes. A student may be instructional in words correct but frustrational in comprehension and/or errors. The evaluator needs to look at all three measures and decide if the student's scores are within the instructional level. For example, if a student's median words correct and errors are well within the instructional level, but comprehension is below instructional level, the evaluator may decide that the student's performance is instructional but that a more in-depth evaluation of comprehension skills is needed. Likewise, if student's median words correct are in the instructional range and the error rate substantially exceeds instructional level, the evaluator may view the student's performance as frustrational, especially if the comprehension

level is less than expected. When the evaluator finds that the child is within the criteria for instructional level, the evaluator moves up the series; if not, the evaluator moves down.

Criteria for frustration, instructional, and mastery levels are provided from the literature and displayed in Table 4.1.

There are several other ways in which one can determine criteria for instructional level. One would be to collect local norms within a particular district or school. The process for collecting these norms is complex and interested readers should consult an excellent description of the procedure by Shinn (1988, 1989). Examples of norms obtained from various settings are provided in Chapter 7 (see Tables 7.1, 7.2, and 7.3). The norms on these tables are given for illustrative purposes only and should not be equally applied to all other settings.

An important distinction between the collection of local norms and those used by Fuchs and Deno (1982) is that the norming of CBA in a district may not be able to suggest the best place in which a child should be instructed. The recommended reading levels of Fuchs and Deno for mastery, instructional, and frustrational levels are based on a "best guess" approach for instruction. Where a student is expected to begin instruction should be at a point at which material has not yet been completely mastered (mastery level), but also is not too difficult (frustration). Thus, although a student may be found to be in the 16th percentile in reading according to local norms, the decision as to where instruction should begin is made by seeing where the student's oral reading rates fall in comparison to students in other grades. For example, if a fourth-grade student's reading places him at the 16th percentile compared to other fourth-graders, but at the 38th percentile compared to third-graders, and at the 75th percentile compared to second graders, it seems that placement at the third-grade level would be meaningful. If local norms are not available, however, decisions based on the Fuchs and Deno criteria for instructional level are acceptable.

TABLE 4.1. Revised Placement Criteria for Direct Reading Assessment

Grade level of materials	Level	Words correct per minute	Errors per minute
1–2	Frustration	< 40	> 4
	Instructional	40–60	4 or less
	Mastery	> 60	4 or less
3–6	Frustration	< 70	> 6
	Instructional	70–100	6 or less
	Mastery	> 100	6 or less

Note. From "Developing Goals and Objectives for Educational Programs [Teaching Guide]" by L. S. Fuchs, and S. L. Deno, 1982, Minneapolis: U.S. Department of Education Grant.

One of the problems that can arise in deciding whether a student's reading level is instructional occurs when a student is moved from the second- to third-grade level materials. As seen in Table 4.1, a student reading in third-grade material at 70 words correct per minute is considered to be at the instructional level. In second-grade material, 40 words correct per minute is instructional. Thus, for example, a third-grade student who is found to read at 60 words correct per minute in third-grade materials is at a frustrational level. The same student when tested in second-grade material may be found to read at 70 words correct per minute, which is mastery. The problem is that the student appears not to have an instructional level. In this case, one would interpret these findings in light of the change in difficulty of material that occurs between second and third grade, along with the ensuing increase in expected performance. This student would be viewed as having an instructional level somewhere between grade 2 and 3 material.

7. The evaluator should continue to give probes until the median scores for at least two sets of scores are instructional, *and* the one above them is frustrational.

The optimal pattern would be something like this:

♦ Level 7—Frustration
♦ Level 6—Instructional
♦ Level 5—Instructional
♦ Level 4—Mastery

Often, this exact pattern will not be obtained. Some children never reach a mastery level and will have a long series of instructional levels. After three consecutive instructional levels, it is unnecessary to continue further. *The child's placement is at the highest instructional level.* The evaluator also may have to use his or her judgment about instructional, frustration, and mastery levels. The criteria provided are not specific cutoffs, but should be viewed as gradual changes. For example, a child scoring at 58 words correct per minute (where 50 is mastery) on one level and 61 on the next is probably close to mastery on both levels.

Interpreting Reading Probe Data

The results of the reading assessment should provide an indication of the level in the reading series where instruction would be most profitable. Defined as the "instructional level," this is the place in the curriculum series where a student is likely to be challenged but make progress if he or she is taught at that level. In contrast, placement in curriculum materials that are at a higher level would be frustrational and too difficult for students to effectively learn. Placement in curriculum materials at a lower level would be at mastery and not present sufficient challenge to the student. This is an important issue, because children many times are being asked to read at levels and in materials that have high probabilities of failure. It is recognized that one cannot always expect a teacher to move a student down to a reading level far below the lowest student in the class. This presents significant practical problems that cannot be addressed easily. Often, consultants need to be creative about this problem and offer suggestions that may be more acceptable within the present classroom structure. For example, if it is found that a fourth-grade student should be in a second-grade book, according to the instructional criteria suggested by Fuchs and Deno (1982), then one may suggest to the teacher the possibility of moving only to the third-grade book, but providing some type of additional individual instructional time with the student. The use of peer tutoring can often significantly assist the teacher when this type of problem arises. For example, a peer who is reading at a higher level may provide sight-word drill for the targeted student. This additional effort can be provided while the student remains in his or her current reading group. Recommendations such as this are discussed in more detail in the next chapter. Regardless of the recommendations made based on the identification of the student's instructional level in reading, these data provide diagnostic information to the evaluator about why a student may be having difficulty in grade-level assigned reading material.

A second important finding based on the reading assessment is the identification of potential goals for reading achievement during the ensuing instructional period. On the basis of current oral reading rates, the teacher can set weekly, biweekly, monthly, and yearly goals for both oral reading rates and numbers of pages covered. When reading probes taken from the year-end goal are readministered, progress on the student's performance across time can be monitored. Again, more detail on this use of CBA data in general, and reading in particular, are included in Chapter 6.

MATHEMATICS

Assessing mathematics begins by obtaining the sequence of instruction for computational skills for your school district. If this is not available, the evaluator may use the list of objectives given in Chapter 3 (see Appendix 3B). There is not much deviation from district to district in the order in which these skills are taught.

Over the last several years, there has been a trend in the instruction of mathematics toward the teaching of problem-solving skills while deemphasizing the teaching of computational competencies. Although obtaining data on a student's skills in problem-solving and other noncomputational aspects of mathematics (e.g., estimation) are certainly considered important, CBA still emphasizes computational objectives as the foundation upon which success in other aspects of mathematics are built.

Math probes can be made for the assessment of either a single skill (such as two-digit addition with regrouping in the 10's column only), or multiple skills (such as all addition and subtraction facts with results less than 10). Single-skill probe sheets are very useful for providing very specific recommendations regarding deficient and mastered math skills and are typically used when in the assessment of instructional placement phase of the academic skills evaluation. These sheets can also be valuable in monitoring the acquisition of newly taught skills during the instructional modification phase of the assessment. Multiple-skill sheets offer the advantage of assessing a broader range of skills at the same time. These sheets are used typically when conducting progress monitoring of student performance (the final phase of the CBA). These are also excellent for determining where additional assessment may be necessary.

Single-Skill Probes

1. The evaluator should define the specific types of math problems that are of interest. This can be determined either by examination of a recent end-of-book (or end-of-level) test (if available), or through the teacher interview. During the teacher interview, it is recommended that the teacher mark on the list of computational skills where the student has attained mastery, where the student is being instructed, and where the student is having significant difficulties. By looking at the range of items between the teacher's rated mastery and frustration levels of the student's computation skills, the evaluator can select the possible types of computational skills to be assessed. It is not necessary to assess every single computational objective between the mastery and frustration levels. Instead, three or four objectives should be selected that will allow the evaluator to assess the range of items between these two points. In selecting these objectives, the evaluator should try to choose those that require different operations (e.g., addition and subtraction), if both types of objectives are listed between mastery and frustration points.

2. The evaluator should write (or type) several sheets of problems of the same type, leaving enough room for computation if necessary (e.g., in the case of long division). For simpler problems, 30–35 to a sheet would be good (e.g., single-digit fact families). Several sheets of the same computa-

TABLE 4.2. Match between Objectives of Milliken Math Sequences Program and Computational Skills Mastery List (see Appendix 3B)

Appendix 3B objective number	Milliken objective number	Appendix 3B objective number	Milliken objective number
1	Addition: 6–8	26	Subtraction: 28
2	Subtraction: 4–8	27	Subtraction: 41–43
3	Addition: 11–20	28	—
4	Addition: 23–25	29	Subtraction: 41–43
5	Addition: 23–25	30	Subtraction: 33–35
6	Addition: 41	31	Subtraction: 35
7	Subtraction: 13–18	32	Subtraction: 40, 44
8	—	33	Multiplication: 6–30
9	Subtraction: 23	34	Addition: 55–58
10	Subtraction: 32	35	Addition: 55–58
11	—	36	Addition: 55–58
12	—	37	Subtraction: 41
13	Addition: 41	38	Multiplication: 31–32, 36
14	—	39	Multiplication: 36
15	Addition: 26–27, 32–34	40	Multiplication: 32
16	Addition: 28–34	41	Multiplication: 37–39
17	Addition: 42–47	42	—
18	Addition: 46–47	43	Division: 36–39, 42
19	Addition: 48–50	44	Division: 40–41, 43–44
20	Addition: 42–45	45	Division: 46–47
21	Addition: 46–47	46	Division: 9–51
22	Addition: 48–50	47	Multiplication: 43–49
23	Addition: 55–58	48	Multiplication: 50–54
24	—	49	Multiplication: 61–62
25	Subtraction: 24–27, 29–31		

tional type may be needed, with the same format, but different numbers. The evaluator should be sure to provide a good sample of all numbers within the parameters that are set and should be careful about using zeros.

There are several excellent computer programs available that will automatically generate specific math probes. The Math Sequences program from Milliken (Milliken Publishing Company, 1100 Research Blvd., St. Louis, MO 63132), available for IBM, Macintosh, and Apple computers, is quite useful in developing these probes. Although the computer program will not generate exact probes for all of the computational skills listed on Appendix 3B, many are included on this program (about 85.7%). Table 4.2 provides a listing of the correspondence of computational objectives from Appendix 3B and the Milliken Math Sequences program.

Multiple-Skill Probes

Two types of multiple-skill probes can be developed. When using multiple-skill probes at the curriculum-placement phase of the evaluation to identify specific strengths and deficiencies in computational skills, the evaluator should define the upper skill of interest and determine how many skills will be assessed at once. A number of problems of each type should be devised as noted earlier. For each sheet, the evaluator should select two or three of each computational skill and place them onto a probe sheet. An example of a multiple-skill probe, adding two- and three-digit numbers without regrouping, is given in Figure 4.1.

When the objective of assessment is to monitor progress, as in the final phase of the CBA, the multiple-skill probe selected needs to reflect all the curriculum objectives that are identified for that grade. In other words, if the evaluator is monitoring progress across curriculum objectives for a third-grade student, the multiple-skill probe needs to contain problems that sample all the skills to be taught across the third-grade curriculum. The Montoring Basic Skills computer program (Fuchs, Hamlett, & Fuchs, 1990a) for the Apple series computer contain a well-developed, well-researched set of these types of probes. Additionally, a set of black-line masters are included that offer 30 probes per grade level.

Administration and Scoring of Math Probes

1. Generally, no more than two different probe sheets for each skill or cluster of skills are administered. The evaluator should give the probe to

```
ADD: 2 & 3 D NO RGRP        Name _____

1.      10   2.      76   3.      78   4.      13   5.      21
      + 64        + 12        + 11        + 86        + 71

6.      20   7.      20   8.      57   9.      68  10.      11
      + 11        + 68        + 32        + 11        + 42

11.    137  12.     607  13.     745  14.     665  15.     637
      +401        +310        +244        +124        +132

16.    370  17.     413  18.     770  19.     517  20.     150
      +618        +416        +105        +260        +503
```

FIGURE 4.1. Example of skill probe: Adding two- and three-digit numbers without regrouping.

the child and tell him or her to work each problem, going from left to right without skipping. If the child does not know how to do a problem, he or she should go on to the next one. For probes in addition or subtraction, the student is stopped after 2 minutes. For probes involving multiplication and/or division, the student is stopped after 5 minutes.

2. If the child's score on the probe sheet is significantly below instructional level, the evaluator should move downward in the curriculum to a less challenging probe. If the evaluator feels the student's performance on the probe was not indicative of the student's best efforts, a second probe of the same skills can certainly be administered. Likewise, if the evaluator finds the student highly frustrated by the skill being assessed, he or she can stop the student short of the 5 minutes permitted for the probe. It is important, however, to note the exact time the student worked on the math probe. If the child scores close to or within the instructional–mastery level, the evaluator should administer one additional probe of those same skills.

3. Each of the probes should be scored as follows: The evaluator should count the separate digits in an answer. For all skills except long division, only digits *below the line* are counted. For example, in a two-digit addition problem with regrouping, digits written above the 10's column are not counted.

The evaluator should count the number of digits correct and incorrect for each probe. If the child completes the worksheet before time is up, the evaluator should divide the number of digits by the total number of seconds and multiply by 60. This equals the digits correct (or incorrect) per minute. The *median* score for all probes of the same skills serve as the score for that skill or cluster.

If a student skips problems on a worksheet, any omitted problems should be scored as *errors*. Obviously, this will inflate the number of incorrect digits per minute and deflate the number of correct digits per minute. It is important to note this deviation, however, because skipping problems usually indicates that a student has mastered only certain skills assessed on the worksheet. For example, if single-digit addition with sums to 18 is being assessed, and a student only completes problems in which a 9 is not one of the addends, this should be reflected in the score obtained on that probe. In addition to scoring the probe with omitted items counting as incorrect, the evaluator should also report the score *without* counting omitted items to demonstrate the discrepancy between these scores.

Another problem that may be encountered in scoring the math probes may occur when students are doing double-digit multiplication. An error in multiplication will result in incorrect scores when the student adds the columns. Even though all operations are correct, a single mistake in multiplication can result in all digits being incorrect. When a student makes an error in multiplication, digits should be scored as correct or incorrect if the addition operations are performed correctly. For example, the problem

$$
\begin{array}{r}
45 \\
\times\ 28 \\
\hline
360 \\
90 \\
\hline
1260
\end{array}
$$

has 10 digits correct (9 digits plus the place holder under the 0). Suppose the problem has been completed as follows:

$$
\begin{array}{r}
45 \\
\times\ 28 \\
\hline
350 \\
80 \\
\hline
1150
\end{array}
$$

The problem is scored as having 8 digits correct (7 digits plus the place holder under the 0), because the student multiplied incorrectly but added correctly.

In addition to scoring the math problems for digits correct and incorrect, it may also be helpful to score the probes for the percentage of problems completed correctly. This is a more commonly used metric in classrooms and may be helpful in communication to the teacher.

Criteria

Criteria are provided from Deno and Mirkin (1977) for frustrational, instructional, and mastery levels in Table 4.3. Additional norms are provided from a Midwestern school district in Table 4.4.

Interpreting Data from Math Probes

Mathematics typically is taught at a single level across students within a classroom. Although students may be divided into math groups, the differences between groups may be reflected more in depth of content than in actual curriculum material covered. As such, deciding placement of a student into a particular level of the curriculum is not an issue.

Much more important here are decisions regarding the particular computational skills present or absent in the student's repertoire. A fourth grader being asked to do division and multiplication, but who does not

TABLE 4.3. Placement Criteria for Direct Assessment of Math

Grade	Level	Criterion	
		Median digits correct per minute	Median digits incorrect per minute
Grades 1–3	Frustration	0–9	8+
	Instructional	10–19	3–7
	Mastery	20+	≤2
Grade 4+	Frustration	0–19	8+
	Instructional	20–39	3–7
	Mastery	40+	≤2

Note. The data are from Deno and Mirkin (1977). The table is reproduced from "Behavioral Assessment of Academic Skills" by E. S. Shapiro and F. E. Lentz, Jr., 1986, in T. R. Kratochwill (Ed.), *Advances in School Psychology*, Vol. 5, p. 124. Copyright 1986 by Lawrence Erlbaum Associates. Reprinted by permission.

have mastery of basic addition and subtraction facts, clearly needs to have additional and substantial instruction on those basic facts before he or she can be expected to learn the material being instructed in the classroom. By contrast, a student who attains high levels of accuracy on expected levels of performance, but at rates that are below expectations, needs to improve in his or her fluency with the material; however, the basic concepts have been learned. For example, a student may know the concept of regrouping (borrowing), but cannot perform the computations fast enough

TABLE 4.4. Norms for Math Computation (2-Minute Timing) from a Rural Midwestern School District, 1985–1986

Grade	Winter		Spring		Winter		Spring	
	MDC	ME	MDC	ME	MDC	ME	MDC	ME
	Addition				Subtraction			
1	24	12	22	2	19	14	29	19
2	65	3	57	2	38	2	40	8
3	68	1	56		35	4	44	3
4	35	1	36	2	17	12	42	5
	Multiplication				Division			
1	—	—	—	—	—	—	—	—
2	—	—	—	—	—	—	—	—
3	51	10	63	5	—	—	—	—
4	11	92	129	2	17	41	37	1

Note. MDC, median digits correct; ME, median errors.

to be at a mastery level. The key findings from these data are to facilitate description of acquired knowledge and to make specific recommendations for future interventions. On the basis of these data, it should be possible to tell a teacher the specific skills on which instruction should be focused.

As with reading data, the results of the assessment of instructional placement in math can serve as a mechanism for setting short- and long-term goals. The repeated administration of these measures over time permits progress toward these goals to be evaluated. Again, more details on this use of the data are discussed in Chapters 5 and 6.

WRITTEN EXPRESSION

The purpose of assessing written expression is to determine the level and type of skills that students have attained. In contrast to reading and math, it is unlikely that there are any particular curriculum objectives to which the written expression assessment can be linked. Instead, the procedure employed is a more general technique that is used across grades.

Construction, Administration, and Scoring of Probes

1. A series of "story starters" should be constructed that can be used to give the initial idea for students to write about. These starters should contain items that most children will find of sufficient interest to generate a written story. Table 4.5 offers an extensive list of possible story starters. During the assessment, the evaluator may choose to give two or three story starters, again using the median scores.

2. The evaluator should give the child a copy of the story starter and read the starter to him or her. The evaluator then tells the student that he or she will be asked to write a story using the starter as the first sentence. The student should be given a minute to think about a story before he or she will be asked to begin writing.

3. After 1 minute, the evaluator should tell the child to begin writing, start the stopwatch, and time for 3 minutes. If the child stops writing before the 3 minutes are up, he or she should be encouraged to keep writing until time is up.

4. The evaluator should count the number of words that are correctly written. "Correct" means that a word can be recognized (even if misspelled). Capitalization and punctuation are ignored. The rates of correct and incorrect words per 3 minutes are calculated. If the child stops writing before the 3 minutes are up, the number of words correct should be divided by the amount of actual time (in seconds) spent in writing, and this should be multiplied by 180 for the number of words correct per 3 minutes.

TABLE 4.5. List of Possible Story Starters

I just saw a monster. The monster was so big it . . .

I made the biggest sandwich in the world.

Bill and Sue were lost in the jungle.

One day Mary brought her pet skunk to school.

One day it rained candy.

Tom woke up in the middle of the night. He heard a loud crash.

Jill got a surprise package in the mail.

One time I got very mad.

The best birthday I ever had . . .

I'll never forget the night I had to stay in a cave.

The most exciting thing about my jungle safari was . . .

When my video game started predicting the future, I knew I had to . . .

I never dreamed that the secret door in my basement would lead to . . .

The day my headphone radio started sending me signals from outer space, I . . .

The worst part about having a talking dog is . . .

When I moved to the desert, I was amazed to find out that cactuses . . .

When I looked out my window this morning, none of the scenery looked familiar.

I've always wanted a time machine that would take me to that wonderful time
  when . . .

I would love to change places with my younger/older brother/sister, because . . .

The best thing about having the robot I got for my birthday is . . .

I always thought my tropical fish were very boring until I found out the secret of their
  language.

I thought it was the end of the world when I lost my magic baseball bat, until I found
  an enchanted . . .

The best trick I ever played on Halloween was . . .

I was most proud of my work as a private detective when I helped solve the case of
  the . . .

If I could create the ideal person, I would make sure that he or she had . . .

You'll never believe how I was able to escape from the pirates who kept me prisoner
  on their ship.

TABLE 4.6. Norms for Written Expression

Grade	Words per 3 minutes
1	15
2	28
3	37
4	41
5	49
6	53

Note. Data are from Mirkin et al. (1981).

TABLE 4.7. Means and Standard Deviations for Grade-Level Local Norms for Total Words Written for Two Midwestern Districts

Grade	District	Fall	Winter	Spring
2	A	11.7	16.7	24.7
		(7.3)	(10.1)	(11.5)
	B	—	—	—
3	A	22.9	27.8	33.8
		(10.3)	(11.9)	(12.4)
	B	—	—	—
4	A	32.7	36.4	41.4
		(12.9)	(12.4)	(12.9)
	B	26.1	36.9	41.6
		(12.1)	(12.2)	(12.5)
5	A	40.3	44.6	46.4
		(14.5)	(13.7)	(13.6)
	B	36.8	38.8	41.5
		(11.7)	(14.7)	(12.5)
6	A	47.4	47.5	53.5
		(13.8)	(14.3)	(15.4)
	B	—	—	—

Note. From "Identifying and Defining Academic Problems: CBM Screening and Eligibility Procedures" by M. R. Shinn, in M. R. Shinn (Ed.), 1989, *Curriculum-Based Measurement: Assessing Special Children*, p. 112. Copyright 1989 by The Guilford Press. Reprinted by permission.

5. Table 4.6 provides norms for written performance per 3 minutes from Mirkin et al. (1981); Table 4.7 provides the norms reported by Shinn (1989) from large urban (District A) and rural (District B) Midwestern school districts, representing data on approximately 1,000 students from grades 1 to 5 across 15 different elementary schools.

The criteria for these probes may be best determined by taking a local sample—for example, 5–10 other children in the same grade who are considered not to have any difficulty. Alternatively, a teacher may administer the story starters to an entire class to determine a local norm. Written expression probes can also be scored and examined for spelling, punctuation, capitalization, and grammatical usage.

Interpreting Written Expression Probes

A significant number of data are obtained from the assessment of written expression. Other than determining where the student's written expression falls relative to that of his or her peers, the probe also offers opportunities to explore related problems, such as spelling errors, grammatical usage, and mechanics of writing. Furthermore, the assessment allows one to examine the creativity a student can generate. Although there are no norms for such a subjective area, stories that reflect imagination and insight can suggest certain capabilities of students. In addition, one can examine the stories for structure (beginning, plot, end) and make specific suggestions to teachers for written expression goals. And, like other parts of the CBA, written expression can offer indications of ongoing progress in meeting goals across the school year.

SPELLING

The assessment of spelling is similar to the CBA of reading and math, since the content of the evaluation is taken directly from the instructional curriculum. It is important to note, however, that there often is not substantial overlap between the reading series and spelling series. Examination of the teacher interview data should show whether spelling is being taught from a separate series, from the reading series, or by using teacher-generated word lists. Probes are typically constructed from the same curricular material in which the student is being instructed. It is important to recognize that many schools today do not teach spelling apart from reading and other language-arts activities. As such, it may be difficult to find a grade-based spelling curriculum to use for assessment. One alternative that is recommended in conducting a CBA in spelling is to use any set of materials that contains the typical skills instructed within a particular grade level. Fuchs, Hamlett, and Fuchs (1990b) offer a computer program for the Apple series that contains such materials for spelling.

Constructing, Administering, and Scoring Spelling Probes

1. From the appropriate curriculum (spelling or basal reader series), the evaluator should select three sets of 20 words taken randomly from across the text or material used as the spelling curriculum.

2. Words should be dictated to the student at the rate of one every 7 seconds.

3. The evaluator should dictate from successive grade-level probes until the following criteria are met:

Grades 1–2	20–39 letter sequences correct per minute
Grades 3–6	40–59 letter sequences correct per minute

4. The evaluator should count the correct letter sequences. Spelling is scored in terms of correct letter sequences. The procedure for scoring is as follows:

a. A "phantom" character is placed before and after each word. For example, the word

__ B U T T E R __

has seven possible letter sequences.

b. The word BUTTER spelled as

__ B U T E R __ has five letter sequences correct.
__ B U T T A R __ has five letter sequences correct.
__ B A T T A R __ has three letter sequences correct.

Rates are calculated as follows:

$$\frac{\text{Letter sequences correct}}{\text{Total seconds dictated}} \times 60 \text{ seconds} =$$
Letter sequences correct per minute

Interpreting Spelling Probe Data

In spelling, as in mathematics, all students are typically placed into the same level of the curriculum, regardless of their particular skill level. Thus, recommendations to move a student to a different level of the spelling curriculum will not usually be logical. Results of the CBA in spelling may suggest the degree to which a student needs to have additional drill and practice on words previously instructed but not mastered. In addition, the data may show the types of errors typically made by the student (e.g., consistently missing middle vowels, but getting beginning and ending consonants correct; correctly identifying all components of words except ending sounds; spelling all words phonetically). These types of error analyses will allow for specific instructional recommendations.

SUMMARIZING THE DATA-COLLECTION PROCESS

CBA, as described here, incorporates the first two phases of the assessment process: collection of data about the instructional environment and the student's instructional placement within the curriculum. Information is obtained through the teacher interview, direct observation, examination of permanent products, student interview, and administration of skill probes. Decisions that can be made from these data include those pertaining to correct placement in the curriculum, potential variables affecting academic performance, recommendations for interventions, relative standing compared to peers on academic skills, setting long- and short-term goals, assessment of progress on goals, and evaluation of the effectiveness of designed interventions. In addition, the data can and have been used in making eligibility decisions (Germann & Tindal, 1985) as well as in program evaluation (Deno, 1985).

To facilitate the process of integrating the data from the teacher interview, direct observation, student interview, and assessment of individual skills, a form is available that provides places to report all the data from each part of the evaluation. A copy of this form is given in Appendix 4A, with an expanded version available in the workbook accompanying this text (Shapiro 1996). Places are available for recording results of skill probes, teacher interview data, student interview data, direct observation data, and any relevant comments about the examination of permanent products. The form has been used across hundreds of cases and has been reported as very useful in integrating the information from the assessment. Evaluators are encouraged to copy and employ this form as they conduct CBA.

The final two steps in the academic assessment process involve the development and implementation of instructional modifications based on the data collected through the assessment of the academic environment and evaluation of instructional placement, and the monitoring of the student's progress using these modifications over time. The next two chapters discuss possible interventions that may be applicable to alter academic performance. The final step in the assessment process, progress monitoring, is then described.

Data Summary Form for Academic Assessment

Child's name: _____ Date: _____
Teacher: _____ School district: _____
Grade: _____
School: _____

READING—SKILLS

Primary type of reading series used

☐ Basal reader
☐ Literature-based
☐ Trade books

Secondary type of reading materials used

☐ Basal reader
☐ Literature-based
☐ Trade books
☐ None

Title of curriculum series: _____
Level/book—target student: _____
Level/book—average student: _____

Results of passages administered:

Grade level/ book	Location in book	WC/ min	Errors/ min	% correct	Median scores for level			Learning level (M, I, F)
					WC	ER	%C	
	Beginning							
	Middle							
	End							
	Beginning							
	Middle							
	End							
	Beginning							
	Middle							
	End							
	Beginning							
	Middle							
	End							

READING—ENVIRONMENT

Instructional Procedures:

Primary type of reading instruction:

- ☐ Basal readers ☐ Whole-language
- ☐ Other (describe) _____

Number of reading groups: _____

Student's reading group (if applicable) _____

Alloted time/day for reading: _____

Contingencies: _____

Teaching procedures: _____

Observations: _____ None completed for this area

System used:

- ☐ SECOS ☐ B.O.S.S.
- ☐ Other _____

Setting of observations:

- ☐ ISW: TPsnt ☐ SmGp: Tled ☐ Coop
- ☐ ISW: TSmGp ☐ LgGp: Tled ☐ Other _____

SECOS results:

ISW%	_____	OCA rate	_____
Non ISW%	_____	TA/SW rate	_____
SIC%	_____	TA/OTH rate	_____
AC rate	_____		

B.O.S.S. results

AET%	_____	OFT-M%	_____
PET%	_____	OFT-V%	_____
		OFT-P%	_____

TEACHER-REPORTED STUDENT BEHAVIOR

Rate the following areas from 1 to 5 (1 = very unsatifactory, 3 = satisfactory, 5 = superior)

Reading Group

- a. Oral reading ability (as evidenced in reading group) _____
- b. Volunteers answers _____
- c. When called upon, gives correct answer _____
- d. Attends to other students when they read aloud _____
- e. Knows the appropriate place in book _____

Independent Seatwork

- a. Stays on task _____
- b. Completes assigned work in required time _____
- c. Work is accurate _____
- d. Works quietly _____
- e. Remains in seat when required _____

Homework (if any)

    a. Handed in on time   _____

    b. Is complete   _____

    c. Is accurate   _____

STUDENT-REPORTED BEHAVIOR   ____ None completed for this area

Understands expectations of teacher	☐ Yes	☐ No	☐ Not sure
Understands assignments	☐ Yes	☐ No	☐ Not sure
Feels he/she can do the assignments	☐ Yes	☐ No	☐ Not sure
Likes the subject	☐ Yes	☐ No	☐ Not sure
Feels he/she is given enough time to complete assignments	☐ Yes	☐ No	☐ Not sure
Feels like he/she is called upon to participate in discussions	☐ Yes	☐ No	☐ Not sure

MATH—SKILLS

Curriculum series used: _____

Specific problems in math: _____

Mastery skill of target student:_____

Mastery skill of average student: _____

Instructional skill of target student: _____

Problems in math applications: _____

Results of math probes:

Probe type	No.	Digits correct/min	Digits incorrect/min	% problems correct	Learning level (M, I, F)

MATH—ENVIRONMENT

Instructional Procedures:

Number of math groups: _____

Student's group (high, middle, low): _____

Allotted time/day: _____

Teaching procedures: _____

Contingencies: _____

Observations: ____ None completed for this area

System used:

   ☐ SECOS   ☐ B.O.S.S.

   ☐ Other _____

Setting of observations:

   ☐ ISW: TPsnt   ☐ SmGp: Tled   ☐ Coop

   ☐ ISW: TSmGp   ☐ LgGp: Tled   ☐ Other _____

SECOS results:

ISW%	_____	OCA rate	_____
Non ISW%	_____	TA/SW rate	_____
SIC%	_____	TA/OTH rate	_____
AC rate	_____		

B.O.S.S. results:

AET%	_____	OFT-M%	_____
PET%	_____	OFT-V%	_____
		OFT-P%	_____

TEACHER-REPORTED STUDENT BEHAVIOR

Rate the following areas from 1 to 5 (1 = very unsatifactory, 3 = satisfactory, 5 = superior)

Math Group (large)

a. Volunteers answers   _____

b. When called upon, gives correct answer   _____

c. Attends to other students when they give answers   _____

d. Knows the appropriate place in math book   _____

Math Group (small)

a. Volunteers answers   _____

b. When called upon, gives correct answer   _____

c. Attends to other students when they give answers   _____

d. Knows the appropriate place in math book   _____

Math Group (cooperative)

a. Volunteers answers   _____

b. Contributes to goup objectives   _____

c. Attends to other students when they give answers   _____

d. Facilitates others in group to participate   _____

e. Shows appropriate social skills in group   _____

Independent Seatwork

a. Stays on task   _____

b. Completes assigned work in required time   _____

c. Work is accurate _____
d. Works from initial directions _____
e. Works quietly _____
f. Remains in seat when required _____

Homework (if any)
a. Handed in on time _____
b. Is complete _____
c. Is accurate _____

STUDENT-REPORTED BEHAVIOR _____ None completed for this area

Understands expectations of teacher	☐ Yes	☐ No	☐ Not sure
Understands assignments	☐ Yes	☐ No	☐ Not sure
Feels he/she can do the assignments	☐ Yes	☐ No	☐ Not sure
Likes the subject	☐ Yes	☐ No	☐ Not sure
Feels he/she is given enough time to complete assignments	☐ Yes	☐ No	☐ Not sure
Feels like he/she is called upon to participate in discussions	☐ Yes	☐ No	☐ Not sure

SPELLING—SKILLS

Type of material used for spelling instruction:

I Published spelling series
   Title of series _____
I Basal reading series
   Title of series _____
I Teacher-made materials
I Other _____

Curriculum series (if applicable): _____

Results of spelling probes:

Grade level of probe	Probe no.	LSC/min	% Words correct	Median LSC for grade level	Level (M, I, F)
	1				
	2				
	3				
	1				
	2				
	3				
	1				
	2				
	3				
	1				
	2				
	3				

SPELLING—ENVIRONMENT

Instructional Procedures:

Allotted time/day: _____

Teaching procedures: _____

Contingencies: _____

Observations: _____ None completed for this area

System used:

□ SECOS   □ B.O.S.S.

□ Other _____

Setting of observations:

□ ISW: TPsnt   □ SmGp: Tled   □ Coop

□ ISW: TSmGp   □ LgGp: Tled   □ Other _____

SECOS results:

ISW%	_____	OCA rate	_____
Non ISW%	_____	TA/SW rate	_____
SIC%	_____	TA/OTH rate	_____
AC rate	_____		

B.O.S.S. results:

AET%	_____	OFT-M%	_____
PET%	_____	OFT-V%	_____
		OFT-P%	_____

STUDENT-REPORTED BEHAVIOR _____ None completed for this area

Understands expectations of teacher   □ Yes   □ No   □ Not sure

Understands assignments   □ Yes   □ No   □ Not sure

Feels he/she can do the assignments   □ Yes   □ No   □ Not sure

Likes the subject   □ Yes   □ No   □ Not sure

Feels he/she is given enough time to
complete assignments   □ Yes   □ No   □ Not sure

Feels like he/she is called upon to
participate in discussions   □ Yes   □ No   □ Not sure

WRITING—SKILLS

Types of writing assignments: _____

Areas of difficulty:

Content: Mechanics:

□ Expressing thoughts   □ Capitalization

□ Story length   □ Punctuation

□ Story depth   □ Grammar

□ Creativity   □ Handwriting

                               □ Spelling

Results of written expression probes:

Story starter	Words written/ 3 min	Instructional level?	Comments

WRITING—ENVIRONMENT

Instructional Procedures:

Allotted time/day: _____

Teaching procedures: _____

Observations: _____ None completed for this area

System used:

☐ SECOS   ☐ B.O.S.S.

☐ Other _____

Setting of observations:

☐ ISW: TPsnt   ☐ SmGp: Tled   ☐ Coop

☐ ISW: TSmGp   ☐ LgGp: Tled   ☐ Other _____

SECOS results:

ISW%	_____	OCA rate	_____
Non ISW%	_____	TA/SW rate	_____
SIC%	_____	TA/OTH rate	_____
AC rate	_____		

B.O.S.S. results

AET%	_____	OFT-M%	_____
PET%	_____	OFT-V%	_____
		OFT-P%	_____

STUDENT-REPORTED BEHAVIOR _____ None completed for this area

Understands expectations of teacher	☐ Yes	☐ No	☐ Not sure
Understands assignments	☐ Yes	☐ No	☐ Not sure
Feels he/she can do the assignments	☐ Yes	☐ No	☐ Not sure
Likes the subject	☐ Yes	☐ No	☐ Not sure
Feels he/she is given enough time to complete assignments	☐ Yes	☐ No	☐ Not sure
Feels like he/she is called upon to participate in discussions	☐ Yes	☐ No	☐ Not sure

CHAPTER 5

♦♦♦

Step 3: Instructional Modification I

General Strategies

♦

BACKGROUND

The selection of interventions to remediate academic problems has long been dominated by attempts to match specific characteristics of student learning styles to specific methods of instruction. Based on the idea that effective matching of learning style and instructional method would result in the most effective and efficient learning, significant efforts have been devoted to both identifying these critical, underlying processes and developing intervention programs aimed at remediating these processes. Effective teaching was felt to be based on identification of aptitude–treatment interactions (ATIs) that were evident for the referred child.

Two general approaches to designing treatment interventions resulted from this model. One strategy was to identify the deficient processes and design interventions that would assist the students in compensating for the problem. For example, students with numerical memory problems might be given concrete cues to assist them in the computation process. Those with poor written expression might be permitted to submit responses on a test by dictating or audiotaping their answers. The second approach to deriving interventions based on the ATI model was to determine the students' modality strengths in learning and to teach specifically to those strengths. For example, students found to be deficient in auditory analysis (phonics) would be taught using a sight-oriented approach to reading. Those students found to be stronger at simultaneous than at sequential processing would be instructed in more holistic means of learning basic skills.

Although the ATI approach to remediating academic problems has intuitive and logical appeal, as well as a long, deep-rooted history in the educational process, there really is little empirical support for the continued use of this strategy. Historically, significant efforts were devoted to developing assessment and remediation programs based on this approach (e.g., Barsch, 1965; Frostig & Horne, 1964; Johnson & Myklebust, 1967; Kephart, 1971; Wepman, 1967). Typically, these programs involved the administration of tests to determine deficient psychological processes underlying acquisition of basic academic skills. Tests attempted to identify within-child processes such as sequential memory, figure–ground perception, auditory perception, and visual–motor integration; training programs aimed at remediating the specific deficiencies were then provided. Substantial reviews of the literature concerning the empirical support for the assessment instruments, as well as their related instructional training programs, have clearly suggested that such approaches to remediating academic problems are likely to fail (Arter & Jenkins, 1979; Cronbach & Snow, 1977; Tarver & Dawson, 1978; Ysseldyke & Mirkin, 1982).

Several individuals have suggested reasons why the search for ATIs are doomed to fail. Cronbach and Snow (1977) have suggested, after reviewing over 90 studies examining ATIs, that no ATI is so well replicated that it can guide the development of instructional strategies. Gordon et al. (1985) noted that many investigators find it hard to dismiss the ATI model because of its intuitive appeal, despite its current lack of empirical validation. Messick (1970), in an early paper, felt that the existing assessment technology cannot effectively identify the complexities of interactions that occur during the learning process.

Perhaps another reason why the ATI model will not succeed in the development of instructional interventions can be seen in the nature of ATI findings. These studies are almost exclusively based on analysis of large groups of students. Conclusions drawn from these findings may not always be applicable to individual students, even if the assessment methodologies suggest that the student has specific deficiencies. In other words, even though studies may suggest that students with strong sequential processing skills as assessed on the Kaufman Assessment Battery for Children (K-ABC) would best be instructed in math by a stepwise approach to computation, these results may not be directly applicable to a specific, individual student. Indeed, some serious questions have been raised about the use of group-design methodologies in general for decision making about effective interventions (e.g., Kratochwill, 1985a; Shapiro, 1987b).

Despite the substantial problems with ATI models for designing academic interventions, the use of these strategies continues to permeate the literature. Continued efforts in assessment measures, such as the K-ABC and the revision of the Detroit Test of Learning Abilities, to identify underlying psychological processes and link them to intervention programs, unfortunately reinforce the idea that there is empirical support for such efforts.

An alternative to the ATI model attempts to examine the *functional* rather than *structural* relationships between individual learners and their academic performance. Instructional strategies are based on empirical data suggesting which procedures are most effective in improving academic skills. Specifically, the targeted problem is identified and divided into component skills needed to acquire the behavior, and these components are taught using a wide variety of techniques designed to facilitate generalization (Zigmond & Miller, 1986). The strategies include practice, rehearsal, increased opportunities to respond, use of feedback and reinforcement principles, and other techniques consistent with effective teaching. Setting short- and long-term goals, monitoring student performance, and adjusting components of instruction are all part of the process. As one can see, these procedures are not related to any particular structural characteristic inherent to individuals.

The important aspect of this model of effective teaching is that instructional procedures remain maximally sensitive to their functional relationship to behavior change. Those procedures that produce improvement in a specific student's performance are retained. Those interventions not found to result in the desired change are discarded, *but only for that individual.* Another student, who may appear equally deficient, may be responsive to the same procedure that failed for a former student. In other words, the procedures remain sensitive to individual differences in student *performance*, but unrelated to any structural differences.

Efforts to describe effective remediations for academic problems based on functional relationships to behavior are not new. For example, Staats, Minke, Finley, Wolf, and Brooks (1964) demonstrated in numerous studies that reading skills of children could be modified through contingent reinforcement programs. Hall, Lund, and Jackson (1968) showed that teacher attention could affect study behavior. Lovitt and Curtiss (1969) found that manipulation of points awarded for academic performance could improve performance on a wide variety of mathematics, reading, and language arts tasks. More recently, Broussard and Northrup (1995), Northrup et al. (1994), and Cooper et al. (1990) showed how a functional analysis of behavior can be applied to academic problems of typical general education classrooms.

Clearly, the functional approach to selection of interventions for academic problems is linked closely to the behavioral assessment procedures previously described. Methods for monitoring the performance of students on the areas targeted for change and for facilitating decisions about altering instructional strategies play critical roles in the model. In addition, the particular interventions that may be effective at improving a child's academic performance are partially evident from the assessment process. Whether interventions need to concentrate on antecedent or consequent events surrounding academic performance (e.g., changing the teacher's pacing of instruction and feedback mechanisms), or on the curriculum material itself (e.g., changing the student's placement in reading material) will be based on the data gathered through the teacher interviews, direct observations, review of permanent products, student interview, and the administration of direct skill probes.

Despite the direct link between the assessment process and the monitoring of interventions, the selection of the particular intervention strategy may not be based entirely on the assessment data. In addition to the data collected, teacher skills, teacher knowledge, and clinical experience may all play an important part in choosing an appropriate intervention. In other words, on the basis of all the information obtained, a decision is made to *try* a specific intervention strategy for any of a number of reasons including the following: (1) It has been effective with other students with similar problems before; (2) the research suggests that this may be effective; (3) the teacher is comfortable with this strategy over other possible strategies; (4) the teacher is skilled with using this type of approach; or (5) the data suggest that this procedure would manipulate a critical variable for improvement. What is crucial is that although logical analysis is used to select the intervention strategy, evaluation of the intervention's effectiveness occurs through ongoing data collection.

Many, many interventions for academic problems based on functional relationships to academic performance exist. The literature contains literally thousands of research articles that document the value of all types of procedures for all types of academic problems. Specific publications exist that are devoted only to the publication of effective instructional interventions (e.g., *Learning Disabilities Forum*; *Learning Disabilities Research and Practice*) An attempt is made in this chapter to describe several general strategies that have been broadly applied across different types of academic skills. Those chosen for review represent strategies with substantial empirical databases (Algozzine & Maheady, 1986); they include self-management, peer tutoring, performance feedback, direct instruction/precision teaching, and cooperative learning. (Selected procedures from the literature described specifically for remediating basic skills in reading, mathematics, spelling, and written language will be described in the next chapter.) Clearly, the descriptions of the procedures in this volume cannot be comprehensive or exhaustive. It is strongly suggested that interested readers examine the numerous source materials listed for each method before trying to implement these strategies.

GENERAL STRATEGIES FOR ACADEMIC PROBLEMS

Self-Management

Significant efforts have been made to design and evaluate behavior-change strategies that place control of the specified contingencies in the hands of the individual whose behavior is being changed. These procedures have substantial appeal, since they potentially may result in generalization across time and setting (e.g., Holman & Baer, 1979). In addition, the procedures may be more efficient, since they require only minimal involvement of significant others. This may be particularly important in school settings, where teachers often legitimately complain that class size inhibits the potential for interventions with individual students. A related advantage of self-management is the potential for these procedures to teach students to be responsible for their own behavior. For many developmentally disabled students, this may be a particularly important issue (e.g., Fowler, 1984; Shapiro, 1981; Shapiro & Cole, 1994).

Several authors have offered varying definitions of self-management (Browder & Shapiro, 1985; Fantuzzo & Polite, 1990; Fantuzzo, Rohrbeck, & Azar, 1986; Mace & West, 1986). Although these definitions emphasize different aspects of the process, the model of self-management suggested by Kanfer (1971) seems to have broad-based appeal. His model contains three primary components: self-monitoring, self-evaluation, and self-reinforcement. Self-monitoring includes both self-observation and self-recording of behavior. At times, this process alone may be reactive and result in behavior change (e.g., Nelson, 1977). Once behavior is monitored, the individual must evaluate his or her response against a known criterion. The process of self-evaluation leads directly to self-reinforcement, because the individual must now decide whether he or she has met the criteria for self-reinforcement, and, if so, must apply the appropriate consequences. Although there have been significant questions regarding the mechanisms operating in self-management (e.g., Bandura, 1976; Brigham, 1980; Hughes & Lloyd, 1993; Mace & Kratochwill, 1985; Mace & West, 1986) Kanfer's model has fairly wide acceptance among researchers (Karoly, 1982).

Self-management procedures can be roughly divided into two categories (Roberts & Dick, 1982; Shapiro & Cole, 1994). One set of procedures is based on principles of contingency management and is designed primarily to manipulate the consequences of behavior. These procedures usually involve self-monitoring of behavior and rewards for attaining specified criteria. The other type of procedure is based more on control of conditions antecedent to behavioral events—specifically, the manipulation of cognitive variables. These procedures typically employ some form of verbal mediation strategy.

Contingency Management Procedures

Self-management procedures based on principles of contingency management are usually straightforward. Individuals are taught to self-monitor (self-observe and self-record) the presence or absence of a specified response. The actual recording mechanism can involve mechanical devices, such as response counters, or tally marks using paper and pencil. The individual can be cued to self-monitor via audio signals (e.g., prerecorded beeps) or via the signaling of others (e.g., teacher's announcement that it is time to record). Individuals may also be taught to self-monitor the completion of a task, (such as a worksheet in school) rather than using an external cuing device. The variety of mechanisms available for setting up a self-monitoring program have been extensively described (e.g., Gardner & Cole, 1988; Nelson, 1977; Shapiro, 1984; Shapiro & Cole, 1994).

Setting up a self-monitoring program requires that the response to be monitored be clearly defined for the student. For example, if students are to monitor their on-task behavior at a given cue, they may have to be trained to discriminate those behaviors defined as "working" from those defined as "not working." Many studies employing self-monitoring procedures include a training period that precedes the actual implementation of the technique. Usually, it does not take long for students to learn the needed discrimination. Studies of developmentally disabled children with multiple handicaps (e.g., Hughes, Korinek, & Gorman, 1991; Shapiro, Browder, & D'Huyvetters, 1984), preschool children (e.g., Connell, Carta, & Baer, 1993; Fowler, 1986), or learning disabled students (e.g., Hallahan et al., 1982; Smith, Young, Nelson, & West, 1992; Trammel, Schloss, & Alper, 1994) have all demonstrated successful self-monitoring with relatively little time needed for training.

Once the target behavior is identified, a procedure to cue students when to self-monitor is needed. In some cases, external cues such as audiotaped beeps can be employed. In at least one case, a 1-minute interlude of music was played to cue students to self-monitor for on-task behavior (Shapiro, McGonigle, & Ollendick, 1981). In some settings, however, use of externally cued signals may be both disruptive to others in the classroom and interfere with instructional processes. In such cases, it is possible to teach students to self-monitor very specific events, such as the completion of a worksheet or an individual problem on a worksheet. These types of cuing mechanisms may require some initial instruction but rarely are disruptive to others or to the teacher.

Selection and design of the self-monitoring device are also important considerations. The procedure chosen should be as simple as possible and require the least amount of effort on the student's part. For younger students, use of a "countoon" (Jenson, Rhode, & Reavis, 1994; Kunzelman,

1970) may be helpful. This is simply a form with stick figure or icon drawings representing the desired behavior already printed on the form. For example, if a student were to self-monitor in-seat behavior, a series of stick figures of a child sitting in a seat might be drawn on a form. The child simply crosses out the figure as a form of self-monitoring.

Self-monitoring alone may be reactive and result in behavior change. Although there is an extensive literature on the reactive effects of self-monitoring (e.g., Nelson & Hayes, 1981), it is clear that the task of simply observing one's own behavior may be sufficient to alter the behavior in the desired direction. It is therefore logical to use self-monitoring alone as an intervention procedure. Many times, students will show desired changes without any additional backup rewards. In such cases, the positive behavioral changes and associated reinforcers (better grades, fewer teacher reprimands, pleased parents) are probably functioning to sustain the observed behavior change. Although reactive self-monitoring is desirable, it does not always occur. Numerous studies have been reported in the literature in which additional rewards were required to facilitate the behavior-change process. One should therefore not be discouraged by the failure of self-monitoring alone to be reactive.

Another important aspect of any self-management program is making sure that student reports of self-monitored behavior are accurate. Some studies have found that teacher checking of the accuracy of student self-monitored behavior is necessary to maintain desired levels of behavior change (e.g., Rhode, Morgan, & Young, 1983; Santogrossi, O'Leary, Romanczyk, & Kaufmann, 1973; Smith et al., 1992). Teachers should plan on "surprise" checks of self-monitoring accuracy throughout the implementation of an intervention program. Obviously, these checks will need to be frequent in the beginning portion of the self-management treatment. Robertson, Simon, Pachman, and Drabman (1980), Rhode et al. (1983), Shapiro and Cole (1994), Smith et al. (1992), Smith, Young, West, Morgan, and Rhode (1988), and Young, West, Smith, and Morgan (1991) offer descriptions for how to gradually reduce the needed teacher-checking procedure.

Applications of contingency-based self-management procedures for academic skills have most often used forms of self-monitoring as the intervention strategy. Many of these investigations have targeted academic skills indirectly by having students self-monitor on-task behavior or its equivalent. For example, in a series of studies conducted as part of the University of Virginia Institute for Research in Learning Disabilities (Hallahan et al., 1982), elementary-age students with learning disabilities were taught to self-monitor their on-task behavior ("Was I paying attention?") at the sound of a beep emitted on a variable-interval 42-second (range 11–92 seconds) schedule. Data were also recorded on the number of math problems completed correctly on a series of three assigned sheets of problems. Results of their study showed significant improvements in on-task behavior, but only modest changes in the number of problems completed correctly. Other studies by these same authors produced similar results (e.g., Hallahan, Marshall, & Lloyd, 1981; Lloyd, Hallahan, Kosiewicz, & Kneedler, 1982). In looking more carefully at this issue, we (Lam et al., 1994) compared the relative effects of self-monitoring on the on-task behavior, academic accuracy, and disruptive behavior of three students with severe behavior disorders. Of special interest in our study was the collateral effect of the self-monitoring of one of these behaviors upon the other. Results showed that in the specific behavior for which self-monitoring was applied (i.e., on-task behavior, academic accuracy, or disruptive behavior), substantial improvement was evident. However, the most improvement in the collateral behaviors was present when self-monitoring was applied to academic accuracy over the other two behaviors. Similar outcomes were found in several other studies (Carr & Punzo, 1993; Harris et al., 1994; Maag et al., 1993; Reid & Harris, 1993). In all cases, self-monitoring was reactive, without any additional contingencies on performance.

McLaughlin, Burgess, and Sackville-West (1982) had 6 students with behavioral disorders record whether they were studying or not studying during an individual reading instruction period at random intervals determined by the students. The procedure was employed within a classroom already using a classwide token economy procedure. In a subsequent phase, students had to match teacher recordings to earn the appropriate points. Results showed that self-monitoring of study behavior significantly improved the percentage of problems completed correctly, with particular gains when teacher matching was required.

Prater, Hogan, and Miller (1992), working with an adolescent student with learning and behavior disorders, used self-monitoring supported by audio and visual prompts to increase on-task behavior and academic performance. After the procedure was implemented in a resource room, a modified version of the self-monitoring procedure using only visual prompts was then implemented in two mainstream classrooms (mathematics and English). Results for improvements in on-task behavior were commensurate with the implementation of the self-monitoring procedures in all three settings.

The use of self-management procedures derived from contingency management principles clearly has applicability in designing intervention strategies for academic problems. Although the procedure has been used more often to target on-task behavior and its equivalents, the procedure can be used successfully with academic targets per se. Indeed, literature reviews have shown that the most significant gains in academic performance are related to strategies (not just self-management) that directly target academic performance rather than treating academic skills as collateral variables to on-task (Hoge & Andrews, 1987; Skinner & Smith, 1992.)

Cognitive-Based Interventions

Procedures that have been developed for the modification of cognitions have typically employed varied forms of self-instruction. Originally described by Meichenbaum and Goodman (1971), self-instruction involves having individuals talk aloud as they perform a task. The self-instructions are designed to refocus the individual's thoughts and teach effective problem solving. Although the technique was first described by Meichenbaum and Goodman for reducing impulsive behavior in children, the procedure has since been applied to many problems, including increasing on-task behavior (e.g., Bornstein & Quevillon, 1976; Manning, 1990), social skills (e.g., Cartledge & Milburn, 1983; Combs & Lahey, 1981; Lochman & Curry, 1986; Maag, 1990), and academic skills (e.g., Fox & Kendall, 1983; Mahn & Greenwood, 1990; Roberts, Nelson, & Olson, 1987; Swanson & Scarpati, 1984).

Johnston et al. (1980) provided an excellent example of a typical self-instruction training program. Three children in classes for the educable mentally retarded were taught to add and subtract with regrouping by training them to make specific self-statements related to performing the task accurately. Training was conducted in a 20- to 30-minute session, during which the children were given problems to complete. The instructor then modeled the use of self-instruction by asking and answering a series of questions. The self-instruction training was conducted following guidelines established by Meichenbaum and Goodman (1971) and involved the following: (1) The trainer first solved the problem using the self-instructions while the subject watched; (2) the child performed the task while the trainer instructed aloud; (3) the child spoke aloud while solving the problem with the help of the trainer; (4) the child performed the self-instructions aloud without trainer prompting; and finally, (5) the child performed the task using private speech. Figure 5.1 shows an example of the self-instructions actually employed in the study. Results of this study demonstrated that self-instruction training can be an effective strategy for teaching such skills. Similar results were found in a follow-up study (Whitman & Johnson, 1983).

Shapiro and Bradley (1995) provided another example of using a self-instruction training procedure to improve the skills of a 10-year-old, fourth-grade boy, Ray, who was having significant problems in math. Specifically, Ray was having difficulties learning to conduct subtraction with regrouping. Using a self-instruction training methodology, a four-step "cue card" was used to teach Ray how to solve two-digit minus one-digit

Q. What kind of a problem is this?

$$\begin{array}{r} 36 \\ +47 \\ \hline \end{array}$$.

A. It's an add problem. I can tell by the sign.

Q. Now what do I do?

A. I start with the top number in the 1's column and I add. Six and 7 (the child points to the 6 on the number line and counts down 7 spaces) is 13. Thirteen has two digits. That means I have to carry. This is hard so I go slowly. I put the 3 in the 1's column (the child writes the 3 in the 1's column in the answer) and the 1 in the 10's column (the child writes the 1 above the top number in the 10's column in the problem).

Q. Now what do I do?

A. I start with the top number in the 10's column. One and 3 (the child points to the 1 on the number line and counts down 3 spaces) is 4. Four and 4 (the child counts down 4 more spaces) is 8 (the child writes the 8 in the 10's column in the answer).

Q. I want to get it right so I check it. How do I check it?

A. I cover up my answer (the child covers the answer with a small piece of paper) and add again starting with the bottom number in the 1's column. Seven and 6 (the child points to the 6 on the number line and counts down 6 spaces) is 13 (the child slides the piece of paper to the left and uncovers the 3; the child sees the 1 which he or she has written over the top number in the 10's column in the problem). Got it right. Four and 3 (the child points to the 4 on the number line and counts down 3 spaces) is 7. Seven and 1 (the child counts down 1 more space) is 8 (the child removes the small piece of paper so the the entire answer is visible). I got it right so I'm doing well. (If, by checking his or her work, the child determines that he or she has made an error, he or she says, "I got it wrong. I can fix it if I go slowly." The child then repeats the self-instruction sequence starting from the beginning.)

FIGURE 5.1. Example of self-instruction training sequence for addition with regrouping. From "Teaching Addition and Subtraction to Mentally Retarded Children: A Self-Instruction Program," by M. B. Johnston, T. L. Whitman, and M. Johnson, 1980, *Applied Research in Mental Retardation, 1,* p. 149. Copyright 1980 by Pergamon Press, Ltd. Reproduced by permission.

subtraction problems with regrouping (see Figure 5.2). Individual sessions were held between Ray and his teacher three times per week across a 4-week period. As seen in Figure 5.3, Ray showed an immediate response to the procedure, with increased performance over the 4-week period.

A very similar approach to cognitive-behavior modification was described by Cullinan, Lloyd, and Epstein (1981) and entitled "academic strategy training." The first step of strategy training involves the design of the approach. To design an attack strategy, tasks are divided through task analysis into several component steps. Figure 5.4 provides an example of an attack strategy used for teaching multiplication facts. Once designed, the strategy is taught directly to students, using multiple examples of appropriate and inappropriate application. Students practice the strategy until they demonstrate mastery, at which time they should be able to perform the task correctly with any items from the response class of the task.

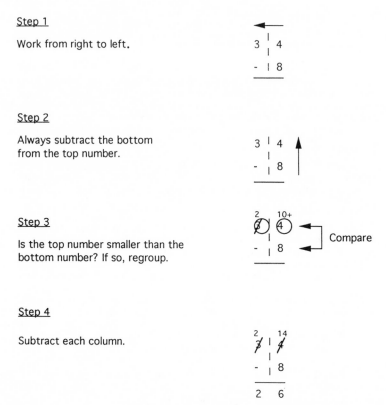

FIGURE 5.2. From "Treatment of Academic Problems" by E. S. Shapiro and K. L. Bradley, 1995, in M. A. Reinecke, F. M. Dattilio, and A. Freeman (Eds.), *Cognitive Therapy with Children and Adolescents*, p. 360. Copyright 1995 by The Guilford Press. Reprinted by permission.

Studies investigating strategy training have shown the procedure to be effective in teaching handwriting and composition skills (Blandford & Lloyd, 1987; Graham & Harris, 1987; Kosiewicz, Hallahan, Lloyd, & Graves, 1982), word reading accuracy (Lloyd, Kneedler, & Cameron, 1982), reading comprehension (Lysynchuk, Pressley, & Vye, 1990; Miller, Giovenco, & Rentiers, 1987; Schunk & Rice, 1992), and arithmetic (Cullinan et al., 1981; Montague, 1989; Montague & Bos, 1986). Conceptually, these procedures are identical to self-instruction training and appear to be applicable across academic areas.

Deshler and Schumaker (1986) described another set of procedures called the "strategies intervention model," designed to facilitate the performance of secondary-level students with mild handicaps. The purpose of

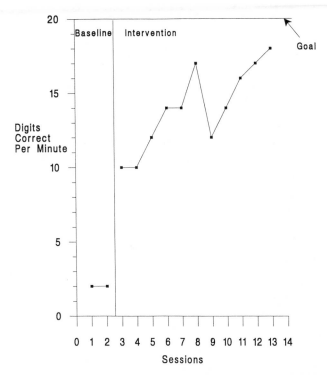

FIGURE 5.3. Results of self-instruction intervention. From "Treatment of Academic Problems" by E. S. Shapiro and K. L. Bradley, 1995, in Reinecke, F. Dattilio, and Freeman (Eds.), *Cognitive Therapy with Children and Adolescents*, p. 361. Copyright 1995 by The Guilford Press. Reprinted by permission.

these procedures is not to teach specific skill areas, as with self-instruction training and strategy training, but to teach students how to learn. For example, an instructional goal in the strategies intervention model would be to teach students skills for summarizing and memorizing material for a social studies test, rather than teaching them actual social studies content. The goal of the approach is to teach strategies that are broadly applicable across content areas.

The strategies intervention model begins by identifying the curriculum demands that the student lacks (e.g., note-taking, writing well-organized paragraphs). Once these deficiencies are identified, a specific teaching strategy is taught. Different strategy programs have been developed for various types of problems and have been packaged into the learning strategies curriculum (Schumaker, Deshler, Alley, & Warner, 1983). The first strand of the curriculum includes the word-identification strategy

TASK CLASS FOR MULTIPLICATION FACTS

Description: Multiplication of any number (0–10) by any number (0–10)
Examples: 0 × 6 = ____; 3 × 9 = ____; 7 × 4 = ____; 8 × 8 = ____; 10 × 1 = ____
Objective: Given a page of unordered multiplication problems written in horizontal form with factors from 0 to 10, the student will write the correct products for the problems at a rate of 25 problems correct per minute with no more than 2 errors per minute.

ATTACK STRATEGY FOR MULTIPLICATION FACTS

Attack Strategy: Count by one number the number of times indicated by the other number.

Steps in Attack Strategy:	Example:
1. Read the problem.	2 × 5 = ____
2. Point to a number that you know how to count by.	Student points to 2
3. Make the number of marks indicated by the other number.	2 × 5 = ____
	/////
4. Begin counting by the number you know how to count by and count up once for each mark, touching each mark.	"2, 4 . . ."
5. Stop counting when you've touched the last mark.	". . . 6, 8, 10"
6. Write the last number you said in the answer space.	2 × 5 = _10_

TASK ANALYSIS SHOWING PRESKILLS FOR MULTIPLICATION ATTACK STRATEGY

1. Say the numbers 0 to 100.
2. Write the number 0 to 100.
3. Name × and = signs.
4. Make the number of marks indicated by numerals 0 to 10.
5. Count by numbers 1 to 10.
6. End counting-by sequences in various positions.
7. Coordinate counting-by and touching-marks actions.

FIGURE 5.4. Task class, attack strategy, and task analysis of preskills for multiplication facts. From "Strategy Training: A Structured Approach to Arithmetic Instruction" by D. Cullinan, J. Lloyd, and M. H. Epstein, 1981, *Exceptional Education Quarterly, 2*, pp. 43–44. Copyright 1981 by Pro-Ed, Inc. Reprinted by permission.

(Lenz, Schumaker, Deshler, & Beals, 1984) and is aimed at teaching decoding of multisyllablic words. Other strategies are used to teach related skills, such as the visual imagery strategy (Clark, Deshler, Schumaker, & Alley, 1984), the self-questioning strategy (Clark et al., 1984), and the paraphrasing strategy (Schumaker, Denton, & Deshler, 1984). The interpreting visual aids strategy (Lenz, Schumaker, Deshler, & Beals, 1984) is used to help students gain information from pictures, diagrams, and figures. Finally, the multipass strategy (Schumaker, Deshler, Alley, & Warner, 1983) is used for attacking textbooks by using methods similar to the

SQ3R (Survey, Question, Read, Recite, Review) method of study. The second strand of the curriculum concentrates on note-taking and memorization skills, and the final strand of the curriculum emphasizes written expression and demonstrations of competence.

Significant field testing and evaluation of the strategies intervention model have been conducted through the University of Kansas Institute for Research in Learning Disabilities and reported in a large number of published journal articles and technical reports (e.g., Deshler & Schumaker, 1986, 1993; Deshler, Schumaker, Alley, Warner, & Clark, 1982; Deshler, Schumaker, Lenz, & Ellis, 1984; Ellis & Lenz, 1987; Ellis, Lenz, & Sabournie, 1987a, 1987b). Results have consistently shown that before training, students showed limited use of these strategies and poor performance on the related academic skills. After training, students showed marked improvements in academic performance. At present, the learning strategies curriculum is being implemented by a wide range of school districts across the country. Deshler and Schumaker (1986) report that although the strategies intervention model has enjoyed substantial success in reports of student outcome, there appear to be significant relationships between the level of staff training implementing the model and academic gains of adolescents. Clearly, caution is warranted for readers interested in this model to secure appropriate and effective training in this model before implementing the procedures in their own districts.

Conclusions

Self-management appears to be a promising intervention for remediating academic problems. Procedures such as self-monitoring are rather simple to employ and may result in significant gains. In particular, the possibility of achieving generalization across tasks, time, and behaviors is exciting.

Equally appealing is the use of cognitive-based procedures such as self-instruction training. Although these procedures obviously require more effort on the part of trainers, they clearly have the potential for teaching academic skills to students. Even more encouraging are the efforts of the researchers from the University of Kansas, who have taken the basic concepts of self-instruction training and cognitive-behavior modification, and applied them to the development of a curriculum for teaching adolescent learning- disabled students how to solve problems for academic tasks.

Peer Tutoring

Another strategy with wide applications across academic content areas has been the use of peer tutoring. Although numerous examples have been reported in the literature, systematic efforts both to demonstrate use of peer tutoring and investigate specific variables that affect academic performance have emerged from the work of Greenwood and his associates at the Juniper Gardens Children's Project in Kansas City, Kansas (e.g., Delquadri, Greenwood, Whorton, Carta, & Hall, 1986; Greenwood, 1991; Greenwood, Delquadri, & Hall, 1989; Greenwood, Carta, & Hall, 1988; Greenwood, Carta, et al., 1992; Greenwood, Terry, et al., 1992; Greenwood, Terry, Utley, Montagna, & Walka, 1993). On the basis of the significant literature suggesting that rates of student engagement in academic tasks are uniformly low across regular and special education settings (Berliner, 1979; Greenwood, 1991; Greenwood, Delquadri, Stanley, Terry, & Hall, 1985; Haynes & Jenkins, 1986; Leinhardt, et al., 1981), Hall et al. (1982) and Greenwood, Delquadri, Stanley, et al. (1981) operationalized academic engagement as opportunities to respond. Specifically, they reasoned that a necessary condition for academic progress is the frequent presentation of antecedents for student responding in academic performance. These concepts were demonstrated empirically in several studies (Greenwood, Delquadri, & Hall, 1984; Greenwood, Dinwiddie, et al., 1984; Greenwood et al., 1989).

Classwide peer tutoring was employed as a logical mechanism for increasing opportunities to respond. In particular, the strategies developed were designed to be employed within larger, regular education classes that contained students identified as learning-disabled or slow-learners. Typical classroom instruction provided by a teacher, even to a small group of students, involves asking a single question and calling upon a single student to respond. When a peer-tutoring procedure is employed, half the students in the class (assuming dyad tutoring) can respond in the same amount of time as a single student using teacher-oriented instruction. Elliott, Hughes, and Delquadri (cited in Delquadri et al., 1986) reported that some children improved their academic behavior from 20% to 70% as a result of peer-tutoring procedures.

Greenwood (1991) reported the long-term impact of time spent engaged in academic instruction across 416 first-grade students who were followed for 2 years. Complete data were collected on a total of 241 of these students at the end of the third grade. Students were divided into three groups: (1) an at-risk group of students with low socioeconomic status (SES) for whom teachers implemented a classwide peer-tutoring program from the second half of first grade through second grade; (2) an equivalent group of at-risk students for whom no peer tutoring was implemented; and (3) a nonrisk group of students from average- to high-SES backgrounds. Data collected on time spent in academic engaged time and scores on the Metropolitan Achievement Test favored the group receiving the classwide peer-tutoring program and the nonrisk group.

It is important to remember that the peer-tutoring procedures described by Greenwood and his associates involve same-age tutors and are classwide procedures. Other investigators have used cross-age (Beirne-Smith, 1991; Cochran, Feng, Cartledge, & Hamilton, 1993; Topping & Whiteley, 1993; Vacc & Cannon, 1991) and cross-ability (Arblaster, Butler, Taylor, Arnold, & Pitchford, 1991) peer tutoring, all showing similar positive effects. Although the procedures to be described here are those described by Greenwood and colleagues for same-age, classwide peer tutoring, these strategies are very similar for other types of peer tutoring procedures.

Procedures for Classwide Peer Tutoring

The procedure for peer tutoring involves the use of: (1) weekly competing teams; (2) tutor–tutee pairs within teams; (3) points earned for correct responding; (4) a modeling error-correction procedure; (5) teacher-mediated point earning for correct tutor behavior; (6) switching of tutor–tutee at midsession; (7) daily tabulation of point totals and public posting on a game chart; (8) selection of a winning team each day and each week; and (9) regular teacher assessments of students' academic performance, independent of tutoring sessions. For most subject areas, the tutoring sessions are divided into 30-minute blocks—10 minutes of tutoring for each student, and 5 to 10 minutes for adding scores and posting team outcomes. (A manual [Greenwood, Delquadri, & Carta, 1988] that describes these procedures in great detail is available from Educational Achievement Systems, Inc., 319 Nickerson, Suite 112, Seattle, WA 98109.)

Each Monday, students are paired through a random selection process. Individual ability levels of students are not considered in the assignment of tutors. Children remain in the same tutor–tutee pairs for the entire week. Each pair of students is also assigned to one of two teams for the week.

When tutoring sessions begin, a timer is set for 10 minutes, and the tutee begins the assigned work. The specific academic skill assigned can be reading sentences aloud, reading words from a word list, spelling dictated words, completing assigned math problems, or any other academic task desired by the teacher. For example, in reading sentences, the tutee begins reading sentences aloud to the tutor. Tutors give 2 points for reading each sentence without errors. One point is earned for successfully correcting an error identified by the tutor. Tutors are instructed to correct errors by pronouncing the correct word or words and having the tutee reread the sentence until it is correct. In spelling, points are based on tutees' orally spelling each word and then writing the word three times if not correct. Throughout the tutoring session, the teacher circulates around the room, providing assistance to tutors and tutees and awarding bonus points to pairs for cooperative tutoring. Tutees are also given bonus points for responding immediately when asked by the tutors.

After 10 minutes, tutors and tutees reverse roles, and the same procedures are followed. At the end of all tutoring sessions for that day, individual points are summed and reported aloud to the teacher. Individual points are recorded on a large chart in the front of the classroom, and team totals are determined. No rewards other than applause for winning efforts are provided to the teams.

On Fridays, the week's tutoring is assessed by the teacher. Each child is assessed using curriculum-based measures in the academic skills tutored that week. Students who continue to have difficulties with certain skills may then be directly instructed outside of tutoring sessions by the teacher.

Before students can begin the tutoring process, they must be trained. Greenwood et al. (1984) indicate that training is conducted using explanation, modeling, role playing, and practice. During the first day of training, the teacher presents a brief overview of the tutoring program, demonstrates with a teacher aide or consultant how errors are to be corrected, demonstrates how points are administered by tutors and how they are recorded on student point sheets, and has students practice tabulating points and reporting these results to the teacher. In the second day of training, students actually practice tutoring with feedback from the teacher and consultant regarding identifying errors, using the correction procedure, using praise, and tabulating points. If needed, a third day of practice is held for students to learn the tutoring process. Typically, students learn the procedures quickly and can begin tutoring after the first or second day. It may be necessary to continue to train younger students for a few more days, however.

The teacher's role during tutoring sessions involves initially determining dyads, timing the sessions, monitoring tutoring and awarding bonus points for correct tutoring, answering questions as needed, and tabulating and posting points. After each session, the teacher reviews point sheets to assess student accuracy and honesty in reporting and assesses academic progress using curriculum-based measures once each week, usually on Fridays.

Conclusions

Procedures for establishing peer tutoring are easy and can be applied to a wide range of academic areas. As demonstrated in the work of Greenwood and colleagues, it is not necessary to be concerned about matching students of differing ability levels. Indeed, some studies have demonstrated that peer tutoring may result in academic improvements in tutors as well as tutees (e.g., Cochran et al., 1993; Dineen, Clark, & Risley, 1977; Franca, Kerr, Reitz, & Lambert, 1990; Houghton & Bain, 1993). After all, one of the best ways to learn something is to try to teach it to someone else!

Beyond the work of Greenwood and colleagues, other investigations have demonstrated generalized effects of peer tutoring in mathematics (DuPaul & Henningson, 1993; Fantuzzo, King, & Heller, 1992; McKenzie & Budd, 1981), the acquisition of peer tutoring through observation of peer models (Stowitschek, Hecimovic, Stowitschek, & Shores, 1982), combining an in-school peer-tutoring procedure with a home-based reinforcement system (Trovato & Bucher, 1980), and using preschool or kindergarten-age students as peer tutors (Eiserman, 1988; Tabacek, McLaughlin, & Howard, 1994; Young, Hecimovic, & Salzberg, 1983). Scruggs, Mastropieri, Veit, and Osguthorpe (1986), and Franca et al. (1990) examined the relationship of peer tutoring to social behaviors for students with behavior disorders. Johnson and Idol-Maestas (1986) showed that access to peer tutoring can serve as an effective contingent reinforcer. Fuchs and her colleagues (Fuchs, Fuchs, Phillips, et al., 1995; Phillips et al., 1993, 1994) have combined classwide peer-tutoring strategies with curriculum-based measurement as a method for individualizing student instruction. Clearly, there are substantial empirical and clinical reports for the effectiveness of peer tutoring to improve academic performance of students. More importantly, these studies have demonstrated that peer-tutoring procedures can be applied across all academic areas, with students of varied academic levels.

Performance Feedback

A simple procedure that has been found to be effective in modifying a variety of academic behaviors is the provision of response-contingent feedback about performance. Van Houten and Lai Fatt (1981) examined the impact of public posting of weekly grades on biology tests with 12th-grade high school students. Results of the first experiment revealed that the effects of public posting plus immediate feedback and praise increased accuracy from 55.7% to 73.2% across the 47 students in the study. In a replication of the study, Van Houten and Lai Fatt showed that public posting alone with biweekly feedback increased student performance. These results were consistent with earlier studies examining the use of explicit timing and public posting in increasing mathematics and composition skills in regular elementary school students (Van Houten et al., 1975; Van Houten & Thompson, 1976). Kastelen, Nickel, and McLaughlin (1984) also showed that public posting of grades, immediate feedback, and praise improved the percentage of task completion in reading among 16 eighth-grade students. In addition, some generalization to spelling and writing tasks were evident.

In another study of public posting in the classroom, Bourque, Dupuis, and Van Houten (1986) compared the posting of student names versus coded numbers for weekly spelling test results in four third-grade classrooms. Results showed performance to be the same regardless of whether student names or codes were used. Other simple forms of public posting, such as placing pictures of students on a bulletin board as a reward for achieving significant improvement on weekly spelling tests, have been successful (Gross & Shapiro, 1981).

Systems for providing contingent feedback to students can be developed in many ways. Typically, a chart is created on which student progress is posted. These charts can vary from simple recording of test scores to some form of visual aid. For example, the use of bar graphs can be particularly helpful for students who have difficulty deciphering daily test scores. It is extremely important, however, that any public posting of scores be done in a positive, constructive manner. Van Houten and Van Houten (1977) described a system in which individual student accomplishments were compared to accomplishments of students as part of a team. Results of their study showed that although increases in performance were present under both conditions, significantly more improvement was present during the team phase.

Not surprisingly, the use of feedback systems and public posting of individual performance can result in significant improvement in academic skills. The procedure can be applied to many academic skills and across age and grade levels of students.

Direct Instruction

The term "direct instruction" has been applied in two related but different ways within the literature. Rosenshine (1979) has used the term "direct instruction" (not capitalized) to refer to instructional strategies that enhance a student's academic engaged time. Specifically, he considers techniques that result in frequent student responses, fast-paced instruction, teacher control of material, and other such methods designed to increase engaged time as indicative of direct instruction. No emphasis is given to the specific curriculum materials.

"Direct Instruction" (capitalized) is the instructional approach conceptualized by Englemann and his colleagues (e.g., Englemann & Carnine, 1982) and implemented and evaluated through Project Follow-

Through in the late 1960s and 1970s. Although Direct Instruction includes all of the characteristics described by Rosenshine (1979), it also includes very specific curricular materials that contain explicit, systematic, step-by-step instructions for teaching.

The underlying principle in the Direct Instruction materials is that for *all* students to learn, materials and teacher presentation must be clear and unambiguous (Gersten, Woodward, & Darch, 1986). Although this sounds simple, many instructional programs, particularly basal reading materials, have not been designed with sufficient precision to allow students with mild handicaps to succeed. Direct Instruction curricula have been developed so that students initially acquiring a skill are presented with questions for which there can only be one, correct response. In addition, materials are generated that offer simple but elegant strategies for application (Gersten et al., 1986). For example, after students are taught to discriminate short and long vowel sounds of three vowels (O, A, I), they are taught a rule: "If the last letter is E, you'll hear a letter *name* in the word. You'll hear the name of the letter that is underlined." Practice using the rule is then implemented, with students constantly being asked to recite the rule as the skill is mastered.

Development of the Direct Instruction model was based on two guiding principles: "Teach more in less time," and "Control the details of what happens" (Becker & Carnine, 1981). All instructional activities are designed to increase academic engaged time and to focus on teaching the general case. For example, rather than teaching single sounds sequentially through the curriculum, 40 different sounds may be taught, with rules provided for linking them together. In this way, general decoding skills can be taught quickly and efficiently. To control the instructional environment, all lessons are scripted for the teacher. What the teacher is to say and do is written out within the teaching manuals. Student progress is monitored using criterion-referenced progress tests, and the methods for obtaining these data are explicitly described in the manuals.

The teaching techniques of the Direct Instruction model vary according to the skill levels of the students (Becker & Carnine, 1981). Whereas initial acquisition of skills in reading relies heavily on small-group instruction and unison responding, later skills are taught through more independent and large-group instruction. In addition, less reliance on unison responding occurs in later grades. Feedback mechanisms also change across grades, with children in the early grades receiving immediate feedback and older children getting delayed feedback. The overriding emphasis in the model is on mastery instruction. Students being instructed in small groups are not advanced until *all* students in the group achieve mastery on the skill being taught. For example, Stein and Goldman (1980) compared performance of students with learning disabilities (ages 6 to 8) being instructed in either the Direct Instruction (DISTAR) reading curriculum or the Palo Alto series. Although the two series are very similar in content, a critical difference in teaching strategy is the insistence of the DISTAR curriculum that each student in the group master the skills at one level before proceeding to the next. By contrast, the Palo Alto curriculum allows teachers to proceed when most students have acquired the instructed skill. Results of their study showed that the mean gain for DISTAR was 15 months (over the 9-month period) compared to a gain of 7 months for the Palo Alto curriculum.

The Direct Instruction model contains at least seven basic principles for teaching strategies. Each of these is presented briefly. Readers interested in more detailed descriptions should see Englemann and Carnine (1982).

Scripted Presentations

Each lesson is scripted for the teacher. The exact words to be used in presenting materials, along with appropriate sequencing of teacher questions and responses to student performance, are offered. Becker and Carnine (1981) stated that this feature of the model is frequently criticized; critics object that scripted lessons may stifle teacher creativity and initiative. The authors point out, however, that the use of scripts allows teachers to use a pretested strategy with proven effectiveness. Scripts also reduce the time needed for teachers to prepare lessons. Furthermore, scripted lessons make the monitoring of student performance easier, since lessons are standardized.

Small-Group Instruction

Much of the teaching in the model, particularly at the earlier grades, is done in small groups. This structure permits frequent student responses, more direct adult contact, teacher-controlled instruction, and opportunities for modeling by other students. These groups often consist of 5 to 10 students and occur throughout the instructional day. In upper grades, reliance on small groups is reduced, and increased large-group and independent instruction is employed.

Unison Responding

During the small-group instruction, students are frequently asked to respond in unison. This creates an atmosphere of fast pace, high intensity, and active participation.

Signals

Another important component of the Direct Instruction model is the use of signals within the instructional process. Signals are used to help pace students through a lesson as to when responses should be given. For example, in sounding out a word, students may be told to say a sound aloud as long as a teacher touches it. This procedure ensures that students blend correctly as the teacher moves from sound to sound across the word. Effective use of signals can also provide opportunities to allow students who need a few extra seconds to formulate a response that is not dominated by the more able students in a group.

Pacing

Through the use of signals, unison responding, and small-group instruction, the pacing of instruction is clearly controlled. Becker and Carnine (1981) point out that students are likely to be more attentive to fast-paced presentation. However, the use of a fast-paced instructional strategy does not mean that teachers rush students into giving responses when more time is needed to formulate answers. Carnine (1976) demonstrated that students answer correctly about 80% of the time when in a fast-paced condition (12 questions per minute), but answer correctly only 30% of the time in a slow-rate condition (5 questions per minute).

Corrections

Correcting errors is an important part of the process of Direct Instruction. Research on correcting errors, although limited, suggests that students need to attend to the feedback and rehearse the corrected strategies for the results of error correction to be effective (Fink & Carnine, 1975). In addition, modeling of correct responses can be effective, but the correction needs to be applied in subsequent situations (Stromer, 1975).

Praise

Not surprisingly, the use of praise within the small-group, fast-paced instructional sessions is a critical component of the Direct Instruction model. The relationship of teacher attention to increasing student attentiveness is well documented (e.g., Cossairt, Hall, & Hopkins, 1973; Hall et al., 1968). It is interesting to note, however, that the role of praise alone within the Direct Instruction model has not been investigated (Becker & Carnine, 1981).

Summary of Direct Instruction

The Direct Instruction model was one of the major models of compensatory education evaluated through Project Follow-Through in the 1970s. Although the evaluation conducted by the Abt Associates (1976, 1977) has been questioned in regard to the fairness of the measures employed, the adequacy of the sample, and the appropriateness of the analysis, the evaluation did provide direct comparisons of eight different models of compensatory education. Each model was based on a different instructional philosophy; their emphases included child self-esteem, child language development, parent education, child cognitive development, behavior analysis, and direct instruction. Comparisons were made using measures of basic skills (word knowledge, spelling, language, math computation), cognitive and conceptual skills (reading, math concepts, math problem solving, Raven's Progressive Matrices), and affective measures (the Coopersmith Self-Esteem Inventory and Intellectual Achievement Responsibility Scale). These measures were combined into a measure entitled the Index of Significant Outcomes (ISO).

Results of the Abt report are clear. Examination of overall ISO scores found that the Direct Instruction model ranked first across cognitive, affective, and basic skills measures. Moreover, in none of the subareas examined did it rank any less than third (Becker & Carnine, 1981). The Abt report also compared the models on four subtests of the Metropolitan Achievement Tests (MAT): Total Reading, Total Math, Spelling, and Language. In all areas, the Direct Instruction model far outscored all other models, with scores across the four basic skills areas ranging from the 40th percentile in Reading to the 50th percentile in Spelling and Language. Total Math fell at the 48th percentile.

Data obtained by Becker and Englemann (1978) at the Direct Instruction sites provide even stronger evidence of the success of the model. Scores obtained on the Wide Range Achievement Test (WRAT), given at the prekindergarten and third-grade periods, found students at or above the 50th percentile on the Reading, Arithmetic, and Spelling subtests. In further follow-up data, Becker and Gersten (1982) reported WRAT and MAT scores for all students who had been in the 3-year Direct Instruction sites and were now in the fifth and sixth grades. Results showed that students who attended the Project Follow-Through programs outperformed a matched group of students who did not. These effects were particularly strong in reading, math problem solving, and spelling. Effects on the MAT Science, Math Concepts, Math Computation, and Word Knowledge subtests were somewhat less. In no case, however, did any comparison favor the control group. One finding of the follow-up study, however, was that compared to a national norm sample, these children began to lose ground after Follow-Through ended. This suggests that without continued instruction using similar strategies, children are unlikely to compete effectively against their peers.

Gersten, Keating, and Becker (1988) presented the results of two long-term studies of the Direct Instruction model. Academic achievement scores of 1,097 students in the fifth and sixth grade who had received direct instruction in grades 1–3 were compared against 970 students who had received traditional education. The second study followed students through high school who had received Direct Instruction or not received it. Outcomes from these studies showed that the fifth- and sixth-grade students performed better on standardized achievement tests in reading, spelling, and mathematics. Students from the second study followed up at high school performed better in reading and math, had been retained in grades fewer times, and had a higher rate of college acceptance than the comparison groups.

The results of the Abt studies and the strong showing of Direct Instruction should not be surprising. Indeed, significant research since the Follow-Through project has continued to demonstrate the superiority of Direct Instruction to other strategies for teaching basic skills to learners with mild handicaps (Gersten et al., 1986; White, 1988). Furthermore, the research on academic engaged time (Greenwood, 1991; Rosenshine, 1981; Rosenshine & Berliner, 1978), opportunities to respond (Greenwood et al., 1985), and other time variables related to educational gains (Gettinger, 1984; Rich & Ross, 1989) has clearly demonstrated that educational processes resulting in increased student engaged time will result in increased student performance.

Perhaps the greatest criticisms of the Direct Instruction model comes from those who feel the method results in stifled creativity and failure to consider individual differences in learning. Although these criticisms may be justified when considering the instructional process for high-achieving students, they seem inappropriate if aimed at students with handicaps or low achievement. These individuals most often are the focus of remedial programs and therefore would benefit most from Direct Instruction approaches.

Future research issues related to Direct Instruction do not need to center upon demonstrations of its effectiveness. These data exist and are convincing. More importantly, efforts need to be devoted to examining how these strategies can be more widely adopted into the educational system for students with handicaps. It is unfortunate that the technology and resources that exist for accelerating the performance of low-achieving youngsters continue to go apparently untapped.

Cooperative Learning and Group Contingencies

Traditional goals in classrooms implicitly assume competition rather than cooperation. Students are compared to each other; this results in discouraging student–student interaction, which might improve performance (Johnson & Johnson, 1985), and it clearly places low achievers at a disadvantage (Slavin, 1977). Several researchers have described and field- tested successful strategies for improving academic skills that are based on principles of cooperation rather than competition (Johnson & Johnson, 1985, 1986; Slavin, 1983a, 1983b).

Several reviews have been published substantiating the effectiveness of cooperative learning strategies (e.g., Axelrod & Greer, 1994; Cosden & Haring, 1992; Johnson, Maruyama, Johnson, Belson, & Skon, 1981; Maheady, Harper, Mallette, & Winstanley, 1991; Nastasi & Clements, 1991; Slavin, 1980; 1983a; 1985). These procedures have been applied across all academic subjects, have occurred in both the United States and other countries, and have incorporated both individual and group reward systems. Of the 27 studies reported by Slavin (1980), 24 (89%) showed significant positive effects on achievement when rewards were based on individual performance of group members, in comparison with control groups .

Within cooperative learning strategies, group contingencies may play a significant part. Litow and Pumroy (1975) identified three types of group contingencies: (1) dependent, in which the group's attainment of a reward requires that the performances of a target student or students meet a specified criterion; (2) interdependent, in which the group's attainment of a reward requires that every member of the group meet a specified criterion or, alternatively, that the group's average performance exceed the criterion; and (3) independent, in which each member of the group's attainment of the reward requires that his or her own performance meet the specified criterion. Several studies have used these contingencies for managing academic skills (Chadwick & Day, 1971; Evans & Oswalt, 1968; Fantuzzo, Polite, & Grayson, 1990; Goldberg & Shapiro, 1995; McLaughlin, 1981; Shapiro & Goldberg, 1986, 1989; Turco & Elliott, 1990).

Procedures for Cooperative Learning

Although cooperative learning can be applied in several ways, Slavin, Madden, and Leavey (1984) provide an excellent example. "Team-assisted individualization" (TAI) consists of several procedures designed to combine cooperative learning strategies and individualized instruction. Students are first assigned to four- or five-member teams. Each team is constructed such that the range of abilities in that skill is represented across team members.

After team assignment, students are pretested on mathematics operations and are placed at the appropriate level of the curriculum, based on their performance. Students then work on their assignments within the team by first forming pairs or triads. After exchanging answer sheets with their partners, students read the instructions for their individualized assignments and begin working on the first skillsheet. After working four problems, students exchange sheets and check their answers. If these are correct, students move to the next skillsheet. If incorrect, the students continue in blocks of four problems on the same skillsheet.

When a student has four in a row correct on the final skillsheet, the first "checkout," a 10-item quiz, is taken. If the student scores at least 8 correct out of 10, the checkout is signed by the teammate, and the student is certified to take the final test. If the student does not score 80%, the teacher is called to assist the student with any problems not understood; a second checkout is taken, and if the criterion is met, the student is again certified to take the final test.

At the end of the week, team scores are computed by averaging all tests taken by team members. If the team reached the preset criterion, all team members receive certificates. Each day, teachers work with students who were at the same point in the curriculum for 5–15 minutes. This provides opportunities for teachers to give instruction on any items that students may find difficult.

Conclusions and Summary

Cooperative learning and group contingencies have a significant logical appeal. Concerns are often raised about mainstreamed students and their social acceptance by peers; greater social acceptance of such students may result from placing them in close, cooperative contact with other students. In addition, the strategies appear to be consistent with other approaches such as peer tutoring, which are based on increasing student engagement rates in classrooms.

Despite these very positive aspects of cooperative learning strategies, there appear to be a number of potential problems in using these procedures. We (Elliott & Shapiro, 1990) noted that in cooperative strategies in which interdependent or dependent group contingencies are employed, low-achieving members of a group may be criticized by high-achieving members of the group. In addition, some strategies (not Slavin's), deemphasize the individualization of instruction. This would be a significant problem for students with handicaps.

Although some questions can be raised about cooperative learning strategies, the procedures clearly have documented effectiveness and acceptability (e.g., Elliott, Turco, & Gresham, 1987; Goldberg & Shapiro, 1995; Shapiro & Goldberg, 1986, 1989; Turco & Elliott, 1990). These procedures, again, can be employed as classwide techniques, not specifically aimed at students with academic deficiencies. As such, they become excellent preventative recommendations for students who remain in regular education classes.

SUMMARY

The many and varied strategies discussed in this chapter represent intervention techniques that can be broadly applied across types of academic problems, age ranges, types of handicapping conditions, and types of school settings. An extensive database supporting each of the strategies exists, along with significant evidence of field testing. Practitioners with limited experiences in using these procedures are strongly encouraged to seek out detailed descriptions of the methods and to experiment with them in their own settings. Although some adaptations of procedures may be needed for specific settings, most techniques can be easily implemented with few modifications. Furthermore, much of the literature cited in this chapter contains descriptions of methods that can be read, understood, and directly implemented.

CHAPTER 6

♦♦♦

Step 3: Instructional Modification II
Specific Skill Areas

♦

Literally hundreds of intervention procedures have been reported in the literature as successful techniques to improve performance in the basic skills of reading, math, spelling, and written language. In addition, a large number of interventions have appeared in the literature designed to improve skills in content areas (e.g., biology, history) and more complex forms of skills, such as creative writing. Obviously, any attempt to provide a comprehensive review of these procedures in any single source would be impossible. This chapter presents a variety of strategies that have repeatedly appeared in the literature in different forms. The choice of particular strategies is partially based on my own experience across a wide age range of students and types of academic problems. Readers are directed to several excellent resources that provide somewhat more in-depth analysis of many of the procedures discussed (e.g., Howell et al., 1993; Maher & Zins, 1987; Stoner et al., 1991; Sulzar-Azaroff & Mayer, 1986).

READING

Probably the most frequently encountered academic difficulties are related to reading and language arts. This is not surprising, given the complexity of skills needed to master reading. A student must understand rules of phonetic analysis, must be capable of effective integration of sounds, must be fluent enough to derive meaning from the material, and must perform these skills at an automatic level. Breakdowns at any single level of skill may have "ripple effects" on the acquisition of subsequent skills. In addition, after learning all the rules for effective decoding, students using the English language must then learn all the exceptions. It is no wonder that reading remains the most difficult academic skill to master.

Assuming that students have the necessary prereading skills, such as letter recognition, letter–sound association, and basic phonetic analysis skills, effective interventions for reading problems must concentrate on the acquisition of two related skills: reading fluency and comprehension. Although these skills are closely interrelated, acquiring fluency alone does not always improve comprehension. We have all come across students who have mastered reading fluently but cannot meaningfully synthesize what they have read (i.e., "word callers"). Students who have still not mastered the prerequisite skills of letter identification, sound–symbol association, and basic phonetic analysis need interventions aimed at teaching these essential reading skills. Procedures such as stimulus delay or delayed prompting (Bradley-Johnson, Sunderman, & Johnson, 1983; Halle, Baer, & Spradlin, 1981; Ingenmey & Van Houten, 1991; Koscinski & Gast, 1993; Touchette & Howard, 1984) and stimulus fading (Ducharme & Worling, 1994; Tawney, 1972) have often been used to teach these skills, primarily to preschool children. Readers interested in these procedures should consult these sources as well as Sulzar-Azaroff and Mayer (1986).

Reading Fluency Problems

Children who do not read with sufficient fluency almost inevitably have severe comprehension problems, typically related to the inability to decode words quickly and automatically. Dysfluent readers will spend significant amounts of time struggling through text, only to discover at the end of the passage that they cannot remember a thing they have read.

Among the procedures that appear to have substantial support for improving the oral reading fluency of students is "previewing," defined by Rose (1984a) as any method that provides the opportunity for a learner to read or listen to a passage prior to instruction and/or testing. Three types of previewing procedures have been identified: (1) oral previewing, or having the learner read the assigned selection aloud prior to the reading lesson; (2) silent previewing, or having the learner read the passage to him- or herself prior to the lesson; and (3) listening previewing, in which the teacher reads the assigned passage aloud and the learner follows silently (Hansen & Eaton, 1978).

Rose and his colleagues have conducted several studies investigating the relative effectiveness of these types of previewing procedures. In one of his initial investigations, Rose (1984a) found that listening and silent previewing were more effective than no previewing with elementary-aged students with learning disabilities, and that the listening procedure was relatively more effective than the silent previewing approach.

The previewing procedures are really quite simple. Materials for instruction and data collection are typically selected from the student's present curriculum. For example, Rose and Sherry (1984) employed the Interesting Reading Series (Follett Educational Corporation), a high-interest, low-vocabulary series, with adolescent students who had learning disabilities. In another study, Rose and Beattie (1986) used the Barnell–Loft Multiple Skills Series (Levels A and B) with elementary-age students who were classified as educable mentally retarded and behavior disordered.

Silent previewing involves asking the student to read the assigned passage silently and then aloud to the teacher. In listening previewing, students are asked to follow along as the teacher reads the passage. Students then read the passage aloud to the teacher. This type of previewing can also be done by tape-recording the passages ahead of time (Rose & Beattie, 1986). Oral previewing requires a student to read the passage aloud once before instruction and then again after instruction. Studies conducted by Rose, McEntire, and Dowdy (1982), and Rose (1984c) have suggested that this latter form of previewing is not effective.

Results of Rose's studies have been consistent and impressive. In almost all cases reported, the levels of highest reading performance were observed with the listening previewing procedure. This was seen in investigations with elementary- and secondary-age students with learning disabilities (Rose, 1984c; Rose & Sherry, 1984), elementary-age students classified as educable mentally retarded (Rose, 1984a), and elementary-age students identified as behavior-disordered populations (1984c). In addition, Rose and Beattie (1986) reported that use of listening previewing without the tape recorder may have a better effect than previewing with the tape recording. Of importance, however, was the equally consistent finding that error rates failed to decrease as a result of the previewing procedure. This may suggest that the technique is useful for improving the rates of slow but accurate readers, but may not affect reducing error rates. Clearly, this procedure offers a simple, straightforward, and easily implemented strategy for improving reading fluency.

Others have also found previewing to be a powerful strategy for improving reading skills. For example, Rousseau, Tam, and Ramnarain (1993) compared the use of presenting key words and previewing to improve the reading comprehension of five Hispanic, 11- and 12-year-old students. Using an alternating treatments design, the key word, listening previewing alone, and the combined interventions were compared. They found that the key-word technique resulted in higher oral reading rates and reading comprehension scores than previewing alone, but that the combination of key word presentation and listening previewing had the best performance. Skinner et al. (1993), in comparing the effects of three different forms of previewing on the oral reading rates of 12 junior and senior high school students with learning disabilities, found that significantly fewer errors were made under slow- compared to fast-rate listening previewing conditions.

Another procedure for improving reading fluency has been described by Freeman and McLaughlin (1984). Students are asked to read aloud a word list simultaneously with a tape recording of the word list being read at a significantly higher reading rate. The idea behind the procedure is for students to model higher reading rates. This procedure is felt to be especially valuable in working with secondary-age students, who may fail to acquire fluency when reading in content areas, because they lack the necessary sight vocabulary.

In the Freeman and McLaughlin (1984) procedure, students all reading below 50 words correct per minute were asked to read aloud with a tape that presented the word lists at 80 words per minute. After reading the words with the tape recorder, they were then assessed on the same list. Results of the study were impressive, with all students showing substantial gains in oral reading rates on the word lists after the intervention was begun.

Despite the positive findings of Freeman and McLaughlin (1984), their conclusions that students using this procedure are modeling high oral reading rates may be erroneous. In a series of investigations, my colleagues and I (Shapiro, Eichman, Body, & Zuber, 1987; Shapiro & McCurdy, 1989; Skinner & Shapiro, 1989) have demonstrated that the increased oral reading rates following the taped-word intervention may be due more to the repeated practice and exposure to the word list then any modeling phenomenon. Moreover, these studies have questioned the generalization of acquiring fluency in word lists to the reading of passages within which these words are to be found.

Despite the questions raised regarding the reasons why the taped-word procedure results in increased oral reading rates, it is clear that the technique can be a useful mechanism for improving reading fluency, particularly on word lists. Continued research to demonstrate if this procedure is effective for increasing reading fluency on passages remains to be conducted.

One of the most critical findings of the research on previewing and the taped-word procedure is the relationship of increased practice and opportunities to respond on fluency. For example, Hargis, Terhaar-Yonkers, Williams, and Reed (1988) determined that students with mild handicaps need an average of 46 repetitions for a word to reach a level of automatic recognition. Two related techniques have been developed that are especially aimed at improving reading fluency through drill and practice: "folding-in" and the "drill sandwich." Full and detailed descriptions of the folding-in technique can be found in the workbook accompanying this text (Shapiro, 1996).

The folding-in technique is based on two well-established principles of learning: arranging an instructional match and providing for enough repetitions for material to move from unknown status to mastery. The instructional match, or instructional level, is the optimal condition under which a student will learn. When being taught at the instructional level, the student is sufficiently challenged, with a realistic opportunity for success. If the level of material becomes too difficult (frustrational), the student is likely to fail and learning will be minimal. Likewise, if the material is too easy, the lack of challenge will result in little gain over current functioning. Gickling and Havertape (1981) and Gickling and Rosenfield (1995) identified the ratio of known to unknown information that must be established to teach students at their instructional level. Table 6.1 displays the instructional levels for reading comprehension and other practice-related activities.

As a drill procedure, the folding-in technique is based on having students learn new words by never allowing more than 15–30% of the material presented to be unknown. Here are the steps in using the technique:

1. Select a passage that the evaluator wishes to have the student read. The passage should be one that the student is currently working on in class. It is important that the passage contain no more than 50% unknown material.

2. Have the student read a portion of the passage (usually a paragraph or two) aloud and time the reading. Mark where the student was in the passage at the end of 1 minute. The number of words read correctly in this minute is designated as the presession reading fluency.

3. As the student reads, note at least three words that the student has

TABLE 6.1. Instructional Levels as Defined by Gickling's Model of CBA

Reading	Practice
93–97% known material	70–85% known material
3–7% unknown material	15–30% unknown material

Note. From "Best Practices in Curriculum-Based Assessment" by E. E. Gickling and S. Rosenfield, 1995, in A. Thomas and J. Grimes (Eds.), *Best Practices in School Psychology—III,* p. 589. Copyright 1995 by the National Association of School Psychologists. Reprinted by permission.

difficulty with or does not seem to understand. On 3″ × 5″ index cards, write the two words. These words are designated as "unknowns."

4. On 3″ × 5″ index cards, write seven words selected from the passage that the student does seem to know. These should be words that are meaningful to the passage, not simply sight words such as "and," "the," or other nonmeaningful expressions.

5. Begin the session by presenting the first unknown word. The evaluator should define the word for the student and use it in a sentence. Next, the evaluator should ask the student to repeat the definition and use it in a different sentence.

6. Now the folding-in begins. After the unknown word is presented, one of the known words is presented. The student is asked to say the word aloud. Next, the unknown word is again presented, followed by the known word previously presented, and then a new known word. This sequence of presentation, unknown followed by knowns, is continued until all seven knowns and the one unknown word have been presented.

Next, the second unknown word is presented. The word is presented in the same way as the first, with its definition given and its use in a sentence, first by the evaluator and then by the student. This second unknown word is then folded-in among the other seven known words and one unknown word. In the course of the multiple presentations of the words, the student is asked to repeat the unknown word's definition and to use it in a sentence whenever he or she hesitates or is incorrect in the pronunciation of the word. Finally, the third unknown is folded-in among the other nine words (two unknown, seven known). Given that the other words were assessed to be known at the starting point, the student should not have any difficulty with these words.

7. Upon completion of the folding-in intervention, the student is asked to reread the passage. The evaluator again marks the word the student was reading at 1 minute. It is important that the student read only to the same point of the passage that he or she read to at the beginning of the session. The number of words read correctly in 1 minute is considered the student's postsession reading score.

8. Both the pre- and postsession scores are graphed (usually by the student).

9. The next session begins by having the student read the next portion of the passage. Following the reading, a review of the ten words (eight known, two unknown) that were used in the previous session is conducted. A mark is placed on one of the unknown words to designate that the student knew the word without hesitation during this session.

10. As each new unknown word is added to the drill procedure, one of the original known words is removed from the pile. The original un-

known words selected on the first session remain in the pile until eight additional unknown words are added. By the time the 11th new unknown word is added, the word that is removed has far exceeded the number of repetitions necessary for new material to reach mastery level.

The folding-in technique provides high levels of repetition with guaranteed success. Given that the student already knows at least 70% of the material throughout the intervention session, he or she is likely to maintain high levels of motivation and concentrate on learning the new items that are being presented. Over time, this technique should result in the student learning more new material faster and retaining it longer than more traditional techniques.

A technique that is very similar to folding-in is the drill-sandwich procedure. Described by Coulter and Coulter (1991), the intervention is based on the same principles of instructional match and frequent repetition. The drill sandwich begins in the same way as folding-in by selecting three unknown and seven known words. However, instead of folding in the unknown words among the known, the total group of ten words is presented sequentially, with the unknown words placed in the third, sixth, and eighth positions. The set of words are then presented multiple times (usually five times through the pack per session), with the known words being shuffled at the end of each time through the set. Rearranging the words prohibits students from simply memorizing the upcoming word in the pack, rather than really reading the word off the index card. The passage is then reread at the end of the session.

I (Shapiro, 1992) provided an illustration of the use of this procedure to improve the reading fluency of four students (ages 6–9). Results of the pre- and postsession fluency for one of the students is shown in Figure 6.1. As the figure shows, the student's performance was consistently higher during postsession reading, with increases of reading fluency from 80 to 120 words correct per minute across the 11 sessions of treatment.

Several studies have examined the importance of the recommended instructional ratios of known to unknown items. For example, Neef, Iwata, and Page (1980) demonstrated that interspersing known items at a ratio of 50% during spelling instruction of new words resulted in superior performance in acquisition and long-term retention relative to other conditions. Roberts and her colleagues (Roberts & Shapiro, in press; Roberts, Turco, & Shapiro, 1991) examined the degree to which one must remain within the specific 70% known, 30% unknown ratio suggested by Gickling. In these studies, the drill-sandwich procedure was used with children scoring in the average to low-average ranges on the reading subtest of the California Test of Basic Skills. In the first study (Roberts et al., 1991), students

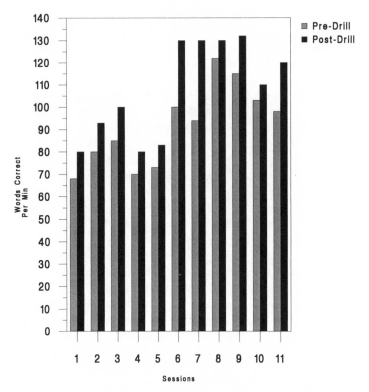

FIGURE 6.1. Oral reading rates of Anthony before and after drill session using the folding-in technique. From "Gickling's Model of Curriculum-Based Assessment to Improve Reading in Elementary Age Students" by E. S. Shapiro, 1992, *School Psychology Review, 21*, p. 172. Copyright 1992 by the National Association of School Psychologists. Reprinted by permission.

were randomly assigned to one of four conditions: (1) 90% known to 10% unknown; (2) 80% known to 20% unknown; (3) 60% known to 40% unknown; and (4) 50% known to 50% unknown. Based on the predictions of Gickling, it was expected that the best student performance would be evident for the 80% known to 20% unknown condition. At the end of 8 weeks of the intervention, results indicated that students acquired new information best in the most frustrating condition (50% known to 50% unknown); however, retention of learned words and the effect on untaught material was highest in the condition predicted by Gickling. In the second study, the ratio of known to unknown was stretched to 90% unknown to 10% known, 50% known to 50% unknown, and 80% known to 20% unknown. Results again indicated that although student acquisition of new information was best in the highly frustrating 90% unknown condition, students retained the information best when they were taught within the ratios recommended by Gickling.

Although research has not always substantiated Gickling's instructional ratios (e.g., Cooke, Guzaukas, Pressley, & Kerr, 1993), there does appear to be enough support for the use of the drill-sandwich and folding-in techniques to make strong suggestions that practitioners consider using them. In my own clinical experience, I have had dozens of successful implementations of the strategy, with only a rare failure.

Probably the most effective way to improve reading skills is to have students increase their time for reading. Using an oral rather than a silent reading strategy, although somewhat controversial (e.g., Taylor & Conner, 1982), does assure the observer that the student is actively engaged in reading behavior. Procedures described in Chapter 5, such as Direct Instruction or peer tutoring, specifically emphasize repeated and frequent practice in their instructional methodologies. Indeed, the folding-in or drill-sandwich techniques can easily be adapted for use under peer-tutoring conditions.

Frequently, when strategies are recommended that increase the amount of time students must spend practicing and rehearsing material, educational professionals express concern about available personnel to conduct such sessions. One program that has been designed and field-tested for teaching paraprofessionals, student tutors, or parents to provide this instruction is called the Success Controlled Optimal Reading Experience (SCORE; Cradler, Bechthold, & Bechthold, 1973). SCORE is a sequential phonics program designed to teach pupils of any age who are deficient in basic word attack skills and/or reading fluency below fourth-grade levels. The program is based on mastery learning and produces high levels of frequent responding.

Comprehension

Whether students master the skills of reading depends not only on their fluency, but also, equally as important, on their ability to comprehend the material they have read. It is important to recognize that comprehension is a skill to be taught, just as phonetic analysis and letter identification are skills to be instructed. Teaching comprehension is typically accomplished using either prereading or postreading strategies.

Postreading techniques tend to be straightforward. These often involve having students complete workbook pages and usually require students to respond to questions, such as identifying the main idea, sequence, and inferences from a previously read passage. Assignments are then graded, and feedback is offered.

Many examples can be found in the literature in which various aspects of postreading have been manipulated. For example, Swanson (1981) found that the use of self-recording, together with free time contingent on improvements in responses to questions asked after reading passages, resulted in increased performance on the comprehension task. This was in contrast to targeting error rates and silent reading rates, which resulted in no observable changes on comprehension measures.

Jenkins, Barksdale, and Clinton (1978) likewise demonstrated that providing monetary rewards for improved percentages of questions answered correctly after reading passages resulted in increased scores on the comprehension measure, but no changes in oral reading rates. Fluency improved only when it became the targeted response. Lahey et al. (1973) also demonstrated that providing contingent praise and pennies for giving correct responses to comprehension questions resulted in substantial improvements in the percentage of questions answered correctly.

Although each of these procedures involves the simple addition of contingent reinforcement on improved responses to comprehension questions, significant questions can be raised about these methods of improving comprehension. In each of these studies, students were told to read the passage and then were given a set of questions to answer. The ability to recall information correctly in order to respond to a question is probably a function of memory as much as understanding of what the student read. Howell et al. (1993) accurately pointed out that we typically read materials because we have specific questions in mind that we would like to have answered. What we read depends much on what we want to get from the material we are reading. Thus, prereading strategies of instruction may be much more logical in teaching comprehension skills.

Howell et al. (1993) provided an excellent example of the difference between prereading and postreading activities. If a teacher asks a student a week after the student has read a passage the question, "How old was Joy in that story?", the teacher is likely not to receive an accurate reply. Suppose, however, the teacher tells the student before he or she reads the passage, "Read this paragraph to find out how old Joy is." Obviously, the latter procedure seems to be more a measure of comprehension than of memory. In a typical prereading exercise, the teacher begins by reviewing the content of the passage and presenting new vocabulary. The student is then given the comprehension questions and asked to read the passage to find the answers. To assist the student in finding the answers, specific problem-solving or learning strategies may be taught.

Idol (1987) and Idol-Maestas and Croll (1987) have described a procedure called "story mapping" to teach comprehension skills. The procedure involves bringing the reader's attention to important and interrelated parts of the passage. Students are taught to organize the story into specific parts, including the setting, problem, goal, action, and outcome. Figure 6.2 illustrates the story map. Idol-Maestas and Croll used the procedure for students with learning disabilities, and found significant improvements in comprehension without continuation of the story-mapping procedure, as well as maintenance of comprehension levels after the procedure was discontinued.

In a follow-up study, Idol (1987) implemented the story-map technique with 27 students in a third/fourth-grade classroom. The strategy employed is a good example of a prereading technique. After showing the set of generic questions that students were to answer after reading the passage (Figure 6.3) and having the students read the story silently, the teacher displayed the story map. Students then completed the story map during a group instruction period led by the teacher. In a subsequent phase, the teacher no longer modeled the use of the story map as students independently completed the map. Students were permitted to fill in the map as they read the story. After the students completed the assignment, the teacher lead the group in completing the map by calling on students in the group. Finally, in the last phase, the teacher discontinued completing the maps. A final phase with baseline conditions was then instituted.

Results of the study showed substantial improvements in student comprehension scores once the story-mapping procedure was instituted. This was especially true for the students with learning disabilities and low achievement in the classroom. An interesting related finding of the study was that gains in comprehension were observed on a variety of measures of comprehension and general application of reading. Similar positive outcomes for story mapping have been reported by several investigators (e.g., Baumann & Bergeron, 1993; Billingsley & Ferro-Almeida, 1993; Davis, 1994).

Other prereading instructional procedures found useful for teaching comprehension are self-instruction training procedures. Very much like learning strategies, these techniques are designed to have students practice asking a series of questions to themselves as they read. Smith and Van Biervliet (1986) described a self-instruction training program used with 6 comprehension-deficient sixth-grade students. The instruction focused on having students practice

(a) reading the title of the story; (b) looking at illustrations; (c) reading the story and looking for the main idea; (d) noting the sequence of

MY STORY MAP

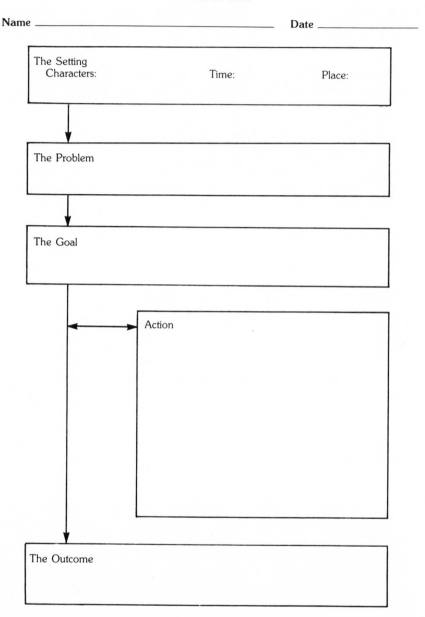

FIGURE 6.2. Form for completing story-mapping exercises. From "Group Story Mapping: A Comprehension Strategy for Both Skilled and Unskilled Readers" by L. Idol, 1987, *Journal of Learning Disabilities, 20*, p. 199. Copyright 1987 by Pro-Ed, Inc. Reprinted by permission.

Name: _____

Date: _____

1. Where did this story take place?
2. When did this story take place?
3. Who were the main characters in the story?
4. Were there any other important characters in the story? Who?
5. What was the problem in the story?
6. How did _____ try to solve the problem?
7. Was it hard to solve the problem? Explain.
8. Was the problem solved? Explain.
9. What did you learn from reading this story? Explain.
10. Can you think of a different ending?

FIGURE 6.3. Questions used to frame story map. From "Group Story Mapping: A Comprehension Strategy for Both Skilled and Unskilled Readers" by L. Idol, 1987, *Journal of Learning Disabilities, 20*, p. 197. Copyright 1987 by Pro-Ed, Inc. Reprinted by permission.

events; (e) reading through the comprehension questions; (f) rereading the story and answering the questions as they came to the answers in the story; and (g) checking the answers by referring again to the section of the story which provided the answers. (p. 47)

Self-instruction training was provided by using the procedures described by Meichenbaum and Goodman (1971) and involved having the student watch the experimenter model the task aloud, having the child perform the task while the experimenter instructed him or her aloud, having the child perform the task self-instructing aloud while the experimenter whispered, having the child perform the task while self-instructing in a whisper, and having the child self-instruct silently. Results of the study showed significant changes in the percentage of comprehension questions answered correctly after training. Three additional students who served as controls showed no change throughout the investigation.

In another study designed to examine self-instruction training, Miller (1986) compared the self-instruction procedure to a control practice technique in which students received equivalent exposure and practice to materials, but were not taught the self-verbalization strategy. Results of the study showed that although no differences in performance were evident between conditions when students were exposed to a single self-instruction training session, significant differences were present when three training sessions were employed.

Graham and Wong (1993) compared teaching students a mnemonic strategy and a self-instruction technique to identify relationships in the text that were implicit, explicit, or script implicit. Using a question–answering method, 45 average readers and 45 poor readers were taught a mnemonic strategy called 3H (Here, Hidden, and In My Head) to cue themselves as to how to find answers to comprehension questions. In one of the conditions, a self-instruction procedure was used to teach students how to use the 3H intervention. Results of the study showed that students in both the self-instruction and didactic teaching groups improved their reading comprehension performance. However, self-instruction training was more effective than the didactic teaching technique in maintaining performance over time.

Although there appears to be a preference in instructional strategies for prereading interventions in teaching comprehension, one postreading procedure may be valuable for improving both fluency and comprehension skills. A problem sometimes faced after conducting an assessment of reading skills is that students are being instructed in texts far beyond their level of effective acquisition. As noted by Lovitt and Hansen (1976a), it becomes difficult for students to achieve academic gains if they are being instructed in materials that clearly exceed their instructional levels. Placing students into lower level materials, however, can present a problem for teachers. For example, it may be unrealistic to expect a teacher to have a single student in curriculum materials that are significantly below the lowest level used by other students in the classroom. In addition, some teachers who are willing to place students into such material may be prevented from doing so by district policy.

Lovitt and Hansen (1976b) described a technique called "contingent skipping and drilling" that may prove useful in these circumstances. After the appropriate level of instruction was determined using curriculum-based assessment, desired performance levels were set for each student so as to achieve 25% improvement over baseline. During the intervention, students were permitted to skip all the remaining stories in the quarter of the basal reader book if, on the same day, all scores equaled or exceeded the preset criterion score. If a student went 7 days without skipping, a drill procedure was instituted. Drills employed for correct oral reading rate required a student to read the last 100 words from the previous day's assignment until he or she could pass at his or her criterion level. For incorrect rate, the teacher showed the student a list of words he or she had misread. The student was required to rehearse all lists of phrases in which these words were embedded until he or she could read all of them to the teacher. The comprehension drill required the student to rework answers to the questions until they were all correct. Students received drills on those aspects of reading performance that were below the desired scores, and could be drilled on all three components. Drill procedures remained in effect until a student skipped a section. After skipping, another 7 days had to elapse before another drill procedure was implemented.

Results of the study showed improvements across students in oral reading rates, reductions in error rates, and improvements in comprehension questions. Lovitt and Hansen (1976b) pointed out that although the measure of skipping in their procedure was a quarter of the text, teachers concerned about the amount of basal material not read could design the skipping procedure so that students could skip the following story rather than the entire quarter of the book.

Over the last several years, the emphasis in teaching reading comprehension skills has been on metacognition. Defined as conscious control of the skills by which one thinks and reasons, "metacognitive techniques" are designed to provide a framework for acquiring information from text. For example, as a student is reading, he or she may be taught to access prior knowledge, ask a set of questions to him- or herself, attempt to predict outcomes, examine relationships among characters, or other such strategies. The idea is to teach the student strategies to approach the information so that the text becomes meaningful as he or she reads it.

The literature exploring the many metacognitive strategies is voluminous. For example, a computerized literature search on the terms "reading comprehension and metacognition" within *Psychlit* between January 1990 and December 1994 resulted in 48 citations. Any attempt to describe the many possible strategies here is beyond the scope of this book. Ward and Traweek (1993) described one strategy, the think-aloud procedure, as illustrative of metacognitive techniques. Grade-level passages were modified using a cloze technique wherein every fifth word of the passage was left blank. In their procedure, replacement with only the exact word was considered correct. In the think-aloud technique, students were asked to tell the examiner the word that was omitted and why they chose that particular word to fit in the blank. In their study, Ward and Traweek compared the think-aloud condition to another condition in which students were simply told to tell the examiner the word left out in the passage. At the end of the intervention, a series of nine comprehension questions were asked. In addition, a set of questions was asked, designed to elicit the metacognitive strategies that students used in completing the cloze technique. Results showed that although both groups of students displayed equivalent performance on word identification and reading tasks, the students who used the think-aloud technique dramatically improved their comprehension scores.

Another metacognitive intervention teaches students to give reasons for responses to questions. In two studies with fifth-grade students, scores on a test of reading comprehension were significantly improved as a result of using the technique. Benito, Foley, Lewis, and Prescott (1993) had students use a question–answer response technique in responding to four types of questions usually asked in content-area textbooks. Although the students showed minimal gains on a global measure of reading comprehension, they all showed a substantial increase in the percentage of questions answered correctly in a social studies text.

In general, using metacognitive and cognitive strategies are the focus of significant interventions to improve reading comprehension skills. Indeed, it appears that the use of these strategies is critical to teaching students with academic skills problems in reading. Readers are encouraged to examine the large array of interventions that have appeared in the literature showing the wide range of strategies that can be selected.

MATHEMATICS

Students typically are referred for two types of problems in mathematics. Difficulties in mastering computational skills are the more common. These problems can range from failure to learn basic addition, subtraction, and multiplication facts to difficulties learning the correct rules for regrouping. Also, some students who are able to learn basic math facts have difficulty reaching levels of fluency. Mathematics is an area in which speed *and* accuracy are particularly important for success.

The other common type of problem in mathematics involves skills requiring the application of math. This would include such areas as time, money, measurement, and geometry. Word problems would also fall into this category.

Although failure in mathematical applications certainly is important, students who cannot master basic computational skills are very unlikely to succeed at applications. As such, intervention procedures designed as prework activities are focused more on applications and conceptual understanding of operations, whereas postwork activities emphasize acquisition of basic computational skills.

Postwork Activities

The procedures that are probably most frequently used for the remediation of computational problems involve contingent reinforcement and feedback. Kirby and Shields (1972) provided praise and immediate correctness feedback to increase the response rate for multiplication problems of a 13-year-old boy. McLaughlin (1981) described a more extensive token economy program that provided points for many behaviors, including increasing math rates on assigned daily worksheets. Points could be exchanged for a variety of activity reinforcers.

In both of these studies, significant improvements in math rates were observed when the procedures were in effect. Employing a reversal design, Kirby and Shields (1972) demonstrated that the changes in rate were directly related to implementing the intervention. Similarly, McLaughlin (1981) showed that earning points for increasing math rates resulted in the observed improved performance.

Contingent free time has also been employed in several investigations to improve math rates. Terry, Deck, Huelecki, and Santogrossi (1978) showed that allowing a student to earn free time if 100% of the problems on a daily math worksheet were correct resulted in improvements from completion of almost no problems to 100% completion immediately. Johnston and McLaughlin (1982) used a similar procedure with a 7-year-old girl in second grade. Before each session, the girl was told how many problems she needed to complete to earn the free time for the rest of the period. After 3 consecutive days at the specified criterion level, the criterion was increased by 5%. Results showed that the girl increased her performance in a stepwise fashion as the criterion changed.

Feedback and contingent praise have also been used to increase arithmetic response rate. Luiselli and Downing (1980), working with a 10-year-old, fifth-grade boy with a learning disability, simply offered the child feedback and praise for correct responding after a specified number of problems were completed. The number of problems was gradually increased across days. Using a reversal design, the investigators found substantial increases in performance that were attributable to the implementation of the intervention.

Blankenship (1978) investigated the use of modeling and corrective feedback in modifying inversion errors in subtraction. This type of problem occurs when students subtract the minuend from the subtrahend in regrouping problems:

$$\begin{array}{r} 37 \\ -\ 9 \\ \hline 32 \end{array} \qquad \begin{array}{r} 466 \\ -\ 89 \\ \hline 423 \end{array}$$

Using 10 children with learning disabilities who had identified inversion problems in subtraction, Blankenship began the intervention by having the teacher provide individual demonstration and modeling of how to perform the regrouping problem correctly. Students then completed a sample problem under teacher supervision and continued until they accurately completed the problem. Beginning on the following day, students were given feedback regarding their accuracy after completing the first group of problems. No additional feedback was provided on the rest of the worksheet. Results were dramatic and showed changes from 0% to almost 100% correct for all students after the intervention was employed.

Skinner and his colleagues in a series of studies have examined the use of a corrective feedback procedure entitled "cover–copy–compare" (CCC) to improve student performance in mathematics (Skinner, Bamberg, Smith, & Powell, 1993; Skinner, Ford, & Yunker, 1991; Skinner, Shapiro, Turco, Cole, & Brown, 1992; Skinner, Ford, & Yunker, 1991). The procedure involves five steps: (1) look at the problem, (2) cover the problem with an index card, (3) write the problem and solution on the right side of the page, (4) uncover the problem and solution, and (5) evaluate the response. In Skinner et al. (1992), a comparison was made between feedback in the CCC procedure given by peers or by the student to themselves for six second-grade students. Results showed that student performance was greater for four of the six students when the feedback was self-directed rather than peer-directed. However, across all students the peer-directed feedback sessions required double the time to complete the intervention. Skinner, Bamberg, et al. (1993) had three third-grade students subvocalize the CCC procedure while working on division problems. Results showed that two of the three students had increased their rate of correct responding to mastery levels. The third student required more directed feedback and goal setting to reach this level of performance. Follow-up data obtained 8 months after the intervention ended showed strong maintenance of division facts.

Clearly, the simple procedure of increased contingent feedback and reward can act as often-needed incentives for improving fluency of basic computational skills. Although this is true, the most straightforward recommendations about increasing fluency in computational skills are hardly novel. Even though students may know their facts, they must be able to perform them at a reasonable pace. Almost all discussions of increasing fluency note that one item is required: practice. Practice through the use of flash cards and oral recitation, practice through writing responses, and practice with and without timing are essential to improving computational skills. This should not be surprising, given what we know about increased opportunities to respond and improved academic skills. Practice alone, however, may not be sufficient to increase *accuracy* of responding effectively. When the difficulties a child is having are not just related to speed or fluency but show problems in accuracy, the use of prework activities become important.

Prework Activities

Two types of prework activities have been described for math problems. Although strategy training and self-instruction training use somewhat different terminology, they are essentially the same procedure. Both procedures involve having students (1) identify the steps needed to solve a particular task, and (2) use a self-talk format for proceeding through these steps.

Cullinan et al. (1981) provided a detailed explanation of strategy training for arithmetic instruction. Before a strategy can be devised to attack a problem, an analysis of the curriculum must be completed. The specific objectives being taught, such as adding one-digit numbers, writing numerical fractions when given pictures that show fractional relationships, or determining speed when given distance and time, provide the content for which strategies can be developed. Obviously, one can subdivide these objectives to even smaller levels. The optimal size of the task to be taught is often based upon the teacher's preference, the student groups being taught, and the judgment of professionals as to which level of tasks would result in the greatest generalization. In Chapter 5, Figure 5.4 displays an example of a task class for multiplication facts described by Cullinan et al. (1981).

Once the objective is determined, an attack strategy is devised. The strategy employed is based on a rational analysis of the problem (Resnick & Ford, 1978); that is, how does a competent learner solve this problem? Figure 5.4 shows the attack strategy developed for performing multiplication facts. After the strategy has been developed, it is important to task-analyze the strategy to determine whether there are specific skills required to perform the attack strategy that the student has not yet acquired. For example, Figure 5.4 shows the task analysis of the multiplication attack strategy. Obviously, a student who cannot count by 2's, 5's, and so on, will not succeed at the strategy devised to teach multiplication facts.

The attack strategy can be taught using any form of direct instruction. If a student has mastered the preskills, however, simply telling him or her the rule for combining skills may be a successful teaching strategy. One way to teach students these strategies has been through self-instruction. Johnson et al. (1980) and Whitman and Johnston (1983) have provided excellent examples of how self-instruction training can be used to teach addition and subtraction regrouping skills. After the appropriate sequence of steps to solve these problems is defined using a task analysis, students are taught to verbalize these steps as they actually solve problems. Initially, the teacher serves as a model for self-instruction while students observe.

Through a series of gradual steps, students begin to self-instruct without teacher prompting. Finally, students are expected to self-instruct "covertly" and talk to themselves. As discussed earlier, these procedures have been widely applied for both academic (Fox & Kendall, 1983) and behavioral problems (Roberts & Dick, 1982). In Chapter 5, Figure 5.1 shows an example of the actual self-instruction procedure used by Johnston et al. (1980).

Beyond the acquisition of mathematical operations, strategy training is expected to have additional benefits of teaching students problem solving. One of the important aspects of strategy training is the anticipated generalization of the strategy across related types of tasks. For example, it is expected that by teaching students problem solving for addition problems involving regrouping, acquisition of subtraction or multiplication problems with regrouping should be easier. Although the evidence is still limited, there does appear to be at least some within-skill (within-operation) generalization (Lloyd, Saltzman, & Kauffman, 1981). Clearly, however, the use of such procedures as strategy training in prework activities may play a significant part in the remediation of mathematics problems.

SPELLING

Procedures to improve spelling have involved mostly efforts aimed at postwork activities. In particular, prompting, modeling, feedback, and rehearsal appear to be the most common interventions employed. Instructors have included peer tutors, parents, teachers, and individuals themselves.

Delquadri et al. (1983) investigated the effects of classwide peer tutoring on spelling performance in a regular third-grade classroom. Students were awarded points for correct performance during tutoring. In addition, demonstration and feedback were employed when errors were made during tutoring sessions. Significant reductions in the numbers of errors made on weekly Friday spelling tests were evident when the peer tutoring procedures were in effect. Gettinger (1985) examined the use of imitation to correct spelling errors as a means of increasing spelling performance. Using an alternating treatments design, Gettinger had students engage in one of four conditions. Following a no-instruction control, in which students were told to study and practice, comparison was made between teacher- and student-directed study with or without cues regarding the incorrect portion of the word. In the teacher-directed condition, students were shown and told the correct spelling of the word. Cues consisted of having the part of the misspelled word circled. Results of the study revealed that the highest performance on posttests occurred when student-directed study with cues was employed. All four conditions, however, were significantly better than the no-instruction control condition.

An interesting procedure used to improve spelling called "Add-a-Word" was described by Pratt-Struthers, Struthers, and Williams (1983). The procedure involves having students copy a list of 10 words, cover each word, and write it a second time, then check each word for correct spelling against the teacher's list. Misspelled words are repeated and remain on the list. If a word is spelled correctly on two consecutive days, the word is dropped from the list and replaced with a new word. Results of this study showed that all nine of the fifth- and sixth-grade students with learning disabilities increased their percentage of correctly spelled words during a creative writing assignment using this procedure.

McLaughlin, Reiter, Mabee, and Byram (1991) replicated the Add-a-Word program across nine 12- to 14-year-old students with mild handicaps. Comparing the program to the more traditional approach of giving a Monday pretest followed by an end of the week posttest, students' overall accuracy in spelling was higher during the Add-a-Word program than during any other form of instruction. Similar findings for the Add-a-Word program were reported by several other investigators (McAuley & McLaughlin, 1992; Struthers, Bartlamay, Bell, & McLaughlin, 1994; Struthers, Bartlamay, Williams, & McLaughlin, 1989).

Although most procedures for academic remediation are based on positive procedures, as is typical in skill acquisition programs, use of a mild aversive technique has also been investigated for improving spelling performance. Foxx and Jones (1978) and Ollendick et al. (1980) examined use of positive practice overcorrection in improving spelling. In the Foxx and Jones study, 29 students between fourth and eighth grade were assigned to one of four conditions. All students took a pretest on Wednesday and a graded spelling test on Friday. In the control condition, no other manipulation was employed. In the second condition, students took only the Friday test, followed by positive practice on Monday. The positive practice procedure involved having students write out for each misspelled word (1) correct spelling, (2) phonetic spelling, (3) part of speech, (4) dictionary definition, and (5) correct usage in five sentences. In the third condition, students took the pretest, did positive practice on those words, and then took the Friday test. Finally, in the fourth condition, students performed positive practice after both pretest and posttest conditions. Results of their study found that all conditions in which positive practice was employed resulted in improved spelling performance over the control condition. Similar findings were observed in the Ollendick et al. study in two single-case design experiments, in which positive practice paired with contingent reinforcement resulted in better performance than did traditional teaching procedures.

Finally, simply providing contingent reward for meeting preset criteria for performance can result in improved spelling performance. We (Goldberg & Shapiro, 1995; Shapiro & Goldberg, 1986, 1989) compared the effects of types of group contingencies on spelling performance of regular sixth-grade students. Students were awarded points that were equivalent to a penny each if they met the preset criterion for performance. Although the findings related to the effectiveness of group contingencies were complex, they strongly suggested that even the poorest spellers significantly improved their performance as a result of contingent rewards.

The procedures employed to teach spelling in these studies are typical of how most spelling is usually taught. Students are assigned a list of words that they memorize and recite back when asked on the spelling test. Practice and rehearsal are conducted daily. Although this strategy appears to work, it may not be the best way to teach spelling (Howell et al., 1993). Students who are poor spellers are usually poor in phonetic decoding. However, if these students have good visualization skills, they may be able to learn to memorize the word lists, repeat them during the test, and score high marks for spelling in school. The real test for these individuals, however, is how they spell when they must produce written language. Thus, teaching spelling is usually linked to instruction and remediation for written language.

WRITTEN LANGUAGE

The area of written language involves many interrelated skills. These include grammar, punctuation, handwriting, spelling, creativity, and expressiveness. Over the last decade, Graham, Harris, and their colleagues have provided extensive descriptions of the best way to teach these skills, especially to children with mild handicaps (e.g., Graham, 1982; Graham, MacArthur, Schwartz, & Page-Voth, 1992; Graham, Harris, MacArthur, & Schwartz, 1991; Graham & Miller, 1980). Their work has focused primarily on the use of strategy instruction as a mechanism to teach the component skills necessary for effective writing.

An excellent review of earlier intervention studies in remediating problem of spelling, handwriting, and creative writing was provided by Kerr and Lambert (1982; see Table 6.2). In handwriting, intervention procedures were almost the same across studies. Typically, students are provided with feedback, modeling, and prompting. In addition, contingent reward is provided for improved performance. These procedures

TABLE 6.2. Applied Behavior Analysis Studies on Spelling

Reference	Subjects	Setting	Experimental design	Behaviors measured	Intervention procedures	Results
Axelrod and Paluska (1975)	22 third- and fourth-graders	Classroom	ABCBA	Number of words spelled correctly	Game I (Good Behavior Game in teams) Games and prizes Game 2 Probes: 6 spelling words daily (7 days)	Class average Baseline 1: 58% Game 1: 61% Games and prizes: 82.5% Game 2: 67% Probes: 58%
Broden et al. (1978)	Experiment I: Third-grader Experiment II: Second-grade sibling	Home	Experiment I: ABAB design with multiple probes Experiment II: ABABA	Weekly spelling scores	Tutor reviewed list until child spelled each word correctly 3 times, praised correct response	Experiment I test scores: Baseline I: 41% Tutor I: 94% Baseline 2: 29% Tutor 2: 93% Experiment II test scores: Baseline I: 39% Tutor I: 97% Baseline 2: 56% Tutor 2: 96% Baseline 3: 91%
Dineen, Clark, and Risley (1977)	Three 9- to 10-year-olds	Classroom	Pre- and posttests within subjects	Gain scores on: Tutor spelling lists Tutee spelling lists Control spelling lists	Peer tutoring, each subject serving as tutor, tutee, and "control"	Mean percent change: Control words: −1% Tutee words: +59% Tutor words: +47%

(cont.)

TABLE 6. 2. (cont.)

Reference	Subjects	Setting	Experimental design	Behaviors measured	Intervention procedures	Results
Foxx and Jones (1978)	29 students in grades 4, 5, 7, and 8	Classroom	5 (condition) × 4 (grade) design; each class received each experimental condition for 4 weeks in a different sequence	Spelling test scores	Pretest/test (PRE): Pretest on weekly spelling words; feedback on words missed, then test Test-positive practice (POS): Weekly spelling tests; students required to remediate each misspelled weekly spelling word; positive practice Pretest/positive practice test (PRE/POS): Pretest: teacher graded tests; students used positive practice; weekly tests Pretest/positive practice test/positive practice (PRE/POS/POS): Like (PRE/POS), with positive practice requirement for words misspelled on weekly test	Positive practice increased spelling averages for all classes; pretest increased averages for fifth grade only Mean percentage point gains: PRE/POS/POS: 14% PRE/POS: 11% POS: 10% PRE: 0%

Harris et al. (1972)	Elementary students	Classroom	ABAB	Spelling scores	Informal peer tutoring, independent study; tutoring, and independent study	Spelling gains: Tutoring 1: 14–25% Independent 1: 7–9% Tutoring 2: 23–24% Independent 2: 8% Tutorial procedure effective across a large number of students across grades
Kauffman et al. (1978)	Experiment I: Two 8-year-old children (IQ 70), educable mentally retarded	Classroom	ABAB: experimental phases were altered weekly	Correctly spelled words	"Modeling Only": Praise for correct spelling. Teacher modeled correctly spelled word "Imitation Plus Model": Praise for correct spelling; teacher modeled and wrote exact imitation of child's error; child wrote word correctly	Imitation Plus Model better than Model Only (faster acquisition and a higher final level of performance)
Lovitt and Curtiss (1969)	32 fourth-graders	Classroom	AB₁B₂	Number of 100% papers recieved	Phase 1: Traditional procedure Phase 2: Contingent free time individually arranged Phase 3: Group contigency was added	Median number of perfect papers out of 30 for each phase: Phase 1: 12 Phase 2: 25.5 Phase 3: 30

(cont.)

TABLE 6.2. (cont.)

Reference	Subjects	Setting	Experimental design	Behaviors measured	Intervention procedures	Results
Rieth et al.	Experiment I: 13-year-old	Classroom	Within-subject $AB_1B_2B_3$ design	Spelling scores on weekly tests	Experiment I: 4 phases—distributing spelling words into units of 5 or 6 words and giving daily quizzes	Experiments I, II, and III: Students did better when they received portion of the words each day and were tested daily than when they received all words at the beginning of the week and had weekly tests
	Experiment II: 8 children	Classroom	Within-subject $AB_1B_2B_3$ design		Experiment II: Same as I, with a larger number	
	Experiment III: 50 fifth graders-	Classroom	Comparisons of different groups of students		Experiment III: Like I and II, but compared different groups of students and included all students	
	Experiment IV: 8 fourth graders	Classroom	$AB_1B_2B_3B_4$		Experiment IV: 5 phases—presented a few words each day without daily testing	Experiment IV: Distributed practice with tests was superior to other conditions

Note. From "Behavior Modification of Children's Written Language" by M. M. Kerr and D. L. Lambert, 1982, in M. Hersen, R. M. Eisler, and P. M. Miller (Eds.), *Progress in Behavior Modification*, Vol. 13, pp. 86–88. Copyright 1982 by Academic Press. Reprinted by permission.

have been applied to manuscript and cursive letter formation. Consistently, students improve their handwriting when these procedures are put into place.

Substantial interventions to teach written language skills have emerged in the literature over the last decade based primarily on a constructivist approach to learning that perceives learning as a series of socially situated events that are functional, meaningful, and authentic (Harris & Graham, 1994), rather than linear and hierarchical. Investigations by Graham, Harris, and their colleagues began by examining the characteristics of writing products produced by students with learning disabilties. (Interested readers should see Graham, Harris, et al., 1991, for a superb description of their research program).

In general, Graham, Harris, and colleagues found that students with learning disabilities do not use very effective strategies in conducting writing tasks. For example, in planning an essay, students with learning disabilities made the task into a question-answering task with little consideration given to the relationship of the questions and the material that was to be written. It was also found that students with learning disabilities have a difficult time accessing the knowledge they do possess. This is especially true, given the mechanical problems many of these student have in producing written work.

Students with learning disabilities are equally ineffective at revising. Graham, Harris, et al. (1991) noted that students with learning disabilities tend to look at revising as an opportunity to improve the appearance of the composition, with little attention to its content. Additionally, students with learning disabilities may be unrealistic about the quality of their writing skills.

Based on these deficiencies, writing strategies have been developed designed to teach students with learning disabilities to self-monitor productivity, frame and plan text, generate content, edit, revise, and write sentences. Through a series of empirical studies, the impact of these strategies has been thoroughly tested. For example, in the area of planning, strategies such as brainstorming, framing text, and goal setting can be taught successfully to students with learning disabilities.

Harris and Graham (1985) taught two sixth-grade students to brainstorm as part of a larger strategy to improve composition skills. Three objectives of instruction were identified as increasing the number of different action words, action helpers, and describing words. Students were taught the attack strategies (brainstorming) for improving their compositions; each of the three objectives were attacked individually. Results of the study showed substantial increases in performance on the type of words used in the composition, as well as an increase in overall quality of writing.

In another set of studies, students were taught strategies for framing by posing and answering questions, each involving different parts of the story. Using a scale developed by Graham and Harris (1989) that scored each composition for the presence and quality of the inclusion of eight story grammar elements (main character, locale, time, starter event, goal, action, ending, and reaction), students increased the number of story grammar parts included significantly. Performance generalized to another writing assignment for a different teacher and was maintained for at least 4 weeks.

Another important part of the planning process in writing is the setting of goals. Graham et al. (1992) reported an investigation in which four fifth-grade students with learning disabilities were taught a specific prewriting strategy. The strategy included three steps:

1. Do PLANS (Pick goals, List ways to meet goals, And, make Notes, Sequence notes).
2. Write and say more.
3. Test goals. (p. 325)

Both product and process goals were selected by having students choose one goal from three or four listed in each area. For product goals, students chose goals for purpose, structure, and fluency. Under purpose, the student could choose from the following: (1) Write a paper that will convince my friends; (2) write a paper that will be fun to read; or (3) write a paper that will teach something. Under structure, the student's choice of goals were as follows: (1) Write an essay that has all the parts; or (2) write a story that has all the parts. Under fluency, the student chose a goal based on word count, adjusted depending on his or her pretest performance.

The second step of the strategy required students to indicate process goals for accomplishing the product goals previously chosen. The students then self-administered prompts to continue planning once they actually started writing. At the final step, students evaluated whether the goals were met.

The strategy was modeled by the instructor using a self-instruction technique that began with a talk-aloud procedure as an essay was written. Planning worksheets were provided for the students and modeled by the instructor. In a typical self-instruction format, the requirements for students to engage in self-talk were increased. Once the steps of the strategy were memorized, the instructor and the students composed an essay jointly and finally, the students completed two or three essays independently.

Results of the study showed that the students improved their writing skills in terms of the number of story elements included, as well as the quality of their writing. Prior to learning the strategy, students spent less than 5 seconds of prewriting time on their stories. This increased to approximately 8 minutes following instruction. Total composing time increased from 12 minutes in baseline to 20 minutes after intervention. In addition, when students were asked to write stories in other areas not discussed as part of the intervention, substantial improvements over baseline scores were evident across students. Other studies (Graham & Harris, 1989; Sawyer, Graham, & Harris, 1992) have also shown the potential value of goal setting as a strategy in improving writing skills.

In the area of revising, the use of peers to react and make suggestions has been a commonly applied strategy. Stoddard and MacArthur (1993) and MacArthur, Schwartz, and Graham (1991) reported the use of peer editors by having an assigned student summarize the main points of the essay in a log with suggestions for revisions. Students are provided with a series of questions to help guide their decisions. The editor and student author then discuss the suggestions. Results from these studies showed that students with learning disabilities made more mechanical and content revisions compared to baseline.

Finally, the impact of self-monitoring productivity has been examined during the writing process. Harris et al., (1994) compared two procedures for self-monitoring. In one condition, they used the procedure reported by Hallahan, Lloyd, Kauffman, and Loper (1983), whereby students are told to ask themselves, "Was I paying attention?" immediately after hearing a tone played on a tape recorder. Tones occurred at random intervals between 10 and 90 seconds. As each tone was heard, students were instructed to mark their response to the self-directed question on a recording sheet. In the other condition, students were told to simply self-record the number of words in the composition and record it on a graph at the conclusion of their writing. Results showed that both forms of self-monitoring improved the students' on-task and writing quality.

Strategy instruction has also been applied in improving the handwriting of students. Traditional techniques for teaching handwriting usually involve modeling the formation of letters by an instructor, followed by practice. Unfortunately, for many students with learning disabilities, these procedures are not always successful.

Kosiewicz et al. (1982) used a self-instruction and self-correction procedure to improve the handwriting of a boy with learning disabilities. Using the self-instruction procedure in combination with self-correction produced substantially better handwriting. Blandford and Lloyd (1987) used a self-instructional training technique to enhance handwriting of two students with learning disabilities. Using a cue card that included self-evaluation questions related to proper handwriting technique, the students were taught to covertly ask and answer each question as they completed their handwriting assignment. After the students improved their performance, the cue cards were removed and maintenance data were collected. Results showed that the self-instructional training procedure improved the handwriting of both students, and these effects were maintained after use of cue cards was discontinued.

Despite these two studies, the outcomes of using self-instruction to improve handwriting have been somewhat mixed. Graham (1983) tried using self-instruction training to improve the handwriting skills of three third- and fourth-grade students with learning disabilities. After extensive training, however, only modest gains on the letters taught were found. No transfer to untaught letters was evident.

A particularly unique study was reported by Campbell and Willis (1979), who implemented a behavioral program to teach creative writing to fifth-grade children. Using Torrance's (1972) definitions for components of creativity, the authors generated operational definitions for fluency, flexibility, elaboration, and originality. Figure 6.4 lists the definitions

Fluency. The number of different but relevant topic-related responses given. This can usually be considered in terms of the number of sentences. In the scoring system, one point was given for each expressed idea relevant to the topic.

Flexibility. The change in perspective of thought or particular pattern set from the previous idea or response (sentence). Flexibility can be distinguished from fluency on the basis of whether the sentence or phrase being rated is an elaboration of an already stated idea (fluency), another example of an idea already stated (also fluency), or the expression of a completely different point (flexibility). In the scoring system, one point was given for each different expressed idea relevant to the topic.

Elaboration. This is the degree of response elaboration, enhancement, or "spelling out" of a particular response or idea. It is the amount of information above and beyond what is necessary to communicate the basic idea. Indicators of this were the use of prepositional phrases, conjunctions, adjectives, adverbs, compound sentences, and so forth. A maximum of two points was given, dependent upon the degree of elaboration.

Originality. The fourth component is not easy to objectively define. With the consensus of the classroom teacher and the first author, however, the response definition for originality was "the improbability of a response occuring within the responses of fifth graders." It was thus considered in light of the total range of responses to the topic by all the students, as well as what the investigator and teacher thought was an original response for this age group. Two points were given for each idea that was thought to be an original response.

FIGURE 6.4. Torrance's (1973) response categories for creative writing task. From "A Behavioral Program to Teach Creative Writing in the Regular Classroom" by J. Campbell and J. Willis, 1979, *Education and Treatment of Children, 2*, p. 8. Copyright 1979 by the Pressley Ridge School. Reprinted by permission.

employed in the study. A token reinforcement system was used; students were awarded points exchangeable for backup rewards if they increased their creativity scores from the previous day. Results of the study showed continued increases in performance when the intervention was employed.

Another prewriting activity that can be a valuable tool in improving the written language skills of students is the use of a web. The web is a nonlinear outline that provides a mechanism for organizing information and linking important concepts together. The web begins with a main idea in the center and then branches to other categories of information. Zipprich (1995) described a study designed to teach webbing as a strategy to improve the written compositions across 13 students with learning and behavior disabilities between ages 9 and 12 years. Prior to the study, students were taught to identify elements of narrative stories using the story-map (Idol, 1987). In baseline, students were asked to write their best story during a 30-minute period, based on a picture cue displayed by the teacher. Following baseline, students were shown a prestructured web to help teach them how to clarify components of the story (see Figure 6.5). The teacher then led the students through a brainstorming session, writ-

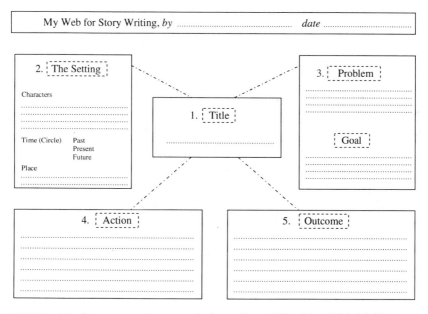

FIGURE 6.5. Prestructured story web form. From "Teaching Web Making as a Guided Planning Tool to Improve Student Narrative Writing" by M. A. Zipprich, 1995, *Remedial and Special Education, 16*, p. 6. Copyright 1995 by Pro-Ed, Inc. Reprinted by permission.

ing their responses on the prestructured web that was displayed on an overhead projector. Next, the students were shown another picture and were told to complete their own individual webs. Students then shared their ideas with the group, and the collective outcomes were recorded by the teacher. Students were then given 30 minutes to write their best story, using either individual ideas or the group ideas from the web. Finally, students were shown another picture and asked to generate a web and a story. Results were scored using a holistic scoring device. Overall, most of the students showed substantial gains in various components of the webbing process. Students were somewhat inconsistent in their improvement across components of the writing process (e.g., number of words, thought units, sentence types), but all showed improvement over baseline in the amount of planning time and quality (holistic score) of their writing.

CONCLUSIONS AND SUMMARY

Interventions for academic problems can be highly complex. Although studies have been conducted with all skills areas employing postwork activities that do not require extensive intervention development (e.g., reinforcement contingencies, feedback, modeling, and prompting), an emphasis on prework activities requiring strategy training is somewhat involved. These strategies, however, may foster generalization across tasks and can be quite powerful in the instructional process.

Missing, by design, from this review of potential intervention techniques are procedures more commonly viewed as based on information-processing approaches to remediation. For example, no recommendations for examining modality of instruction or altering curriculum materials based on learning approaches of students were made. These types of recommendations, common in the past, are not considered likely to result in improved student performance. Instead, the targets for intervention (i.e., reading, arithmetic, spelling, and writing) become the focus of the interventions. If a student is having problems reading, strategies to improve reading, and not some hypothesized set of underlying skills, should be implemented. If a student is having trouble learning basic math facts, basic math facts should be taught, not any perceptual process. Indeed, this approach works; it has worked well; and it is consistently reinforced through the research.

Given this wide range of intervention procedures, which strategies should we choose? This is where we leave the realm of empirical decision making and use the "artistic" nature of clinical decision making. Educational professionals have a significant amount of experience upon which they can draw to make judgments about what might or might not work.

What works with a particular student may not work with the next student who has a similar problem. Yet, there are procedures that appear to be more effective with certain types of problems. This is the point at which we begin the journey into problem solving for effective intervention. We begin where our experience tells us we will have success. Where we go next depends on the research and analysis of our data.

CHAPTER 7

♦♦♦

Step 4: Progress Monitoring

♦

Regardless of which instructional modifications identified in step 3 of the assessment model are implemented, a key decision for the evaluator is to determine whether the intervention is effective in improving the academic performance of the student. Setting goals for performance is an important element of ensuring student success. Likewise, determining whether a student is making progress toward his or her goal is an essential ingredient in conducting an effective evaluation of academic skills. Failing to evaluate a student's academic progress after starting an intervention program is tantamount to undergoing months of diagnostic tests for a medical condition, being prescribed with extensive pharmacotherapy by a physician, but never checking back with the physician to see if the therapy is working. Indeed, progress monitoring is a primary component of any system of problem-solving assessment.

Within my model of CBA, progress monitoring can be used to determine both short- and long-term outcomes of academic interventions. In either case, the measures must be direct (use direct observation of the outcome response), repeated (be taken frequently throughout the intervention period), and incorporate a time series analysis (graphed; Marston & Magnusson, 1988; Marston & Tindal, 1995). When short-term progress monitoring is used, the evaluator is trying to determine if the specific instructional objective that is being taught is being learned. For example, suppose it is determined during the assessment of instructional placement and instructional modification that a student does not understand the algorithm for regrouping in subtraction. The evaluator constructs a self-instruction procedure to help guide the student through the steps of the process as the intervention. To determine if the student is learning the strategy, a math probe is constructed, consisting of subtracting two-digit from three-digit numbers with regrouping to the 10's and 100's columns. Repeated twice per week, the percentage of problems correct, as well as the number of digits correct per minute, are calculated. Increases evident in the graphed data would indicate that the student is learning the instructional objective being taught. Once the student reaches mastery level on this objective, the evaluator would repeat the process for any additional objectives that need to be taught. As one can see, this process informs the evaluator that the student has accomplished the short-term goals that were set when the intervention was begun. This process is very consistent with the specific sub-skill mastery model of CBA described in Chapter 2.

Although a student may show consistent acquisition of short-term goals and objectives, the degree to which these accomplishments translate into reaching the year-long curriculum goals set by the teacher are unknown. For example, just because a student increases his or her performance in computational objectives of regrouping in subtraction may or may not impact on the student's overall performance to acquire mastery across all curriculum objectives of that grade level. The assessment process for long-term measurement is best described by the type of progress monitoring developed in the curriculum-based measurement model and is consistent with other general outcome measurement models of CBA (see Chapter 2).

The process of CBM or long-term progress monitoring uses a standardized, systematic, and repeated process of assessing students directly from material that reflects student outcomes from across all the curriculum objectives for that year. For example, to assess a third-grade student in mathematics computation, the evaluator would first identify all computational objectives required for that student during the entire third grade. Drawing randomly from across these objectives, a set of probes consisting of approximately 20 to 30 problems would be developed. Each probe would then contain problems that reflect the expected performance across the curriculum. A student's score on these probes across time would reflect the degree to which the instructional processes occurring in the classroom were effective.

To illustrate, suppose the third grade curriculum for mathematics computation indicates that students will be taught up to three-digit addition and subtraction with regrouping. Using CBM procedures, the evaluator develops a series of 72 probes (36 weeks of school × 2 probes per week) consisting of two- and three-digit addition and subtraction problems with regrouping. These probes are given to the students weekly. During the first few weeks of school, student performance on these probes may not be very high. However, as the teacher begins the process of teaching addition with regrouping, student performance on the probes should improve if the instruction is effective. After all, the material being taught is appearing on the test and the student's performance should reflect the learning that is occurring. As the year progresses the student's performance should steadily increase as the skills are learned. Should the probes begin to show a pattern of no improvement or decline, the teacher would know that the instructional processes that had been working previously were no longer effective. Thus, the progress monitoring data offers a clear message that something in the instructional process needs to change.

Effective progress monitoring requires data collection for the assessment of both short- and long-term objectives. It is impossible to cover the details of all types of progress monitoring in the scope of this book. Readers are directed to several excellent sources that provide superb detail regarding the many forms of progress monitoring (see Howell et al., 1993; Marston & Magnusson, 1988; Shinn, 1989). A very good set of video- and audiotapes are also available, providing the reader with clear examples and explanations of the process of long-term progress monitoring (Problem Solving Assessment Videotape Series, Iowa Department of Education, 1989; available from the National Association of School Psychologists, 4340 East West Hwy., Suite 402, Bethesda, MD 20814). In this chapter, basic principles and examples of short- and long-term progress monitoring in reading, math, spelling, and written language are provided.

READING

Long-Term Monitoring

Selecting Probes

As with the assessment of instructional placement, the rate of a student's reading aloud of passages is used for long-term progress monitoring. However, unlike the earlier part of the assessment, the passages chosen to monitor the student are taken from goal-level material (i.e., material the student is expected to complete by the end of the assessment period). The determination of the material appropriate for monitoring was made during the assessment for instructional placement. In other words, if a fourth-grade student was found to be instructional at the second-grade level, using fourth-grade material to monitor his or her performance would likely result in little growth, because we are expecting him or her to demonstrate skills at a level that is clearly too difficult (i.e., frustration level). Likewise, monitoring the student in second-grade material may be too easy and result in a ceiling effect, thus showing no sensitivity to instruction. It is also possible that if the student was assessed in material in which he or she was being instructed, practice effects would impact the measurement. Thus, the selection of material for monitoring in this case would be to choose third-grade material. Although this material might be above the student's current instructional level, it represents material that is likely to be sensitive to the instructional process.

In general, the material selected for monitoring should be at a level at which the student's performance is either instructional or just slightly frustrational. Selecting material that is too far from the student's assessed instructional level (as determined in step 2 of the model) is likely to result in floor effects and show little change over time. Material that is too close to the instructional level may reflect ceiling or practice effects and again not be sensitive to student growth.

Developing Probes

Once the material for assessment is selected, a set of passages are developed from that material in the same way as described in Chapter 3. Each passage is randomly selected from across the curriculum materials and re-typed onto a separate page. Readability of published texts can vary widely. It is recommended that the readability level of the passage be checked so that it remains within ± 1 grade level of the material from which it was selected. Several formulas exist for checking readability such as the Fry (1968), Flesch (1952), and Gunning (1952) indices. Computer programs are available that will automatically determine these indexes. Enough probes should be developed to assess students twice per week for an entire school year. Usually, this requires between 70 and 80 passages.

Administering and Scoring Probes

Students are asked to read each passage aloud for 1 minute. If students are unable to pronounce or phonetically decode words, they are prompted to continue after 3 seconds. Errors are scored only for omissions and mispronunciations, with self-corrections being scored as correct. The total number of words read correctly and incorrectly per minute are calculated.

Unlike the assessment of instructional progress, progress monitoring involves only a 1-minute reading sample, with no assessment for comprehension. Studies have shown that this procedure can be conducted under conditions of self-, peer-, or teacher-monitoring with high levels of integrity and reliability (Bentz, Shinn, & Gleason, 1990; McCurdy & Shapiro, 1992).

Selecting Long-Range Goals

In order to provide meaningful interpretation of the data, it is important to select a long- range goal. Several approaches to establishing the goal are available, including the use of local norms, average learning rate, and mastery criteria (Marston & Tindal, 1995).

Use of local norms offers several advantages. First, the data to be used to set goal levels are based on the performance of large numbers of students from the same educational environment. As such, these students are likely to be representative of the performance levels expected of the student being assessed. Several sources are available for readers interested in the procedures to develop and maintain local norms (Canter, 1995; Shinn, 1988, 1989). Although establishing local norms can be time-consuming and initially expensive in terms of manpower, the data can be quite valuable in selecting appropriate goals for students, as well as establishing expected levels of performance over time.

Given that not all districts will have local norms available, it is possible to use several of the excellent sets of norms that have been reported in the literature. Shinn (1989) provided data in reading taken at fall, winter, and spring assessment from a large Midwestern school district (see Table 7.1). Table 7.2 reports norms reported by Hasbrouck and Tindal (1992),

TABLE 7.1. Quartiles for Local Norms in Reading from Grade-Level Basal Reading Material for a Large, Metropolitan Midwestern School District

Grade	Quartile	Fall	Winter	Spring
1	1st	0	8	35
	2nd	2	19	69
	3rd	9	52	94
2	1st	17	41	60
	2nd	40	81	98
	3rd	77	119	133
3	1st	52	67	86
	2nd	79	101	119
	3rd	110	132	141
4	1st	61	80	87
	2nd	87	106	115
	3rd	117	135	142
5	1st	73	86	98
	2nd	102	115	124
	3rd	130	144	153
6	1st	102	111	117
	2nd	130	133	144
	3rd	155	166	171

Note. From "Identifying and Defining Academic Problems: CBM Screening and Eligibility Procedures" by M. R. Shinn, in M. R. Shinn (Ed.), 1989, *Curriculum-Based Measurement: Assessing Special Children*, p. 113. Copyright 1989 by The Guilford Press. Reprinted by permission.

TABLE 7.2. Quartiles for Oral Reading Fluency Averaged across Up to Eight Different School Districts

Grade	Percentile	Fall	Winter	Spring	*SD* of raw scores
2	25	23	46	65	39
	50	53	78	94	
	75	82	106	124	
3	25	65	70	87	39
	50	79	93	114	
	75	107	123	142	
4	25	72	89	92	37
	50	99	112	118	
	75	125	133	143	
5	25	77	93	100	35
	50	105	118	128	
	75	126	143	151	

Note. From "Curriculum-Based Oral Reading Fluency Norms for Students in Grades 2 through 5" by J. E. Hasbrouck and G. Tindal, 1992, *Teaching Exceptional Children*, *24*(3), p. 42. Copyright 1992 by the Council of Exceptional Children. Reprinted by permission.

TABLE 7.3. Quartiles for Local Norms in Reading from Grade-Level Basal Reading Material for a Small, Metropolitan Northeastern School District

Grade	Percentile	Fall	Winter	Spring
1	25th	1	6	16
	50th	4	15	48
	75th	7	24	80
2	25th	18	27	42
	50th	39	59	77
	75th	59	91	111
3	25th	40	50	61
	50th	62	76	87
	75th	84	102	112
4	25th	66	80	88
	50th	85	102	112
	75th	104	124	135
5	25th	78	88	97
	50th	104	116	129
	75th	129	147	160

who summarized normative data taken from numerous districts (over 9,000 students) across the country. Table 7.3 reports norms that I (Shapiro, 1991) collected on reading rates from a small, urban city in the Northeast (see Table 7.3).

In selecting goals for students, the evaluator should examine the current level of the student's performance and select a goal that is realistic yet ambitious. Using normative data can help the evaluator make this decision. For example, looking at Table 7.3, a fourth-grade student is found in the fall to be reading at 45 words correct per minute in fourth-grade material. Students in this district, in the fall, scoring at the 25th percentile were found to be reading at 66 words correct per minute (WCPM). In establishing a year-long goal for the target student, one may decide that a reasonable goal would be to move the student to a level equal to at least the 25th percentile of the fourth grade. Looking at Table 7.3, students at the 25th percentile in the spring are reading at 88 WCPM. Thus, a goal of 90 WCPM (rounding upward) is set for the target student. This information is then added to the graph on which progress monitoring will be plotted.

A second method for establishing goals is to use an average learning rate for students. Used in combination with local norms, average learning rates establish the amount of gain that students are expected to make over each year of instruction. Fuchs et al. (1993) reported progress monitoring data from 2 years across over 3,000 students in the areas of reading, math, and spelling. Table 7.4 shows the data for reading. These data can be used to establish the average expected levels of gain in oral reading rate across a year for other students. Although using data that come directly from the district where the student is enrolled would be better, the data provided by Fuchs et al. can be very helpful. For example, in the case of our fourth-

TABLE 7.4. Mean and Standard Deviation for Average Gains across 1 Year for Students across Five Midwestern School Districts.

Grade	Mean	*SD*
1	2.10	1.01
2	1.46	0.69
3	1.08	0.52
4	0.84	0.30
5	0.49	0.28
6	0.32	0.33

Note. Adapted from "Formative Evaluation of Academic Progress: How Much Growth Can We Expect?" by L. S. Fuchs, D. Fuchs, C. L. Hamlett, L. Walz, and G. Germann, 1993, *School Psychology Review, 22*, p. 34. Copyright 1993 by the National Association of School Psychologists. Adapted by permission of authors.

grade student, it can be seen that the average fourth grader should make 0.84 WCPM gain per week when instructed in fourth-grade materials. Since our student will be taught in third-grade materials, we may select the third-grade rate of improvement, 1.08 WCPM, as our target.

The slope of improvement, or average learning rate, can be plotted on our graph by simply multiplying the rate by the number of weeks over which the student will be instructed. In our example using 35 weeks, the expected performance level of our student, using an average rate of gain of 1.08 words per week, would result in a goal of 104 (66 + 38) WCPM at the end of the 35 weeks of school.

A final method for selecting a goal is to use the criteria for instructional levels described in Chapter 3. These data offer general guidelines for expected levels of oral reading rates and can be useful in suggesting appropriate goals for performance. For example, with our fourth-grade student, we note that 70–100 WCPM represents the instructional level for third- and fourth-grade reading material. Given that our student is currently reading 45 WCPM in fourth-grade material, we might select a level of performance halfway between 70 and 100 (85) as our long-term goal. Although not as precise as using local norms, this procedure will offer a rough guideline for making goal-setting decisions.

Graphing Data

As already mentioned, the graphic depiction of progress monitoring is an essential feature of the procedure. Without graphic displays of the data, decisions about a student's progress are impossible. For most purposes, a simple equal interval graph is used. Time is indicated on the horizontal axis, with performance in oral reading rate scaled along the vertical axis. Marston (1988), in comparing both equal interval and semilogarithmic graphs, found that predictions of goals were more accurate with equal interval graphs. In addition, this type of graph is more understandable by teachers, parents, and students.

Graphs are designed to display student progress across the entire time period during which progress monitoring is being conducted. The graph contains the student's baseline level performance, a goal, an aim line (the line of progress that a student needs to establish to reach their goal), and the data collected during each progress monitoring period.

Making Instructional Decisions

The most important part of the entire process of academic assessment occurs in this phase. The data collected must be used to make instructional decisions in order for the entire process to be valuable. For example, Fuchs et al., (1992) and Fuchs et al. (1991) found that when a computerized expert system to assist teachers with making instructional decisions based on CBM data was not used, students showed poorer performance than when the expert system was used.

In order to use the data from progress monitoring to make effective instructional decisions, it is important to establish a set of decision-rules that guide the evaluator in determining if the student is making progress toward the set goal. For example, in their computerized progress monitoring system, Fuchs, Hamlett, and Fuchs (1990a, 1990b, 1990c) use specific rules for evaluating the appropriateness of goals and determining whether teaching changes are needed. To monitor goal appropriateness, when at least six scores and at least 3 weeks had passed since the last goal was set, the four most recent scores are examined. If all scores are above the aim line, the program recommends that the goal be raised. Increasing the goal is also recommended if, after at least eight assessments and 3 weeks have passed, the program finds that the best line of fit (trend estimate) through the most recent 8–10 data points is steeper than the goal line. Others may simply set initial performance requirements, such as "If four consecutive data points fall below the aim line, a change in instructional intervention should be made."

Trend estimation can also be used. There are several approaches to trend estimation. Two of the more commonly used approaches in the special education literature are the split middle or quarter-intersect (White & Liberty, 1976) methods. Both techniques require that 9–12 data points be collected. In the split-middle technique, the entire data set is divided at the median data point. Next, the median score of each set of data is calculated and the two points are connected. This results in a trend estimation of the entire data set.

A more precise method of trend estimation is to calculate the ordinary least squares (OLS) regression line that fits the data series. This statistic is available with most computer programs that can be used to graph data (e.g., Microsoft Excel™, Quatro-pro™, Cricket Graph™). In addition, Shinn, Good, and Stein (1989) provide a program written in the BASIC language that can be used with most computers. Shinn et al. found that the OLS can result in more accurate predictions than the split-middle technique.

Regardless of which method is used to analyze the data, evaluators need to make instructionally relevant decisions based on their data. Should the data show that the student is easily exceeding his or her goal early on in the instructional process, the goal should be increased. If applying the decision rules shows that the student's performance is not sufficient to make the year-end goal, a change in instructional procedures needs to be implemented. The exact nature of the change is based on an examination of the data that have been collected through the progress monitoring procedure, the informal observation of the instructor, an examination of the data that had been collected during the implementation of the instructional modifications, as well as any "best educational guesses" suggested by the many professionals working with the student. Whatever type of change is suggested, this is noted on the graph (usually by a solid line) and progress monitoring is continued.

Figure 7.1 shows the progress monitoring in reading over 10 weeks (two assessment sessions per week) of a student, Brandon. Following an assessment of the academic environment and instructional placement, a previewing intervention was implemented after a baseline period (see Chapter 6 for a discussion of this intervention). A goal of 70 WCPM over 20 weeks was set, depicted by the dashed line. After 4 weeks of data collection, it was found that Brandon was not making adequate progress to meet his goal. A folding-in intervention was added to the previewing. The combination of these two interventions resulted in an immediate and substantial improvement in Brandon's performance. An analysis of Brandon's trend using the OLS statistic completed after the 8th week showed that he would meet or exceed his goal by the end of the 20-week intervention period.

An Alternative to Oral Reading Fluency

Although there is strong and substantial research supporting the use of the oral reading fluency metric as a key indicator of student progress in read-

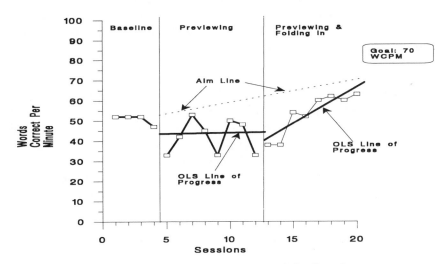

FIGURE 7.1. Progress monitoring graph for Brandon.

ing over time, there remains a significant suspicion among many educators that oral reading fluency does not effectively reflect acquisition of comprehension. Indeed, perhaps the greatest criticism of CBM comes from those in the reading field who doubt that a student's reading can be adequately reflected in oral fluency rates alone. Recognizing this problem, Fuchs and Fuchs (1992) identified an alternative to oral reading fluency that has a stronger comprehension component but can equally be sensitive to student growth over time. The technique required students to read a passage in which every seventh word was omitted. Students were provided with three choices to replace the blank, only one of which made any sense in the context of the paragraph. This modified maze technique was implemented, using a computer program that generated graphic displays of student results. In the study, they compared the modified maze technique to a written cloze requiring an exact replacement, written retell using total words written as the score, and a written retell with a matched words written score. Results showed that the retell and cloze techniques were inadequate to reflect ongoing student progress in reading, whereas the criterion validity of the maze technique was very strong. Fuchs and Fuchs also reported that teachers saw the maze technique as an acceptable measure of decoding, fluency, and comprehension. Fuchs et al. (1993) provided normative data on the amount of progress students are expected to make over a year on this measure.

Short-Term Monitoring

When intervention strategies developed for instructional modification involve specific instructional objectives, the monitoring process for the mastery of those objectives requires the development of a teacher- or evaluator-made test that actually assesses the skill. The primary purpose of this form of assessment is to assist the evaluator in deciding what types of skills need to be taught and to potentially provide information about instructional modifications that may be effective. Howell et al., (1993) have identified this type of assessment as a "specific level assessment."

One type of specific level assessment would be a miscue analysis of oral reading fluency. Parker, Hasbrouck, and Tindal (1992) found that this type of analysis could be useful in some forms of progress monitoring. Figure 7.2 provides an example of the type of analysis that might be used when examining a student's performance on an oral reading task (Howell et al., 1993). Using these data, the evaluator can design an instructionally relevant program to impact the skills that are weak. Repeated use of this type of measure can be effective in determining if the student is making progress in mastering these goals.

Another method for conducting short-term monitoring of reading

ERROR PATTERN ANALYSIS

student's name _____*Flara*_____ date _____

Content Categories	No. of Errors

Words: errors involving whole words

polysyllabic words | monitor(monshur *mon·fior* / *mornish*) also(always)

compound words |

sight words | the (that), were (was), those (these), I'd (I'lld)

silent letters |

Units: errors involving combined letter units

endings (suffixes) |

r-controlled vowels | person (preson)

vowel teams | thought (that)

consonant digraphs(th, sh, ch, etc) | thought (that)

consonant clusters (bl, br, ld, etc) |

CVC words |

Conversions: errors involving sound modification

double consonant words | Pepper (Petter)

vowel plus e conversions |

Sounds: errors involving individual letters and sounds

vowels | those (these), the (that), Mrs. (miss)

consonants |

sequence |

sounds |

symbols |

FIGURE 7.2. Error pattern analysis for decoding. From *Multilevel Academic Skills Inventory* by K. W. Howell, S. H. Zucker, and M. K. Morehead, 1982. Copyright 1982 by The Psychological Corporation. Reprinted by permission.

progress can be the repeated use of a teacher rating scale. This may be a particularly useful technique when the instructional objective focuses on improving reading comprehension. These measures again tend to be teacher- or evaluator-made and are tailored specifically to the instructional lessons being taught.

For example, a sixth-grade student, Ray, was found to have oral reading fluency commensurate with a sixth-grade level. However, an evaluation of his comprehension skills showed that he had great difficulty comprehending what he had read. Specifically, the evaluation showed that he had great problems recognizing main ideas, discriminating relevant from irrelevant details, and making inferences beyond the factual information provided in the story read. After the assessment of the academic environment and instructional placement, the evaluator recommended that Ray be taught a webbing technique (see Chapter 6) to increase his comprehension skills. To assess the acquisition of his comprehension skills, a brief five-item checklist was created (see Figure 7.3). Twice each week, Ray was given a new passage to read. After completing his web, Ray was asked to discuss the story with his teacher, who then completed the checklist. Scores across 5 weeks on each item are shown in Table 7.5. These data reflect the impact of the webbing strategy on Ray's performance.

Another technique that can be useful for short-term monitoring in reading is the use of an oral retell technique. This is particular valuable for narrative text. In the technique, the student is asked to read a passage of 200–300 words. Immediately following the reading, students are asked to tell what they read in their own words. The retell can be scored for the presence or absence of elements of the story, such as theme, problem, goal, setting, and so forth. If the retell is aided by the examiner, this can also be indicated. Figure 7.4 illustrates such a scoring technique. Although the retell technique has not fared well in terms of being sensitive to growth across curriculum objectives (Fuchs & Fuchs, 1992), it may be useful as an

TEACHER RATING MEASURE FOR COMPREHENSION

	Poor				Excellent
1. Ability to recognize main ideas	1	2	3	4	5
2. Recognition of relevant detail	1	2	3	4	5
3. Discriminates relevant from irrelevant detail	1	2	3	4	5
4. Inferences beyond story detail	1	2	3	4	5
5. Overall comprehension skill rating	1	2	3	4	5

FIGURE 7.3. Example of teacher rating measure for assessment of reading comprehension.

TABLE 7.5. Scores on Biweekly Comprehension Probes by Ray's Teachers

	Ray's Scores on Teacher Comprehension Rating Form				
Probe no.	MI	DET	D/I	INF	OVR
1	2	3	1	1	2
2	2	3	1	1	2
3	3	3	2	1	2
4	3	3	2	1	2
5	3	3	1	2	2
6	4	4	2	1	3
7	4	4	2	2	3
8	4	4	3	2	3
9	3	4	3	2	3
10	4	4	3	1	3

Note. MI, main idea; DET, relevant detail; D/I, discriminates relevant/irrelevant detail; INF, inferences beyond story; OVR, overall comprehension rating.

QUANTIFICATION OF RETELLING FOR NARRATIVE TEXT

Book/Page: _____   Date: _____

Directions: Place a 1 next to each item the student includes in his or her retelling. Credit the gist as well as the obvious recall. Place an "*" if you ask the child questions to aid his or her recall.

Story Sense

Theme:	Main idea or moral of story	☐ (1)
Problem:	Difficulty to overcome	☐ (1)
Goal:	What the character wants to happen	☐ (1)
Title:	Name of the story (if possible)	☐ (1)

Setting

When and where the story occurs ☐ (1)

Characters

Name the main characters ☐ (1)

Events/Episodes

Initiation event	☐ (1)
Major events (climax)	☐ (1)
Sequence: retells in structural order	☐ (1)

Resolution

Name problem solution for the goal	☐ (0.5)
End the story	☐ (0.5)

TOTAL   _____ (10)

FIGURE 7.4. Scoring form for quantification of retelling task for narrative text.

indicator of improvement when specific comprehension skills are being taught.

It is important to remember that the use of short-term monitoring is primarily focused on diagnosing the instructional process. As such, it does not meet the psychometric standards of typical progress monitoring measures. Consistent with a specific subskill mastery model, these methods of monitoring student progress will vary each time a new instructional objective is developed. However, the measures can be very helpful in assisting an evaluator in making effective and relevant recommendations for whether the recommended changes in instruction have been effective in teaching the student the specific skill that the instructional method was designed to teach.

MATHEMATICS

Long-Term Monitoring

Selecting Probes

As noted in Chapter 3, CBA of math focuses on the acquisition of computational skills. In choosing the material for assessment, it is important to understand how curricula in math are structured. An examination of the scope and sequence for computational objectives of any published math curriculum shows that the curriculum is recursive. Skills are often introduced and practiced in one grade and then reappear over the next several grades. Mastery of the skill is not expected until several grades after the skill is first taught.

Given that computational objectives are repeated over several grades makes selection of material for monitoring important. If the examiner selects the content of the assessment from the objectives being taught at the grade level of instruction, the student is likely to have some problems where mastery is expected, and other problems in the acquisition (instructional) stage of the learning process. Such information would be valuable in informing the evaluator as to the level of student performance within grade-level material. On the other hand, if the material chosen for assessment comes only from instructional objectives where mastery is expected, the outcomes provide the evaluator with information about the student's long-term mastery of computation.

In most CBA long-term progress monitoring, the material selected for assessment involves multiple-skill probes taken from across grade-level computational objectives. Material selected for assessment is usually taken from the grade level at which the student is being instructed. This is determined through the teacher interview conducted as part of the assessment of the academic environment. It is important to realize that if a student is found during the assessment of instructional placement to have significant deficiencies in computational objectives occurring far below his or her grade level, conducting the progress monitoring process at grade level may result in a potential floor effect. As such, it may be necessary to select grade-level material a year or two below current grade-level functioning, if progress monitoring is to be effective. For example, suppose a fourth-grade student is found to be frustrational in addition with regrouping, a skill initially introduced in the third grade of the curriculum. Using fourth-grade level material for progress monitoring, that contains many computational objectives for which addition with regrouping is a prerequisite skill, is likely to result in a lack of sensitivity to instruction, and thus the student shows little growth over time. In such a case, using third-grade level computational probes would be recommended.

Developing Probes

Probes for the long-term monitoring in mathematics are developed by randomly selecting problems from across the grade-level curriculum objectives chosen for assessment. A total of 70–80 probes, each containing 20 to 30 problems, is usually developed to allow monitoring to occur approximately twice per week for a full academic year. Because each probe contains items that were selected from across grade-level curriculum objectives, the administered CBM test should reflect student gains in the curriculum over time.

Obviously, it would be somewhat time-consuming to develop a set of 70–80 math probes per grade level, each containing a set of problems that represents the entire curriculum. There are several computer programs, however, that can be used to generate these problems. Milliken Math Sequences provides the user with sets of single-skill math probes for each computational objective. Users of this program can then combine the printed copy from the program by cutting and pasting the problems to generate the grade-level math probe useful for progress monitoring.

Fuchs, Hamlett, and Fuchs (1990a) in their program, Monitoring Basic Skills Progress: Basic Math, provide a set of black-line masters consisting of grade-level problems that have already been developed. These can be scored by the teacher or student using the computer program.

The advantage of the Milliken program is that one can individualize the material for each specific curriculum; that is, once the evaluator obtains the scope and sequence of computational objectives for the student, a series of single-skill probes can be printed and combined so that the probes given for that student will represent the particular curriculum of instruction. The disadvantage of this approach is the time involved in doing the cutting and pasting to generate the probes.

The advantage of the Fuchs et al. (1990a) program is that multiple grade-level probes are already created. Unfortunately, the specific computational skills included in their grade-level probes may differ somewhat from the curriculum objectives of the student being assessed. It is important for the evaluator to look at the overlap of the skills included in the Fuchs et al. program and the curriculum of instruction before using these probes.

Administering and Scoring Probes

Probes are administered in much the same way as the assessment of instructional placement described in Chapter 3. Students are given between 3 and 5 minutes to complete as many problems as they can. As the grade level of the students increases, so does the complexity of the problems. As such, the amount of time permitted to complete the probe increases. Usually, 3 minutes are allowed for probes at the first- and second-grade levels. A total of 4 minutes is permitted for third- and fourth-grade probes, 5 minutes for fifth-grade and up. Instructions to the students are to do the problems in sequence, only skipping problems they cannot do after trying. Students are given the probes once or twice per week. Students are stopped when the time expires or when they have completed all the problems on the sheet.

The probes are scored for digits correct and incorrect per minute, as described in Chapter 3. (Detailed descriptions of the use of this metric, along with several practice exercises, can be found in the workbook accompanying this text [Shapiro, 1996].) An error analysis can also be performed by looking at results of individual items to examine which of the computational objectives the student has mastered, partially mastered, or not mastered. The computer program by Fuchs et al. (1990a) conducts such an analysis automatically. Results of this analysis can be useful in planning future instructional objectives.

Setting Long-Term Goals

Long-term goals in computational math are determined in the same ways as in reading. Local normative data collected in fall, winter, and spring can be developed and used to signal the expected performance in terms of digits correct per minute per grade level. Average learning rate normative data can also be collected. Fuchs et al. (1993) provided such data for a large number of students, and these data are reported in Table 7.6. In ad-

TABLE 7.6. Mean and Standard Deviation for Average Gains on Digits and Problems Correct in Math across 1 Year for Students across Five Midwestern School Districts

Grade	Digits		Problems	
	Mean	SD	Mean	SD
1	.34	.19	.26	.14
2	.28	.20	.14	.12
3	.30	.23	.24	.12
4	.69	.46	.25	.17
5	.74	.44	.23	.17
6	.42	.49	.13	.13

Note. Data from Fuchs, Fuchs, Hamlett, Walz, and Germann (1993).

dition, the evaluator can use the mastery criterion provided in Chapter 3 as a guideline for selecting appropriate goals.

Graphing

Graphic display of the data remains an essential feature of the progress monitoring process. These graphs can be either hand drawn or computer generated. For example, the Fuchs et al. (1990a) computer program automatically draws and updates student graphs as the data are collected. These graphs offer opportunities for feedback to students and can be very useful for student motivation, as well as helping teachers make instructional recommendations.

Making Instructional Decisions

The data obtained from progress monitoring in math are interpreted in much the same way as in reading. Using a priori decision rules, outcomes generated by the data tell the evaluator whether the current instructional procedures are having their desired impact. When the data series suggests that the goal needs to be altered or an instructional change needs to be made, the graphic display of the progress monitoring data is used to verify that the new procedures are indeed effective.

Progress monitoring data in math can also be used to identify what potential skills may need specific instruction. The evaluator can examine each probe produced by the student for an analysis of the types of problems at which the student is experiencing difficulties. This would help the instructor plan the teaching necessary for the student to learn this skill. As noted previously, the computer program developed by Fuchs et al. (1990a) does this automatically as the data are entered. Using this program, Fuchs,

Fuchs, Phillips, Hamlett, and Karns (1995) combined a classwide peer-tutoring program in mathematics with progress monitoring. Using the results of weekly CBM tests, computerized feedback was provided to select the instructional objectives to be taught through a peer-tutoring format. Results of the study showed that the combination of these two procedures was very powerful in producing substantial improvements in the mathematics performance of students.

Short-Term Monitoring

As noted previously for reading, the primary objective of short-term monitoring is to assess whether a student has acquired the specific curriculum objective that has been instructed. In addition, through short-term monitoring, an error analysis can be performed to reveal the patterns of mistakes that a student is making. This assessment involves the use of single-skill probes.

Single-skill math probes, as described in Chapter 3, are used. Performance on these probes, before and after instruction on a particular objective, provides the data for determining if the student is reaching mastery. For example, if the assessment of instructional placement shows a student to be deficient in knowing the algorithm for two-digit by two-digit multiplication, the repeated administration of a probe after the strategy was developed to teach this skill would demonstrate the short-term monitoring procedure for acquiring this skill. Although it is possible to obtain such data from the long-term monitoring process as well, because the probes will contain some problems derived from all grade-level curriculum objectives, it is important to recognize that the long-term monitoring probes may only have one or two problems that are representative of the skill being taught. As such, there may be limited opportunities to carefully assess exactly the types of errors that students are making. Use of single-skill probes, often given under untimed conditions, permits the evaluator to get a more detailed picture of how a student attacks a particular type of computational problem.

Math probes are analyzed to determine whether students are demonstrating difficulties with knowledge of facts, operations, place value, algorithms, or problem solving. Problems with math facts are seen when students consistently add, subtract, multiply, or divide incorrectly. These problems are due to the lack of mastery of basic math facts, such as multiplying 9×7 and getting 56. Errors in operations occur when students add instead of subtract or add instead of multiply. For example, Figure 7.5 shows the performance of a student with problems in operation. This student understands the concept of subtraction but consistently performs subtraction rather than attending to the sign indicated for each problem.

```
   8         3          5          3
 - 5       + 3        - 2        + 1
 ───       ───        ───        ───
   3         0          3          2


   7         4          7          4
 - 5       + 2        - 2        + 1
 ───       ───        ───        ───
   2         2          5          3
```

FIGURE 7.5. Example of errors in operation.

Errors in place value usually occur if students are having difficulty with the concept of regrouping. Here, students fail to align numerals properly and do not recognize the properties of placing numbers into their respective columns (1's, 10's, 100's, etc.). Algorithm problems are a common source of error in math computation. Students showing problems in this area do not understand the correct sequence of steps in completing the problem. For example, as seen in Figure 7.6, although Bill knows his addition math facts, he does not understand the algorithm for adding two-digit numbers. In fact, Bill's approach to the problem is to simply add everything. An interesting question that might be raised about Bill's behavior is that the algorithm he is apparently using to add is similar to one used in the process of multiplying two-digit numbers. It might be useful to examine whether multiplication is a skill being currently taught in the classroom and this is partially causing some of Bill's confusion.

A final area of error analysis in math computation is the examination of a student's problem-solving skills. In particular, it is possible to see if a student uses or understands the process of estimation. For example, Bill's responses to the addition problem show clear signs that he does not use any form of estimation in determining whether his answers are correct. This may point to another area that is ripe for possible intervention.

Readers interested in more detailed examples and exercises to ana-

```
    7          11          15          12
  + 8         + 7        + 33        + 26
  ───         ───        ────        ────
   15          18         4848        3478


    4          15          26          11
  + 8         + 5        + 32        + 67
  ───         ───        ────        ────
   12          20         5948        7788
```

FIGURE 7.6. Example of errors in algorithm for Bill.

lyze common sources of errors in math should see the workbook accompanying this text (Shapiro, 1996) as well as excellent texts by Howell et al., (1993), Salvia and Hughes (1990), and Rosenfield (1987).

SPELLING

Long-Term Monitoring

Selecting Probes

The decisions that guide the selection of material for long-term progress monitoring of spelling are similar to those in reading. Using the information from the assessment of the academic environment and the assessment of instructional placement, the grade level at which the student is instructional was identified. In choosing material for monitoring, it is typical that the evaluator uses this level of material for monitoring. Rather than selecting material somewhat beyond the current instructional level, as was recommended for reading, it is more common that the level where the student is actually being instructed is used in spelling. Although this may present some problems in terms of practice effects, using the instructional level material will assure the evaluator of good sensitivity in the data to the instructional process.

Developing Probes

When spelling is being taught from a published spelling series, finding the material to select for developing probes is relatively simple. Once the level in the series where the student is instructional has been identified (in Step 2, Instructional Placement Assessment), the evaluator will find listed at the end of each level of the series a list of new spelling words taught from that level. The probes are developed by randomly selecting a list of 20 words from the entire pool of words that the student will be taught across the school year. Approximately 70–80 word lists are developed to permit up to two assessments per week.

In recent years, the frequency of spelling instruction delivered from published spelling curricula has steadily diminished. More and more, spelling is being taught as a subject integrated within language arts, reading, and other content areas. When spelling lists are generated for the typical Friday spelling test, found in many elementary schools, the words on the list are coming from various nonstandardized sources. Given that long-term progress monitoring needs to use a systematic, standardized methodology, using such material for progress monitoring would be difficult and is not recommended.

An alternative to long-term progress monitoring when the instruction is not from a published spelling curriculum is to use already prepared graded word lists. Fuchs et al. (1990c) in their computerized program Monitoring Basic Skills Progress: Spelling, provide a set of such word lists for grades 1–6. Derived from the Harris–Jacobson (1972) word lists, the evaluator can use these lists to assess a student's progress in spelling, even if spelling is being taught from nonstandard material.

Administering and Scoring Probes

Spelling probes are administered and scored in the same way as the probes used in the assessment of instructional placement (Chapter 3). Words are dictated at a rate of one every 7 seconds until the list is exhausted. Scoring is done using letters-in-a-sequence (see Chapter 3) and the percentage of words spelled correctly. (More detailed explanation of letters-in-a-sequence and practice exercises for learning how to score spelling this way are provided in the workbook accompanying this text.) In the Fuchs et al. (1990c) computerized spelling program, the results of the spelling probes are entered and automatically scored for both metrics.

Setting Long-Term Goals

The procedures for selecting long-term goals in spelling are no different than they were for reading or math. Use of local norms, learning-rate norms, and use of the criteria used for the assessment of instructional placement can all be applied. Table 7.7 provides normative data from Fuchs et al. (1993), indicating the average learning rates across over 3,000 students from grades 1–5.

TABLE 7.7. Mean and Standard Deviation for Average Gains (Slope) on Letter Sequences and Words Correct in Spelling across 1 Year for Students across Five Midwestern School Districts

Grade	Letter sequences		Words correct	
	Mean	*SD*	Mean	*SD*
2	.92	.48	.17	.10
3	.57	.34	.11	.09
4	.48	.50	.09	.07
5	.41	.41	.06	.07

Note. Data from Fuchs, Fuchs, Hamlett, Walz, and Germann (1993).

Graphing

As with all other areas of long-term progress monitoring, data from the assessment of spelling are graphed. Usually, the letters-in-a-sequence data are used, because these data tend to be more sensitive to small changes in performance than percentage of words spelled correctly. The Fuchs et al. (1990c) computer program automatically provides this graph.

Making Instructional Decisions

The data from the long-term progress monitoring in spelling indicate the degree to which student performance is being affected by the instructional process. The same types of decision rules applied for reading and math are used to determine if a change in goals or instructional methods is warranted.

Short-Term Monitoring

Like other areas of instruction, the short-term progress monitoring of spelling is designed to assist the evaluator in identifying the specific skills that the student may be having difficulty learning and involves the use of primarily teacher-made tests. The primary purpose of the monitoring process, however, is to diagnose the student's performance and to identify clear targets for instruction. Unlike the areas of reading and math, however, short-term monitoring of spelling can be ascertained directly from the long-term progress monitoring probes.

By conducting an analysis of error types, the evaluator is able to determine the kinds of skills a student may need to be taught. This is accomplished most easily if a computerized program is used, such as the one developed by Fuchs et al. (1990c). As seen in Figure 7.7, the computer program examines the last 50 words of the student's progress monitoring tests and provides a list of the error types and their frequency. From this information, evaluators can design instructional methods that will emphasize the teaching of these skills. The repeated assessment process used in long-term progress monitoring allows the evaluator to see if the student reduces the frequency of a specific type of error over time.

WRITTEN LANGUAGE

Long-Term Monitoring

The long-term monitoring of performance in written language is identical to the technique for monitoring described in Chapter 3 for assessing instructional placement. Students are asked to write for 3 minutes, using a

```
-----------------------------------------------------------------------
NAME: Charles Landrum          Spelling 4            Date: 4/10      Page 1
-----------------------------------------------------------------------
Corrects (100% LS)                     14 word(s)
Near Misses (60-99% LS)                19 word(s)
Moderate Misses (20-59% LS)            16 word(s)
Far Misses (0-19% LS)                   1 word(s)
```

Type	Correct	Possible	Pct	Type	Correct	Possible	Pct
Sing cons	48	50	96	Final vow	3	7	42
Blend	7	10	70	Double	3	4	75
FSLZ	0	0	100	c/s	0	1	0
Single vow	21	31	67	c/ck	0	2	0
Digraph	6	8	75	-le	4	7	57
Vowel + N	6	8	75	ch/tch	2	2	100
Dual cons	13	25	52	-dge	0	1	0
Final e	1	5	20	Vowel team	4	12	33
igh/ign	0	0	100	Suffix	5	6	83
ild/old	0	0	100	tion/sion	0	1	0
a+l+cons	0	0	100	ance/ence	0	0	100
Vowel + R	9	14	64	sure/ture	0	0	100

KEY ERRORS

Dual cons	Final e	Final vow
learner-leaner	alone-alon	taste-tast
sample-samble	knife-knif	hero-hearow
chart-chard	rare-rar	lazy-lazz
mumble-mobble	cube-cub	unlucky-unluke
tractor-trater		
apart-apeot		

FIGURE 7.7. Example of skills analysis in spelling from Monitoring Basic Skills Progress. From "Effects of Expert System Advice within Curriculum-Based Measurement on Teacher-Planning and Student Achievement in Spelling" by L. S. Fuchs, D. Fuchs, C. L. Hamlett, and R. M. Allinder, 1991, *School Psychology Review*, *20*, p. 56. Copyright 1991 by the National Association of School Psychologists. Reprinted by permission.

story starter provided by the evaluator. Outcomes are scored for total words written, but can also be scored for the presence or absence of specific skills. Performance is graphed, and decision rules are applied to determine if the goals or instructional methods need to be altered.

Short-Term Monitoring

More attention in progress monitoring of written language is devoted to short-term monitoring than to many other areas. Because written language involves the integration of multiple skills, all of which are needed for producing good written products (i.e., grammar, handwriting, planning, punctuation, creativity, thought, etc.), the short-term monitoring process is usually designed to evaluate if the instructional methods are resulting in the acquisition of these skills.

Scoring of written language samples usually relies on the use of both quantitative and qualitative (subjective judgment) measurement. For example, Table 7.8 shows a list of 12 measures developed by Zipprich (1995) to score narrative written essays of children aged 9 to 12 years. She also developed a holistic scoring checklist and a scale for evaluating the student's performance for scoring these essays (see Figure 7.8). The repeated administration, along with graphing of these data, can be used to determine if specific instructional techniques developed to improve the student's skills are evident. Zipprich found that teaching webbing techniques was successful at improving over baseline the number of words for 9 of 13 students, the number of thought units for 7 students, the density factor (ideas in thought units) for 7 students, and the planning time for all students. Holistic scores for all students improved over baseline. Although beyond the study reported by Zipprich, the data from the individual students across these skills could be used to design instructional programs aimed to improve the specific skills not impacted by the webbing technique.

Graham and Harris (1989) described a similar scale to assess writing skills. In their scale, the presence or absence of eight elements of story grammar were assessed: main character, locale, time, starter event, goal, action, ending, and reaction. For each element, scores from 0 to 4 were assigned. Likewise, a holistic scale using a 1 (lowest quality) to 7 (highest quality) rating was employed. These measures were used to assess change in student writing performance over time, following a self-instruction training procedure.

SUMMARY

The final step in the assessment of academic skills involves the assessment of student progress over time. Goals are set for short- and long-term objectives, and progress toward these goals is measured. Progress monitoring in all four areas of basic skills instruction contains both long- and short-term objectives. The primary purpose of long-term monitoring is to determine the impact of the instructional process on the accomplishment of long-range curriculum goals set by the instructor. Typically, these are year-long goals.

Long-term data are always graphed. Viewed as an essential element of progress monitoring, the graphic display of the data offers continual

TABLE 7.8. Target Behaviors Used to Score Narrative Essay Exams

Behavior	Definition	Measurement
1. Planning time	Length of time, measured in minutes, a student requires to complete "My Web for Story Writing."	Teacher records minutes on blackboard.
2. Words produced	Individual words produced by a student within a story.	Evaluator count.
3. Thought unit	A group of words that cannot be further divided without the disappearance of its essential meaning.	Evaluator count.
Sentence types		
4. Fragment	An incomplete thought.	Evaluator count.
5. Simple	A sentence expressing a complete thought that contains a subject and predicate.	Evaluator count.
6. Compound	A sentence containing two or more simple sentences but no subordinate clauses.	Evaluator count.
7. Compound/ complex	A sentence containing two or more simple sentences and one or more subordinate clauses.	Evaluator count.
8. Holistic score	A quality-of-writing factor developed by this researcher.	A 14-item criteria checklist used to render a score that converts to a Likert Scale score of 1.0–3.0.
Mechanics		
9. Spelling	A subjective evaluation of overall spelling accuracy.	Scale developed by researcher.
10. Capitals	A subjective evaluation of correct use of capitalization as taught through standard English language text.	Scale developed by researcher
11. Punctuation	A subjective evaluation of correct use of punctuation as taught through standard English language text.	Scale developed by researcher.
12. Density factor	A quality factor developed by researcher to measure amount of information contained in each thought unit.	A criteria checklist used to render a score for number of ideas included in a thought unit.

Note. From "Teaching Web Making as a Guided Planning Tool to Improve Student Narrative Writing" by M. A. Zipprich, 1995, *Remedial Special Education, 16,* p. 7. Copyright 1995 by Pro-Ed, Inc. Reprinted by permission.

	Evaluator	Checker	Comparison
	Yes No	Yes No	
1. Did the student include a title?	__ __	__ __	_____
2. Did the student have a clear introduction to the story (i.e., a statement of the problem or beginning of the story line)?	__ __	__ __	_____
3. Did the student identify characters?	__ __	__ __	_____
4. Did the student state the goal of the story?	__ __	__ __	_____
5. Did the student add action to the story?	__ __	__ __	_____
6. Did the student sate an outcome?	__ __	__ __	_____
7. Did the student write more than one paragraph?	__ __	__ __	_____
8. Did each paragraph deal with only one topic?	__ __	__ __	_____
9. Are the major points in each paragraph presented in a correct sequence?	__ __	__ __	_____
10. Do the paragraphs have a beginning sentence that adequately introduces the idea discussed?	__ __	__ __	_____
11. Is each paragraph started on a new line?	__ __	__ __	_____
12. Did the student sequence the story appropriately?	__ __	__ __	_____
13. Did the student sequence the story appropriately?	__ __	__ __	_____
14. Did the student include only relevant information			
Total "YES"	__ __	__ __	_____
Conversion Score*	__ __	__ __	_____

*Holistic Score Conversion Scale:

Total =	Score =	Status
0–3	1.0	Unacceptable
4–7	1.5	Unacceptable/some improvement
8–10	2.0	Acceptable with errors/needs improvement
11–12	2.5	Acceptable with errors/showing improvement
13–14	3.0	Acceptable/meets crtieria

FIGURE 7.8. Holistic scoring device used for evaluating written language skills. From "Teaching Web Making as a Guided Planning Tool to Improve Student Narrative Writing" by M. A. Zipprich, 1995, *Remedial and Special Education, 16*, p. 8. Copyright 1995 by Pro-Ed, Inc. Reprinted by permission.

feedback to the evaluator and student about progress toward these goals. Using decision rules established before the monitoring begins, decisions to change goals or alter instructional methods are made. In most cases, however, the long-term monitoring data do not tell the evaluator about the specific skills areas needed to be targeted, nor the possible instructional techniques that may be useful to improve student performance.

To determine the specific skills that may have to be targeted for improvement, short-term progress monitoring is used. The primary objective of these data is to guide the evaluator in developing effective intervention techniques. By knowing the specific skills that a student needs to master, strategies aimed at teaching those skills can be developed.

It is critical to recognize that both types of progress monitoring are needed to provide a clear picture of a student's progress. The evaluator usually starts with long-term progress monitoring because a student maintaining performance along the designated aim line under long-term monitoring conditions suggests to the evaluator that the current instructional methods are working fine, and there is no need to change. However, when the instructional methods are no longer successful, short-term monitoring offers the evaluator a methodology for better determining the targets for intervention, as well as assisting in development of better strategies for instruction.

CHAPTER 8

♦♦♦

Case Illustrations

♦

In this chapter, a number of examples illustrating the use of the assessment procedures and some of the interventions described in the text are presented. Obviously, it would be impossible to offer examples of all of the intervention procedures described in Chapters 5 and 6. Interested readers are directed to texts by Howell et al., (1993), Sulzar-Azaroff and Mayer (1986), Rosenfield (1987), Stoner et al., (1991), and Maher and Zins (1987) for a wider variety of examples of curriculum-based assessment and behavioral interventions for academic problems.

CASE EXAMPLES FOR ACADEMIC ASSESSMENT

Two cases are presented that illustrate the use of CBA in assessing the instructional environment and instructional placement. These cases were briefly mentioned at the beginning of Chapter 1. The first case is that of Brian, a second-grade boy who was referred by his teacher because of academic problems, as well as a high degree of distractibility. An important question related to this case is the boy's eligibility for special education.

The second case, that of Maria, illustrates the evaluation of a fifth-grade girl, who had been enrolled in a self-contained classroom for students with learning disabilities and was being considered for mainstreaming. A major question of this evaluation was to assess the status of this child's academic skills in terms of the expectations of the mainstreaming environment.

Each assessment case is presented in the form of a psychological report. Completed teacher interview, observation, and assessment forms for the cases are also included, along with narrative material describing the forms.

Case 1: Brian

Name:	Brian	*Chronological age*:	9 years, 3 months
Date:	4/30/87	*Grade*:	2
Birth date:	1/27/78	*School*:	Salter
Teacher:	Mrs. Roberts		

Background Information

Brian, a second-grade student, has attended Salter Elementary School since November 13, 1986. He was retained in kindergarten and is on the list this year for possible retention.

On the referral request, the teacher reported that Brian is distracted easily and has difficulty concentrating. Mrs. Salter reports that he has great difficulty sitting still in his seat, which has resulted in his desk being removed from the area near his peers and placed adjacent to the teacher's desk. During remedial math, Brian is also removed from the rest of the students.

Assessment Methods

- ◆ Structured teacher interview
- ◆ Direct classroom observation
- ◆ Student interview
- ◆ Direct assessment of reading, mathematics, spelling, written expression, and oral expression

Assessment Results: Reading

Teacher Interview. According to his teacher (see Figure 8.1), Brian is currently placed in Level 9 (Grade 1; *Colors*) of the Macmillan-R reading series. Reading instruction is given for 90 minutes per day. During the week, he spends 5 hours in reading instruction within the regular classroom (half in small-group instruction and half in individual seatwork), and 2 ½ hours per week in remedial reading. No specific contingencies are set by the teacher for completion of work in either small-group or individual seatwork conditions. Currently, Brian is placed in the lowest of the three reading groups in the classroom.

According to his teacher, Brian's oral reading skills are about the same as those of his peers. Other skills, such as sight word recognition and comprehension, are much worse than those of others in his group. His teacher notes that he shows some sporadic efforts at word attack and can be successful when he tries. On a brief behavior rating scale, Mrs. Roberts

TEACHER INTERVIEW FORM FOR ACADEMIC PROBLEMS

Student: __Brian__   Teacher: __Mrs. Roberts__
Birthdate: __1/27/78__   Date: __4/30/87__
Grade: __2__   School: __Salter__
                                                Interviewer: __Roberta Simon__

GENERAL

Why was this student referred? __Academic difficulties and disruptiveness, repeated__
__kindergarten, on retention list for next year__

What type of academic problem(s) does this student have? _____
__Reading, math, spelling__

READING

Primary type of reading series used   Secondary type of reading materials used
  ☒ Basal reader   ☐ Basal reader
  ☐ Literature-based   ☐ Literature-based
  ☐ Trade books   ☐ Trade books
                                               ☐ None

Reading series title (if applicable) __Macmillan-R__

Grade level of series currently placed __first__

Title of book in series currently placed __Colors__

How many groups do you teach? __3__

Which group is this student assigned to? __Lowest__

At this point in the school year, where is the average student in your class reading?

   Level and book __Level 11 (2nd grade)__

   Place in book (beginning, middle, end, specific page) __Beginning__

Time allotted/day for reading __Approx. 90 minutes__

How is time divided? (Independent seatwork? Small group? Cooperative groups?)
__Mostly small group with independent reading during day__

How is placement in reading program determined? __Pick up where left off at end of__
__1st grade–reading specialist test__

How are changes made in the program? __Reading specialist tests__

Does this student participate in Chapter 1 (remedial) reading programs? How much?
__Yes, 5 days a week, approx. 1/2 hr each day__

Typical daily instructional procedures __Small-group work, independent seatwork while__
__other 2 groups meet__

Contingencies for accuracy? __None__

Contingencies for completion? __None__

Daily scores (if available) for past 2 weeks __See permanent products__

Group standardized test results (if available) __Stanford Achievement Test total reading__
__= 25th percentile nationally__

FIGURE 8.1. Completed teacher interview form in reading for Brian.

ORAL READING

How does he/she read orally compared to others in the reading group?
___ Much worse   ___ Somewhat worse   _X_ About the same
___ Somewhat better   ___ Much better

In the class?
___ Much worse   _X_ Somewhat worse   ___ About the same
___ Somewhat better   ___ Much better

WORD ATTACK

Does he/she attempt unknown words? _Yes—sporadic effort and success_

SIGHT WORDS

How is the student's sight vocabulary, compared to that of others in his/her reading group?
___ Much worse   _X_ Somewhat worse   ___ About the same
___ Somewhat better   ___ Much better

In the class?
_X_ Much worse   ___ Somewhat worse   ___ About the same
___ Somewhat better   ___ Much better

COMPREHENSION

How well does the student seem to understand what he/she reads, compared to others in his/her reading group?
_X_ Much worse   ___ Somewhat worse   ___ About the same
___ Somewhat better   ___ Much better

In the class?
_X_ Much worse   ___ Somewhat worse   ___ About the same
___ Somewhat better   ___ Much better

BEHAVIOR DURING READING

Rate the following areas from 1 to 5 (1 = very unsatisfactory, 3 = satisfactory, 5 = superior)

Reading Group

a. Oral reading ability (as evidenced in reading group)	3
b. Volunteers answers	3
c. When called upon, gives correct answer	1
d. Attends to other students when they read aloud	1
e. Knows the appropriate place in book	1

Independent Seatwork

a. Stays on task	1
b. Completes assigned work in required time	1
c. Work is accurate	1
d. Works quietly	1
e. Remains in seat when required	1

Homework (if any)

a. Handed in on time	3
b. Is complete	3
c. Is accurate	3

indicates that Brian has great difficulty staying on task, completing work on time, remaining in his seat, and attending to others in small-group activities.

Direct Observation. Data were collected during observations in the regular classroom and in the remedial reading program using the State–Event Classroom Observation System (SECOS; see Table 8.1). Observations were conducted for a total of 43 minutes in the regular classroom while Brian was engaged in independent seatwork for reading and the teacher worked with another reading group, and for 20 minutes of independent seatwork during remedial reading while the teacher circulated around the room. These particular settings were chosen for observation as the most likely to result in the levels of distractible behavior indicated by

TABLE 8.1. Direct observation data during reading from the SECOS Collected during Reading for Brian

	ISW: TSmGp (reg. class) 43 min		ISW: TPsnt (Chapter 1 class) 20 min	
	Brian	Peers	Brian	Peers
	Student behavior			
States				
SW	84	86	80	85
OS	3	0	10	5
LK	11	14	8	5
SIC	0	0	1	5
SIT	3	11	19	20
OACT	2	0	0	0
Events				
RH	0.39	0.6	0	0
CAL	0.11	0.1	0.1	0
AC	0.04	0.32	0.2	0
OAC	0.07	0.1	0.15	0.2
OS	0.04	0	0.3	0.2
	Teacher behavior			
States				
TA/SW	0.02	0	0.25	0.6
TA/OTH	0.04	0.1	0.1	0.4
APP	0.02	0.32	0.4	1.6
DIS	0.02	0	0	0

Note. ISW: TSmGp, independent seatwork, teacher working with a small group; ISW: TPsnt, independent seatwork, teacher present. Other abbreviations as in Table 3.2 (see Chapter 3).

Mrs. Roberts. Comparison data were obtained by using a randomly select-ed peer once every minute. (Data for comparison students are reported in parentheses following Brian's data.)

These observations failed to confirm the teacher's report of a highly distractible child during reading. Indeed, Brian's behavior during these observations showed that he had sustained on-task levels with minimal teacher contact.

Student Interview. Brian was interviewed after the observation was conducted and was asked questions about his assignment. Results of the interview suggested that Brian was well aware of the assignment's objec-tives. He indicated accurately that the task was related to a story he had recently read in his reading group, and that the teacher wanted to know if he remembered what he had read. Brian was confident about his ability to complete the assignment, although he reported that he really did not like reading that much. When asked to rate how much time he got to complete his assignments on a scale from 1 (not enough) to 3 (too much), Brian re-ported that the amount of time given was usually enough. He did feel that his teacher tended to call on him more than other students in class.

In general, the interview with Brian suggested that he has fairly good self-esteem related to completing reading tasks. Brian also seems to have a good understanding of the classroom expectations, knows the means to access help when its required, and is able to complete his tasks, even though he dislikes the subject matter.

Direct Assessment. Administration of oral reading probes from books at the second-grade, first-grade, and primer levels (see Figure 8.2) showed that Brian is at an instructional level within the first-grade book, where he is currently placed. Brian does appear to have good comprehension skills along with his oral reading skills at the first-grade level.

Assessment Results: Mathematics

Teacher Interview. In the teacher interview for mathematics (see Fig-ure 8.3), Mrs. Roberts indicates that Brian is placed in the second-grade book of the Addison-Wesley series. Fifty minutes per day are allotted for math. The teacher introduces the lesson in a large-group activity, and stu-dents complete independent seatwork as the teacher circulates among them. Brian also receives an additional 30 minutes of math instruction three times per week through the remedial math program. No specific contingencies are used for accuracy or completion of work.

According to his teacher, Brian does not yet have mastery of basic

Data Summary Form for Academic Assessment

Child's name: Brian   School: Salter

Teacher: Mrs. Roberts   Date: 4/30/87

Grade: 2   School District: Parkland

READING—SKILLS

Primary type of reading series used
- ☒ Basal reader
- ☐ Literature-based
- ☐ Trade books

Secondary type of reading materials used
- ☐ Basal reader
- ☐ Literature-based
- ☒ Trade books
- ☐ None

Title of curriculum series: Macmillan-R

Level/book—target student: Level 9, Grade 1, Colors

Level/book—average student: Level 11, Grade 2, Believe It

STUDENT-REPORTED BEHAVIOR _____ None completed for this area

Understands expectations of teacher	☒ Yes	☐ No	☐ Not sure
Understands assignments	☒ Yes	☐ No	☐ Not sure
Feels he/she can do the assignments	☒ Yes	☐ No	☐ Not sure
Likes the subject	☐ Yes	☒ No	☐ Not sure
Feels he/she is given enough time to complete assignments	☒ Yes	☐ No	☐ Not sure
Feels like he/she is called upon to participate in discussions	☒ Yes	☐ No	☐ Not sure

Grade level/book	Location in book	WC/ min	Errors/ min	% correct	Median scores for level WC	ER	%C	Learning level (M, I, F)
Primer:	Beginning	68	5	80	68	2	100	Mastery
You Can (Level 4)	Middle	72	2	100				
I Can Too (Level 5)	End	65	0	100				
1:	Beginning	55	2	100	50	2	100	Instructional
We Can Read (6)	Middle	49	3	100				
Ups and Downs (8)	End	50	2	40				
Being Me (10)								
2:	Beginning	33	5	20	23	5	20	Frustrational
Believe It (11)	Middle	22	8	0				
Stand Tall (13)	End	23	6	20				

FIGURE 8.2. Reading probe data for Brian. WC, words correct.

TEACHER INTERVIEW FORM FOR ACADEMIC PROBLEMS

Student: ___Brian___   Teacher: ___Mrs. Roberts___

Birthdate: ___1/27/78___   Date: ___4/30/87___

Grade: ___2___   School: ___Salter___

                                     Interviewer: ___Roberta Simon___

MATHEMATICS

Curriculum series ___Addison-Wesley___

What are the specific problems in math? ___No math facts, no regrouping skills,___ ___discouraged when he sees poor performance___

Time allotted/day for math ___Approx. 50 min___

How is time divided? (Independent seatwork? Small group? Large group? Cooperative groups?) ___Group instruction, math games, math drills, independent seatwork, with___ ___teacher supervision___

For an average performing student in your class, at what point in the planned course format would you consider this student at mastery? (See computational mastery form.) ___Finished addition and subtraction without regrouping___

For an average-performing student in your class, at what point in the planned course format would you consider this student instructional? (See computational mastery form.) ___Addition and subtraction with regrouping to 10's column___

For an average performing student in your class, at what point in the planned course format would you consider this student frustrational? (See computational mastery form.) ___Addition and subtraction with regrouping beyond the 10's column___

For the targeted student in your class, at what point in the planned course format would you consider this student at mastery? (See computational mastery form.) ___None, no math facts, way behind peers—performance recently worsened___

For the targeted student in your class, at what point in the planned course format would you consider this student instructional? (See computational mastery form.) ___Basic addition facts with sums to 10___

For the targeted student in your class, at what point in the planned course format would you consider this student frustrational? (See computational mastery form.) ___Addition with more than single digits; all subtraction facts___

How is mastery assessed? ___Chapter tests, teacher evaluations, no % criterion for success___

Describe any difficulties this student has in applying math skills? (measurement, time, money, geometry, problem solving) ___All areas___

Are your students grouped in math? ___No___

If so, how many groups do you have, and in which group is this student placed? ___Not applicable___

How are changes made in the student's math program? ___None made___

Does this student participate in Chapter 1 (remedial) math programs? ___Yes, 3 times___ ___per week, 1/2 hr each___

Typical daily instructional procedures ___See "How time is divided?"___

Contingencies for accuracy? ___None___

Contingencies for completion? ___None___

(cont.)

FIGURE 8.3. Completed teacher interview form in math for Brian.

FIGURE 8.3. *(cont.)*

Daily scores (if available) for past 2 weeks Not available

Group standardized test results (if available) 15th percentile on Stanford Achievement
 Test total math

BEHAVIOR DURING MATH

Rate the following areas from 1 to 5 (1 = very unsatisfactory, 3 = satisfactory,
5 = superior)

Math Group (large)

a. Volunteers answers	3
b. When called upon, gives correct answer	1
c. Attends to other students when they give answers	1
d. Knows the appropriate place in math book	3

Math Group (small)

a. Volunteers answers	3
b. When called upon, gives correct answer	1
c. Attends to other students when they give answers	1
d. Knows the appropriate place in math book	3

Math Group (cooperative)

a. Volunteers answers	2
b. Contributes to group objectives	2
c. Attends to other students when they give answers	1
d. Facilitates others in group to participate	2
e. Shows appropriate social skills in group	3

Independent Seatwork

a. Stays on task	1
b. Completes assigned work in required time	1
c. Work is accurate	1
d. Works from initial directions	1
e. Works quietly	1
f. Remains in seat when required	1

Homework (if any)

a. Handed in on time	3
b. Is complete	3
c. Is accurate	1

facts and therefore has been unable to acquire regrouping skills, which is
where the average student in her class is being instructed. On a brief behavior rating form, Mrs. Roberts again reports very low levels of attentive
behavior for Brian.

Direct Observation. Data were collected through direct observation
in one 15-minute, independent seatwork period in the remedial math
classroom (see Table 8.2). No time was available for observation of math

TABLE 8.2. Direct Observation Data from the SECOS
Collected during Math for Brian

	ISW: TPsnt (reg. class) 15 min	
	Brian	Peers
	Student behavior	
States		
SW	68	47
OS	2	0
LK	27	47
SIC	0	0
SIT	0	0
OACT	3	7
Events		
RH	0	0
CAL	0.13	1.06
AC	0	0.26
OAC	0	0.53
OS	0.06	0.26
	Teacher behavior	
States		
TA/SW	0.13	0.26
TA/OTH	0	0
APP	0.06	0.26
DIS	0	0

in the regular classroom setting. Peer-comparison data were again collected by random selection of peers on every fourth observation interval.

These data suggest that although Brian is somewhat more distractible during math than reading, his levels of attentive behavior are comparatively higher than those of his classmates in the remedial math program. In addition, Brian appears to be able to sustain his level of on-task behavior without extensive teacher or peer contact.

Student Interview. Brian was interviewed after the observation of his independent seatwork. Unlike reading, Brian reported less assurance of the required task. When specifically asked about the purpose of the assignment, Brian responded with a vague, "I guess the teacher wants me to learn this," rather than the specific response outlining the requirements of the reading task. Brian indicated that math was his hardest subject and that he was not very confident he could accurately complete the task. In addition, Brian told the examiner that his "mind wanders" during math and that he often just writes down numbers that might be right, without really completing the computations. When asked if he feels the teacher calls on him too often in math, Brian told the examiner that the teacher seems to call on him often, especially when he does not know the right answer. Brian also was unsure about what he should do when he had a problem he could not do, and often just sat and daydreamed when he had trouble with an assignment.

Direct Assessment. The administration of five sets of math probes (see Figure 8.4) showed that Brian has mastery of single- and double-digit addition with sums to 19, and single- and double-digit subtraction with results less than 19. He is instructional in skills requiring regrouping; he is at a frustrational level in subtraction skills involving regrouping.

Assessment Results: Spelling

Teacher Interview. Brian is currently placed in the second-grade book of the McGraw-Hill series. Fifteen minutes per day are allotted for group instruction of spelling, and no contingencies for accuracy or completion are provided. Mrs. Roberts indicates that Brian is failing all material in spelling, seldom completes his work, and is inaccurate when work is completed.

Direct Observation. A 42-minute observation of spelling/language arts (see Table 8.3) produced results similar to the observations collected during reading. Brian was engaged in schoolwork for a substantial portion of the intervals. He did not contribute to the discussion as much as his peers during the large-group instruction and was approached by the teacher about twice as often as his peers.

Student Interview. No student interview was conducted for this skill area.

Direct Assessment. According to probes given from the first- and second-grade levels of the spelling series (see Figure 8.5), Brian is at an instructional level at both the first- and second-grade levels in terms of letter sequences correct per minute. However, his median percentage of words correct was 53% at Level 1 and 35% for Level 2. These low percentages explain his teacher's evaluation of poor spelling, despite his being at the instructional level.

Data Summary Form for Academic Assessment

Child's name: ___Brian___ School: ___Salter___
Teacher: ___Mrs. Roberts___ Date: ___4/30/87___
Grade: ___2___ School District: _Parkland_

MATH—SKILLS

Curriculum series used: _Addison-Wesley_

Specific problems in math: _No math facts_

Mastery skill of target student: _None_

Mastery skill of average student: _Addition and subtraction without regrouping_

Instructional skill of target student: _Addition facts: sums less than 10_

Instructional skill of average student: _Addition and subtraction with regrouping_

Problems in math applications: _All areas_

STUDENT-REPORTED BEHAVIOR ____ None completed for this area

Understands expectations of teacher	☐ Yes	☐ No	☒ Not sure
Understands assignments	☐ Yes	☒ No	☐ Not sure
Feels he/she can do the assignments	☐ Yes	☒ No	☐ Not sure
Likes the subject	☐ Yes	☒ No	☐ Not sure
Feels he/she is given enough time to complete assignment	☐ Yes	☐ No	☒ Not sure
Feels like he/she is called upon to participate in discussions	☒ Yes	☐ No	☐ Not sure

Results of math probes:

Probe type	No.	Digits correct/ min	Digits incorrect/ min	% problems correct	Learning level (M, I, F)
3. Add two one-digit numbers: sums 11–19	1	20	10	10	Mastery
	2	13	1	12	
	3	26	1	1	
7. Subtract a one-digit number from a one- or two-digit number: combinations to 18	1	26	0	26	Mastery
8. Subtract one-digit from two-digit number-no regrouping	1	15	1	14	Instructional
	2	18	1	17	
15. Add a one-digit number to a two-digit number with regrouping	1	15	0	15	Instructional
	2	13	1	12	
25 Subtract a one-digit number from a two-digit number with regrouping	1	6	19	0	Frustrational
	2	5	17	1	

FIGURE 8.4. Math probe and interview data for Brian.

TABLE 8.3. Direct Observation Data from the SECOS Collected during Spelling for Brian

	LgGp: Tled (reg. class) 15 min	
	Brian	Peers
	Student behavior	
States		
SW	81	70
OS	0	6
LK	15	18
SIC	0	6
SIT	8	3
OACT	4	0
Events		
RH	0.2	1.7
CAL	0.02	0.24
AC	0	0.36
OAC	0	0.12
OS	0	0.24
	Teacher behavior	
States		
TA/SW	0.4	0.72
TA/OTH	0.07	0.24
APP	0.3	0.72
DIS	0.12	0.24

Assessment Results: Writing

Teacher Interview. Writing assignments are made periodically and include sentence writing. The completed interview form is not provided, because the teacher indicates that Brian had difficulties in all areas of written language, including mechanics, handwriting, grammatical usage, and spelling.

Direct Observation. There was no opportunity to observe a writing lesson.

Student Interview. No student interview was conducted for this skill area.

Direct Assessment. When story starters were administered to Brian (see Figure 8.6), his stories all fell below instructional levels for a second grader in the spring (see Table 4.6 for normative data). Examination of

Data Summary Form for Academic Assessment

Child's name: ___Brian___   School: ___Salter___

Teacher: ___Mrs. Roberts___   Date: ___4/30/87___

Grade: ___2___   School District: ___Parkland___

SPELLING

Type of material used for spelling instruction:

☒ Published spelling series
    Title of series ___Basic Goals in Spelling—McGraw-Hill___
□ Basal reading series
    Title of series _____
□ Teacher-made materials
□ Other _____

Curriculum series (if applicable) _____

STUDENT-REPORTED BEHAVIOR ✓ None completed for this area

Understands expectations of teacher	□ Yes	□ No	□ Not sure
Understands assignments	□ Yes	□ No	□ Not sure
Feels he/she can do the assignments	□ Yes	□ No	□ Not sure
Likes the subject	□ Yes	□ No	□ Not sure
Feels he/she is given enough time to complete assignment	□ Yes	□ No	□ Not sure
Feels like he/she is called upon to participate in discussions	□ Yes	□ No	□ Not sure

Results of spelling probes:

Grade level of probe	Probe #	LSC/min	% words correct	Median LSC for grade level	Level (M, I, F)
1	1	35	53	47	Instructional
	2	71	36		
	3	47	31		
2	1	35	75	41	Instructional
	2	56	28		

FIGURE 8.5. Spelling probe data for Brian.

writing samples shows mechanical and grammatical insufficiencies, poor organization in writing, and some spelling difficulties (see Figure 8.7).

One 3-minute oral expression probe was administered to determine whether the difficulties evident in the written language samples are related to problems in writing or expression of thought. Brian told a coherent story using 360 words, indicating that he is capable of organizing his thoughts and presenting a sample with a logical beginning, middle, and end.

Data Summary Form for Academic Assessment

Child's name: _Brian_   School: _Salter_

Teacher: _Mrs. Roberts_   Date: _4/30/87_

Grade: _2_   School District: _Parkland_

WRITING—SKILLS

Types of writing assignments: _Sentence writing_

Areas of difficulty:

Content

- ☐ Expressing thoughts
- ☒ Story length
- ☒ Story depth
- ☒ Creativity

Mechanics:

- ☐ Capitalization
- ☐ Punctuation
- ☒ Grammar
- ☒ Handwriting
- ☒ Spelling

STUDENT-REPORTED BEHAVIOR ✓ None completed for this area

Understands expectations of teacher	☐ Yes	☐ No	☐ Not sure
Understands assignments	☐ Yes	☐ No	☐ Not sure
Feels he/she can do the assignments	☐ Yes	☐ No	☐ Not sure
Likes the subject	☐ Yes	☐ No	☐ Not sure
Feels he/she is given enough time to complete assignment	☐ Yes	☐ No	☐ Not sure
Feels like he/she is called upon to participate in discussions	☐ Yes	☐ No	☐ Not sure

Results of written probes:

Story starter	Words written/ 3 min	Instructional level?	Comments
The thing I like most about school . . .	10	Frustrational	Poor sentence structure evident
When I grow up . . .	18	Frustrational	Excited to tell story although not legible
I am happiest . . .	12	Frustrational	

FIGURE 8.6. Data from story starter probes for Brian.

Conclusions

Brian is a second-grade student who is described as distractible by his teacher. He is reported to be having academic difficulty in all subject areas.

In reading, Brian is placed at the first-grade level, where he has been found to be at an instructional level for words correct and incorrect, and at a mastery level for comprehension. Results of the assessment indicate that

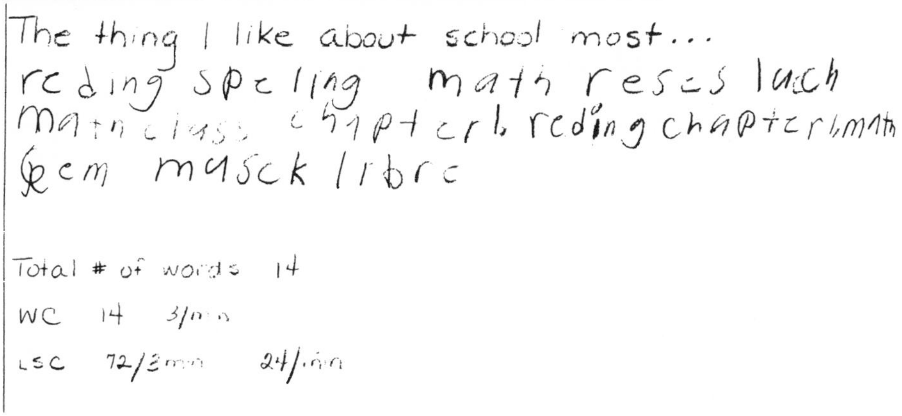

The thing I like about school most...
reding spelling math reses luch
math class chapterl. reding chapterl,math
poem musck librc

Total # of words 14

WC 14 3/min

LSC 72/3min 24/min

FIGURE 8.7. Example of story starter completed by Brian.

he is placed appropriately and that instruction should continue at this level.

In math, Brian is described by his teacher as lacking all math facts. Data collected in the direct assessment are inconsistent with this report. Brian has acquired math facts and can successfully solve numerous problems with use of his fingers. At this time, however, he has not achieved automatic recall of math facts. He has mastered computational skills up to the addition and subtraction of a two-digit number without regrouping. It is very possible that the teacher's perception of Brian's difficulties in math is related to his failure to have reached an automatic recall level with his facts. Brian needs to work on automatic recall and reduce the reliance on his fingers for computation.

The two areas in which Brian may be having the greatest difficulties are spelling and written language. Although Brian appears to have acquired some phonetic skills in learning spelling sequences, his overall poor performance on percentage of words correct is unacceptable to his teacher. Written language is at a frustration level in all skills and needs to be given significant attention.

One of the teacher's main concerns about Brian is his distractibility. Across all observations conducted in the regular classroom and remedial classroom during math, reading, and spelling, Brian's level of attentive behavior either matched or exceeded that of his peers. In addition, during lengthy periods of independent seatwork, Brian appeared to work well without teacher or peer contact. Interestingly, Brian self-reported that he often finds his mind wandering during math, a subject area in which his teacher often reported him to be especially distractible. These findings are in contrast to the teacher's stated reasons for referral.

One possible explanation for these findings is that Brian's poor written language skills result in very low levels of academic productivity. Although Brian is on-task, the quality of his work may be quite poor. Indeed, his work samples show inconsistent performance (see Figure 8.8). Clearly, whether Brian is actually distractible or not, his current level of academic performance is not acceptable to his teacher. It is suggested, however, that

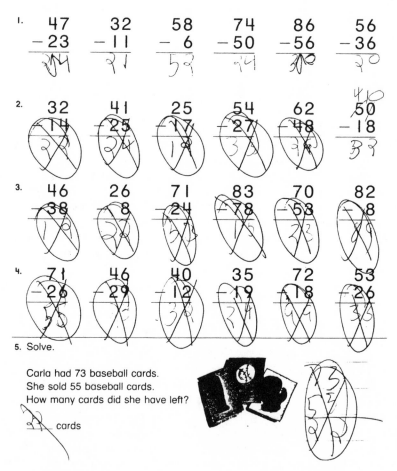

FIGURE 8.8. Example of math paper completed by Brian.

alternatives to his distractibility be considered as the potential reasons for his lack of performance.

Recommendations

1. Placement in reading at the first-grade level appears to be appropriate.

2. Continued use of the Barnell–Loft Specific Skills Series may help Brian maintain his level of comprehension. In particular, books that drill the student in locating answers, drawing conclusions, and finding the main idea should be employed.

3. Placement in the second-grade math book appears appropriate.

4. Daily timed probes and practice with both addition and subtraction math facts, combined with reinforcement for not using finger or number line prompts should be employed to improve Brian's automatic recall of math facts.

5. Placement in the second-grade spelling book appears appropriate.

6. Brian's performance in spelling may benefit from an Add-a-Word procedure. In this procedure, a list of 10 words from the spelling book is compiled using a "copy, cover, and compare" method. Words are tested daily and are dropped from the list after they have been spelled correctly for 2 consecutive days; every time a word is dropped, a new word is added. Dropped words are retested again after 5 days and at the end of 2 months.

7. Brian's level of written expression needs improvement. Writing opportunities should be increased. Instruction in using correct capitalization and punctuation should be included. Emphasis on letter and number formation in handwriting should be added to his instructional program. Use of a self-monitoring program, in which Brian writes, checks, and scores his own work, may be very useful.

8. Brian's behavior does not appear to be highly distractible. It is possible that his behavior is being effectively maintained by his removal in distance from his peers in the classroom. Perhaps Brian could have two seats in the classroom—one for instruction and one for seatwork. The instructional seat could be placed strategically to minimize interaction with other students. For seatwork, he could be placed among his peers. Through the use of a contingency contract, Brian could earn time at the table with the rest of the children. Time could be earned for being on task, remaining seated, attending to others during academic responding, and ignoring others' negative behaviors. In particular, the contract should require that Brian's independent seatwork be accurate and complete.

ROBERTA SIMON
School Psychologist

Comments about Brian's Case

This case illustrates several excellent issues related to academic assessment. The case demonstrates the first two steps of the four-step model of academic assessment: Assessing the Instructional Environment and Instructional Placement.

The child was referred by the teacher due to academic failure and distractibility. Interview data with the teacher suggested that the psychologist would find a child who was off-task, was disruptive to himself and others, and had poor academic skills in all areas. Results of the direct observations revealed the opposite about the child's behavior. He was on task, at least as much as his peers; he could work for sustained periods without teacher contact; and his on-task behavior was evident across situations. It was interesting that Brian himself reported that he sometimes finds himself to be more distracted in some subjects, especially math. The major question raised by the psychologist was why the child was seen as distractible by the teacher.

Several hypotheses were formulated to answer this question. One was related to the child's poor written language skills. It was suggested that Brian's poor handwriting, mechanics, and spelling on written assignments often resulted in inaccurate work. As such, the academic products seen by the teacher following independent seatwork showed poor performance. Given an apparent problem with bothering others in the past (his desk had been moved to isolate him from the others), the teacher may have attributed the poor academic performance to distractibility when it never really occurred.

Another hypothesis was that the current intervention, removing his desk, was effective at controlling the distractibility problem. However, this should not be a permanent solution. Because the intervention apparently resulted in some significant changes in behavior, an excellent suggestion made by the psychologist was to use Brian's high levels of on-task behavior to earn reentry to a regular seat in the classroom among his peers.

Regarding academic skills, results of the administration of skill probes showed that Brian was being instructed at the level he should have been in all skills areas. Some additional time, however, needs to be devoted to written language. In terms of deciding whether he had a learning disability, additional testing to meet state guidelines (usually administration of an individual intelligence test and possibly a test of visual–motor integration) would be necessary. As it turned out, Brian was tested and found not to be eligible for classes for the learning disabled.

Case 2: Maria

Name:	Maria	*Chronological age*:	10 years, 5 months
Date:	4/15/87	*Grade*:	5
Birth date:	12/12/76	*School*:	Carnell
Teacher:	Mrs. Sklar		

Background Information

Maria is in the fifth-grade class at Carnell Elementary School. She has been in a self-contained classroom for students with learning disabilities since the beginning of second grade and is currently being considered for mainstreaming. The purpose of this evaluation is to determine Maria's strengths and weaknesses and to make recommendations for appropriate objectives and goals.

Assessment Methods

- ◆ Review of records
- ◆ Teacher interview
- ◆ Student interview
- ◆ Direct classroom observation
- ◆ Direct assessment of reading, math, spelling, and writing

Assessment Results: Reading

Teacher Interview. The reading portion of the completed teacher interview (see Figure 8.9) shows that Maria is currently placed in the Houghton Mifflin series, level 4-1. Although about 1 year behind other fifth-grade students, she is 1 year ahead of the average student in her current classroom. Mrs. Sklar has the 15 students in the class divided into five reading groups, with Maria being in the next to the highest. Two hours are allotted daily for language arts, which include reading, spelling, and sometimes writing. No group contingencies are employed for accuracy or completion; however, each student has specific individual goals that earn free time when met. In-class work not completed is assigned as homework. The teacher-completed brief rating form indicates Maria to be satisfactory or above in all work-related academic behaviors.

Direct Observation. Reading was observed for 15 minutes during a period of independent seatwork while the teacher circulated around the room and for 10 minutes during a small- group, teacher-led activity (see Table 8.4) using the B.O.S.S. Data were also collected on randomly selected peers who were observed simultaneously with Maria. During these observations, Maria had levels of overall on-task behavior equal to those of her peers. However, whereas her peers tended to have higher levels of active engaged time, Maria spent the largest portion of her time in passive engagement. When Maria was off-task, she tended to be off-task in mostly a passive, inattentive way.

Student Interview. Maria was interviewed following the direct observation. She reported accurately the purpose of the assignment, as well as

TEACHER INTERVIEW FORM FOR ACADEMIC PROBLEMS

Student: __Maria__   Teacher: __Mrs. Sklar__
Birthdate: __12/12/76__   Date: __4/15/87__
Grade: __5__   School: __Carnell__
                                             Interviewer: __Greg Astor__

GENERAL

Why was this student referred? __Considered for mainstreaming__

What type of academic problem(s) does this student have? __Language problems__

READING

Primary type of reading series used
  ☒ Basal reader
  ☐ Literature-based
  ☐ Trade books

Secondary type of reading materials used
  ☐ Basal reader
  ☒ Literature-based
  ☐ Trade books
  ☐ None

Reading series title (if applicable) __Houghton Mifflin__

Grade level of series currently placed __4-1__

Title of book in series currently placed __Gateways__

How many groups do you teach? __5__

Which group is this student assigned to? __Next to highest__

At this point in the school year, where is the average student in your class reading?

  Level and book __3-2, Weavers__

  Place in book (beginning, middle, end, specific page) __Beginning__

Time allotted/day for reading __120 min__

How is time divided? (Independent seatwork? Small group? Cooperative groups?)
__Small group with teacher and independent seatwork__

How is placement in reading program determined? __Previous records, end-of-book tests__

How are changes made in the program? __Teacher observations or testing__

Does this student participate in Chapter 1 (remedial) reading programs? How much?
__No__

Typical daily instructional procedures __Work with teacher in small group, check independent seatwork, silent reading__

Contingencies for accuracy? __Individual goals__

Contingencies for completion? __None__

Daily scores (if available) for past 2 weeks __Not available__

Group standardized test results (if available) __Not available__

FIGURE 8.9. Completed teacher interview form in reading for Maria.

ORAL READING

How does he/sheshe read orally compared to others in the reading group?
___ Much worse   ___ Somewhat worse   _X_ About the same
___ Somewhat better   ___ Much better

In the class?
___ Much worse   ___ Somewhat worse   _X_ About the same
___ Somewhat better   ___ Much better

WORD ATTACK

Does he/she attempt unknown words? _Syllabification and common words_

SIGHT WORDS

How is the student's sight vocabulary, compared to others in his/her reading group?
___ Much worse   ___ Somewhat worse   ___ About the same
_X_ Somewhat better   ___ Much better

In the class?
___ Much worse   ___ Somewhat worse   ___ About the same
_X_ Somewhat better   ___ Much better

COMPREHENSION

How well does the student seem to understand what he/she reads, compared to others in his/her reading group?
___ Much worse   ___ Somewhat worse   ___ About the same
_X_ Somewhat better   ___ Much better

In the class?
___ Much worse   ___ Somewhat worse   _X_ About the same
___ Somewhat better   ___ Much better

BEHAVIOR DURING READING

Rate the following areas from 1 to 5 (1 = very unsatisfactory, 3 = satisfactory, 5 = superior)

Reading Group

a. Oral reading ability (as evidenced in reading group)   _3_
b. Volunteers answers   _5_
c. When called upon, gives correct answer   _4_
d. Attends to other students when they read aloud   _5_
e. Knows the appropriate place in book   _5_

Independent Seatwork

a. Stays on task   _5_
b. Completes assigned work in required time   _5_
c. Work is accurate   _4_
d. Works quietly   _4_
e. Remains in seat when required   _5_

Homework (if any)

a. Handed in on time   _5_
b. Is complete   _5_
c. Is accurate   _4_

TABLE 8.4. Direct Observation Data from the B.O.S.S.
Collected during Reading for Maria.

| | ISW: TPsnt 15 min | |
	Maria	Peers
Behaviors		
AET	22%	41%
PET	53%	37%
TOTAL OT	75%	78%
OFT-V	0%	3%
OFT-M	3%	5%
OFT-P	18%	5%

the overall objective of the reading activity. When asked whether she thought that she could do the assigned work, Maria reported that she always thinks she can do the task, even when she knows that it might be too difficult. Maria did indicate she knows how to find help if a problem arises. In regard to being called on by the teacher, Maria thought that the she was being called on about the right amount of time. She did report that often she feels rushed to complete her assignments and, unfortunately, has to take a lot of her work home because it was not completed during the time allotted in class.

Direct Assessment. The administration of oral reading probes at levels 3-2, 4-1, and 4-2 (see Figure 8.10) showed that Maria is functioning at an instructional level in the book where she is currently being taught (book 4-1), and appears to be at a frustrational level in book 4-2. Although instructional in book 4-1 in which she achieved a median oral reading rate of 75 words correct per minute and 100% comprehension she did make a few too many errors in oral reading. Errors made reflect a lack of word attack skills, frequently looking at the first letter of a word and guessing, omitting suffixes, and occasionally substituting and adding words. Interestingly, words mispronounced during reading were pronounced correctly when used in answers to comprehension questions. Maria does appear to be accurately placed in her reading series.

Assessment Results: Mathematics

Teacher Interview. Maria is currently placed in the fifth-grade book of the Heath math series. Mrs. Sklar indicates no concern for Maria's math ability, indicating that she is on grade level in all skills. No behavioral difficulties related to performing math tasks are indicated. Instruction in math is given for 40—45 minutes per day, with time divided into indepen-

Data Summary Form for Academic Assessment

Child's name: Maria   School: Carnell
Teacher: Mrs. Sklar   Date: 4/15/87
Grade: 5   School District: Orefield

READING—SKILLS

Primary type of reading series used
   ☒ Basal reader
   ☐ Literature-based
   ☐ Trade books

Secondary type of reading materials used
   ☐ Basal reader
   ☒ Literature-based
   ☒ Trade books
   ☐ None

Title of curriculum series: Houghton Mifflin

Level/book—target student: 4-1, Gateways

Level/book—average student: 3-2, Weavers

STUDENT-REPORTED BEHAVIOR   _____ None completed for this area

Understands expectations of teacher	☒ Yes	☐ No	☐ Not sure
Understands assignments	☒ Yes	☐ No	☐ Not sure
Feels he/she can do the assignments	☒ Yes	☐ No	☐ Not sure
Likes the subject	☒ Yes	☐ No	☐ Not sure
Feels he/she is given enough time to complete assignment	☐ Yes	☒ No	☐ Not sure
Feels like he/she is called upon to participate in discussions	☒ Yes	☐ No	☐ Not sure

Results of reading probes:

Grade level/book	Location in book	WC/ min	Errors/ min	% correct	Median scores for level WC	ER	%C	Learning level (M, I, F)
4-1, *Gateways*	Beginning	91	6		75	6	100	Instructional
	Middle	75	10	100				
	End	64	5					
4-2, *Banners*	Beginning	48	8	80	48	8	80	Frustrational
	Middle	53	8					
	End	34	4					
3-2, *Weavers*	Beginning	98	2		101	2	100	Mastery
	Middle	102	4					
	End	101	2	100				

FIGURE 8.10. Reading probe data for Maria.

dent seatwork, small-group, and infrequent large-group instruction. Similar contingencies to reading are set in math, with students having individual goals for performance.

Direct Observation. Data for the 10 minutes of independent seatwork in math observed (see Table 8.5), show that Maria remained on task for 75% (peers, 62%) of the observed intervals, with the majority of nonengaged time involving off-task passive behavior 18% (peers, 8%). Consistent with data collected in reading, Maria is a well-behaved student with high rates of passive engagement that reflect a student who appears to be working well on assigned tasks.

Student Interview. Maria's report in math was similar to that in reading. She seemed to have a good idea of the requirements of the task and the expectations of the teacher. In addition, Maria felt confident in her abilities to be successful on the task. Unlike reading, Maria felt that the teacher called on her too often in math.

Direct Assessment. Four different sets of math probes were given to confirm the teacher report (see Figure 8.11). Maria was tested on multiplication and division involving regrouping and remainders. These objectives represented objectives 41, 44, 46, and 49 on the computational mastery form shown in Appendix 3B.

Data from the math probes showed that Maria is at an instructional level on all objectives except multiplying three-digit numbers with regrouping. Here she had a very high error rate. Examination of the probes shows that she made a number of careless positioning errors. During the assessment, Maria commented that she finds math pretty easy and that it is her best subject.

TABLE 8.5. Direct Observation Data from the B.O.S.S. Collected during Math for Maria

	ISW: TPsnt 10 min	
	Maria	Peers
Behaviors		
AET	14%	39%
PET	61%	23%
TOTAL OT	75%	62%
OFT-V	0%	0%
OFT-M	6%	12%
OFT-P	18%	9%

Data Summary Form for Academic Assessment

Child's name: Maria   School: Carnell

Teacher: Mrs. Sklar   Date: 4/15/87

Grade: 5   School District: Orefield

MATH—SKILLS

Curriculum series used: Heath

Specific problems in math: None

Mastery skill of target student: Division

Mastery skill of average student: Multiplication

Instructional skill of target student: N/A

Instructional skill of average student: Division

Problems in math applications: None

STUDENT-REPORTED BEHAVIOR ____ None completed for this area

Understands expectations of teacher	☒ Yes	☐ No	☐ Not sure
Understands assignments	☒ Yes	☐ No	☐ Not sure
Feels he/she can do the assignments	☒ Yes	☐ No	☐ Not sure
Likes the subject	☐ Yes	☐ No	☒ Not sure
Feels he/she is given enough time to complete assignment	☒ Yes	☐ No	☐ Not sure
Feels like he/she is called upon to participate in discussions	☒ Yes	☐ No	☐ Not sure

Results from math probes:

Probe type	No.	Digits correct/ min	Digits incorrect/ min	% problems correct	Learning level (M, I, F)
4. Multiplying a three digit number by a one-digit number with regrouping	1	28	0	9	Instructional
	2	32	0	11	
44. Divide a two-digit number by a one-digit number with remainder	1	39	0	13	Instructional
	2	44	0	14	
46. Divide a four-digit number by a one-digit number with remainder	1	31	0	10	Instructional
	2	34	0	12	
49. Multiply a three-digit number by a three-digit number with regrouping	1	30	10	6	Frustrational
	2	25	12	4	

FIGURE 8.11. Probe data for math for Maria.

Assessment Results: Spelling

Teacher Interview. Maria is currently placed in the fifth-grade book of Economy, *Keys to Spelling Mastery*. The teacher reports Maria to be halfway through the book and doing well on her spelling tests. Mrs. Sklar does indicate that Maria appears to have difficulty learning the endings of words, which obviously hinders her mastery of spelling. She also states that Maria has some trouble remembering spelling rules. Although Maria usually does well on tests, Mrs. Sklar notes that she appears to have a retention problem.

Direct Observation. Maria was observed for 15 minutes during an independent seatwork task. During this observation, she was on task only 63% (peers, 67%) of the observed intervals (active engagement 21%; passive engagement 42%). Most of her off-task behavior was spent as passive off-task, 23% (peers, 25%). Although these levels of on- and off-task behavior appear low, the peer comparison data showed that her levels were comparable to those of her peers.

Student Interview. Maria recognized that spelling was an area of great frustration for her. She reported consistently that she is unable to accurately spell words when she writes stories, as well as on weekly spelling tests. When assignments are given, Maria reported that she understands their purpose ("to learn how to spell"), but she fails to see the specific objective of the work. Often, Maria reported that she is unsure of her likely success in completing an assignment.

Direct Assessment. Word lists from the fifth- and sixth- grade books were administered to Maria. For both books, Maria had a low percentage of words correct (44–50% for fifth grade, 17–31% for sixth grade), but scored at an instructional level on the fifth-grade list and a frustrational level on the sixth-grade list in terms of letters in correct sequence per minute. These results suggest appropriate placement of Maria in the spelling series; however, the low percentage of words spelled correctly and high scores on in-class spelling tests confirm the teacher- reported problem of word retention.

Assessment Results: Writing

Teacher Interview. According to the teacher, writing assignments are given infrequently. When assigned, they involve short stories and creative writing. No specific instructional strategies are employed for teaching writing skills. All papers written must be legible or they are returned to be redone.

Data Summary Form for Academic Assessment

Child's name: <u>Maria</u>   School: <u>Carnell</u>

Teacher: <u>Mrs. Sklar</u>   Date: <u>4/15/87</u>

Grade: <u>5</u>   School District: <u>Orefield</u>

WRITING—SKILLS

Types of writing assignments: <u>Short stories, creative writing</u>

Areas of difficulty:

Content	Mechanics:
☐ Expressing thoughts	☒ Capitalization
☒ Story length	☒ Punctuation
☒ Story depth	☒ Grammar
☐ Creativity	☐ Handwriting
	☒ Spelling

Story starter	Words written/ 3 min	Instructional level?	Comments
My favorite vacation . . .	41	Below	Poor grammar, poor mechanics
The worst time I ever had was . . .	36	Below	Poor sequence of action

FIGURE 8.12. Data from story starter probes for Maria.

Mrs. Sklar stated that Maria has writing problems in the areas of expression, mechanics, grammar, and spelling. Maria confuses verb tenses, mixes singulars and plurals, and has punctuation problems. She also writes base words without appropriate endings.

Direct Assessment. Three story starters were administered (see Figure 8.12). All three resulted in scores below criteria for her grade on words correct per 3 minutes, placing her at a frustrational level in written language. Errors in spelling, capitalization, punctuation, and grammar were present. Also, the stories were very short, given the 3 minutes of time allowed. Maria was very quick to begin writing, taking only 5 seconds of her allowed minute to think of a story. Her handwriting was found to be excellent.

Conclusions

Maria appears to be placed appropriately in the areas of reading, math, and spelling. In reading, Maria shows good comprehension, as well as enthusiasm and motivation for reading. Math skills are excellent, aside from some careless errors. She is at an instructional level in long division and three-digit multiplication, both of which are fifth-grade skills.

Spelling appears to be somewhat of a problem. Although Maria seems to be accurately placed and doing well when memorizing spelling words for tests, she fails to apply these skills effectively when writing. Many of her spelling errors involve letter omissions (particularly word endings), substitutions, and reversals. She also appears to have poor knowledge of spelling rules.

Written language appears to be a big problem for Maria, given her poor spelling skills. Although her handwriting is excellent, she makes frequent errors in punctuation, capitalization, and grammar. She is slow to express her thoughts on paper; this is evident in her slow writing rate.

Recommendations

1. More practice in reading skills may be useful in enhancing Maria's reading performance. Peer tutoring, involving a classmate who reads at a higher level, may be an effective alternative. Listing the mispronounced words and practicing these in isolation may then enhance Maria's reading skills further.

2. Maria needs to be taught spelling rules rather than memorization of words. In addition, spelling drills that incorporate previously learned words should be added to the weekly spelling instruction. A procedure that may facilitate this is the Add-a-Word procedure.* Lists of words may be derived from those most frequently misspelled on writing assignments or mispronounced during oral reading, in addition to those in the spelling curriculum.

3. More opportunities to practice written expression are needed. Concentration should be on speed of expression, mechanics, grammar, and spelling. Evaluative teacher feedback, plus increased practice in proofreading and in specific problem areas, may increase accuracy in writing. In addition, teaching organization of stories prior to instruction may be useful.

4. Maria appears to be ready for full mainstreaming. Her reading skills, although behind expected levels for her grade, are at a level where she should be able to succeed, perhaps in the lowest reading group of her grade. Additional support through peer tutoring, direct instruction, and practice will be needed to maintain skill levels in reading. In math, Maria should have no difficulties in the mainstreamed classroom; her skills appear to be at a fifth-grade level. The greatest problem will occur in written language. Special efforts will be needed to have Maria practice written expression outside of regular classroom assignments. This may be an excellent opportunity to have her parents provide daily practice and feedback on writing skills. Emphasis should be placed on mechanics as well as thought production.

GREG ASTOR
School Psychologist

*See recommendations for Brian, above.

Comments on Maria's Case

This case represents an example of how CBA can provide an empirical method for determining where a student stands in relationship to regular education peers. In this case, Maria had been in a self-contained class-room for children with learning disabilities. It sounds as if she could have been mainstreamed earlier than this for math; it appears that she would have no difficulty in this area given her skills. In reading, she would need to be monitored closely.

One clear point from this case was the obvious area in which she would encounter trouble. From the evaluation, Maria would need to have additional support in the area of written language. She would be likely to experience significant difficulties in regular classrooms, and preparations to provide this support could be made.

This case also illustrates the use of data to confirm the teacher re-port. In Maria's case, all data obtained through teacher interview were confirmed through the evaluation. Direct observation suggested that she had attention levels equivalent to peers, that she could sustain attention with minimal teacher contact, and that she would do well behaviorally within the mainstream setting. Again, these data offered empirical support to making a critical decision in the educational life of Maria.

CASE EXAMPLES FOR ACADEMIC INTERVENTIONS

The next two cases are designed to illustrate the last two steps of the four-step assessment process: Instructional Modification and Progress Monitor-ing. It would be impossible to provide case illustrations for even a small portion of the many academic interventions covered in Chapters 5 and 6. Readers are encouraged to examine the publications cited in those chap-ters for specific examples of the procedures of interest. Two types of inter-vention cases were chosen for presentation here. One illustrates how CBA can be employed as a monitoring device for a child in a special education resource room to assess the effectiveness of different intervention strate-gies. The other case provides a demonstration of the effectiveness of the skip-and-drill reading procedure applied to a child not found eligible for special education. For the first case, an example of the type of data col-lected for long-term and short-term progress monitoring is provided.

Case 1: Josh

Name:	Josh	*Chronological age*:	11 years, 1 month
Date:	5/12/87	*Grade*:	4
Birth date:	3/6/76	*School*:	Rogers
Teacher:	Mr. Zack		

Background Information

Josh was referred for evaluation as part of a biannual assessment of progress. He has been in the special education resource room for children with learning disabilities since October 1985. At the time of the referral, he attended the resource room for 1 hour per day, where he received instruction in reading. His resource room teacher, Mrs. Roust, reported that he was making excellent progress in his reading skills and that Josh should be considered for mainstreaming for reading into the regular classroom beginning the following fall.

Procedure for Monitoring Progress

At the beginning of the school year, a CBA was administered to determine a baseline rate of Josh's oral reading rates. After it was determined that instruction should begin at the 3-1 level of the Ginn series (about 1 year behind his peers), baseline probes were selected from the 3-1 and 3-2 levels of the reading series, because his teacher indicated that she was setting a goal to move Josh through both the 3-1 and 3-2 books that year. Baseline probes were constructed by having Josh read a 150-word passage taken from the middle of the 3-1 and 3-2 books each day for 5 days. Across these days, Josh's mean reading rate was 55 words correct per minute in the 3-1 text and 38 words correct per minute in the 3-2 text. These data, along with data collected throughout the year, are displayed in Figure 8.13.

Two goals were set for Josh. First, a long-term monitoring goal were obtained by collecting normative data on Josh's fourth-grade classmates. These data showed that the median oral reading rates at the same levels of the text were at 103 words correct per minute. A goal of having Josh read 100 words correct per minute by the end of May was set. The second goal, for short-term monitoring, was to have Josh master the content of both the 3-1 and 3-2 books during the year. This represented mastery of 460 pages of material across the two books. When this figure was divided by 180 school days per year, a goal was set for Josh to master approximately 2.5 pages per day. Mastery was assessed by assigning Josh sets of comprehension questions that were to be answered after reading the passages. In addition, end-of-level tests were administered. Josh needed to score at least 85% or better on both measures for material to be considered mastered.

Figure 8.13 shows the data for Josh's progress toward his oral reading rate goal. The dashed line represents his aim line, or the slope of progress necessary to meet the stated goal of 100 words correct per minute by the end of May. The solid line shows Josh's long-range goal across all interventions during the entire year. Figure 8.14 shows Josh's progress toward his pages-mastered goal across the first 15 weeks of the year. Again, the

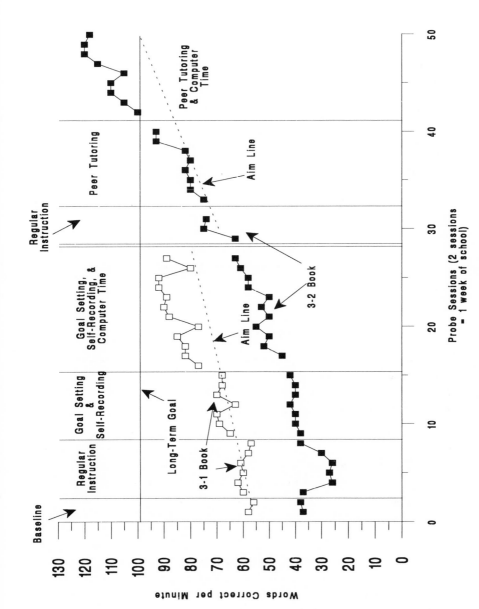

FIGURE 8.13. Progress monitoring chart (words per minute) for Josh in reading.

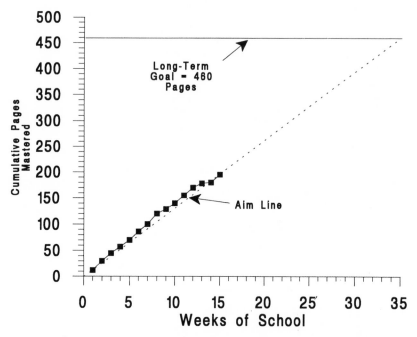

FIGURE 8.14. Progress monitoring chart (cumulative pages mastered) for Josh in reading.

dashed line shows his expected rate of progress if he met his goal; the solid line shows his long-range goal.

Results of Progress Monitoring and Interventions

During the first 3 weeks of school, no special instruction was employed for reading other than what Josh received through the resource room. Data were collected on reading probes twice a week, in the same way as during baseline. Little progress was made in reading rate on either the 3-1 or 3-2 texts during this period. After consultation with the teacher, it was decided to implement a weekly goal-setting strategy along with a self-recording procedure.

Each Monday, the teacher and Josh met to discuss the weekly goal. Goals were established so that Josh would increase his correct oral reading rate each week by at least five words correct per minute. His weekly goal for pages mastered remained at 12 pages per week. After each probe was administered, Josh plotted his score on a graph that he and his teacher had developed.

This intervention resulted in greater progress. During the 4 weeks this program was in place, Josh's oral reading rate increased to about 70 words correct per minute on the 3-1 text. In addition, some increases were shown on the 3-2 text, to about 40 words correct per minute.

It was then decided to add a backup reward to the program. If Josh met his weekly goal, he was given 15 minutes of additional computer time. In an initial interview with Josh's teacher, it was determined that Josh found the computer extremely reinforcing and would probably work harder to earn additional computer time beyond that which he already was given. Furthermore, because Josh's teacher felt that it might be unfair to other students if only Josh received the opportunity to earn extra computer time, two students were randomly selected from the class each week to share the reward with Josh, should he earn the extra time.

Not unexpectedly, the addition of the computer time contingency enhanced Josh's oral reading rate even further. By the end of the 6 weeks of this intervention, Josh was reading at about 90 words correct per minute at level 3-1 and had increased his correct reading rate at level 3-2 to about 60 words per minute. In addition, Josh had completed the 3-1 book and was about to begin book 3-2.

The same set of interventions—weekly goal setting, self-recording, and earning additional computer time—was used for 2 weeks in the new book. Josh maintained his reading level at about 70 words correct per minute. The teacher decided to switch to a peer-tutoring intervention with the entire class, using the procedures described in Chapter 5. Josh's performance showed significant acceleration using this procedure. After 5 weeks of peer tutoring, Josh's correct reading rate in the 3-2 book was again at about 80 words correct per minute. Finally, the teacher added extra computer time to the peer-tutoring procedure, and Josh began to read at between 100—120 words correct per minute, exceeding his long-term goal.

Figure 8.14 shows Josh's progress in pages mastered across the first half of the year. His progress was steady and showed continual meeting of his weekly page goals.

Conclusions and Comments about Josh's Case

As one can see from the case of Josh, a number of different interventions were attempted. These included goal setting with self-recording; a combination of goal setting, self-recording, plus a powerful reward for meeting goals; peer tutoring without rewards; and peer tutoring with rewards. The particular strategies chosen were based on consultation with the teacher and knowledge of specific interventions that would be powerful for Josh.

It is entirely possible that the same set of interventions would have been ineffective for another student. What is critical is that the interventions employed for Josh's problems in reading were evaluated through ongoing progress monitoring. As a result, the success of these particular interventions are well documented.

Case 2: Marla

Name: Marla   *Chronological age*: 9 years, 9 months
Date: 1/7/87   *Grade*:   3
Birth date: 10/1/77   *School*:   Riverview
Teacher: Mrs. Richards

Background Information

Marla was referred for evaluation because of failure to make adequate progress in reading and math. Results of the evaluation revealed that although Marla was about a half to a full year behind in all academic subjects, she did not qualify for placement into a special education classroom. The team recommended that the psychologist and educational consultant work together to formulate interventions that might improve her academic progress in reading and math. After consultation, direct observation, and CBA of Marla's reading and math skills, it was determined that Marla be placed in the basal reading series at a frustrational level and that one part of the intervention would be to instruct her at a lower level of the reading series. In math, it was shown that Marla had not mastered basic addition and subtraction facts, which resulted in failure at third-grade level skills. Drill and practice interventions using reinforcement contingencies were designed for this area.

Interventions for Reading

When Marla was assessed in reading, it was found that she was currently placed in the 3-1 level of the reading series. Based on the assessment, however, she was instructional at the 2-2 level and at a frustration level in the 3-1 book. Discussions with Marla's teacher suggested that it would not be practical to move Marla to the 2-2 book, as she would then constitute a single-child reading group. As an alternative, it was suggested that Marla continue to attend the small reading group where the 3-1 book was being employed. During the 30–45 minutes of daily individual seatwork, however, Marla was to complete the workbook exercises from the 2-2 book. Additionally, she would spend 15 minutes each day in reading practice from the 2-2 book with a peer from the high reading group and/or the teacher.

The teacher agreed to these changes but was concerned that Marla would still be significantly behind the other students. In conjunction with these changes, a skip-and-drill procedure was implemented. The entire 2-2 book was divided into 10 sections, each with about 20 pages. After baseline data were obtained across a 5-day period, desired performance to meet the skip contingency was defined as improvement of at least 25%. For Marla, this meant that she had to demonstrate correct oral reading rates of 75 words per minute with less than four errors, and at least 80% correct on the comprehension questions. Levels of desired performance increased until she reached levels equivalent to her classmates of 98 words correct per minute with less than four errors, and 90% correct on the comprehension questions.

When the skip-and-drill intervention was implemented, Marla would be asked to read the assigned passage and answer the comprehension questions. The rates of correct and incorrect oral reading were kept by the teacher. If she met the criterion for skipping, Marla was permitted to by-pass the remainder of the section and move directly to the next part of the text. If she failed to meet the criterion for skipping, three different types of drill procedures were employed. For correct reading rate, Marla was required to read the last 100 words of the passage from the assignment. She continued to read until she could complete it at the criterion level.

For incorrect reading rate, a list of misread words was completed. These words were embedded in phrases from the reader and Marla was required to rehearse the list of phrases until she could read all of them correctly.

Finally, for comprehension drill, Marla's answer sheet was returned to her with the incorrect responses checked. She was then required to re-work the answers until they were correct.

The drill procedure was instituted if Marla went 5 days without skipping any passages. Once drill was implemented, another 5 days had to pass before drill was again instituted. If Marla did not meet the criterion for skipping, but drill was not required, she simply continued to read the next section of the book without any additional drill.

Figure 8.15 shows the results of this intervention for Marla's reading. Each week, Marla was assessed using a curriculum-based probe taken from her current reading book. The probe was selected from material that she had not yet been required to read. The procedure shows significant improvements in her correct and incorrect reading rates as soon as the program was begun. In fact, Marla only had to go through the drill procedure once throughout the entire 20 days that the intervention was employed. Furthermore, at the end of the intervention, Marla was placed in the 4-1 book, reintegrated fully with her reading group, and the skip-and-drill technique was no longer employed.

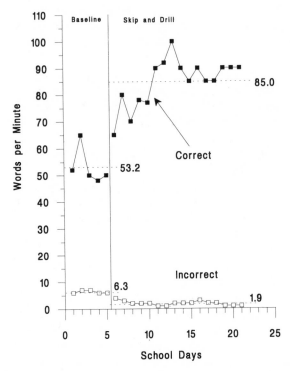

FIGURE 8.15. Results of skip-and-drill procedure in reading for Marla.

Math Intervention

After consultation with the teacher, it was decided to use a drill and self-monitoring procedure for math. Each day, Marla and her teacher decided on a goal for performance. A new set of problems was then generated by means of the Milliken Math Sequences Computer Program. After Marla was taught how to generate the math problems via computer, she was told to time herself for 2 minutes. Marla was then taught how to score her own math, using digits correct per minute as the measure. Results of her performance were then charted by Marla and shown to the teacher upon request.

Results of this intervention, following baseline on sets of addition and subtraction problems, are shown in Figure 8.16. This intervention alone did not result in substantial improvement in Marla's skills. After consultation with the teacher, it was decided to add a peer-tutoring component to the program. Although some progress was made with this, the teacher felt an additional intervention was necessary. The teacher then added backup rewards contingent upon meeting the daily goals. These rewards were chosen by Marla prior to her actual performance on the task. Again, little progress was made.

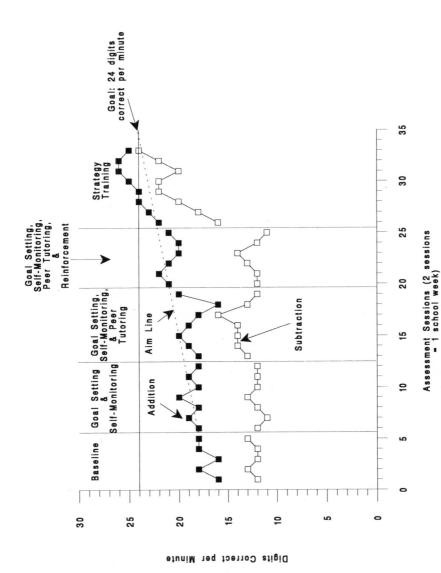

FIGURE 8.16. Progress monitoring in math (digits correct) for Marla.

At this point, the teacher decided to use strategy training as described in Chapters 5 and 6. After the addition and subtraction of single-digit and double-digit numbers without regrouping were task analyzed, strategies for solving these problems were derived. Marla was taught via a self-instruction format how to solve these problems, initially with number lines. Assessment was always conducted, however, without access to the number line. As noted in Figure 8.16, the use of strategy training significantly improved Marla's skills in addition and subtraction.

Conclusions and Comments about Marla's Case

This case shows how a specific intervention can be employed effectively for a student within a regular classroom setting. The case illustrates the problems typically encountered by many classroom consultants when ideal recommendations (i.e., placing the student into a lower level reading book) cannot be accomplished in practice. The alternatives to such recommendations that were employed in the present case, however, offer effective options for this type of problem. Also shown in the case is how a procedure such as skip-and-drill can be employed to move a student quickly through material that has been previously covered but not effectively mastered.

In math, the case illustrates how a number of procedures expected to be effective may not be. One may wonder why Marla's teacher did not move immediately to strategy training when goal setting and self-monitoring were not successful. Furthermore, one may question the consultant's judgment in not recommending strategy training as an initial step in the intervention sequence. Actually, there was no evidence from the assessment that Marla had a skills problem. The difficulty appeared to be primarily a rate problem, for which a practice-and-drill strategy alone should have been effective. In the ongoing collection of assessment data, however, the failure of these procedures to improve Marla's performance became evident.

A CASE EXAMPLE OF THE FOUR-STEP MODEL OF DIRECT ACADEMIC ASSESSMENT

The final case presented here illustrates how all four steps of the model described in this text translate into practice. Although assessment data were collected for the student across academic areas, only the data and intervention technique for reading are presented. During the instructional modification phase, the folding-in procedure, discussed in Chapter 6, for the remediation of problems in reading fluency is presented. Readers interested in an example of the four-step assessment model applied to problems in math computation is provided by Shapiro and Ager (1992).

Case: Shawn*

Name:	Shawn	*Chronological age*:	8 years, 1 month
Date:	4/3/94	*Grade*:	2
Birth date:	3/1/87	*School*:	Kennedy
Teacher:	Mrs. Kregel		

Background Information

Shawn was referred due to his poor reading abilities, as well as other academic skills problems. At the time of referral, his teachers reported that he

TABLE 8.6. Direct Observation Data from the SECOS Collected during Reading for Shawn

	Silent reading 20 min		Oral reading/ teacher-directed instruction 40 min
	Shawn	Peers	Shawn
	Student behavior		
States			
SW	44%	56%	56%
OS	0%	0%	0%
LK	30%	25%	24%
SIC	0%	0%	2%
SIT	31%	13%	14%
OACT	3%	6%	4%
Events			
RH	1 (8 min)	0	1 (20 min)
CAL	0	1 (4 min)	1 (20 min)
AC	0	1 (4 min)	1 (13 min)
OAC	1 (8 min)	0	1 (10 min)
OS	0	0	1 (40 min)
	Teacher behavior		
States			
TA/SW	1 (2 min)	1 (2 min)	1 (5 min)
TA/OTH	1 (8 min)	1 (4 min)	1 (13 min)
APP	0	0	1 (10 min)
DIS	1 (5 min)	1 (2 min)	1 (13 min)

*Many thanks to Amy Kregel, graduate student in school psychology at Lehigh University, for this case example.

had been absent often from school. Currently he attends a general education classroom and is not being considered for special education. However, his teacher reports that Shawn is not making the progress expected compared to other second graders.

Step 1: Assessment of the Instructional Environment

Teacher Interview. Mrs. Kregel reported that Shawn is currently being instructed in the Houghton Mifflin reading series, recently finishing the second book of Level 1 (grade 1) and has started in the first book of Level 2 (grade 2). Unfortunately, Shawn missed a considerable amount of material as a result of a 6-week absence from school during a family trip abroad. According to his teacher, Shawn is experiencing difficulties reading. In particular, Mrs. Kregel noted that Shawn lacks phonetic analysis skills, has a poor sight vocabulary, and poor oral reading ability.

Although Shawn is placed in a book consistent with his grade level, he is instructed in a below-average reading group. He and six other students receive remedial reading with another teacher for 90 minutes per day. During the allotted time, Shawn receives a considerable amount of one-to-one instruction attention. Typically, the first 30 minutes of the instructional period are spent in silent reading and reviewing vocabulary. Students than read aloud to the group and complete written assignments. Any tasks not completed during the reading period are assigned as homework. A chart is displayed prominently in front of the classroom, on which accurate assignment completion is noted by stickers.

In terms of behavior, Mrs. Kregel reported that Shawn is generally on-task and works quietly to complete his assigned work. Although he volunteers in class, he rarely gives the correct answer when called upon. The teacher's primary concern surrounds the accuracy of Shawn's work in reading.

Mrs. Kregel also completed the Academic Performance Rating Scale (DuPaul et al., 1991). She indicated that all aspects of language arts (reading, spelling, and writing) are the most significant problem for Shawn. Math was noted as one of Shawn's strengths.

Direct Observation. Using the SECOS, Shawn was observed during one 20-minute silent reading and one 40-minute oral reading, teacher-directed instruction period. Comparison to peers from Shawn's classroom was made during the silent reading period only. As can be seen in Table 8.6, during both sessions, Shawn was found to be engaged in schoolwork and/or teacher interaction about schoolwork for at least 70% of the intervals. These levels of engagement were similar to those of his peers. Disruptive behaviors, such as calling out, socializing with peers, or getting out of his or her seat were infrequent for both Shawn and his classmates.

During silent reading, Shawn received one-to-one instruction from his teacher for 31% of the intervals, compared to his peers, who received this type of instruction for only 13% of the intervals. Most of the time, the teacher was trying to teach Shawn phonetic analysis. Teacher approval was minimal throughout the observation, despite the high frequency of teacher contact. It was observed during the oral reading, teacher-directed instruction that Shawn was having great difficulty in identifying basic sight vocabulary and using context cues to answer questions about the material being read. A high degree of on-task behavior was evident, despite Shawn's academic problems.

Student Interview. When asked about school, Shawn stated that he enjoyed math and felt that it was his strongest area. He thought that most of his problems were in spelling, although he acknowledged having trouble with the reading assignment he had just been asked to complete. Shawn noted that he sometimes did not understand the assignments he was given and was not interested in the work, especially if it was related to language arts. Although he thought the time he was given to do his work was fair, he disliked the fact that he often had homework in reading and spelling because he had trouble with class assignments. Shawn noted that he often had trouble sounding out words. When asked to explain the procedure he should use if he were confused about his assignments, Shawn demonstrated that he knew how to access help from his teacher or peers.

Permanent Product Review. Shawn's reading journal and written reading comprehension assignments for the past week were examined. Examination of these materials showed that Shawn had good knowledge of beginning consonant sounds. Areas of difficulty appeared to be in consonant blends, punctuation, and medial vowels. Although all assignments were completed, they lacked accuracy.

Summary. The assessment of the academic environment shows that Shawn's classroom instruction follows fairly traditional approaches to teaching reading. Students are grouped by ability and much of the instruction is teacher directed in small groups. Indeed, Shawn receives significant teacher attention for his reading problems and is paired with students of similar ability levels. Although Shawn is now reading in material consistent with his grade level, he lacks many of the skills needed for success in reading.

The direct observation of Shawn's behavior reveals that he is an attentive child, who appears to try hard to overcome his academic problems. He appears to maintain this good level of engaged behavior despite low levels of teacher approval. Examination of Shawn's products, as well as the classroom observation is very consistent with the information reported through the teacher interview.

Step 2: Assessing Instructional Placement

Timed passages were administered to Shawn across five levels of the reading series. As seen in Figure 8.17, Shawn was found to be instructional at the Preprimer B level but frustrational at all other levels. Because Shawn was found to be frustrational at all levels below the level where he is currently placed (level 2-1), passages from that level were not administered. During the reading of these passages, Shawn was observed to be very dysfluent. He would often lose his place, read a line more than once, and replace unknown words rather than sound them out. However, he was able to answer the comprehension screening questions with at least 80% accuracy for all passages.

In general, the direct assessment of reading showed that Shawn is being instructed at a level far beyond his current instructional level. He is likely to experience little success at the 2-1 level at which he is being taught.

Grade level/book	Location in book	WC/ min	Errors/ min	% correct	Median scores for level			Learning level (M, I, F)
					WC	ER	%C	
Preprimer B—*Bells*	Beginning	54	0		45	0	100	Instructional
	Middle	42	0					
	End	45	0	100				
Preprimer C—*Drums*	Beginning	38	6		38	5	100	Frustrational
	Middle	40	5	100				
	End	29	2					
Preprimer D—*Trumpets*	Beginning	43	4		39	8	80	Frustrational
	Middle	39	12					
	End	25	8	80				
Primer—*Parades*	Beginning	31	10	80	31	10	80	Frustrational
	Middle	35	3					
	End	22	10					
1-2—*Carousels*	Beginning	19	6		18	6	100	Frustrational
	Middle	15	6	100				
	End	18	4					

FIGURE 8.17. Results of reading probes for Shawn.

Step 3: Instructional Modification

In reviewing the data from steps 1 and 2 with the teacher, it was decided to construct an intervention to increase Shawn's sight word recognition and reading fluency in grade-level material. This was considered an essential ingredient for Shawn to succeed, especially because his teacher indicated that she was reluctant to move him back to a lower level in the reading series.

The folding-in technique was selected to be implemented three times per week in one-to-one sessions led by an instructional assistant. Baseline data were first collected by the evaluator in the 2-1 level of the reading series where Shawn was being taught. Material selected for instruction during the folding-in technique was selected from the story just ahead of where the class was presently reading. This would permit Shawn the opportunity to preview and practice reading material prior to his classmates.

Each session began with Shawn first being asked to read a passage (usually a paragraph or two consisting of about 100 words) from the upcoming story. The number of words read correctly per minute was calculated and plotted on Shawn's bargraph. From the passage, a list of seven words read correctly (identified as "known words") and three words read incorrectly (identified as "unknown words") were selected. The known words selected consisted of words relevant to the content of the story and not simply articles such as "the," "and," and similar types of words. All of the words were written on 3″ × 5″ index cards.

The unknown words were then interspersed among the known words by folding each unknown word into a review of the seven known words. This was done by having the instructional assistant present the first unknown word to Shawn. The instructional assistant taught the word to Shawn by saying the word, spelling the word, and using the word in a sentence. Shawn was then asked to do the same. After the unknown word was taught, it was presented to Shawn, followed by the first known word. Next, the unknown word was presented, followed by the first known word and then the second known word. This sequence continued until all seven known and the first unknown word had been presented. If at any point in the process Shawn hesitated or responded incorrectly, he was asked to again say the word, spell the word, and use it in a sentence.

The second unknown word was then introduced in the same way and folded in among the seven known and one unknown word already presented. The third unknown was then folded in, using the same procedures. The entire procedure took 7–10 minutes.

After the folding-in procedure was completed, Shawn was asked to read the same passage he had read at the beginning of the session. His words correct per minute were again calculated and plotted on his bar graph. Shawn was also asked to again read the words that were used during the folding-in procedure. If he identified a word for 2 consecutive days that had been classified as an unknown, the word was then considered known. The next session, a previous word from the known pile was discarded and replaced by this previously unknown word. The number of words that moved from unknown to known status was also plotted on a graph by Shawn. Each session that Shawn learned at least one new word was rewarded with an opportunity to select an item from a prize bag.

Step 4: Progress Monitoring

Both long- and short-term progress monitoring of Shawn's performance were conducted. In consultation with Shawn's teacher, a short-term goal of learning five new words per week was selected. In addition, at the end of the 4-week intervention, Shawn would be able to read at least 40 words per minute during the presession reading. A long-term (end-of-year) goal was selected by examining the normative data for students in the 25th percentile of grade 2 in Shawn's school district. Those data suggested that Shawn should be able to read at least 40 words per minute in the grade 2-1 book.

Short-term monitoring was reflected in Shawn's performance on the passage read before and after each folding-in session. In addition, the cumulative number of words learned per week was used to show the acquisition of new words for Shawn. Long-term monitoring was obtained through the collection of curriculum-based measurements taken twice per week by randomly selecting passages from across the second half of the level 2-1 book.

Results

The results of the four-step process are shown in Figures 8.18, 8.19, and 8.20. Shawn demonstrated consistent improvement in his reading fluency from pre- to postsession readings during each time the folding-in intervention was conducted. As seen in Figure 8.18, Shawn initially had a reading rate of 12 words correct per minute in the materials being taught. Following each folding-in session, Shawn improved his rate by 10–20 words correct per minute. An examination of his presession reading rate reflects steady improvement toward the goal of 40 words correct per minute in presession reading performance over the 4 weeks of intervention. As seen in Figure 8.18, Shawn also displayed consistent gains each day in the number of new words learned.

Given Shawn's strong performance on short-term objectives, an increase from five to six new words per week occurred after the eighth session. As is evident from Figure 8.19, Shawn was able to easily achieve this

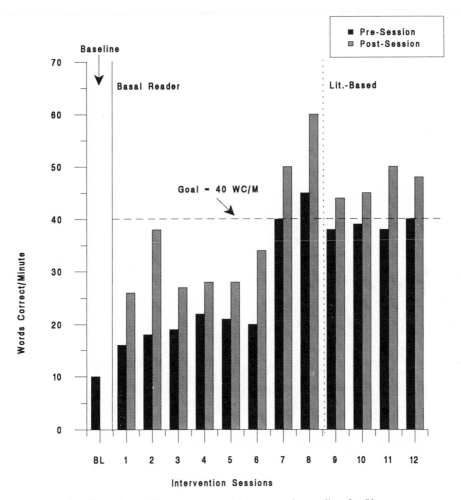

FIGURE 8.18. Pre- and postsession scores in reading for Shawn.

goal throughout the rest of the intervention. Also, at the end of the eighth sessions, the teacher decided to shift Shawn (as well as the rest of the class) to a literature-based reading series. Across the last four intervention sessions, the words and passages used for the folding-in technique were taken from the new instructional material. Passages for CBM were still taken from the latter portion of the 2-1 level basal reading series. Shawn maintained his performance across the final week of the intervention using this new material.

An examination of Figure 8.20 shows that Shawn was moving to-

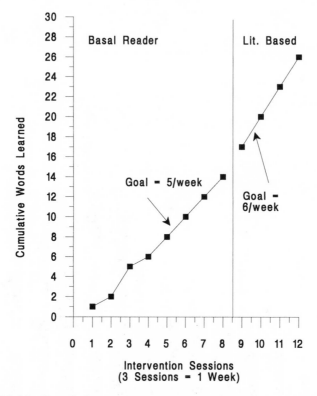

FIGURE 8.19. Cumulative words learned across intervention sessions for Shawn.

ward the long-term goal set for him by his teacher. Despite a change in the instructional material, the data show that Shawn was making excellent progress.

Comments about Shawn's Case

This case illustrates how the full, four-step model discussed throughout this text can be applied. In this particular example, an assessment of the instructional environment showed that Shawn was receiving substantial assistance from the teacher. Indeed, despite high levels of teacher-directed instruction, he was not succeeding. In addition, he had been moved through curriculum materials, even though he clearly lacked mastery with those materials. The teacher was unable or unwilling to move him to material that would be instructional for his fluency level.

Using these data, the evaluator was able to pinpoint what might be keystone behaviors to predict future success. Specifically, the evaluator rec-

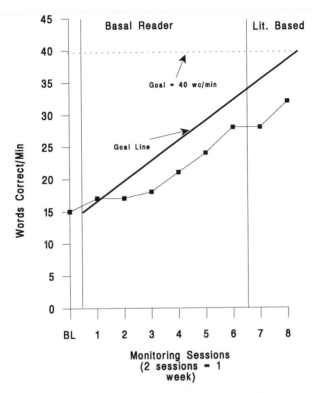

FIGURE 8.20. Long-term progress monitoring in reading for Shawn.

ognized that increasing sight word recognition and fluency were likely to result in Shawn increasing his effective participation in class, as well as, maintain himself within the present classroom environment. By constructing an intervention that included opportunities to preview upcoming material, the probabilities that Shawn would succeed were enhanced.

The case also illustrates the use of the powerful folding-in technique. Because this intervention mixes known and unknown material in a way that guarantees student success, it is likely to result in increased motivation of students to learn. Indeed, the use of bar graphs and other visual displays of the data are known to be excellent mechanisms to motivate challenging students.

Finally, the case illustrates how the data can be used to make instructional decisions. In this case, Shawn had demonstrated the ability to meet the short-term goals set for him (five new words per week). Seeing this, the evaluator determined that the goal could be increased to six words. When this change was made, Shawn's performance improved.

The case also shows the outcomes of an unexpected change, an alteration in the instructional materials. Although the data collection ended as the school year came to a close, the results did show that Shawn could maintain his performance when a new set of reading materials were introduced.

CONCLUSIONS

Interventions that may be effective in improving academic performance cannot always be predicted on the basis of assessment data. Although the evaluation may provide clues as to the best choices of potentially potent strategies, it is through the ongoing collection of data that one can best determine whether a procedure is working as planned. What works for Marla may not work for Shawn. What works for Shawn now may not work for him as well later. These are the realities of academic interventions, and they make the collection of data to assess progress almost imperative.

The cases provided here are only a brief sampling of the richness of possible cases that could have been selected. These cases represent the performance of actual students and are not hypothetical. Obviously, many other cases could have been chosen.

The future of effective academic interventions most likely will rely on the ability to convince teachers, psychologists, school administrators, and consultants of the importance of data collection to evaluate student progress. Being aware of the range of potential interventions to improve academic skills surely will help the consultant in planning effective teaching procedures. However, even those less skilled in developing interventions can greatly facilitate the process of intervention by understanding how to collect data on student progress. Many teachers offer a wealth of experience, knowledge, and training to suggest interventions. It may be unnecessary for those working in a consultative arrangement with these teachers ever to suggest interventions. Data collection, however, appears to be the key to effective intervention. Without the data, we are left to guess the effectiveness of our procedures.

This text has presented a wealth of techniques and strategies for assessing academic problems, as well as potential interventions for solving these complex problems. Reading about them, however, is only the first step. Readers should not be fearful of "trying out" these procedures with one or two representative cases, with teachers who are willing to experiment, and situations likely to result in success. Such readers will probably find that the procedures are extremely easy to implement, are time-efficient, and will result in successful and rewarding delivery of services.

References

♦

Abt Associates. (1976). *Education as experimentation* (Vol. III). Cambridge, MA: Author.

Abt Associates. (1977). *Education as experimentation* (Vol. IV). Cambridge, MA: Author.

Ager, C. L., & Shapiro, E. S. (1995). Template matching as a strategy for assessment of and intervention for preschool students with disabilities. *Topics in Early Childhood Special Education, 15,* 187–218.

Alessi, G., & Kaye, J. H. (1983). *Behavior assessment for school psychologists.* Kent, OH: National Association of School Psychologists.

Algozzine, B., & Maheady, L. (Eds.), (1986). In search of excellence: Instruction that works in special education classrooms [Special issue]. *Exceptional Children, 52*(6).

Allen, L. J., Howard, V. F., Sweeney, W. J., & McLaughlin, T. F. (1993). Use of contingency contracting to increase on-task behavior with primary students. *Psychological Reports, 72,* 905–906.

Allyn & Bacon. (1978). *Pathfinder—Allyn & Bacon reading program.* Boston: Author.

American Psychiatric Association. (1994). *Diagnostic and statistical manual of mental disorders* (4th ed.). Washington, DC: author.

Arblaster, G. R., Butler, A. L., Taylor, C. A., Arnold, C., & Pitchford, M. (1991). Same-age tutoring, mastery learning and the mixed ability teaching of reading. *School Psychology International, 12,* 111–118.

Armbruster, B. B., Stevens, R. J., & Rosenshine, B. V. (1977). *Analyzing content coverage and emphasis: A study of three curricula and two tests* (Technical Report No. 26). Urbana–Champaign: Center for the Study of Reading, University of Illinois.

Arter, J. A., & Jenkins, J. R. (1979). Differential diagnosis–prescriptive teaching: A critical appraisal. *Review of Educational Research, 49,* 517–555.

Axelrod, S., & Greer, R. D. (1994). Cooperative learning revisisted. *Journal of Behavioral Education, 4,* 41–48.

Axelrod, S., & Paluska, J. (1975). A component analysis of the effects of a classroom game on spelling performance. In E. Ramp & G. Semb (Eds.), *Behavior analysis: Areas of research and application* (pp. 277–282). New York: Prentice-Hall.

Ayllon, T., & Roberts, M. D. (1974). Eliminating discipline problems by strengthening academic performance. *Journal of Applied Behavior Analysis, 7,* 71–76

Ayres, R. R., & Cooley, E. J. (1986). Sequential and simultaneous processing on the K-ABC: Validity in predicting learning success. *Journal of Psychoeducational Assessment, 4,* 211–220.

Ayres, R. R., Cooley, E. J., & Severson, H. H. (1988). Educational translation of the Kaufman Assessment Battery for Children: A construct validity study. *School Psychology Review, 17,* 113–124.

Bandura, A. (1976). Self-reinforcement. Theoretical and methodological considerations. *Behaviorism, 4,* 135–155.

Barlow, D. H., & Wolfe, B. E. (1981). Behavioral approaches to anxiety disorders: A report of the NIMH-SUNY, Albany, research conference. *Journal of Consulting and Clinical Psychology, 49,* 448–454.

Barsch, R. H. (1965). *A moviegenic curriculum.* Madison, WI: Bureau for Handicapped Children.

Baumann, J. F., & Bergeron, B. S. (1993). Story map instruction using children's literature: Effects on first graders' comprehension of central narrative elements. *Journal of Reading Behavior, 25,* 407–437.

Beck, A. T., Rush., A. J., Shaw, B. F., & Emery, G. (1979). *Cognitive therapy of depression.* New York: Guilford Press.

Becker, W. C., & Carnine, D. W. (1981). Direct instruction: A behavior theory model for comprehensive educational intervention with the disadvantaged. In S. W. Bijou & R. Ruiz (Eds.), *Behavior modification: Contributions to education* (pp. 145–210). Hillsdale, NJ: Erlbaum.

Becker, W. C., & Engelmann, S. (1978). Systems for basic instruction: Theory and applications. In A. C. Cantania & T. A. Brigham (Eds.), *Handbook of applied behavior research* (pp. 325–377). New York: Irvington.

Becker, W. C., & Gersten, R. (1982). A follow-up of Follow-Through: The later effects of the Direct Instruction model on children in the fifth and sixth grades. *American Educational Research Journal, 19,* 75–92.

Beirne-Smith, M. (1991). Peer tutoring in arithmetic for children with learning disabilities. *Exceptional Children, 57,* 330–337.

Bell, P. F., Lentz, F. E., & Graden, J. L. (1992). Effects of curriculum-test overlap on standardized test scores: Identifying systematic confounds in educational decision making. *School Psychology Review, 21,* 644–655.

Benito, Y. M., Foley, C. L., Lewis, C. D., & Prescott, P. (1993). The effect of instruction in question-answer relationships and metacognition on social studies comprehension. *Journal of Research in Reading, 16*(1), 20–29.

Bentz, J., Shinn, M. R., & Gleason, M. M. (1990). Training general education pupils to monitor reading using curriculum-based measurement procedures. *School Psychology Review, 19,* 23–32.

Bergan, J. R. (1977). *Behavioral consultation,* Columbus, OH: Charles E. Merrill.

Bergan, J. R., & Kratochwill, T. R. (1990). *Behavioral consultation and therapy.* New York: Plenum Press.

Bergan, J. R., & Tombari, M. L. (1975). The analysis of verbal interactions occurring during consultation. *Journal of School Psychology, 13,* 209–226.

Berliner, D. C. (1979). Tempus educare. In P. L. Peterson & H. J. Walberg (Eds.), *Research on teaching* (pp. 120–135). Berkley, CA: McCutchan.

Berliner, D. C. (1988). Effective classroom management and instruction: A knowledge base for consultation. In J. L. Graden, J. E. Zins, & M. J. Curtis (Eds.), *Alternate educational delivery systems: Enhancing instructional options for all students* (pp. 309–326). Washington, DC: National Association of School Psychologists.

Betts, E. A. (1946). *Foundations of reading instruction.* New York: American Book.

Bijou, S., & Grimm, J. A. (1972, October). *Behavioral diagnosis and assessment in teaching young handicapped children.* Washington, DC: Division of Research, Bureau of Education for the Handicapped.

Billingsley, B. S., & Ferro-Almeida, S. C. (1993). Strategies to facilitate reading comprehension in students with learning disabilities. *Reading and Writing Quarterly: Overcoming Learning Difficulties, 9,* 263–278.

Blandford, B. J., & Lloyd, J. W. (1987). Effects of a self-instructional procedure on handwriting. *Journal of Learning Disabilities, 20,* 342–346.

Blankenship, C. S. (1978). Remediating systematic inversion errors in subtraction through the use of demonstration and feedback. *Learning Disability Quarterly, 1,* 12–22.

Blankenship, C. S. (1985). Using curriculum-based assessment data to make instructional management decisions. *Exceptional Children, 42,* 233–238.

Bornstein, P. H., & Quevillon, R. P (1976). The effects of a self-instructional package on overaction preschool boys. *Journal of Applied Behavior Analysis, 9,* 179–188.

Bourque, P., Dupuis, N., & Van Houten, R. (1986). Public posting in the classroom: Comparison of posting names and coded numbers of individual students. *Psychological Reports, 59,* 295–298.

Bradley, K. L., Shapiro, E. S., Lutz, J. G., DuPaul, G. J. (in press). Evaluation of oral reading rate as a curriculum-based measure within literature-based curriculum. *Journal of School Psychology.*

Bradley-Johnson, S., Sunderman, P., & Johnson, C. M. (1983). Comparison of delayed prompting and fading for teaching preschoolers easily confused letters and numbers. *Journal of School Psychology, 21,* 327–335.

Brigance, A. (1977). *Brigance Diagnostic Inventory of Basic Skills.* North Billerica, MA: Curriculum Associates.

Brigance, A. (1978). *Brigance Inventory of Early Skills.* North Billerica, MA: Curriculum Associates.

Brigance, A., (1980). *Brigance Diagnostic Inventory of Essential Skills,* North Billerica, MA: Curriculum Associates. Brigham, T. A. (1980). Self-control revisited: Or why doesn't anyone actually read Skinner (1953). *Behaviorism, 3,* 25–33.

Broden, M., Beasley, A., & Hall, R. V. (1978). In-class spelling performance. *Behavior Modification, 2,* 511–529.

Broughton, S. F., & Lahey, B. B. (1978). Direct and collateral effects of positive reinforcement, response cost, and mixed contingencies for academic performance. *Journal of School Psychology, 16,* 126–136.

Broussard, C. D., & Northrup, J. (1995). An approach to functional assessment and analysis of disruptive behavior in regular educational classrooms. *School Psychology Quarterly, 10*, 151–164.

Browder, D. M., & Shapiro, E. S. (1985). Applications of self-management to individuals with severe handicaps: A review. *Journal of the Association for Persons with Severe Handicaps, 10*, 200–208.

Caldwell, J. H., Huitt, W. G., & Graeber, A. O. (1982). Time spent in learning: Implications from research. *Elementary School Journal, 82*, 471–480.

Campbell, J. A., & Willis, J. (1978). Modifying components of creative behavior in the natural environment. *Behavior Modification, 2*, 549–564.

Campbell, J. A., & Willis, J. (1979). A behavioral program to teach creative writing in the regular classroom. *Education and Treatment of Children, 2*, 5–15.

Cancelli, A. A., & Kratochwill, T. R. (1981). Advances in criterion-referenced assessment. In T. R. Kratochwill (Ed.), *Advances in school psychology* (Vol. 1, pp. 213–254). Hillsdale, NJ: Erlbaum.

Canter, A. (1995). Best practices in developing local norms in behavioral assessment. In A. Thomas & J. Grimes (Eds.), *Best practices in school psychology-III* (pp. 689–700). Washington, DC: National Association of School Psychologists.

Carnine, D. (1976). Effects of two teacher presentation rates on off-task behavior, answering correctly, and participation. *Journal of Applied Behavior Analysis, 9*, 199–206.

Carr, E. G., Newson, C., & Binkoff, J. (1980). Escape as a factor in the aggressive behavior of two retarded children. *Journal of Applied Behavior Analysis, 13*, 101–117.

Carr, S. C., & Punzo, R. P. (1993). The effects of self-monitoring of academic accuracy and productivity on the performance of students with behavioral disorders. *Behavioral Disorders, 18*, 241–250.

Carroll, J. B. (1963). A model of school learning. *Teachers College Record, 64*, 723–733.

Carta, J. J., Atwater, J. B., Schwartz, I. S., & Miller, P. A. (1990). Applications of ecobehavioral analysis to the study of transitions across early education. *Education and Treatment of Children, 13*, 298–315.

Carta, J. J., Greenwood, C. R., & Atwater, J. (1985). *Ecobehavioral system for complex assessments of preschool environments (ESCAPE).* Kansas City: Juniper Gardens Children's Project, Bureau of Child Resarch, University of Kansas.

Carta, J. J., Greenwood, C. R., Schulte, D., Arreaga-Mayer, C., & Terry, B. (1988). *The mainstream code for instructional structure and student academic response (MS-CIS-SAR): Observer training manual.* Kansas City: Juniper Garden Children's Project, Burear of Child Research, University of Kansas.

Cartledge, G., & Milburn, J. F. (1983). Social skill assessment and teaching in the schools. In T. R. Kratochwill (Ed.), *Advances in school psychology* (Vol. 3, pp. 175–236). Hillsdale, NJ: Erlbaum.

Carver, R. P. (1974). Two dimensions of tests: Psychometric and edumetric. *American Psychologist, 29*, 512–518.

Chadwick, B. A., & Day, R. C. (1971). Systematic reinforcement: Academic performance of underachieving students. *Journal of Applied Behavior Analysis, 4*, 311–319.

Clark, F. L., Deshler, D. D., Schumaker, J. B., & Alley, G. R. (1984). Visual imagery and self-questioning: Strategies to improve comprhension of written materials. *Journal of Learning Disabilities, 17,* 145–149.

Clark, L., & Elliott, S. N. (1988). The influence of treatment strength information of knowledgable teachers' pretreatment evaluation of social skills training methods. *Professional School Psychology, 3,* 241–251.

Clymer, T., & Fenn, T. (1979). *Ginn Reading 720, Rainbow Edition.* Lexington, MA: Ginn.

Cobbs, J. A., & Hopps, H. (1973). Effects of academic survival skill training on low achieving first graders. *Journal of Educational Research, 67,* 108–113.

Cochran, L., Feng, H., Cartledge, G., & Hamilton, S. (1993). The effects of cross-age tutoring on the academic achievement, social behavior, and self-perceptions of low-achieving African-American males with behavior disorders. *Behavioral Disorders, 18,* 292–302.

Combs, M. L., & Lahey, B. B. (1981). A cognitive social skills traning program: Evaluation with young children. *Behavior Modification, 5,* 39–60.

Cone, J. D. (1978). The Behavioral Assessment Grid (BAG): A conceptual framework and a taxonomy. *Behavior Therapy, 9,* 882–888.

Cone, J. D. (1981). Psychometric considerations. In M. Hersen & A. S. Bellack (Eds.), *Behavioral assessment: A practical* handbook (2nd ed., pp. 38–68). New York: Pergamon Press.

Cone, J. D., & Hoier, T. S. (1986). Assessing children: The radical behavioral perspective. In R. Prinz (Ed.), *Advances in behavioral assessment of children and families* (Vol. 2, pp. 1– 27). New York: JAI Press.

Connell, M. C., Carta, J. J., & Baer, D. M. (1993). Programming generalization of in-class transition skills: Teaching preschoolers with developmental delays to self-assess and recruit contingent praise. *Journal of Applied Behavior Analysis, 26,* 345–352.

Connoley, A. J. (1988). *Key Math revised: A diagnostic inventory of essential mathematics.* Circle Pines, MN: American Guidance Service.

Cooke, N. L., Guzaukas, R., Pressley, J. S., & Kerr, K. (1993). Effects of using a ratio of new items to review items during drill and practice: Three experiments. *Education and Treatment of Children, 16,* 213–234.

Cooper, J. O., Heward, T. E., & Herron, W. L. (1987). *Applied behavior analysis.* Columbus, OH: Charles E. Merrill.

Cooper, L. J., Wacker, D. P., Thursby, D., Plagmann, L. A., Harding, J., Millard, T., & Derby, M. (1992). Analysis of the effects of task preferences, task demands, and adult attention on child behavior in outpatient and classroom settings. *Journal of Applied Behavior Analysis, 25,* 823–840.

Cooper, L. J., Wacker, D. P., Sasso, G. M., Reimers, T. M., & Donn, L. K. (1990). Using parents as therapists to evaluate the appropriate behavior of their children: Applications to a tertiary diagnostic clinic. *Journal of Applied Behavior Analysis, 23,* 285–296.

Cosden, M. A., & Haring, T. G. (1992). Cooperative learning in the classroom: Contingencies, group interactions, and students with special needs. *Journal of Behavioral Education, 2,* 53–71.

Cossairt, A., Hall, R. V., & Hopkins, B. L. (1973). The effects of experimenter's instruction, feedback, and praise on teacher praise and student attending behavior. *Journal of Applied Behavior Analysis, 6*, 89–100.

Coulter, W. A., & Coulter, E. M. B. (1991). *C. B. A. I. D.: Curriculum-based assessment for instructional design* [Training manual]. New Orleans: Louisiana State University Medical Center.

Cradler, J. D., Bechthold D. L., & Bechthold, C. C. (1973). *Success controlled optimal reading experience.* Hillsborough, CA: Learning Guidance Systems.

Cronbach, L. J., & Snow, R. E. (1977). *Aptitudes and instructional methods.* New York: Irvington.

Cullinan, D., Lloyd, J., & Epstein, M. H. (1981). Strategy training: A structured approach to arithmetic instruction. *Exceptional Education Quarterly, 2*, 41–49.

Daly, E. J., & Martens, B. K. (1994). A comparison of three interventions for increasing oral reading performance: Application of the instructional hierarchy. *Journal of Applied Behavior Analysis, 27*, 459–469.

Das, J. P., Kirby, J., & Jarman, R. F. (1975). Simultaneous and successive syntheses: An alternative model for cognitive abilities. *Psychological Bulletin, 82*, 87–103.

Das, J. P., Kirby, J. R., & Jarman, R. F. (1979). *Simultaneous and successive cognitive processes.* New York: Academic Press.

Davis, Z. T. (1994). Effects of prereading story mapping on elementary readers' comprehension. *Journal of Educational Research, 87*, 353–360.

Delquadri, J. C., Greenwood, C. R., Stretton, K., & Hall, R. V. (1983). The peer tutoring spelling game: A classroom procedure for increasing opportunties to respond and spelling performance. *Education and Treatment of Children, 6*, 225–239.

Delquadri, J., Greenwood, C. R., Whorton, D., Carta, J., & Hall, R. V. (1986). Classwide peer tutoring. *Exceptional Children, 52*, 535–542.

Denham, C., & Lieberman, P. (1980). *Time to learn.* Washington, DC: National Institute of Education.

Deno, S. L. (1985). Curriculum-based measurement: The ermerging alternative. *Exceptional Children, 52*, 219–232.

Deno, S. L., King, R., Skiba, R., Sevcik, B., & Wesson, C. (1983). *The structure of instruction rating scale (SIRS): Development and technical characteristics* (Research Report No. 107). Minneapolis: University of Minnesota, Institute for Research on Learning Disabilities.

Deno, S. L., Marston, D., & Mirkin, P. K. (1982). Valid measurement procedures for continuous evaluation of written expression. *Exceptional Children, 48*, 368–371.

Deno, S. L., Marston, D., & Tindal, G. (1986). Direct and frequent curriculum-based measurement: An alternative for educational decision making. *Special Services in the Schools, 2*, 5–27.

Deno, S. L., & Mirkin, P. K. (1977). *Data-based program modification: A manual.* Reston, VA: Council for Exceptional Children.

Deno, S. L., Mirkin, P. K., & Chiang, B. (1982). Identifying valid measures of reading. *Exceptional Children, 49*, 36–47.

Deno, S. L., Mirkin, P. K., Lowry, L., & Kuehnle, K. (1980). *Relationships among simple measures of spelling and performance on standardized achievement tests* (Research

Report No. 21). Minneapolis: University of Minnesota, Institute for Research on Learning Disabilities. (ERIC Document Reproduction Service No. ED 197 508)

Derr, T. F., & Shapiro, E. S. (1989). A behavioral evaluation of curriculum-based assessment of reading. *Journal of Psychoeducational Assessment, 7,* 148–160.

Derr-Minneci, T. F., & Shapiro, E. S. (1992). Validating curriculum-based measurement in reading from a behavioral perspective. *School Psychology Quarterly, 7,* 2–16.

Deshler, D. D., & Schumaker, J. B. (1986). Learning strategies: An instructional alternative for low-achieving adolescents. *Exceptional Children, 52,* 583–590.

Deshler, D. D., & Schumaker, J. B. (1993). Strategy mastery by at-risk students: Not a simple matter. *Elementary School Journal, 94,* 153–167.

Deshler, D. D., Schumaker, J. B., Alley, G. R., Warner, M. M., & Clark, F. L. (1982). Learning disabilities in adolescent and young adult populations: Research implications (Part I). *Focus on Exceptional Children, 15*(1), 1–12.

Deshler, D. D., Schumaker, J. B., Lenz, B. K., & Ellis, E. S. (1984). Academic and cognitive interventions for LD adolescents (Part II). *Journal of Learning Disabilities, 17,* 170–187.

Dineen, J. P., Clark, H. B., & Risley, T. R. (1977). Peer tutoring among elementary students: Educational benefits to the tutor. *Journal of Applied Behavior Analysis, 10,* 231–238.

Duarte, A. M. M., & Baer, D. M. (1994). The effects of self-instruction on preschool children's sorting of generalized in-common tasks. *Journal of Experimental Child Psychology, 57,* 1– 25.

Ducharme, J. M., & Worling, D. E. (1994). Behavioral momentum and stimulus fading in the acquisition and maintenance of child compliance in the home. *Journal of Applied Behavior Analysis, 27,* 639–647.

Dunlap, G., Kern-Dunlap, L., Clarke, S., & Robbins, F. R. (1991). Functional assessment, curricular revision, and severe behavior problems. *Journal of Applied Behavior Analysis, 24,* 387–397.

Dunn, L. M., & Markwardt, F. C. (1970). *Peabody Individual Achievement Test.* Circle Pines, MN: American Guidance Services.

DuPaul, G. J., & Henningson, P. N. (1993). Peer tutoring effects on the classroom performance of children with attention deficit hyperactivity disorder. *School Psychology Review, 22,* 134–142.

DuPaul, G. J., Rapport, M. D., & Perriello, L. M. (1991). Teacher ratings of academic skills: The development of the Academic Performance Rating Scale. *School Psychology Review, 20,* 284–300.

Durost, W., Bixler, H., Wrightstone, J. W., Prescott, G., & Balow, I. (1970). *Metropolitan Achievement Test: Primary I and II Battery.* New York: Harcourt Brace Jovanovich.

Eckert, T. L., Shapiro, E. S., & Lutz, J. G. (1995). Teacher's ratings of the acceptability of curriculum-based assessment methods. *School Psychology Review, 24,* 499–510.

Eiserman, W. D. (1988). Three types of peer tutoring: Effects on the attitudes of students with learning disabilities and their regular class peers. *Journal of Learning Disabilities, 21,* 249–252.

Elliott, S. N., & Shapiro, E. S. (1990). Intervention techniques and programs for academic performance problems. In T. B. Gutkin & C. R. Reynolds (Eds.), *The handbook of school psychology* (2nd ed., pp. 637–662). New York: Wiley.

Elliott, S. N., Turco, T. L., & Gresham, F. M. (1987). Consumers and clients' pretreatment acceptability ratings of classroom group contingencies. *Journal of School Psychology, 25,* 145–154.

Ellis, E. S., & Lenz, B. K. (1987). A component analysis of effective learning strategies for LD students. *Learning Disabilities Focus, 2,* 94–107.

Ellis, E. S., Lenz, B. K., & Sabournie, E. J. (1987a). Generalization and adaptation of learning strategies to natural environments: Part I. Critical agents. *Remedial and Special Education, 8*(1), 6–20

Ellis, E. S., Lenz, B. K., & Sabournie, E. J. (1987b). Generalization and adaptation of learning strategies to natural environments: Part 2. Research into practice. *Remedial and Special Education, 8*(2), 6–23.

Englemann, S., & Carnine, D. (1982). *Theory of instruction.* New York: Irvington.

Epps, S., McGue, M., & Ysseldyke, J. E. (1982). Interjudge agreement in classifying students as learning disabled. *Psychology in the Schools, 19,* 208–220.

Epps, S., Ysseldyke, J. E., & McGue, M. (1984). "I know one when I see one"—Differentiating LD and non-LD students. *Learning Disabilty Quarterly, 7,* 89–101.

Erchul, W. P., Covington, C. G., Hughes, J. N., & Meyers, J. (1995). Further explorations of request-centered relational communication within school consultation. *School Psychology Review, 24,* 621–632.

Evans, G. W. (1985). Building systems model as a strategy for target behavior in clinical assessment. *Behavioral Assessment, 7,* 21–32.

Evans, G. W., & Oswaldt, G. L. (1968). Acceleration of academic progress through the manipulation of peer influence. *Behaviour Research and Therapy, 6,* 189–195.

Fantuzzo, J. W., & Polite, K. (1990). School-based, behavioral self-management: A review and analysis. *School Psychology Quarterly, 5,* 180–198.

Fantuzzo, J. W., Polite, K., & Grayson, N. (1990). An evaluation of reciprocal peer tutoring across elementary school settings. *Journal of School Psychology, 28,* 209–224.

Fantuzzo, J. W., Rhorbeck, C. A., & Azar, S. T. (1986). A component analysis of behavioral self-management interventions with elementary school students. *Child and Family Behavior Therapy, 9,* 33–43.

Felton, J. L., & Nelson, R. O. (1984). Inter-assessor agreement on hypothesized controlling variables and treatment proposals. *Behavioral Assessment, 6,* 199–208.

Ferster, C. B. (1965). Classification of behavioral pathology. In L. Krasner & L. P. Ullmann (Eds.), *Research in behavior modification* (pp. 6–26). New York: Holt, Rinehart & Winston.

Fink, W. T., & Carnine, D. W. (1975). Control of arithmetic errors using informational feedback and errors. *Journal of Applied Behavior Analysis, 8,* 461.

Fisher, C., & Berliner, D. C. (1985). *Perspectives on instructional time.* New York: Longman.

Flesch, R. (1951). *How to test readability.* New York: Harper.

Fowler, S. A. (1984). Introductory comments: The pragmatics of self-management for the developmentally disabled. *Analysis and Intervention in Developmental Disabilities, 4*, 85–90.

Fowler, S. A. (1986). Peer-monitoring and self-monitoring: Alternatives to traditional teacher management. *Exceptional Children, 52*, 573–582.

Fox, D. E. C., & Kendall, P. C. (1983). Thinking through academic problems: Applications of cognitive behavior therapy to learning. In T. R. Kratochwill (Ed.), *Advances in school psychology* (Vol. 3, pp. 269–301). Hillsdale, NJ: Erlbaum.

Foxx, R. M. & Jones, J. R. (1978). A remediation program for increasing the spelling achievement of elementary and junior high students. *Behavior Modification, 2*, 211–230.

Franca, V. M., Kerr, M. M., Reitz, A. L., & Lambert, D. (1990). Peer tutoring among behaviorally disordered students: Academic and social benefits to tutor and tutee. *Education and Treatment of Children, 13*, 109–128.

Frederick, W. C., Walberg, H. J., & Rasher, S. P. (1979). Time, teacher comments, and achievement in urban high schools. *Journal of Educational Research, 13*, 63–65.

Freeman, T. J., & McLaughlin, T. F. (1984). Effects of a taped-words treatment procedure on learning disabled students' sight-word reading. *Learning Disability Quarterly, 7*, 49–54.

Friedling, C., & O'Leary, S. G. (1979). Effects of self-instruction on second and third grade hyperactive children: A failure to replicate. *Journal of Applied Behavior Analysis, 12*, 211–219.

Friedman, D. L., Cancelli, A. A., & Yoshida, R. K. (1988). Academic engagement of elementary school children with learning disabilities. *Journal of School Psychology, 26*, 327–340.

Frostig, M., & Horne, D. (1964). *The Frostig Program for the Development of Visual Perception: Teachers guide.* Chicago: Follett.

Fry, E. (1968). A readability formula that saves time. *Journal of Reading, 11*, 513–516.

Fuchs, L. S. (1986). Monitoring progress among mildly handicapped pupils: Review of current practice and research. *Remedial and Special Education, 7*(5), 5–12.

Fuchs, L. S., & Deno, S. L. (1982). *Developing goals and objectives for educational programs.* [Teaching guide]. Minneapolis: Institute for Research in Learning Disabilities, University of Minnesota.

Fuchs, L. S., & Deno, S. L. (1991). Paradigmatic distinctions between instructionally relevant measurement models. *Exceptional Children, 57*, 488–500.

Fuchs, L. S., & Deno, S. L. (1992). Effects of curriculum within curriculum-based measurement. *Exceptional Children, 58*, 232–243.

Fuchs, L. S., & Deno, S. L. (1994). Must instructionally useful performance assessment be based in the curriculum? *Exceptional Children, 61*, 15–24.

Fuchs, L. S., Deno, S. L., & Marston, D. (1983). Improving the reliabilty of curriculum-based measures of academic skills for psychoeducational decision making, *Diagnostique, 8*, 135–149.

Fuchs, L. S., Deno, S. L., & Mirkin, P. K. (1984). The effects of frequent curriculum-based measures and evaluation on pedagogy, student achievement, and student awareness of learning. *American Educational Research Journal, 21,* 449–460.

Fuchs, L. S., & Fuchs, D. (1986a). Curriculum-based assessment of progress toward long-term and short-term goals. *Journal of Special Education, 20,* 69–82.

Fuchs L. S., & Fuchs, D. (1986b). Effects of systematic formative evaluation: A meta-analysis. *Exceptional Children, 53,* 199–208.

Fuchs, L. S., & Fuchs, D. (1992). Identifying a measure for monitoring student reading progress. *School Psychology Review, 21,* 45–58.

Fuchs, D., Fuchs, L. S., Benowitz, S., & Barringer, K. (1987). Norm-referenced tests: Are they valid for use with handicapped students? *Exceptional Children, 54,* 263–271. Fuchs, L. S., Fuchs, D., & Bishop, N. (1992). Instructional adaptation for students at risk. *Journal of Educational Research, 86,* 70–84.

Fuchs, L. S., Fuchs, D., & Bishop, N. (1992). Teacher planning for students with learning disabilities: Differences between general and special educators. *Learning Disabilities Research and Practice, 7,* 120–128.

Fuchs, L. S., Fuchs, D., Hamlett, C. L., & Allinder, R. M. (1991a). The contribution of skills analysis within curriculum-based measurement in spelling. *Exceptional Children, 57,* 443–452.

Fuchs, L. S., Fuchs, D., Hamlett, C. L., & Allinder, R. M. (1991b). Effects of expert system advice within curriculum-based measurement on teacher planning and student achievement in spelling. *School Psychology Review, 20,* 49–66.

Fuchs, L. S., Fuchs, D., Hamlett, C. L., & Ferguson, C. (1992). Effects of expert system consultation within curriculum-based measurement using a reading maze task. *Exceptional Children, 58,* 436–450.

Fuchs, L. S., Fuchs, D., Hamlett, C. L., Phillips, N. B., & Bentz, J. (1994). Classwide curriculum-based measurement: Helping general educators meet the challenge of student diversity. *Exceptional Children, 60,* 518–537.

Fuchs, L. S., Fuchs, D., Hamlett, C. L., Phillips, N. B., & Karns, K. (1995). General educators' specialized adaptation for students with learning disabilities. *Exceptional Children, 61,* 440–459.

Fuchs, L. S., Fuchs, D., Hamlett, C. L., & Stecker, P. M. (1991). Effects of curriculum-based measurement and consultation on teacher planning and student achievement in mathematics operations. *American Educational Research Journal, 28,* 617–641.

Fuchs, L. S., Fuchs, D., Hamlett, C. L., Walz, L., & Germann, G. (1993). Formative evaluation of academic progress: How much growth can we expect? *School Psychology Review, 22,* 27–48.

Fuchs, L. S., Fuchs, D., Hamlett, C. L., & Whinnery, K. (1991). Effects of goal line feedback on level, slope, and stability of performance within curriculum-based measurement. *Learning Disabilities Research and Practice, 6*(2), 66–74.

Fuchs, L. S., Fuchs, D., Phillips, N. B., Hamlett, C. L., & Karns, K. (1995). Acquisition and transfer effects of classwide peer-assisted learning strategies in mathematics for students with varying learning histories. *School Psychology Review, 24,* 604–620.

Fuchs, L. S., Hamlett, C. L., & Fuchs, D. (1990a). *Monitoring Basic Skills Progress: Basic Math* [Computer program]. Austin, TX: Pro-Ed.

Fuchs, L. S., Hamlett, C. L., & Fuchs, D. (1990b). *Monitoring Basic Skills Progress: Basic Reading* [Computer program]. Austin, TX: Pro-Ed.

Fuchs, L. S., Hamlett, C. L., & Fuchs, D. (1990c). *Monitoring Basic Skills Progress: Basic Spelling* [Computer program]. Austin, TX: Pro-Ed.

Fuchs, L. S., Tindal, G., & Deno, S. L. (1984). Methodological issues in curriculum-based reading assessment. *Diagnostique, 9*, 191–207.

Gardner, W. I., & Cole, C. L. (1988). Self-monitoring procedures. In E. S. Shapiro, & T. R. Kratochwill (Eds.), *Behavioral assessment in schools: Conceptual foundations and practical applications* (pp. 206–246). New York: Guilford Press.

Germann, G., & Tindal, G. (1985). An application of curriculum-based measurement: The use of direct and repeated measurement. *Exceptional Children, 52*, 244–265.

Gersten, R., Keating, T., & Becker, W. (1988). The continued impact of the direct instruction model: Longitudinal studies of follow through students. *Education and Treatment of Children, 11*, 318–327.

Gersten, R., Woodward, J., & Darch, C. (1986). Direct instruction: A research-based approach to curriculum design and teaching. *Exceptional Children, 53*, 17–31.

Gettinger, M. (1984). Achievement as a function of time spent in learning and time needed for learning. *American Educational Research Journal, 21*, 617–628.

Gettinger, M. (1985). Time allocated and time spent relative to time needed for learning as determinants of achievement. *Journal of Educational Psychology, 77*, 3–11.

Gettinger, M. (1986). Issues and trends in academic engaged time of students. *Special Services in the Schools, 2*, 1–17.

Gickling, E., & Havertape, J. (1981). *Curriculum-based assessment.* Minneapolis, MN: National School Psychology Inservice Training Network.

Gickling, E. E., Rosenfield, S. (1995). Best practices in curriculum-based assessment. In A. Thomas & J. Grimes (Eds.), *Best practices in school psychology—III* (pp. 587–595). Washington, DC: National Association of School Psychologists.

Gickling, E. E., & Thompson, V. P. (1985). A personal view of curriculum-based assessment. *Exceptional Children, 52*, 205–218.

Goh, D. S., Teslow, C. J., & Fuller, G. B. (1981). The practices of psychological assessment among school psychologists. *Professional Psychology, 12*, 699–706.

Goldberg, R., & Shapiro, E. S. (1995). In-vivo rating of treatment acceptability by children: Effects of probability instruction on student's spelling performance under group contingency conditions. *Journal of Behavioral Education, 5*, 415–432.

Good, R. H., III, & Salvia, J. (1988). Curriculum bias in published, norm-referenced reading tests: Demonstrable effects. *School Psychology Review, 17*, 51–60.

Good, R. H., III, Vollmer, M., Creek, R. J., Katz, L., & Chowdhri, S. (1993). Treatment utility of the Kaufman Assessment Battery for Children: Effects of matching instruction and student processing strength. *School Psychology Review, 22*, 8–26.

Goodman, L. (1990). *Time and learning in the special education classroom.* Albany, NY: State University of New York Press.

Gordon, E. W., DeStefano, L., & Shipman, S. (1985). Characteristics of learning persons and the adaptation of learning environments. In M. C. Wang, & H. J. Walberg (Eds.), *Adapting instruction to individual differences* (pp. 44–65). Berkeley, CA: McCutchan.

Graden, J. L., Casey, A., & Bonstrom, O. (1985). Implementing a prereferral intervention system: Part II. The Data. *Exceptional Children, 51*, 487–496.

Graden, J. L., Casey, A., & Christensen, S. L. (1985). Implementing a prereferral intervention system: Part I. The model. *Exceptional Children, 51*, 377–384.

Graham, L., & Wong, B. Y. (1993). Comparing two modes of teaching a question-answering strategy for enhancing reading comprehension: Didactic and self-instructional training. *Journal of Learning Disabilities, 26*, 270–279.

Graham, S. (1982). Composition research and practice: A unified approach. *Focus on Exceptional Children, 14*(8).

Graham, S. (1983). The effects of self-instructional procedures on LD students' handwriting performance. *Learning Disability Quarterly, 6*, 231–234.

Graham, S., & Harris, K. R. (1987). Improving composition skills of inefficient learners with self-instructional strategy training. *Topics in Language Disorders, 7*(4), 66–77.

Graham, S., & Harris, K. R. (1989). A components analysis of cognitive strategy instruction: Effects on learning disabled students' compositions and self-efficacy. *Journal of Educational Psychology, 81*, 353–361

Graham, S., Harris, K. R., MacArthur, C. A., & Schwartz, S. (1991). Writing and writing instruction for students with learning disabilities: Review of a research program. *Learning Disabilities Quarterly, 14*, 89–114.

Graham, S., MacArthur, C. A., Schwartz, S., & Page-Voth, V. (1992). Improving the compositions of students with learning disabilties using a strategy involving product and process goal setting. *Exceptional Children, 58*, 322–334.

Graham, S., & Miller, L. (1980). Handwriting research and practice: A unified approach. *Focus on Exceptional Children. 13*(2).

Greenwood, C. R. (1991). Longitudinal analysis of time, engagement, and achievement in at-risk versus non-risk students. *Exceptional Children, 57*, 521–535.

Greenwood, C. R., Carta, J. J., & Atwater, J. J. (1991). Ecobehavioral analysis in the classroom: Review and implications. *Journal of Behavioral Education, 1*, 59–77.

Greenwood, C. R., Carta, J. J., & Hall, R. V. (1988). The use of peer tutoring strategies in classroom management and educational instruction. *School Psychology Review, 17*, 258–275.

Greenwood, C. R., Carta, J. J., Hart, B., Kamos, D., Terry, B., & Delquadri, J. C. (1992). Out of the laboratory and into the community: Twenty-six years of applied behavior analysis at the Juniper Gardens Children's Project. *American Psychologist, 47*, 1464–1474.

Greenwood, C. R., Carta, J. J., Kamps, D., & Delquadri, J. (1993). *Ecobehavioral assessment systems software (EBASS): Observational instrumentation for school psychologists.* Kansas City: Juniper Gardens Children's Project, University of Kansas.

Greenwood, C. R., Carta, J. J., Kamps, D., Terry, B., & Delquadri, J. (1994). Development and validation of standard classroom observation systems for school practitioners: Ecobehavioral assessment systems software (EBASS). *Exceptional Children, 61,* 197–210.

Greenwood, C. R., Delquadri, J. C., & Carta, J. J. (1988). ClassWide Peer Tutoring (CWPT): Programs for spelling, math, and reading. [Training manual.] Delray Beach, FL: Educational Achievement Systems.

Greenwood, C. R., Delquadri, J. C. & Hall, R. V. (1984). Opportunity to respond and student academic performance. In U. L. Heward, T. E. Heron, D. S. Hill, & J. Trap-Porter (Eds.), *Focus on behavior analysis in education* (pp. 58–88). Columbus, OH: Charles E. Merrill.

Greenwood, C. R., Delquadri, J. C., & Hall, R. V. (1989). Longitudinal effects of classwide peer tutoring. *Journal of Educational Psychology, 81,* 371–383.

Greenwood, C. R., Delquadri, J., Stanley, S., Sasso, G. Whorton, D., & Schulte, D. (1981). Allocating opportunity to learn as a basis for academic remediation: A developing model for teaching. *Monograph in Behavioral Disorders, Summer,* 22–23.

Greenwood, C. R., Delquadri, J. C., Stanley, S. O., Terry, B., & Hall, R. V. (1985). Assessment of eco-behavioral interaction in school settings. *Behavioral Assessment, 7,* 331–347.

Greenwood, C. R., Dinwiddie, G., Bailey, V., Carta, J. J., Kohler, F. W., Nelson, C., Rotholz, C., & Schulte, D. (1987). Field replication of classwide peer tutoring. *Journal of Applied Behavior Analysis, 20,* 151–160.

Greenwood, C. R., Dinwiddie, G., Terry, B., Wade, L., Stanley, S. O., Thibadeau, S., & Delquadri, J. C. (1984). Teacher- versus peer-mediated instruction: An ecobehavioral analysis of achievement outcomes. *Journal of Applied Behavior Analysis, 17,* 521–538.

Greenwood, C. R., Hops, H., & Walker, H. M. (1977). Issues in social interaction/withdrawal assessment. *Exceptional Children, 43,* 490–501.

Greenwood, C. R., Hops, H., Walker, H. M., Guild, J. J., Stokes, J., Young, K. R., Keleman, K. S., & Willardson, M. (1979). Standardized classroom management program: Social validation and replication studies in Utah and Oregon. *Journal of Applied Behavior Analysis, 12,* 235–253.

Greenwood, C. R., Terry, B., Arreaga-Mayer, C., & Finney, R. (1992). The classwide peer tutoring program: Implementation factors moderating students' achievement. *Journal of Applied Behavior Analysis, 25,* 101–116.

Greenwood, C. R., Terry, B., Utley, C. A., Montagna, D., & Walker, D. (1993). Achievement, placement, and services: Middle school benefits of Classwide Peer Tutoring used at the elementary school. *School Psychology Review, 22,* 497–516.

Gresham, F. M. (1984). Behavioral interviews in school psychology: Issues in psychometric adequacy and research. *School Psychology Review, 13,* 17–25.

Gresham, F. M., & Elliott, S. N. (1990). *Social skills rating system.* Circle Pines, MN: American Guidance Service.

Gross, A. M., & Shapiro, R. (1981). Public posting of photographs: A new classroom reinforcer. *Child Behavior Therapy, 3,* 81–82.

Gunning, R. (1952). *The technique of clear writing.* New York: McGraw-Hill.

Haile-Griffey, L., Saudargas, R. A., Hulse-Trotter, K., & Zanolli, K. (1993). *The classroom behavior of elementary school children during independent seatwork: Establishing local norms.* Unpublished manuscript, Department of Psychology, University of Tennessee, Knoxville, TN.

Hall, R. V., Delquadri, J. C., Greenwood, C. R., & Thurston, L. (1982). The importance of opportunity to respond in children's academic success. In E. B. Edgar, N. G. Haring, J. R. Jenkins, & C. G. Pious (Eds.), *Mentally handicapped children: Education and training* (pp. 107–140). Baltimore: University Park Press.

Hall, R. V., Lund, D. E., & Jackson, D. (1968). Effects of teacher attention on study behavior. *Journal of Applied Behavior Analysis, 1,* 1–12.

Hallahan, D. P., Lloyd, J. W., Kauffman, J., & Loper, A. B. (1983). Summary of research findings at the University of Virginia Learning Disabilities Institute. *Exceptional Education Quarterly, 4*(1), 95–114.

Hallahan, D. P., Lloyd, J. W., Kneedler, R. D., & Marshall, K. J. (1982). A comparison of the effects of self- versus teacher-assessment of on-task behavior. *Behavior Therapy, 13,* 715–723.

Hallahan, D. P., Marshall, K. J., & Lloyd, J. W. (1981). Self-recording during group instruction: Effects on attention to task. *Learning Disability Quarterly, 4,* 407–413.

Halle, J. W., Baer, D. M., & Spradlin, J. E. (1981). Teachers' generalized use of delay as a stimulus control procedure to increase language in handicapped children. *Journal of Applied Behavior Analysis, 14,* 389–409.

Hammill, D., & Larsen, S. (1978). *Test of Written Language.* Austin, TX: Pro-Ed.

Hansen C. L., & Eaton, M. (1978). Reading. In N. Haring, T. Lovitt, M. Eaton, & C. Hansen (Eds.), *The fourth R: Research in the classroom* (pp. 41–92). Columbus, OH: Charles E. Merrill.

Hargis, C. H., Terhaar-Yonker, M., Williams, P. C., & Reed, M. T. (1988). Repetition requirements for word recognition. *Journal of Reading, 31,* 320–327.

Harris, A. J., & Jacobson, M. D. (1972). *Basic elementary reading vocabularies.* New York: Macmillan.

Harris, K. R., & Graham, S. (1985). Improving learning disabled students' composition skills: Self-control strategy training. *Learning Disability Quarterly, 8,* 27–36.

Harris, K. R., & Graham, S. (1994). Constructivism: Principles, paradigms, and integration. *Journal of Special Education, 28,* 233–247.

Harris, K. R., Graham, S., Reid, R., McElroy, K., & Hamby, R. (1994). Self-monitoring of attention versus self-monitoring of performance: Replication and cross-task comparison. *Learning Disability Quarterly, 17,* 121–139.

Harris, V. W., Sherman, J. A., Henderson, D. G., & Harris, M. S. (1972). The effect of a tutoring procedure on spelling performance of elementary classroom students. In G. Semb (Ed.), *Behavior analysis in education* (pp. 222–231). Lawrence: University of Kansas Press.

Hasazi J. E. & Hasazi, S. E. (1972). Effects of teacher attention on digit reversal behavior in an elementary school child. *Journal of Applied Behavior Analysis, 5,* 157–162.

Hasbrouck, J. E., & Tindal, G. (1992). Curriculum-based oral reading fluency norms for students in grades 2 through 5. *Teaching Exceptional Children, 24*(3), 41–44.

Hay, W. M., Hay, L. R., & Nelson, R. O. (1977). Direct and collateral changes in on-task and academic behavior resulting from on-task versus academic contingencies. *Behavior Therapy, 8*, 431–441.

Haynes, M. C., & Jenkins, J. R. (1986). Reading instruction in special education resource rooms. *American Educational Research Journal, 23*, 161–190.

Heller, K. A., Holtzman, W. H., & Messick, S. (Eds.). (1982). *Placing children in special education: A strategy for equity*. Washington, DC: National Academy Press.

Hendrickson, J. M., & Gable, R. A. (1981). The use of modeling tactics to promote academic skill development of exceptional learners. *Journal of Special Education Technology, 4*, 20–29.

Hendrickson, J. M., Roberts, M., & Shores, R. E. (1978). Antecedent and contingent modeling to teach basic sight vocabulary to learning disabled children. *Journal of Learning Disabilities, 11*, 69–73.

Hintze, J. M., & Shapiro, E. S. (1995). *Curriculum-based measurement and literature-based reading: Is curriculum-based measurement meeting the needs of changing reading curricula?* Manuscript submitted for publication.

Hintze, J. M., Shapiro, E. S., & Lutz, J. G. (1994). The effects of curriculum on the sensitivity of curriculum-based measurement in reading. *Journal of Special Education, 28*, 188–202.

Hively, W., & Reynolds, M. C. (Eds.). (1975). *Domain-reference testing in special education*. Minneapolis: University of Minnesota, Leadership Training Institute.

Hoge, R. D., & Andrews, D. A. (1987). Enhancing academic performance: Issues in target selection. *School Psychology Review, 16*, 228–238.

Hoier, T. S., & Cone, J. D. (1987). Target selection of social skills for children: The template-matching procedure. *Behavior Modification, 11*, 137–164.

Hoier, T. S., McConnell, S., & Pallay, A. G. (1987). Observational assessment for planning and evaluating educational transitions: An initial analysis of template matching. *Behavioral Assessment, 9*, 6–20.

Holman, J., & Baer, D. M. (1979). Facilitating generalization of on-task behavior through self-monitoring of academic tasks. *Journal of Autism and Developmental Disabilities, 9*, 429–446.

Hopkins, B. L., Schultz, R. C., & Garton, K. L. (1971). The effects of access to a playroom on the rate and quality of printing and writing of first and second grade students. *Journal of Applied Behavior Analysis, 10*, 121–126.

Houghton, S., & Bain, A. (1993). Peer tutoring with ESL and below-average readers. *Journal of Behavioral Education, 3*, 125–142.

Howell, K. W., Fox, S. L., Moorhead, M. K. (1993). *Curriculum-based evaluation: Teaching and decision making* (2nd ed.). Pacific Grove, CA: Brooks/Cole.

Howell, K. W., Zucker, S. H., & Morehead, M. K. (1982). *Multilevel academic skills inventory*. San Antonio, TX: The Psychological Corporation.

Hughes, C. A., Korinek, L., & Gorman, J. (1991). Self-management for students with mental retardation in public school settings: A research review. *Education and Training in Mental Retardation, 26*, 271–291.

Hughes, C. A., & Lloyd, J. W. (1993). An analysis of self-management. *Journal of Behavioral Education, 3*, 405–425.

Hutton, J. B., Dubes, R., & Muir, S. (1992). Assessment practices of school psychologists: Ten years later. *School Psychology Review, 21*, 271–284.

Idol, L. (1987). Group story mapping: A comprehension strategy for both skilled and unskilled readers. *Journal of Learning Disabilities, 20*, 196–205.

Idol-Maestas, L. (1983). *Special educator's consultation handbook*. Rockville, MD: Aspen.

Idol, L., & Croll, V. J. (1987). The effects of training in story mapping procedures on the reading comprehension of poor readers. *Learning Disability Quarterly, 10*, 214–229.

Idol, L., Nevin, A., & Paolucci-Whitcomb, P. (1986). *Models of curriculum-based assessment*. Rockville, MD: Aspen.

Ingenmey, R., & Van Houten, R. (1991). Using time delay to promote spontaneous speech in an autistic child. *Journal of Applied Behavior Analysis, 24*, 591–596.

Iowa Department of Education. (1989). *Problem solving assessment videotape series* [Videotape series]. Des Moines, IA: Author. [Available from the National Association of School Psychologists, Bethesda, MD.]

Iwata, B., Dorsey, M., Slifer, K., Bauman, K., & Richman, G. (1982). Toward a functional analysis of self-injury. *Analysis and Intervention in Developmental Disabilities, 2*, 3–20.

Jastak, J., & Jastak, S. (1978). *Wide Range Achievement Test*. Wilmington, DE: Jastak Associates.

Jastak, S., & Wilkinson, G. S. (1984). *Wide Range Achievement Test-Revised*. Wilmington, DE: Jastak Associates, Inc.

Jenkins, J. R., Barksdale, A., & Clinton, L. (1978). Improving reading comprehension and oral reading: Generalization across behaviors, settings, and time. *Journal of Learning Disabilities, 11*(10), 5–12.

Jenkins, J. R., Deno, S. L., & Mirkin, P. K. (1979). Measuring progress toward the least restrictive alternative. *Learning Disability Quarterly, 2*, 81–91.

Jenkins, J. R., Larson, K., & Fleisher, L. (1983). Effects of error correction on word recognition and reading comprehension. *Learning Disability Quarterly, 6*, 139–145.

Jenkins, J. R., & Pany, D. (1978). Standardized achievement tests: How useful for special education? *Exceptional Children, 44*, 448–453.

Jenson, W. R., Rhode, G., & Reavis, H. K. (1994). *The tough kid tool box*. Longmont, CO: Sopris West.

Johnson, D. J., & Myklebust, H. R. (1967). *Learning disabilities: Educational principles and practices*. New York: Grune & Stratton.

Johnson, D. W., Maruyama, G., Johnson, R., Nelson, D., & Skon, L. (1981). The effects of cooperative, competitive, and individualistic goal structures on achievement: A meta-analysis. *Psychological Bulletin, 89*, 47–62.

Johnson, L. J., & Idol-Maestes, L. (1986). Peer tutoring as a reinforcer for appropriate tutee behavior. *Journal of Special Education Technology, 7*(4), 14–21.

Johnston, M. B., Whitman, T. L., & Johnson, M. (1980). Teaching addition and subtraction to mentally retarded children: A self-instructional program. *Applied Research in Mental Retardation, 1*, 141–160.

Johnston, R. J., & McLaughlin, T. F. (1982). The effects of free time on assignment completion and accuracy in arithmetic: A case study. *Education and Treatment of Children, 5*, 33–40.

Kamps, D., Leonard, B. R., Dugan, E. P., & Boland, B. (1991). The use of ecobehavioral assessment to identify naturally occurring effective procedures in classrooms serving students with autism and developmental disabilities. *Journal of Behavioral Education, 4,* 367–397.

Kanfer, F. H. (1971). The maintenance of behavior by self-generated stimuli and reinforcement. In A. Jacobs & L. B. Sachs (Eds.), *The psychology of private event* (pp. 39–58). New York: Academic Press.

Karlsen, B., Madden, R., & Gardner, E. F. (1975). *Stanford Diagnostic Reading Test* (Green level form B). New York: Harcourt Brace Jovanovich.

Karoly, P. (1982). Perspectives on self-management and behavior change. In P. Karoly & F. H. Kanfer (Eds.), *Self-management and behavior change. From theory to practice* (pp. 3–31). New York: Pergamon Press.

Karweit, N. L. (1983). *Time on task: A research review.* (Report No. 332). Baltimore: Johns Hopkins University, Center for Social Organization of Schools.

Karweit, N. L., & Slavin, R. E. (1981). Measurement and modeling choices in studies of time and learning. *American Educational Research Journal, 18,* 157–171.

Kastelen, L., Nickel, M., & McLaughlin, T. F. (1984). A performance feedback system: Generalization of effects across tasks and time with eighth-grade English students. *Education and Treatment of Children, 7,* 141–155.

Kauffman, J. M., Hallahan, D. P., Haask, B. T., Boren, R. (1978). Imitating children's errors to improve their spellings performance. *Journal of Learning Disabilities, 11,* 219–222.

Kaufman, A. S., & Kaufman, N. L. (1983). *Administration and scoring manual for the Kaufman Assessment Battery for Children.* Circle Pines, MN: American Guidance Service.

Kaufman, A. S., & Kaufman, N. L. (1985). *Kaufman Test of Educational Achievement.* Circle Pines, MN: American Guidance Service.

Kavale, K. A., & Forness, S. R. (1987). Substance over style: Assessing the efficacy of modality testing and teaching. *Exceptional Children, 54,* 228–239.

Kazdin, A. E. (1985). Selection of target behaviors: The relationship of the treatment focus to clinical dysfunction. *Behavioral Assessment, 7,* 33–48.

Kelly, M. L., & Stokes, T. F. (1982). Contingency contracting with disadvantaged youths: Improving classroom performance. *Journal of Applied Behavior Analysis, 15,* 447–454.

Kelly, M. L., & Stokes, T. F. (1984). Student–teacher contracting with goal setting for maintenance. *Behavior Modification, 8,* 223–244.

Kephart, N. C. (1971). *The slow-learner in the classroom.* Columbus, OH: Charles E. Merrill.

Kerr, M. M., & Lambert, D. L. (1982). Behavior modification of children's written language. In M. Hersen, R. M. Eisler, & P. M. Miller (Eds.), *Progress in behavior modification* (Vol. 13, pp. 79–108). New York: Academic Press.

Kirby, F. D., & Shields, F. (1972). Modification of arithmetic response rate and attending behavior in a seventh grade student. *Journal of Applied Behavior Analysis, 5,* 79–84.

Koscinski, S. T., & Gast, D. L. (1993). Use of a constant time delay in teaching multiplication facts to students with learning disabilities. *Journal of Learning Disabilities, 26,* 533–544.

Kosiewicz, M. M., Hallahan, D. P., Lloyd, J., & Graves, A. W. (1982). Effects of self-instruction and self-correction procedures on handwriting performance. *Learning Disability Quarterly, 5,* 71–78.

Kratochwill, T. R. (1985a). Case study research in school psychology. *School Psychology Review, 14,* 204–215.

Kratochwill, T. R. (1985b). Selection of target behaviors in behavioral consultation. *Behavioral Consultation 7,* 49–62.

Kratochwill, T. R., & Bergan, J. R. (1990). *Behavioral consultation in applied settings: An individual guide.* New York: Plenum Press.

Kratochwill, T. R., Elliott, S. R., & Busse, R. T. (1995). Behavioral consultation: A five-year evaluation of consultant and client outcomes. *School Psychology Quarterly, 10,* 87–110.

Kunzelmann, H. D. (Ed.). (1970). *Precision teaching.* Seattle: Special Child Publications.

Lahey, B. B. (1976). Behavior modification with learning disabilities and related problems. In M. Hersen, R. Eisler, & P. M. Miller (Eds.), *Progress in behavior modification* (Vol. 3, pp. 173–206). New York: Academic Press.

Lahey, B. B., Busmeyer, M. K., Beggs, V., & O'Hara, C. (1977). Treatment of severe perceptual–motor disorders in children diagnosed as learning disabled. *Behavior Modification, 1,* 123–140.

Lahey, B. B., & Drabman, R. S. (1973). Facilitation of the acquisition and retention of sight word vocabulary through token reinforcement. *Journal of Applied Behavior Analysis, 6,* 101–104.

Lahey, B. B., McNees, M. P., & Brown, C. C. (1973). Modification of deficits in reading for comprehension. *Journal of Applied Behavior Analysis, 6,* 475–480.

Lahey, B. B., Vosk, B. N., & Habif, V. L. (1981). Behavioral assessment of learning disabled children: A rationale and strategy. *Behavioral Assessment, 3,* 3–14.

Lalli, J. S., Browder, D. M., Mace, F. C., & Brown, D. K. (1993). Teacher use of descriptive analysis data to implement interventions to decrease students' problem behaviors. *Journal of Applied Behavior Analysis, 26,* 227–238.

Lam, A., Cole, C. L., Shapiro, E. S., & Bambara, L. M. (1994). Relative effects of self-monitoring on-task behavior, academic accuracy, and disruptive behavior in students with behavior disorders. *School Psychology Review, 23,* 44–58.

Larsen, S. C., & Hammill, D. D. (1976). *Test of Written Spelling.* Austin, TX: Empiric Press.

Leach, D. J., & Dolan, N. K. (1985). Helping teacher increase student academic engagement rates: The evaluation of a minimal feedback procedure. *Behavior Modification, 9,* 55–71.

Lee, C., & Tindal, G. A. (1994). Self-recording and goal-setting: Effects on on-task and math productivity with low-achieving Korean elementary school students. *Journal of Behavioral Education, 4,* 459–479.

Lee, L., & Canter, S. M. (1971). Developmental sentence scoring. *Journal of Speech and Hearing Disorders, 36,* 335–340.

Leinhardt, G., Zigmond, N., & Cooley, W. W. (1981). Reading instruction and its effects. *American Educational Research Journal, 18,* 343–361.

Lentz, F. E. Jr. (1988). Direct observation and measurement of academic skills: A conceptual review. In E. S. Shapiro & T. R. Kratochwill (Eds.), *Behavioral as-*

sessment in schools: Conceptual foundations and practical applications (pp. 76–120). New York: Guilford.

Lentz, F. E., Jr., & Shapiro, E. S. (1985). Behavioral school psychology: A conceptual model for the delivery of psychological services. In T. R. Kratochwill (Ed.), *Advances in school psychology* (Vol. 4, pp. 191–232). Hillsdale, NJ: Erlbaum.

Lentz, F. E., Jr., & Shapiro, E. S. (1986). Functional assessment of the academic environment. *School Psychology Review, 15*, 346–357.

Lentz, F. E., Jr., & Wehmann, B. A. (1995). Interviewing. In A. Thomas & J. Grimes (Eds.), *Best practices in school psychology—III* (pp. 637–650). Washington, DC: National Association of School Psychologists.

Lenz, B. K., Ehren, B. J., & Smiley, L. R. (1991). A goal attainment approach to improve completion of project-type assignments by adolescents with learning disabilities. *Learning Disabilities Research & Practice, 6*(3), 166–176.

Lenz, B. K., Schumaker, J. B., Deshler, D. D., & Beals, V. L. (1984). *Learning strategies curriculum: The word identification strategy.* Lawrence: University of Kansas.

Lindsley, O. R. (1971). Precision teaching in perspective: An interview with Ogden R. Lindsley. *Teaching Exceptional Children, 3*, 114–119.

Litow, L., & Pumroy, D. K. (1975). A brief review of classroom group-oriented contingencies. *Journal of Applied Behavior Analysis, 8*, 341–347.

Lloyd, J. W. (1980). Academic instruction and cognitive behavior modification: The need for attack strategy training. *Exceptional Education Quarterly, 1*, 53–63.

Lloyd, J. W., Hallahan, D. P., Kosciewitz, M. M., & Kneedler, R. D. (1982). Reactive effects of self-assessment and self-recording on attention to task and academic productivity. *Learning Disability Quarterly, 5*, 216–227.

Lloyd, J. W., Kneedler, R. D., & Cameron, N. A. (1982). Effects of verbal self-guidance on word reading accuracy. *Reading Improvement, 19*, 84–89.

Lloyd, J. W., Saltzman, N. J., & Kaufman, J. M. (1981). Predictable generalization in academic learning as a result of preskills and strategy training. *Learning Disability Quarterly, 4*, 203–216.

Lochman, J. E., & Curry, J. F. (1986). Effects of social problem-solving training and self-instruction training with aggressive boys. *Journal of Clinical Child Psychology, 15*, 159–164.

Lovaas, O. I. (1977). *The autistic child: Language development through behavior modification.* New York: Irvington.

Lovaas, O. I., Koegel, R., Simmons, J. Q., & Long, J. S. (1973). Some generalization and follow-up measures on autistic children in behavior therapy. *Journal of Applied Behavior Analysis, 6*, 131–166.

Lovitt, T. C. (1978). Arithmetic. In N. Haring, M. Eaton, & C. Hansen (Eds.), *The fourth R: Research in the classroom* (pp. 127–167). New York: Charles E. Merrill.

Lovitt, T. C. & Curtiss, K. A. (1969). Academic response rate as a function of teacher- and self-imposed contingencies. *Journal of Applied Behavior Analysis, 2*, 49–53.

Lovitt, T. C., Eaton, M., Kirkwood, M. E., & Perlander, A. (1971). Effects of various reinforcment contingencies on oral reading rate. In E. Ramp & B. L. Hopkins (Eds.), *A new direction for education: Behavior analysis* (pp. 54–71). Lawrence: University of Kansas Press.

Lovitt, T. C., & Hansen, C. C. (1976a). The use of contingent skipping and drilling to improve oral reading and comprehension. *Journal of Learning Disabilities, 9,* 481–487.

Lovitt, T. C., & Hansen, C. C. (1976b). Round one- placing the child in the right reader. *Journal of Learning Disabilities, 9,* 347–353.

Luiselli, J. K., & Downing, J. N. (1980). Improving a student's arithmetic performance using feedback and reinforcement procedures. *Education and Treatment of Children, 3,* 45–49.

Lysynchuk, L. M., Pressley, M., & Vye, N. J. (1990). Reciprocal instruction improves standardized reading comprehension performance in poor gradeschool comprehenders. *Elementary School Journal, 90,* 469–484.

Maag, J. W. (1990). Social skills training in schools. *Special Services in the Schools, 6,* 1–19.

Maag, J. W., Reid, R., & DiGangi, S. A. (1993). Differential effects of self-monitoring attention, accuracy, and productivity. *Journal of Applied Behavior Analysis, 26,* 329–344.

MacArthur, C. A., Schwartz, S. S., & Graham, S. (1991). Effects of a reciprocal peer revision strategy in special education classrooms. *Learning Disabilities Research and Practice, 6,* 201–210.

Mace, F. C., Browder, D. M., & Lin, Y. (1987). Analysis of demand conditions associated with stereotypy. *Journal of Behavior Therapy and Experimental Psychiatry, 18,* 25–31.

Mace, F. C., & Knight, D. (1986). Functional analysis and treatment of severe pica. *Journal of Applied Behavior Analysis, 19,* 411–416.

Mace, F. C., & Kratochwill, T. R. (1985). Theories of reactivity in self-monitoring: A comparison of cognitive-behavioral and operant models. *Behavior Modification, 9,* 323–343.

Mace, F. C., Page, T. J., Ivancic, M. T., & O'Brien, S. (1986). Analysis of environmental determinants of aggression and disruption in mentally retarded children. *Applied Research in Mental Retardation, 7,* 203–221.

Mace, F. C., & West, B. J. (1986). Unresolved theoretical issues in self-management: Implications for research and practice. *Professional School Psychology, 1,* 149–163.

Mace, F. C., Yankanich, M. A., & West, B. (1988). Toward a methodology of experimental analysis and treatment of aberrant classroom behaviors. *Special Services in the Schools, 4* (3/4), 71–88.

Madden, R., Gardener, E. R., Rudman, H. C., Karlsen, B., & Merwin, J. C. (1973). *Stanford achievement test.* New York: Harcourt Brace Jovanovich.

Maheady, L., Harper, G., Mallette, B., & Winstanley, N. (1991). Training and implementation requirements associated with the use of a classwide peer tutoring system. *Education and Treatment of Children, 14,* 177–198.

Maher, C. A., & Zins, J. E. (1987). *Psychoeducational interventions in the schools: Methods and procedures for enhancing student competence.* New York: Pergamon Press.

Mahn, C., & Greenwood, G. E. (1990). Cognitive behavior modification: Use of self-instruction strategies by first graders on academic tasks. *Journal of Educational Research, 83,* 158–161.

Manning, B. H. (1990). Cognitive self-instruction for an off-task fourth grader during independent academic tasks: A case study. *Contemporary Educational Psychology, 15*, 46–46.

Marholin, D., II, & Steinman, W. M. (1977). Stimulus control in the classroom as a function of the behavior reinforced. *Journal of Applied Behavior Analysis, 10*, 465–478.

Marholin, D., II, Steinman, W. M., McInnis, E. T., & Heads, T. B. (1975). The effect of a teachers' presence on the classroom behavior of conduct problem children. *Journal of Abnormal Child Psychology, 3*, 11–25.

Markwardt, F. C. (1989). *Peabody Individual Achievement Test—Revised*. Circle Pines, MN: American Guidance Service.

Marston, D., Fuchs, L. S., & Deno, S. L. (1986). Measuring pupil progress: A comparison of standardized achievement tests and curriculum-related measures. *Diagnostique, 11*, 77–90.

Marston, D., & Magnusson, D. (1985). Implementing curriculum-based measurement in special and regular settings. *Exceptional Children, 52*, 266–276.

Marston, D., & Magnusson, D. (1988). Curriculum-based measurement: District level implementation. In J. L. Graden, J. E. Zins, & M. J. Curtis (Eds.), *Alternative educational delivery systems: Enhancing instructional options for all students* (pp. 137–177). Washington, DC: National Association of School Psychologists.

Marston, D., & Tindal, G. (1995). Best practices in performance monitoring. In A. Thomas & J. Grimes (Eds.), *Best practices in school psychology—III* (pp. 597–607). Washington, DC: National Association of School Psychologists.

Martens, B. K., Steele, E. S., Massie, D. R., & Diskin, M. J. (1995). Curriculum bias in standardized tests of reading decoding. *Journal of School Psychology, 33*, 287–296.

Mash, E. J., & Terdal, L. G. (Eds.). (1981). *Behavioral assessment of childhood disorders*. New York: Guilford Press.

McAuley, S. M., & McLaughlin, T. F. (1992). Comparison of add-a-word and compu-spell programs with low-achieveing students. *Journal of Educational Research, 85*, 362–369.

McCurdy, B. L., & Shapiro, E. S. (1992). A comparison of teacher-, peer-, and self-monitoring with curriculum-based measurement in reading among students with learning disabilities. *Journal of Special Education, 26*, 162–180.

McFall, R. M. (1976). Behavioral training: A skill-acquisition approach to clinical problems. In J. T. Spence, R. C. Carson, & J. W. Thibaut (Eds.), *Behavioral approaches to therapy* (pp. 227–260). Morristown, NJ: General Learning Press.

McKenzie, M. L., & Budd, K. S. (1981). A peer tutoring package to increase mathematics performance: Examination of generalized changes in classroom behavior. *Education and Treatment of Children, 4*, 1–15.

McKinney, J. D., Mason, J., Perkersen, K., & Clifford, M. (1975). Relationship between classroom behavior and academic achievement. *Journal of Educational Psychology, 67*, 198–203.

McKnight, D. L., Nelson, R. O., Hayes, S. C., & Jarrett, R. B. (1984). Importance of treating individually-assessed response classes in the amelioration of depression. *Behavior Therapy, 15*, 315–335.

McLaughlin, T. F. (1981). The effects of a classroom token economy on math performance in an intermediate grade class. *Education and Treatment of Children, 4,* 139–147.

McLaughlin, T. F., Burgess, N., & Sackville-West, L. (1982). Effects of self-recording and self-recording + matching on academic performance. *Child Behavior Therapy, 3*(2/3), 17–27.

McLaughlin, T. F., & Helm, J. L. (1993). Use of contingent music to icrease academic performance of middle-school students. *Psychological Reports, 72,* 658.

McLaughlin, T. F., Reiter, S. M., Mabee, W. S., & Byram, B. J. (1991). An analysis and replication of the add-a-word spelling program with mildly handicapped middle school students. *Journal of Behavioral Education, 1,* 413–426.

Meichenbaum, D. H., & Goodman, J. (1971). Training impulsive children to talk to themselves: A means of developing self-control. *Journal of Abnormal Psychology, 77,* 117–126.

Messick, S. (1970). The criterion problem in the evaluation of instruction: Assessing possible, not just intended, outcomes. In M. C. Wittrock & D. W. Wiley (Eds.), *The evaluation of instruction: Issues and problems* (pp. 183–201). New York: Holt, Rinehart & Winston.

Miller, G. (1986, August). *Fostering comprehension monitoring in less-skilled readers through self-instruction training.* Paper presented at the American Psychological Association, New York.

Miller, G., Giovenco, A., & Rentiers, K. A. (1987). Fostering comprehension monitoring in below average readers through self-instruction training. *Journal of Reading Behavior, 19,* 379–394.

Miltenberger, R. G. (1990). Assessment of treatment acceptability: A review of the literature. *Topics in Early Childhood Special Education, 10*(3), 24–38.

Miltenberger, R. G., & Fuqua, R. W. (1985). Evaluation of a training manual for the acquisition of behavioral assessment interviewing skills. *Journal of Applied Behavior Analysis, 18,* 323–328.

Mirkin, P. K., Deno, S. L., Fuchs, S. L., Wesson, C., Tidal, G., Marston, D., & Kuehnle, K. (1981). *Procedures to develop and monitor progress on IEP goals.* Minneapolis: University of Minnesota, Institute for Research on Learning Disabilities.

Montague, M. (1989). Strategy instruction and mathematical problem solving. *Journal of Reading, Writing, and Learning Disabilities International, 4,* 275–290.

Montague, M., & Bos, C. S. (1986). Verbal mathematical problem solving and learning disabilities: A review. *Focus on Learning Problems in Mathematics, 8*(2), 7–21.

Myers, S. S. (1990). The management of curriculum time as it relates to student engaged time. *Educational Review, 42,* 13–23.

Naslund, R. A., Thorpe, L. P., & Lefever, D. W. (1978). *SRA Achievement Series.* Chicago: Science Research Associates.

Nastasi, B. K., & Clements, D. H. (1991). Research on cooperative learning: Implications for practice. *School Psychology Review, 20,* 110–131.

Neef, N. A., Iwata, B. A., & Page, T. J. (1980). The effects of interspersal training versus high density reinforcement on spelling acquisition and retention. *Journal of Applied Behavior Analysis, 13,* 153–158.

Neill, M., & Medina, N. (1989). "Standardized testing" harmful to educational health. *Phi Delta Kappan, 70,* 688–697.

Nelson, R. O. (1977). Methodological issues in assessment via self-monitoring. In J. D. Cone & R. P. Hawkins (Eds.), *Behavioral assessment: New directions in clinical psychology* (pp. 217–240). New York: Brunner/Mazel

Nelson, R. O. (1985). Behavioral assessment in the school setting. In T. R. Kratochwill (Ed.), *Advances in school psychology* (Vol. 4, pp. 45–88). Hillsdale, NJ: Erlbaum.

Nelson, R. O. (1988). Relationships between assessment and treatment within a behavioral perspective. *Journal of Psychopathology and Behavioral Assessment, 10,* 155–170.

Nelson, R. O., & Hayes, S. C. (1981). Theoretical explanations for reactivity in self-monitoring. *Behavior Modification, 5,* 3–14.

Nelson, R. O., & Hayes, S. C. (Eds.). (1986). *Conceptual foundations of behavioral assessment.* New York: Guilford.

Noll, M. B., Kamps, D., & Seaborn, C. F. (1993). Prereferral intervention for students with emotional or behavioral risks: Use of a behavioral consultation model. *Journal of Emotional and Behavioral Disorders, 1,* 203–214.

Northrup, J., Wacker, D. P., Berg, W. K., Kelly, L., Sasso, G., & DeRaad, A. (1994). The treatment of severe behavior problems in school settings using a technical assistance model. *Journal of Applied Behavior Analysis, 27,* 33–48.

O'Leary, K. D., & Becker, W. C. (1967). Behavior modification of an adjustment class: A token reinforcement program. *Exceptional Children, 33,* 637–642.

O'Leary, K. D., Kaufman, K. F., Kass, R. E., & Drabman, R. E. (1970). The effects of loud and soft reprimands on the behavior of disruptive students. *Exceptional Children, 37,* 145–155.

O'Leary, K. D., Pelham, W. E., Rosenbaum, A., & Price, G. H. (1976). Behavioral treatment of hyperkinetic children: An experimental evaluation of its usefulness. *Clinical Pediatrics, 15,* 510–515.

O'Leary, K. D., Romanczyk, R., Kass, R. E., Dietz, A., & Santogrossi, D. A. (1979). *Procedures for classroom observation of teachers and children.* Stony Brook: Psychology Department, State University of New York.

Ollendick, T. H., & Hersen, M. (1984). *Child behavioral assessment: Principles and procedures.* New York: Pergamon Press.

Ollendick, T. H., Matson, J. L., Esvelt-Dawson, K., & Shapiro, E. S. (1980). Increasing spelling achievement: An analysis of treatment procedures utilizing an alternating treatments design. *Journal of Applied Behavior Analysis, 13,* 645–654.

Ownby, R. L., Wallbrown, F., D'Atri, A., & Armstrong, B. (1985). Patterns of referrals for school psychological services: Replication of the referral problems category system. *Special Services in the School, 1*(4), 53–66.

Parker, R., Hasbrouck, J. E., & Tindal, G. (1992). Greater validity for oral reading fluency: Can miscues help? *Journal of Special Education, 25,* 492–503.

Phillips, N. B., Fuchs, L. S., & Fuchs, D. (1994). Effects of classwide curriculum-based measurement and peer tutoring: A collaborative research–practitioner interview study. *Journal of Learning Disabilities, 27,* 420–434.

Phillips, N. B., Hamlett, C. L., Fuchs, L. S., & Fuchs, D. (1993). Combining classwide curriculum-based measurement and peer tutoring to help general educators provide adaptive education. *Learning Disabilities Research and Practice, 8*(3), 148–156.

Pickens, J., & McNaughton, S. (1988). Peer tutoring of comprehension strategies. *Educational Psychology, 8*(1–2), 67–80.

Piersel, W. C., & Kratochwill, T. R. (1979). Self-observation and behavior change: Applications to academic and adjustment problems through behavioral consultation. *Journal of School Psychology, 17,* 151–161.

Prater, M. A., Hogan, S., & Miller, S. R. (1992). Using self-monitoring to improve on-task behavior and academic skills of an adolescent with mild handicaps across special and regular education settings. *Education and Treatment of Children, 15,* 43–55.

Pratt-Struthers, J., Struthers, B., & Williams, R. L. (1983). The effects of the add-a-word spelling program on spelling accuracy during creative writing. *Education and Treatment of Children, 6,* 277–283.

Reid, R., & Harris, K. R. (1993). Self-monitoring of attention versus self-monitoring of performance: Effects on attention and aademic performance. *Exceptional Children, 60,* 29–40.

Reimers, T. M., Wacker, D. P., Cooper, L. J., & deRaad, A. O. (1992). Acceptability of behavioral treatments for children: Analog and naturalistic evaluations by parents. *School Psychology Review, 21,* 628–643.

Reimers, T. M., Wacker, D. P., Derby, K. M., & Cooper, L. J. (1995). Relation between parental attributions and the acceptability of behavioral treatments for their child's behavior problems. *Behavioral Disorders, 20,* 171–178.

Reschly, D. J., & Grimes, J. P. (1991). State department and university cooperation: Evaluation of continuing education in consultation and curriculum-based assessment. *School Psychology Review, 20,* 522–529.

Resnick, L. B., & Ford, W. W. (1978). The analysis of tasks for instruction: An information-processing approach. In A. C. Cantania & T. A. Brigham (Eds.), *Handbook of applied behavior analysis: Social and instructional processes* (pp. 378–409). Englewood Cliffs: Prentice Hall.

Reynolds, M. C. (1984). Classification of students with handicaps. In E. W. Gordon (Ed.), *Review of research in education* (pp. 63–92). Washington: American Educational Research Association.

Rhode, G., Morgan, D. P., & Young, K. R. (1983). Generalization and maintenance of treatment gains of behaviorally handicapped students from resource rooms to regular classrooms using self-evaluation procedures. *Journal of Applied Behavior Analysis, 16,* 171–188.

Rich, H. L., & Ross, S. M. (1989). Students' time on learning tasks in special education. *Exceptional Children, 55,* 508–515.

Rieth, H. J., Axelrod, S., Anderson, R., Hathaway, F., Wood, K., & Fitzgerald, C. (1974). Influence of distributed practice and daily testing on weekly spelling tests. *Journal of Educational Research, 68,* 73–77.

Roberts, A. H., & Rust, J. O. (1994). Role and function of school psychologists, 1992–93: A comparative study. *Psychology in the Schools, 31,* 113–119.

Roberts, M., & Smith, D. D. (1980). The relationship among correct and error oral reading rates and comprehension. *Learning Disability Quarterly, 3,* 54–64.

Roberts, M. L., & Shapiro, E. S. (in press). The effects of instructional ratios on students' reading performance in a regular education program. *Journal of School Psychology.*

Roberts, M. L., Turco, T., & Shapiro, E. S. (1991). Differential effects of fixed instructional ratios on student's progress in reading. *Journal of Psychoeducational Assessment, 9,* 308–318.

Roberts, R. N., & Dick, M. L. (1982). Self-control in the classroom: Theoretical issues and practical applications. In T. R. Kratochwill (Ed.), *Advances in school psychology* (Vol. 2, pp. 275–314). Hillsdale, NJ: Erlbaum.

Roberts, R. N., Nelson, R. O., & Olsen, T. W. (1987). Self-instruction: An analysis of the differential effects of instruction and reinforcement. *Journal of Applied Behavior Analysis, 20,* 235–242.

Robertson, S. J., Simon, S. J., Pachman, J. S., & Drabman, R. S. (1980). Self-control and generalization procedures in a classroom of disruptive retarded children. *Child Behavior Therapy, 1,* 347–362.

Rose, T. L. (1984a). The effects of two prepractice procedures on oral reading. *Journal of Learning Disabilities, 17,* 544–548.

Rose, T. L. (1984b). The effects of previewing on retarded learners' oral reading. *Education and Treatment of the Mentally Retarded, 19,* 49–52.

Rose, T. L. (1984c). Effects of previewing on the oral reading on mainstreamed behaviorally disordered students. *Behavior Disorders, 10,* 33–39.

Rose, T. L., & Beattie, J. R. (1986). Relative effects of teacher-directed and taped previewing on oral reading. *Learning Disability Quarterly, 9,* 193–199.

Rose, T. L., McEntire, E., & Dowdy, C. (1982). Effects of two error correction procedures on oral reading. *Learning Disability Quarterly, 5,* 100–105.

Rose, T. L., & Sherry, L. (1984). Relative effects of two previewing procedures on LD adolescents' oral reading performance. *Learning Disabilities Quarterly, 7,* 39–44.

Rosenfield, S. A. (1987). *Instructional consultation.* Hillsdale, NJ: Erlbaum.

Rosenfield, S., & Kuralt, S. (1990). Best practices in curriculum-based assessment. In A. Thomas & J. Grimes (Eds.), *Best practices in school psychology-II* (pp. 275–286). Washington, DC: National Association of School Psychologists.

Rosenshine, B. V. (1979). Content, time, and direct instruction. In P. L. Peterson & H. J. Walberg (Eds.), *Research on teaching* (pp. 28–56). Berkeley, CA: McCutchan.

Rosenshine, B. V. (1981). Academic engaged time, content covered, and direct instruction. *Journal of Education, 3,* 38–66.

Rosenshine, B. V., & Berliner, D. C. (1978). Academic engaged time. *British Journal of Teacher Education, 4,* 3–16.

Rousseau, M. K., Tam, B. K., & Ramnarain, R. (1993). Increasing reading proficiency of language-minority students with speech and language impairments. *Education and Treatment of Children, 16,* 254–271.

Salvia, J. A., & Hughes, C. (1990). Curriculum-based assessment: Testing what is taught. New York: Macmillan.

Salvia, J. A., & Ysseldyke, J. E. (1995). *Assessment in special and remedial education* (6th ed.). Boston: Houghton Mifflin.

Santogrossi, D. A., O'Leary, K. D., Romanczyk, R. G., & Kaufman, K. F. (1973).

Self-evaluation by adolescents in a psychiatric hospital school token program. *Journal of Applied Behavior Analysis, 6,* 277–287.

Saudargas, R. A. (1992). State–Event Classroom Observation System (SECOS). Knoxville: Department of Psychology, University of Tennessee.

Saudargas, R. A., & Creed, V. (1980). *State–Event Classroom Observation System.* Knoxville: University of Tennessee, Department of Psychology.

Saudargas, R. A., & Lentz, F. E. (1986). Estimating percent of time and rate via direct observation: A suggested observational procedure and format. *School Psychology Review 15,* 36–48.

Sawyer, R. J., Graham, S., & Harris, K. R. (1992). Direct teaching, strategy instruction, and strategy instruction with explicit self-regulation: Effects on the composition skills and self-efficacy of students with learning disabilities. *Journal of Educational Psychology, 84,* 340–352.

Schumaker, J. B., Denton, P. H., & Deshler, D. D. (1984). *The paraphrasing strategy.* Lawrence: The University of Kansas Press.

Schumaker, J. B., Deshler, D. D., Alley, G. R., & Warner, M. M. (1983). Toward the development of an intervention model for learning disabled adolescents. *Exceptional Education Quarterly, 3*(4), 45–50.

Schunk, D. H., & Rice, J. M. (1992). Influence of reading-comprehension strategy information on children's achievement outcomes. *Learning Disability Quarterly, 15,* 51–64.

Schunk, D. H., & Schwartz, C. W. (1993). Goals and progress feedback: Effects on self-efficacy and writing achievement. *Contemporary Educational Psychology, 18,* 337–354.

Scruggs, T. E., Mastropieri, M., Veit, D. T., & Osguthorpe, R. T. (1986). Behaviorally disordered students as tutors: Effects on social behavior. *Behavioral Disorders, 11*(4), 36–43.

Shapiro, E. S. (1981). Self-control procedures with the mentally retarded. In M. Hersen, R. M. Eisler, & P. M. Miller (Eds.), *Progress in behavior modification* (Vol. 12, pp. 265–297). New York: Academic Press.

Shapiro, E. S. (1984). Self-monitoring. In T. H. Ollendick & M. Hersen (Eds.), *Child behavior assessment: Principles and procedures* (pp. 148–165). New York: Pergamon Press.

Shapiro, E. S. (1987a). *Behavioral assessment in school psychology.* Hillsdale, NJ: Erlbaum.

Shapiro, E. S. (1987b). Intervention research methodology in school psychology. *School Psychology Review, 16,* 290–305.

Shapiro, E. S. (1987c). Academic problems. In M. Hersen & V. Van Hasselt (Eds.), *Behavior therapy with children and adolescents: A clinical approach* (pp. 363–384). New York: Wiley.

Shapiro, E. S. (1989). *Academic skills problems: Direct assessment and intervention.* New York: Guilford Press.

Shapiro, E. S. (1990). An integrated model for curriculum-based assessment. *School Psychology Review, 19,* 331–349.

Shapiro, E. S. (1991). *Allentown School District: Curriculum-based measurement norms—fall, winter, spring 1990–91.* Unpublished technical report, Lehigh University, Bethelehem, PA.

Shapiro, E. S. (1992). Gickling's model of curriculum-based assessment to improve reading in elementary age students. *School Psychology Review, 21,* 168–176.

Shapiro, E. S. (1996). *Academic skills problems workbook.* New York: Guilford Press.

Shapiro, E. S., & Ager, C. L. (1992). Assessment of special education students in regular education programs: Linking assessment to instruction. Elementary School Journal, 92, 283–296.

Shapiro, E. S., & Bradley, K. L. (1995). Treatment of academic problems. In M. A. Reinecke, F. M. Dattilio, & A. Freeman (Eds.), *Cognitive therapy with children and adolescents* (pp. 344–366). New York: Guilford Press.

Shapiro, E. S., Browder, D. M., & D'Huyvetters, K. K. (1984). Increasing academic productivity of severely multi-handicapped children with self-management: Idiosyncratic effects. *Analysis and Intervention in Developmental Disabilities, 4,* 171–188.

Shapiro, E. S., & Cole, C. L. (1994). *Behavior change in the classroom: Self-management interventions.* New York: Guilford Press.

Shapiro, E. S., & Derr, T. F. (1987). An examination of overlap between reading curricula and standardized achievement tests. *Journal of Special Education, 21,* 59–67.

Shapiro, E. S., & Eckert, T. L. (1993). Curriculum-based assessment among school psychologists: Knowledge, attitudes, and use. *Journal of School Psychology, 31,* 375–384.

Shapiro, E. S., & Eckert, T. L. (1994). Acceptability of curriculum-based assessment by school psychologists. *Journal of School Psychology, 32,* 167–184.

Shapiro, E. S., Eichman, M. J., Body, J., & Zuber, A. M. (1987, May). *Generalization effects of a taped-word intervention on reading.* Paper presented at the Association of Behavior Analysis, Nashville, TN.

Shapiro, E. S., & Goldberg, R. (1986). A comparison of group contingencies in increasing spelling performance across sixth grade students. *School Psychology Review, 15,* 546–559.

Shapiro, E. S., & Goldberg, R. (1989). In vivo rating of treatment acceptability by children: Group size effects in group contingencies to improve spelling performance. *Journal of School Psychology, 28,* 233–250.

Shapiro, E. S., & Kratochwill, T. R. (Eds.). (1988). *Behavioral assessment in schools: Conceptual foundations and practical applications.* New York: Guilford Press.

Shapiro, E. S., & Lentz, F. E. (1985). Assessing academic behavior: A behavioral approach. *School Psychology Review, 14,* 325–338.

Shapiro, E. S., & Lentz, F. E. (1986). Behavioral assessment of academic behavior. In T. R. Kratochwill (Ed.), *Advances in school psychology* (Vol. 5, pp. 87–139). Hillsdale, NJ: Erlbaum.

Shapiro, E. S., & McCurdy, B. L. (1989). Direct and generalized effects of a taped-words treatment on reading proficiency. *Exceptional Children, 55,* 321–326.

Shapiro, E. S., McGonigle, J. J., & Ollendick, T. H. (1981). An analysis of self-assessment and self-reinforcement in a self-managed token economy with mentally retarded children. *Applied Research in Mental Retardation, 1,* 227–240.

Shepard, L. (1991). Interview on assessment issues with Lorrie Shepard. *Educational Research, 20,* 21–23,27.

Shinn, M. R. (1988). Development of curriculum-based local norms for use in special education decision-making. *School Psychology Review, 17,* 61–80.

Shinn, M. R. (Ed.). (1989). *Curriculum-based Measurement: Assessing Special Children.* New York: Guilford Press.

Shinn, M. R., Good, R. H., III, & Stein, S. (1989). Summarizing trend in student achievement: A comparison of models. *School Psychology Review, 18,* 356–370.

Shinn, M. R., Habedank, L., Rodden-Nord, L., & Knutson, N. (1993). Using curriculum-based measurement to identify potential candidates for reintegraton into general education. *Journal of Special Education, 27,* 202–221.

Shinn, M. R., & Marston, D. (1985). Differentiating mildly handicapped, low achieving and regular education students: A curriculum-based approach. *Remedial and Special Education, 6,* 31–45.

Shinn, M. R., Tindal, G., Spira, D., & Marston, D. (1987). Practice of learning disabilities as social policy. *Learning Disabilities Quarterly, 10,* 17–28.

Shinn, M. R., Tindal, G., & Stein, S. (1988). Curriculum-based assessment and the identification of mildly handicapped students: A research review. *Professional School Psychology, 3,* 69–86.

Shinn, M. R., Ysseldyke, J. E., Deno, S. L., & Tindal, G. (1986). A comparison of differences between students labeled learning disabled and low achieving on measures of classroom performance. *Journal of Learning Disabilities, 19,* 545–551.

Shriner, J., & Salvia, J. (1988). Chronic noncorrespondence between elementary math curricula and arithmetic tests. *Exceptional Children, 55,* 240–248.

Skinner, C. H., Adamson, K. L., Woodward, J. R., Jackson, R., Atchison, L. A., & Mimms, J. W. (1993). A comparison of fast-rate, slow-rate, and silent previewing interventions on reading performance. *Journal of Learning Disabilities, 26,* 674–681.

Skinner, C. H., Bamberg, H. W., Smith, E. S., & Powell, S. S. (1993). Cognitive cover, copy, and compare: Subvocal responding to increase rates of accurate division responding. *RASE: Remedial and Special Education, 14*(1), 49–56.

Skinner, C. H., Ford, J. M., & Yunker, B. D. (1991). A comparison of instructional response requirements on the multiplication performance of behaviorally disordered students. *Behavioral Disorders, 17,* 56–65.

Skinner, C. H., & Shapiro, E. S. (1989). A comparison of a taped-words and drill interventions on reading fluency in adolescents with behavior disorders. *Education and Treatment of Children, 12,* 123–133.

Skinner, C. H., Shapiro, E. S., Turco, T. L., Cole, C. L., & Brown, D. K. (1992). A comparison of self- and peer-delivered immediate corrective feedback on multiplication performance. *Journal of School Psychology, 30,* 101–116.

Skinner, C. H., & Smith, E. S. (1992). Issues surrounding the use of self-management interventions for increasing academic performance. *School Psychology Review, 21,* 202–210.

Slate, J. R., & Saudargas, R. A. (1986). Differences in learning disabled and average students classroom behaviors. *Learning Disability Quarterly, 9,* 61–67.

Slavin, R. E. (1977). Classroom reward structure: An analytic and practical review. *Review of Educational Research 47,* 633–650.

Slavin, R. E. (1980). Cooperative learning. *Review of Educational Research, 50,* 315–342.

Slavin, R. E. (1983a). *Cooperative learning.* New York: Longman.

Slavin, R. E. (1983b). Team assisted individualization: A cooperative learning solution for adaptive instruction in mathematics. In M. C. Wang & H. J. Walberg (Eds.), *Adapting instruction to individual differences* (pp. 236–253). Berkeley, CA: McCutchan.

Slavin, R. E. (1985). Cooperative learning: Applying contact theory in desegregated schools. *Journal of Social Issues, 41*(3), 43–62.

Slavin, R. E., Madden, N. A., & Leavey, M. (1984). Effects of cooperative learning and individualized instruction on mainstreamed students. *Exceptional Children, 50,* 434–443.

Smith, C., & Arnold, V. (1986). *Macmillan-R series.* New York: Macmillan.

Smith, A. M., & Van Biervliet, A. (1986). Enhancing reading comprehension through the use of a self-instructional package. *Education and Treatment of Children, 9,* 40–55.

Smith, D. J., Young, K. R., Nelson, J. R., & West, R. P. (1992). The effect of a self-management procedure on the classroom academic behavior of students with mild handicaps. *School Psychology Review, 21,* 59–72.

Smith, D. J., Young, K. R., West, R. P., Morgan, D. P., & Rhode, G. (1988). Reducing the disruptive behavior of junior high school students: A classroom self-management procedure. *Behavioral Disorders, 13,* 231–239.

Speltz, L. L., Shimaura, J. W., & McReynolds, W. T. (1982). Procedural variations in group contingencies: Effects on children's academic and social behaviors. *Journal of Applied Behavior Analysis, 15,* 533–544.

Staats, A. W., Minke, K. A., Finley, J. R., Wolf, M. M., & Brooks, L. O. A. (1964). Reinforcer system and experimental procedure for the laboratory study of reading acquisition. *Child Development, 36,* 925–942.

Stanley, S. D., & Greenwood, C. R. (1981). *CISSAR: Code for Instructional Structure and Student Academic Response: Observer's manual.* Kansas City: Junipar Gardens Children's Project, Bureau of Child Research, University of Kansas.

Stanley, S. D., & Greenwood, C. R. (1983). Assessing opportunity to respond in classroom environments through direct observation: How much opportunity to respond does the minority, disadvantaged student receive in school? *Exceptional Children, 49,* 370–373.

Stein, C., & Goldman, J. (1980). Beginning reading instruction for children with minimal brain dysfunction. *Journal of Learning Disabilities, 13,* 219–222.

Stevenson H. C., & Fantuzzo, J. W. (1984). Application of the "generalization map" to a self-control intervention with school-aged children. *Journal of Applied Behavior Analysis, 17,* 203–212.

Stoddard, B., & MacArthur, C. A. (1993). A peer editor strategy: Guiding learning-disabled students in response and revision. *Research in the Teaching of English, 27*(1), 76–103.

Stoner, G., Carey, S. P., Ikeda, M. J., & Shinn, M. R. (1994). The utility of curriculum-based measurement for evaluating the effects of methylphenidate on academic performance. *Journal of Applied Behavior Analysis, 27,* 101–113.

Stoner, G., Shinn, M. R., & Walker, H. M. (Eds.). (1991). *Interventions for achievement and behavior problems.* Washington, DC: National Association of School Psychologists.

Stowitschek, C. E., Hecimovic, A., Stowitschek, J. J., & Shores, R. E. (1982). Behaviorally disordered adolescents as peer tutors: Immediate and generative effects on instructional performance and spelling achievement. *Behavior Disorders, 7,* 136–147.

Stowitschek, C. E., Lewis, B., Shores, R., & Ezzell, D. (1981). Procedures for analyzing student performance data to generate hypothesis for the purpose of educational decision making. *Behavior Disorders, 5,* 136–150.

Stromer, R. (1975). Modifying letter and number reversals in elementary school children. *Journal of Applied Behavior Analysis, 8,* 211.

Struthers, J. P., Bartlamay, H., Bell, S., & McLaughlin, T. F. (1994). An analysis of the add-a-word spelling program and public posting across three categories of children with special needs. *Reading Improvement, 31*(1), 28–36.

Struthers, J. P., Bartlamay, H. R., Williams, R. L., & McLaughlin, T. F. (1989). Effects of the add-a-word spelling program on spelling accuracy during creative writing: A replication across two classrooms. *British Columbia Journal of Special Education, 13*(2), 151–158.

Sulzar-Azaroff, B., & Mayer, G. R. (1977). *Applying behavior analysis procedures with children and youth.* New York: Holt, Rinehart & Winston.

Sulzar-Azaroff, B., & Mayer, G. R. (1986). *Achieving educational excellence: Using behavioral strategies.* New York: Holt, Rinehart & Winston.

Swanson, H. L. (1981). Modification of comprehension deficits in learning disabled children. *Learning Disability Quarterly, 4,* 189–202.

Swanson, H. L., & Scarpati, S. (1984). Self-instruction training to increase academic performance of educationally handicapped children. *Child and Family Behavior Therapy, 6*(4), 23–39.

Szykula, S., Saudargas, R. A., & Wahler, R. G. (1981). The generality of self-control procedures following a change in the classroom teacher. *Education and Treatment of Children, 4,* 253–264.

Tabacek, D. A., McLaughlin, T. F., & Howard, V. F. (1994). Teaching preschool children with disabilities tutoring skills: Effects on preacademic behaviors. *Child and Family Behavior Therapy, 16*(2), 43–63.

Tarver, S. G., & Dawson, M. M. (1978). Modality preference and the teaching of reading: A review. *Journal of Learning Disabilities, 11,* 5–7.

Tawney, J. W. (1972). Training letter discrimination in four-year-old children. *Journal of Applied Behavior Analysis, 5,* 455–465.

Taylor, N. E., & Conner, U. (1982). Silent vs. oral reading: The rational instructional use of both processes. *Reading Teacher, 35,* 440–443.

Terry, M. N., Deck, D., Huelecki, M. B., & Santogrossi, D. A. (1978). Increasing arithmetic output of a fourth-grade student. *Behavior Disorders, 7,* 136–147.

Thomas, D. R., Becker, W. C., & Armstrong, M. (1968). Production and elimination of disruptive classroom behavior by systematically varying teachers' behavior. *Journal of Applied Behavior Analysis, 1,* 35–45.

Thurlow, M. L., Graden, J., Greener, J. W., & Ysseldyke, J. E. (1983). LD and non-LD student's opportunities to learn. *Learning Disability Quarterly, 6,* 172–183.

Thurlow, M. L., & Ysseldyke, J. E. (1982). Instructional planning: Information collected by school psychologists vs. information considered useful by teachers. *Journal of School Psychology, 20,* 3–10.

Thurlow, M. L., Ysseldyke, J. E., Graden, J. L., & Algozzine, B. (1983). What's "special" about the special education resource room for learning disabled students? *Learning Disability Quarterly, 6,* 283–288.

Thurlow, M. L., Ysseldyke, J. E., Graden, J., & Algozzine, B. (1984). Opportunity to learn for LD students receiving different levels of special education services. *Learning Disabilities Quarterly, 7,* 55–67.

Thurlow, M. L., Ysseldyke, J. E., Wotruba, J. W., & Algozzine, B. (1993). Instruction in special education classrooms under varying student-teacher ratios. *Elementary School Journal, 93,* 305–320.

Tiegs, E. W., & Clarke, W. W. (1970). *California Achievement Test.* Monterey, CA: CTB/McGraw-Hill.

Tindal, G., Fuchs, L. S., Fuchs, D., Shinn, M. R., Deno, S. L., & Germann, G, (1985). Empirical validation of criterion-referenced tests. *Journal of Educational Research, 78,* 203–209.

Tindal, G., & Parker, R. (1989). Development of written retell as a curriculum-based measurement in secondary programs. *School Psychology Review, 18,* 328–343.

Tindal, G., Wesson, C., Deno, S. L., Germann, G., & Mirkin, P. K. (1985). The Pine County model for special education delivery: A data-based system. In T. R. Kratochwill (Ed.), *Advances in school psychology* (Vol. 4, pp. 223–250). Hillsdale, NJ: Erlbaum.

Topping, K., & Whiteley, M. (1993). Sex differences in the effectiveness of peer tutoring. *School Psychology International, 14,* 57–67.

Torrance, E. P. (1972). Can we teach children to think creatively? *Journal of Creative Behavior, 6,* 114–137.

Touchette, P. E., & Howard, J. S. (1984). Errorless learning: Reinforcement contingencies and stimulus control transfer in delayed prompting. *Journal of Applied Behavior Analysis, 17,* 175–188.

Trammel, D. L., Schloss, P. J., & Alper, S. (1994). Using self-recording, evaluation, and graphing to increase completion of homework assignments. *Journal of Learning Disabilities, 27,* 75–81.

Trice, A. D., Parker, F. C., & Furrow, F. (1981). Written conversations and contingent free time to increase reading and writing in a non-reading adolescent. *Education and Treatment of Children, 1,* 25–29.

Trovato, J., & Bucher, B. (1980). Peer tutoring with or without home-based reinforcement for reading remediation. *Journal of Applied Behavior Analysis, 13,* 129–141.

Tucker, J. A. (1985). Curriculum-based asessment: An introduction. *Exceptional Children, 52,* 199–204.

Turco, T. L., & Elliott, S. N. (1990). Acceptability and effectiveness of group contingencies for improving spelling achievement. *Journal of School Psychology, 28,* 27–37.

U. S. Department of Education. *Sixteenth annal report to Congress on the implementation of the Individuals with Disabilities Education Act.* Washington, DC: Author.

Vacc, N. N., & Cannon, S. J. (1991). Cross-age tutoring in mathematics: Sixth graders helping students who are moderately handicapped. *Education and Training in Mental Retardation, 26,* 89–97.

Van Houten, R., Hill, S., & Parsons, M. (1975). An analysis of a performance feedback system: The effects of timing and feedback, public posting, and praise upon academic performance and peer interaction. *Journal of Applied Behavior Analysis, 8,* 449–457.

Van Houten, R., & Lai Fatt, D. (1981). The effects of public posting on high school biology test performance. *Education and Treatment of Children, 4,* 217–226.

Van Houten, R., & Thompson, C. (1976). The effect of explicit timing on math performance. *Journal of Applied Behavior Analysis, 9,* 227–230.

Van Houten, R., & Van Houten, J. (1977). The performance feedback system in a special education classroom: An analysis of public posting and peer comments. *Behavior Therapy, 8,* 366–376.

Wahler, R. G., & Fox, J. J., III. (1980). Solitary toy play and time out: A family package for children with aggressive and oppositional behavior. *Journal of Applied Behavior Analysis, 13,* 23–40.

Wahler, R. G., & Hann, D. M. (1984). The communication patterns of troubled mothers: In search of a keystone in the generalization of parenting skills. Special issue: Ecobehavioral approaches with children. *Education and Treatment of Children, 7,* 335–350.

Ward, L., & Traweek, D. (1993). Application of a metacognitive strategy to assessment, intervention, and consultation: A think-aloud technique. *Journal of School Psychology, 31,* 469–485.

Wechsler, D. (1991). *Wechsler Intelligence Scale for Children—III* San Antonio, TX: Psychological Corporation, Harcourt Brace Jovanovich.

Wechsler, D. (1992). *Wechlser Individual Achievement Test.* San Antonio, TX: Psychological Corporation, Harcourt Brace Jovanovich.

Wepman, J. (1967). The perceptual basis for learning. In E. C. Frierson & W. B. Barbe (Eds.), *Educating children with learning disabilities: Selected readings* (pp. 353–362). New York: Appleton-Century Crofts.

Whinnery, K. W., & Fuchs, L. S. (1993). Effects of goal and test-taking strategies on the computation performance of students with learning disabilities. *Learning Disabilities Research and Practice, 8,* 204–214.

White, O. R., & Haring, N. G. (1980). *Exceptional teaching* (2nd ed.). Columbus, OH: Charles E. Merrill.

White, O. R., & Liberty, K. (1976). Behavioral assessment and precise educational measurement. In R. L. Schiefelbusch and N. G. Haring (Eds.), *Teaching special children* (pp. 31–71). New York: McGraw-Hill.

White, W. A. T. (1988). A meta-analysis of the effects of direct instruction in special education. *Education and Treatment of Children, 11,* 364–374.

Whitman, T., & Johnston, M. B. (1983). Teaching addition and subtraction with regrouping to educable mentally retarded children: A group self-instructional training program. *Behavior Therapy, 14,* 127–143.

Wiggins, G. (1989). A true test: Toward a more authentic and equitable assessment. *Phi Delta Kappan, 70,* 703–713.

Wilkinison, G. S. (1993). *Wide Range Achievement Test 3* (3rd ed). Wilmington, DE: Wide Range.

Wilson,F. E., & Evans, I. M. (1983). The reliability of target-behavior selection in behavioral assessment. *Behavioral Assessment, 5,* 15–32.

Witt, J. C. (1990). Complaining, pre-Copernican thought, and the univariate linear mind: Questions for school-based behavioral consultation research. *School Psychology Review, 19,* 367–377.

Witt, J. C., & Elliott, S. N. (1983). Assessment in behavioral consultation: The initial interview. *School Psychology Review, 12,* 42–49.

Witt, J. C., & Elliott, S. N. (1985). Acceptability of classroom intervention strategies. In T. R. Kratochwill (Ed.), *Advances in school psychology* (Vol. 4, pp. 251–288). Hillsdale, NJ: Erlbaum.

Witt, J. C., Erchul, W. P., McKee, W. T., Pardue, M., & Wickstron, K. F. (1991). Conversational control in school-based consultation: The relationship between consultant and consultee topic determination and consultation outcome. *Journal of Educational and Psychological Consultation, 2,* 101–116.

Witt, J. C., & Martens, B. K. (1983). Assessing the acceptability of behavioral interventions used in classrooms. *Psychology in the Schools, 20,* 510–517.

Wood, D. A., Rosenberg, M. S., & Carran, D. T. (1993). The effects of tape-recorded self-instruction cues on the mathematics performance of students with learning disabilities. *Journal of Learning Disabilities, 26,* 250–258, 269.

Woodcock, R. W. (1987). *Woodcock Reading Mastery Tests—Revised.* Circle Pines, MN: American Guidance Service.

Woodcock, R. W., & Johnson, M. (1989, 1990). *Woodcock–Johnson Tests of Achievement.* Allen, TX: Riverside.

Young, C., Hecimovic, A., & Salzberg, C. L. (1983). Tutor–tutee behavior of disadvantaged kindergarten children during peer tutoring. *Education and Treatment of Children, 6,* 123–135.

Young, K. R., West, R. P., Smith, D. J., & Morgan, D. P. (1991). *Teaching self-management strategies to adolescents.* Longmont, CO: Sopris West.

Ysseldyke, J. E., & Christenson, S. (1987). *The Instructional Environment Scale.* Austin, TX: Pro-Ed.

Ysseldyke, J. E., & Christenon, S. (1993). *TIES-II, The Instructional Environment System II.* Longmont, CO: Sopris West.

Ysseldyke, J. E., & Mirkin, P. K. (1982). The use of assessment information to plan instructional interventions: A review of the research. In C. R. Reynolds & T. B. Gutkin (Eds.), *The handbook of school psychology* (pp. 395–409). New York: Wiley.

Ysseldyke, J. E., Regan, R., Thurlow, M. L., & Schwartz, S. (1981). Current assessment practices: The "cattle dip" approach. *Diagnostique, 6*(2), 16–27.

Ysseldyke, J. E., Thurlow, M. L., Christenson, S. L., & McVicar, R. (1988). Instructional grouping arrangements used with mentally retarded, learning disabled, emotionally disturbed, and nonhandicapped elementary students. *Journal of Educational Research, 81,* 305–311.

Ysseldyke, J. E., Thurlow, M. L., Graden, J., Wesson, C., Algozzine, B. & Deno, S.

L. (1983). Generalization from five years of research on assessment and decision making: The University of Minnesota Institute. *Exceptional Education Quarterly, 4*(1), 75–93.

Ysseldyke, J. E., Thurlow, M. L., Mecklenberg, C., Graden, J., & Algozzine, B. (1984). Changes in academic engaged time as a function of assessment and special education intervention. *Special Services in the Schools, 1*(2), 31–44.

Zigmond, N., & Miller, S. E. (1986). Assessment for instructional planning. *Exceptional Children, 52,* 501–509.

Zipprich, M. A. (1995). Teaching web making as a guided planning tool to improve student narrative writing. *RASE: Remedial and Special Education, 16,* 3–15.

Index

♦